NATHANIEL LORD CREWE

NATHANIEL CREWE.
By permission of the Director of the National Portrait Gallery.

Frontispiece.

NATHANIEL LORD CREWE

BISHOP OF DURHAM (1674–1721)

AND

HIS DIOCESE

BY

C. E. WHITING, D.D., B.C.L., F.S.A.

Emeritus Professor of History in the University of Durham;
Hon. Canon of Durham

Published for the Church Historical Society

LONDON
SOCIETY FOR PROMOTING
CHRISTIAN KNOWLEDGE
NORTHUMBERLAND AVENUE, W.C. 2
NEW YORK: THE MACMILLAN COMPANY
1940

Made in Great Britain

CONTENTS

LIST OF ILLUSTRATIONS

PREFACE

SEVERAL brief lives of Nathaniel Lord Crewe, Bishop of Durham, were written in the eighteenth century. There is a quarto MS. entitled "Memoirs of Nathaniel, Lord Crewe," which was bought by the Crewe Trustees in 1891 and is now preserved in the library at Bamburgh Castle.[1] It is not the original document, which is no longer to be found, but is a copy, perhaps, as Andrew Clark suggested, by an illiterate writing master, who wrote a good hand but had some difficulty in making out the original. A second scribe has added a few notes and tells us that the memoir had been compiled from the minutes of Prebendary John Smith of Durham. This manuscript was edited for the Camden Society by Andrew Clark in 1895,[2] and is referred to in these pages as the *Memoirs*. In 1790 there was published in London *An Examination of the Life and Character of Nathaniel Crewe, Bishop of Durham*: wherein the Writings of his several Biographers and other Authors are critically reviewed and compared with a Manuscript never before published, containing Curious Anecdotes of that Prelate. The unknown person who published this refers to a manuscript life which he had obtained from a bookseller who had purchased it among the contents of a library "of a learned gentleman in the city of Durham." This gentleman was a relative of Mr. Trotter, one of Crewe's officials, and the original of this manuscript is said to have belonged to Trotter, though there were several other copies in private hands at the time. This manuscript or "notebook" speaks of Steane as the place of Crewe's "present residence, where his ancestors are buried and where he himself will lie." It tells how the bishop set up his own monument in 1720 and there it ends. So its date is determined as 1720–21. The writer was evidently a great

---

[1] I, v, 52.
[2] See his preface to it, *Camden Miscellany*, No. ix.

admirer of Crewe, but the editor, who has added many notes
and continued the work to include his death and last will, was
a follower of the Whig tradition, an admirer of Burnet, and
had a very unfavourable opinion of Crewe. William Hutchinson in the first volume of his *History and Antiquities of the
County Palatine of Durham*, first published in 1786, gave a
series of lives of the Bishops of Durham, including of course a
life of Crewe. The editor of the *Examination* says of this:
" Some of his authorities are to be discredited : he collected
indiscriminately, and yet with a specious degree of justice
referred the reader to consult the originals." The writer of the
Examination (henceforth so called) professes to correct
Hutchinson's errors. Some further information about the
bishop and his bishopric may be gathered from *An Enquiry
into the Ancient and Present State of the County Palatine of
Durham*. The author is given as John Spearman, but he only
wrote the first part, which was finished in 1697. The second
and third parts were added at a later date by his son George
and published at Edinburgh in 1729.

The recently published volume, *The Surtees Society 1834–
1934*, says (p. 95) that in 1873 that society proposed to
publish diaries and other papers of three Durham bishops,
Matthew, Neile and Crewe, and that in 1885 the chosen editor
found himself unable " to continue his work on those documents." The wording of the proposal was somewhat indefinite
and the present writer has been unable to find any trace of a
diary by Crewe. If he ever wrote one it is doubtful if it
survived him (see pp. 194, 237) and perhaps one of the lives
above mentioned is meant.

The first problem which meets a would-be biographer of
Nathaniel, by divine providence Lord Bishop of Durham,
is how to spell his surname. Everyone in Durham and
Oxford to-day spells it Crewe. In his own day it was commonly spelt Crew. Though he came of a Cheshire family, he
was not connected with the town of Crewe, except that his
great-uncle, Sir Randolph, was described as of Crewe Hall
in the county of Chester. The editors of the *Complete
Peerage* have made a distinction : the seventeenth century

PREFACE xi.

holders of the barony are given as Crew, the holders of the
nineteenth century peerage as Crewe. After he became a
peer, however, examples of Crewe's signature show us
" Nathaniel Crewe Duresme." Seventeenth century vagaries
of spelling do not help us much. In the House of Lords
Journals he appears variously as Episcopus Dunelm and Crew,
Duresme and Crew and Duresme and Crewe. Though purists
may be shocked, there seems then no need to shock the
diocese of Durham, the Crewe Trustees, or the University of
the Creweian oration by spelling his name otherwise than as
the bishop often spelt it himself.

The same difficulty arises about the spelling of Dean Granville's name. He, his father and grandfather had usually
spelt it Grenvile or Greenville, though before their time there
had been ten or a dozen variations. But when Charles II
granted an earldom to Sir John of that name, he was created
Baron Granville of Kilkhampton and Bideford, Viscount
Granville of Lansdown and Earl of Bath. Lord Bath's next
brother Bernard adopted the spelling Granville at once, but
his brother Denis did not do so till after he became Dean of
Durham. The name has been thus spelt in that family ever
since.[3]

This book is an attempt to write a life of Nathaniel Crewe
against the background of his times; it is also an attempt
to picture English Church life, in what was then a comparatively obscure part of England, during the latter part of
the seventeenth and the early part of the eighteenth centuries.
A bishop cannot be considered apart from his diocese, but it
may be objected that there is as much about the diocese here
as about the bishop. An intensive study of a small portion
of a wide field may perhaps have its uses, more particularly
in the case of a diocese with the peculiar rights and traditions
of the palatine see of Durham.

The writer has to express his warmest thanks for help and
information to the Rev. E. W. Sealey, Rector of Hinton-cum-
Steane, to Professor G. M. Trevelyan, to Dr. Cyril Bailey, to
Mr. R. Cartwright of Aynho Park, a collateral descendant of

[3] Roger Granville, *Life of Dean Granville*, Exeter 1902, p. 359.

Crewe, to the Rev. Canon Ollard, to the late Mr. John
Oxberry, F.S.A., to Mr. H. L. Honeyman, to Mr. C. F. Battis-
combe, Secretary to the Crewe Trustees, to Mrs. M. C. N.
Munro of Lincoln College, Oxford, to the Rev. W. S.
Wickenden of Blanchland, to Mr. W. H. Gibson, City
Librarian of Newcastle, to Mr. C. H. Hunter Blair, to Dr.
Decima L. Douie and to Lord Armstrong. He has also to
thank the Dean of Durham and the Master of University
College, Durham, for permission to photograph pictures and
portraits in their charge.

CHAPTER I

EARLY LIFE AND EDUCATION

JOHN CREWE of Wich Malbank, in Cheshire, married Alice, the daughter of Humphrey Mainwaring, and by her had, amongst other children, two sons, Randolph and Thomas, both of whom became serjeants-at-law in 1624. The line of Sir Randolph Crew, or Crewe (his name was written both ways), of Crewe Hall, in the county of Chester, was by maternal descent represented at the beginning of the nineteenth century by John Lord Crewe, created Baron Crewe of Crewe in 1806.

Both these lawyer brothers had distinguished careers. Sir Ranulphe, or Randolph, was Member of Parliament for Brackley in 1597, and was knighted in 1614, in which year he was Speaker of the House of Commons in the Addled Parliament. In 1615 Edmund Peacham, who had recently been deprived of the living of Hinton St. George, in Somersetshire, on a charge of libel, was sent to the Tower for a collection of sermon materials which were thought to be treasonable, and which certainly contained an attack on the constituted authorities of the kingdom. Winwood, Secretary of State; Helwys, Lieutenant of the Tower; together with Bacon, Attorney-General; Yelverton, Solicitor-General; Montague and Crewe, two serjeants-at-law; the four law advisers of the Crown, were ordered to examine the prisoner, with authority, which they exercised, to put him to the torture with a view to obtaining from him information of a conspiracy. Nothing was extracted from him, probably because there was nothing to extract. He was sentenced to death at the Taunton Assizes, though the sentence was not executed and he died in prison. In the same year, 1615, Crewe was appointed as one of the Commissioners to enquire into the complicity of Weston in the murder of Sir Thomas Overbury. When the Earl of Somerset was tried for the same murder Bacon opened the case for the prosecution, and Montague and Crewe followed.

In 1621 Floyd, an elderly Roman Catholic barrister, was accused of contemptuous words about Frederick, the Elector Palatine, and his wife Elizabeth, though he stoutly denied that he had ever used the words of which he was accused. A wave of madness swept over the House of Commons, each member clamouring for a more savage punishment than the last. As it was, they agreed on a punishment far in excess of the crime even if the man had been guilty. Crewe was one of the few who dared to say that the Lower House had no jurisdiction over Floyd at all. On January 26th, 1625 Sir Randolph Crewe was made Chief Justice of the King's Bench. In that capacity he delivered the famous opinion of the judges on the claim of Robert de Vere to the earldom of Oxford and the Chamberlainship. In 1626 there arose trouble about a forced loan. The judges expressed their willingness to pay their share towards it; but one and all refused to sign their consent to the demand, which would be taken as expressing their approval of its legality. Charles promptly sent for the Lord Chief Justice and, as he could not prevail on him to give way, he dismissed him on November 9th, 1626. Sir Randolph lived to a ripe old age and died in 1646.

Thomas Crewe, who was the third son of John Crewe, had perhaps a less distinguished legal and political career. He was Member of Parliament for Lichfield in 1603, for Northampton in 1621, for Aylesbury in 1623, and for Gatton in 1625, and in 1623 received the honour of knighthood. He was one of the Lords Justices of Ireland " before the war." [1] He had a reputation for ability and honesty, and was one of those who in 1621 opposed the Spanish match,[2] and who declared that the privileges of Parliament were their " ancient and undoubted right and inheritance." In 1623 he was elected Speaker of the House of Commons and was re-elected Speaker in Charles I's first parliament, but after that he gave up politics. He was made a member of the ecclesiastical commission in 1633; but died on 31st January, 1634, at the age

[1] *Memoirs*, p. 1.
[2] Gardiner, *Hist. Eng.*, IV, pp. 237–8.

STEANE IN THE SEVENTEENTH CENTURY.
From a painting in University College, Durham.

Facing page 3.

of sixty-eight. He had married Temperance, the fourth daughter of Reginald Bray of Steane, in Northamptonshire, about two miles from Brackley.

Bray died in 1583 leaving five daughters as co-heiresses. Sir Thomas bought up the portions of the other four sisters and so acquired the whole property. He seems to have rebuilt much of the manor house, which stood in a walled park of about a hundred and fifty acres. A picture of it hangs in the senior common room of University College, Durham, and obviously dates from Bishop Crewe's time. It was a long building with mullioned windows, many gables and an arcade on the ground floor. An oblong artificial lake edged with trees was in the foreground, the chapel was on the left and a large outbuilding on the right. The old chapel of the manor was replaced by one built by Sir Thomas Crewe in 1620, though he evidently adapted some of the earlier fourteenth century work, especially in some of the windows. It is dedicated to St. Peter. In the centre of the pediment of the west front there is an inscription " Built by T.C. 1620 " and over the west door the words " Holiness becometh Thy house, O Lord, for ever." Most of the building is in the classical Jacobean style though the south doorway and the carving under the double sun-dial suggest a somewhat later date. There is no tower and the parapet is decorated with a number of small pinnacles. Inside the church, which measures 46 feet 4 inches from north to south and 31 feet from east to west, the white-washed walls, two-decker pulpit, clear glass windows and high pews, all have a seventeenth century appearance. Services are still held in it occasionally in the summer though the living is now united with that of Hinton. On the north side, entered under a narrow pointed arch upon clustered multangular pillars is a chapel which was the burying place of the family and contains their monuments, one of the most elaborate of which is that of Sir Thomas himself and his wife Temperance.[3]

[3] G. Baker, *Hist. and Antiq. Northamptonshire*, London, 1822–30, I, pp. 684–8. A. Oswald, " The Chapel at Steane Park," *Country Life*, 2nd July, 1938.

Sir Thomas Crewe had four sons. John Crewe, born in 1598, was the eldest of these. He was for a time at Magdalen College, Oxford, which he entered in 1616, where he seems to have gained a reputation for critical Latin scholarship, though he never seems to have troubled to take a degree. He was trained for the law, but does not appear to have emulated his two uncles in a brilliant career at one of the inns of court, and he never practised. He was a wealthy young man and so had no great incentive to hard work. However, instead of indulging in a life of leisure he took up politics, and became a member of Parliament. He sat for Amersham in 1625, Brackley in 1626, Banbury 1628–9, Northamptonshire in 1640, and Brackley again from 1640–8. In the earlier parliaments of Charles I not much was heard of him; but in the Short and Long Parliaments he found himself in the opposition. He was chairman of the Parliamentary Committee on Religion in 1640. Petitions for the redress of grievances were sent to him, and the King and Council ordered him to give them up: but to him such a course seemed a betrayal of a trust; so he refused, and was sent to the Tower on May 8th, 1640.[4] Smith says he went in at the Traitors' Gate. He favoured the impeachment of Strafford; but he was in the country during the trial. Letters were sent to him calling him a Straffordian and a papist. Nevertheless, when he returned to town he voted against the bill of attainder. He subscribed £200 to the parliamentary cause, took the Covenant, voted for the Self-Denying Ordinance, and was one of the parliamentary commissioners for the negotiations at Uxbridge in January, 1644. Charles walked with him in the gardens of Christ Church, Oxford, and discussed episcopacy with him. Crewe afterwards said that as far as he could judge, the King understood the controversy as well as any of his chaplains.[5] In spite of his attitude on the treaty, the King said of him, "Crewe, though he be against me, is an honest man." Two years later he was one of the parliamentary commissioners who received Charles

---

[4] Gardiner, IX, 129.
[5] *Memoirs*, p. 2.

from the Scots at Newcastle and conveyed him to Holmby House. On June 4th, 1647 the King and all the Commissioners were seized and carried off by Cornet Joyce. On September 15th, 1648 Crewe was one of the members sent by Parliament to treat with Charles in the Isle of Wight. On December 5th in that year he voted that the King's concessions were a sufficient basis for a treaty, and consequently, with forty others, was expelled the next day by Colonel Pride and confined to his lodgings in the Strand. He disapproved of the trial of the King, and was under arrest from December 6th to 29th. During the Commonwealth he sat as member of parliament for Northamptonshire in 1654–5, and was nominated a member of Cromwell's "Other House" in 1657, but never took his seat. He and all the other excluded members of parliament were restored by Monk on February 21st, 1660. To consider means to accomplish the Restoration there was a meeting at Crewe's house in Queen Street with Monk and some eminent citizens of London. They had not been there above an hour before a troop of horse beset the house; upon which all the company went out the back way through the stables and so escaped capture. Crewe was a member of the Council of State which was appointed on February 23rd, 1660 and consisted of thirty-one members. Wood says of John Crewe that he was "a Presbyterian, Independent, and I know not what" and that "when he saw to what ruin he and the Presbyterians had brought the nation he worked for the Restoration." [6] So did many others. The nation was tired of changes and anarchy and John Crewe was not by any means the only Presbyterian who sought to bring back the King. In the Parliament which met on April 25th he took his seat for Northamptonshire and he was one of the deputation sent to the Hague. He was created Baron Crewe of Steane on April 20th, 1661 and it is said could have become Chancellor of the Exchequer had he so desired; but though the office was kept open for him three months he declined it. [7] After the Restoration he took little part in

---

[6] Wood, *Life and Times*, II, p. 16.
[7] *Memoirs*, p. 2. *Examination*, p. 10.

politics and was wont to say that if he had had to begin the world again he would never have concerned himself with public affairs. He was " a studious man and a good scholar, a man of manners and good breeding, and a critic in the Latin tongue." [8]

John Crewe married Jemima, daughter of Edward Walgrave of Lawford in the county of Essex, by his second wife, Dame Sarah Bingham, daughter of Clement Heigham of Suffolk. Sir Symonds D'Ewes had been a previous but unsuccessful suitor for the hand of the " gracious mistress Jemima " in 1621,[9] but it was on John that her favour, or perhaps her parents' favour, ultimately fell. She bore to her husband six sons and two daughters. The sons were Thomas, who succeeded his father in the barony, John who died unmarried in France in September 1681, Edward who died unmarried in 1680, Samuel who died unmarried in 1661, Nathaniel, the subject of this book, and Walgrave who married Susannah, daughter of Robert Mellor of Derby, and died at the age of thirty-six in 1673. The daughters were Jemima and Anne. Jemima was born in 1625 and married Edward Montagu, first Earl of Sandwich, Pepys' friend, who died at sea in 1672. Anne married Sir Henry Wright of Dagenham in Essex and died a widow September 27th, 1708.

Nathaniel Crewe was born on January 31st, 1633 at Steane. If he did not come into the world with a silver spoon in his mouth, he was at least born heir to £100, for his grandfather, Sir Thomas, died only six hours after he was born, leaving that sum to each of his grandchildren.

In the previous year, ten miles away from Steane, at Compton Winyates, had been born another boy who was to become a bishop, Henry Compton afterwards Bishop of London. The two boys had the same wet nurse, but they grew up very different in character and disposition. They both spent a great part of their childhood and youth away from their birthplace and we have little or no ground for sup-

[8] *Memoirs.*
[9] Gibbs and Doubleday, *Complete Peerage,* III, p. 533.

posing that they knew one another until one crossed the other's path in the days of their maturity.

Nathaniel was baptized according to the rites of the Church of England, his godfathers being his uncle, Nathaniel Crewe, and Major Ingoldsby, and his godmother Lady Curzon. He seems to have been rather a delicate child, with a frequent cough, which made his parents fear consumption. He had, we are told, a very delicate ear for music, so much so, that even in his nurse's arms he was heard to say, " The music cries " when he heard a discord. Allowing that children then remained later in their nurse's charge he was at any rate somewhat precocious. Another curious statement is that he was taught English by his maid Stratford. We may suppose that she taught him to read and write and we hear that he could " read the Bible very perfectly at six years old." Quite early in life he was described as " of quick apprehension and a good mimic." In short he was a very bright child, and it would seem that he was expected to be so, because his father " often told him of the exploits of fifth sons."

In the October of 1642 Nathaniel, with his brothers and sister, removed to London, and three days after they had departed Steane was plundered by some of the King's forces. In London he was placed under the care of Henry Bishop, an old Westminster boy and student of Christ Church, Oxford, who lived near the Temple Bar. Under his tuition he became proficient in Latin, read Terence, and acted a part in two of the latter writer's plays. All his life long he was given to quoting Terence. His father prophesied that he would become " head of a house," meaning at Oxford, but the boy rejoined that that was for old men, but he intended to be a schoolmaster. In 1648 he was sent to a school at Cheynies, near Amersham, in Buckinghamshire. The master of this school was Mr. Azall, who had a reputation for training up many excellent scholars. Here Nathaniel became senior of the school, and "very early showed a particular genius for government." School hours in those days were long and the boys spent all their time at Latin and Greek, so that when he left Cheynies he possessed a fair mastery of the two languages. He

does not seem to have taken much interest in sports. Even as
a schoolboy he preferred to retire to the neighbouring groves
with his books.

Schooldays over he should have gone straight to the
university. But civil wars, parliamentary visitors, expulsions
of students, heads of houses, professors and lecturers, and
intrusion of others whose theological views were more pleasing
to the new rulers of the country, had produced serious results.
Some of the colleges were in great financial difficulties : in
many quarters the new regime met with an acquiescence
which was at least sullen : old customs had been abolished,
the whole system of divine service had been changed. The
numbers of students consequently declined very considerably.
So for a time Nathaniel remained at home and worked with a
private tutor, Henry Hickman, an Oxford scholar, now
lecturer or preacher at Brackley, who [10] came to read logic
and other subjects with him. Crewe had other tutors,
including music masters, and under them he became a good
performer on the fiddle and the theorbo lute. On one occasion
Lord Sandwich carried him to Whitehall where he heard
" Oliver's music," the band of musicians which Cromwell
maintained, and on this occasion Oliver spoke to him.

As the country settled down the life of the university
gradually became normal again and students arrived in their
old numbers. In September 1652 Nathaniel and his brother
Samuel entered Lincoln College, Oxford, as commoners. They
did not matriculate till May 23rd, 1653. Their servitor Agus
was a hard-working student of whom it was reported that he
could live on little and only slept four hours a night. He
ultimately became a fellow of Corpus and since the times
were troublous and it was necessary to have an eye to the
future, he took up medicine, and for that purpose studied
Arabic, to enable him to read the treatises on medical matters
written by Mohammedan scholars. Agus and Nathaniel often
compared notes on their studies for they were both very
diligent. In sheer emulation they would get up at unearthly

[10] See Wood, *Ath. Ox.*, II, p. 893. Palmer, *Nonconformists' Memorial*,
I, p. 245 ; III, p. 130.

hours and spend the whole day in close application, each
striving not to be beaten by the other. Crewe took especial
delight in the Greek authors and was in the habit of repeating
a book of Homer's *Iliad* every Saturday night for his own
diversion, and he used to say that if a certain person [11] could
have puzzled him in Homer he would have given him leave
to whip him. His studies were not confined to the classical
writers only; he gained early credit for his knowledge of
philosophy. His father used to send him books and urged
upon him that his motto should be *multum non multa.* One
of his father's sayings was that " Seneca pleases but Plutarch
sticks by the ribs." Crewe's tutor was John Barnard, fellow
of Lincoln. He was afflicted with a squint, and Crewe used
to say, " *Bernardus non vidit omnia.*" Barnard introduced
him to Peter Heylyn, who made him heartily welcome at his
home in Lacey's Court in Abingdon where the historian was
then leading a secluded life. Barnard referred to this in
1683, when he dedicated to " My Honour'd Lord " Crewe his
*Theologo-Historicus, Or, the True Life of the Most Reverend
Divine and Excellent Historian Peter Heylyn D.D.* In his
epistle dedicatory he refers to the days " when I had the
honour to dictate the first principles of academical learning to
you, which God has since so well blessed, that you are one
(and I wish may long continue so) of the chief prelates in this
realm." Barnard was at that time Rector of Waddington in
Lincolnshire.

[11] The name of the MS. has been destroyed by the bookworm. Probably
the servitor.

CHAPTER II

OXFORD

THE two brothers were admitted to the B.A. degree on February 1st, 1656. Nathaniel's " good parts and diligence recommended him so effectually to the favour of the society " that he was elected to a fellowship on May 9th, 1656. On November 6th in the same year he was chosen Moderator in Logic and Philosophy. The Moderator in Logic presided over the disputations of the undergraduates, the Moderator in Philosophy over those of the bachelors of arts. Crewe held both offices for two years. It was unusual for one man to hold both offices at once, and Mr. Andrew Clark suggested that it may have been due to domestic dissensions in the college. He was young as yet, but well qualified for the offices by his learning, and the story is told that Dr. Gilbert Watts, who had been senior fellow since 1645, said when he heard of the appointment, " Aye, and if the Rector lives one seven years, I tell you that Mr. Crewe will be head of this House."

On June 29th, 1658, he proceeded M.A. and in the Act in July that year was appointed by the proctors the " senior inceptor " in Arts. The Act was generally held in the first week in July and was the great week of the academic year, during which were held the formal disputations completing the degree of M.A. and that of Doctor in either of the Faculties. Oxford was generally full of visitors that week. The senior inceptor took precedence over all the Masters of Arts of his year. It was an honourable dignity, but an expensive one and the proctors chose a man of means, for he had to entertain the vice-chancellor, heads of houses, proctors and doctors at what was called a vesper supper, a banquet given in this instance in Lincoln College hall. With his ability, good breeding and wealth (his father's income was not less than £4,000 a year) and with some reputation as a scholar, he was now one of the most prominent members of his college.[1]

Times were changing, people were wearying of the Commonwealth. One night in 1658 Mr. Thomas Thynne, a gentleman commoner of Christ Church, who in 1682 became Lord Weymouth, happened to be locked out of college, and Crewe put him up for the night, and when all was quiet and they were safe from interruption Crewe confided in his guest that he was in favour of the restoration of the King and the bishops, and he then drank to the return of Charles and the prosperity of the Church. Thynne talked about this in Cavalier circles after the Restoration and it was looked upon as being much to Crewe's credit, but the story, or a similar story, must have got about before the Restoration, because on one occasion Dean Owen (he ceased to be dean when the King came back), seeing Crewe pass by, said " There goes a rotten cavalier."

At Lincoln College every November 6th it was the custom to elect a bursar and a sub-rector for the ensuing year. The custom was that on the evening of November 5th the rector inquired of the fellows which of them " offered himself " for the bursarship or sub-rectorship, and the election took place in the college chapel next morning.[2] Crewe offered himself for the bursarship in 1659, but was elected sub-rector. He was chosen for this office again in 1660 and from November 1663 every year till he was elected rector. The duty of the sub-rector was, of course, to govern in the rector's absence, but he also had the oversight of the exercises of the undergraduates, and was required to act as Moderator in the Bachelors' disputations in physics and metaphysics, and the divinity disputations of the fellows. The last were held in the chapel and took place every Friday in term and were compulsory for all resident members of M.A. standing or over.[3] In that same year, 1650, Crewe was admitted *ad eundem* at Cambridge, and as he had been senior of the Act at Oxford Cambridge made him a member of the Caput Senatus.

[1] A. Clark, *Lincoln*, 1898, p. 129.
[2] *Memoirs*, p. 5, and Andrew Clark's note.
[3] *Ibid.*, p. 5 n.

The Caput Senatus was a small body consisting of the vice-chancellor sitting *ex officio,* a doctor from each of the three faculties, divinity, law and medicine, a regent master of arts and a non-regent master of arts. The members were elected annually by the heads of houses, the doctors and the two scrutators who were the tellers in the non-regent house. The election was conducted in the following manner. The vice-chancellor and the two proctors presented separate lists of three doctors and two masters, and the choice of the electors was confined to the names on these lists. In actual practice the choice was limited to the names on the vice-chancellor's list and he named such persons as were likely to be agreeable to his successor. The Caput thus might be completely subservient to the vice-chancellor. On the other hand it restrained the action of the senate in the interest of the governing authorities of the university, and a grace was submitted to the Senate after it had been approved by the Caput.[4] It was remarkable that an Oxford man should have been elected a member of the Caput, but perhaps it was only as a compliment with no intention that he should be an active member.

Since Oxford passed from the hands of the King to the power of Parliament, the university had been ruled by a resident body of visitors or delegates whose control was only limited by a Standing Parliamentary Committee in London who had power to hear appeals from them. The personnel of the Board of Visitors had been changed twice, in 1652 and in 1654 respectively. In 1658 their activities stopped, their last order was issued on April 8th that year and before long they seem to have quietly disappeared. But there was always a possibility that Parliament might appoint others in their place and a petition to abolish such visitors was drawn up in February 1659. Crewe had a great deal to do with it. Anthony Wood writes, under date February 11th, 1659: " I set my hand to a petition against visitors. Mr. Crewe of Lincoln College brought it to me. The godly party they put

[4] Winstanley, *Unreformed Cambridge,* Cambridge, 1935, pp. 24–5. The writer is indebted for this reference to Prof. G. M. Trevelyan.

up another petition and say ' it is for the cause of Christ.'
Dr. Conant the vice-chancellor sent a letter to Dr. Owen
then at London and told him that he must make haste to
Oxon for godliness lay a-gasping, i.e. there was a petition to
the Parliament to put down visitors. . . . No person was
more ready than Crewe, a presbyterian, to have the said
visitors put down, notwithstanding he had before submitted
to them, and had paid them reverence and obedience." [5]   In
the September of that same year Wood noted that Crewe
and another fellow of Lincoln College, Richard Knightley,
though they had been "notorious compliers in hopes of
preferment," had become "wonderful zealots for the
prelatical cause." Crewe in particular had "planted and
nourished a beard for several years, and had put on such a
starched formality, not at all suitable to his age, that he not
only became ridiculous to the presbyterian but also to the
royal party." [6]

At Lincoln College the Restoration brought few changes.
Among the fellows there were only five ejections, " but these
were chiefly due to tension between the Presbyterians, who
supported Hood, and the Independents who had but little
liking for Crewe or for the rector." [7] Crewe was now firmly
on the Anglican side in ecclesiastical matters. He shaved off
his " plentiful beard," dropped his " Scottish habit," and was
the first to come to chapel in a cassock and surplice, doing so
even before the order for restoring the surplice came out.
Dr. Hood, the Rector of Lincoln, questioned him about it,
and thought he should wait till some definite order was
issued by the college. Crewe replied that he thought every
one knew his duty in so plain a case, and therefore there
seemed no necessity for a meeting of the society to settle it.
The rector, perhaps with a touch of sarcasm, advised him to
aim at the rectorship, for then he would have a long life. But
before he actually wore his surplice it had been the subject of
an undergraduate " rag." Wood tells the story that one of

[5] Wood, *Life and Times*, Oxford Hist. Soc., I, p. 268.
[6] *Ibid.*, I, pp. 332–3.
[7] C. E. Mallet, *Hist. Univ. Ox.*, 1914, II, p. 417.

the gentlemen commoners got possession of it one night after supper, Crewe being temporarily out of the way, put it on, blacked his face, and appeared in the common room, apparently in the hope of frightening those who were gathered there with his ghostly appearance. Then, with half a dozen men at his heels, he went to other places in the college with the same intent. The sub-rector recovered his surplice, which had been rendered filthy; but said that as it had been profaned it should never go into God's house. Wood sneeringly says that "though he was persuaded to use some sanctified soap to purify it again, yet that would not serve his turn," but he sold it to Mr. Rowland Sherrard, one of the fellows, for half its price and bought himself another.[8]

On December 13th, 1662, William Adams, a Bachelor of Arts of Wadham College, was elected to a fellowship at Lincoln. An appeal was made to the Visitor by John Robinson and Henry Foulis, both fellows of the college, on behalf of Christopher Pike, M.A. There was some question about preference being given by the statutes to natives of Rotherham parish in Yorkshire. By statute the Visitor of Lincoln College is the Bishop of Lincoln, so Crewe was sent with an appeal to Bishop Sanderson at Bugden. He had a somewhat perilous journey, as it was winter time and the floods were out. He had to cross the bridges on foot and when he had passed over the flooded region he found he had lost his sword, whereupon he returned in search of it and found it lying on a plank less than a foot broad. Arriving at Bugden he found none of the bishop's officials present and drew up an appeal himself the same evening. Next day he had an interview with Dr. Sanderson who listened while he read the appeal but, being in bad health which made it impossible for him to deal with the matter himself, he appointed a commission consisting of three heads of houses, Dr. Pierce (St. John's), Dr. Bailey (Magdalen) and Dr. Fell (Christ Church) to settle the matter, and they decided in favour of Adams. The bishop was much struck with the ability Crewe had shown in the affair and said

[8] Wood, *Life and Times*, App. VIII, Feb. 17th, 1660/1. Vol. III, p. 514.

that he was a man of " excellent parts." [9] In 1663 it was the
turn of Lincoln College to choose a proctor and on April 29th,
1663 the choice fell on Crewe, whose colleague was Thomas
Tomkyns of All Souls. The King visited Oxford that year and
the vice-chancellor asked for delegates to be nominated to
make all the necessary arrangements. Crewe, as senior
proctor, nominated several doctors and masters, but the
masters for the most part were thought insufficient, " being by
reason of their standing unfit for such an employment." They
were all young, Henry Bagshaw of Christ Church, the senior
of them, was only of six years standing from M.A., while the
youngest, Francis Turner, had only taken his degree that
year. So, says Wood, " it was a very weak choice." [10]

Charles II arrived in Oxford on September 23rd and was
received first by the university, the doctors, masters and
scholars " in all their formalities," the junior scholars " so rude
and brutish that they could scarcely be ordered." The vice-
chancellor made a speech and then presented the King with
" a large fair Bible gilt, covered with black plush and bossed
and clasped with silver, double gilt," and the Queen and the
Duke and Duchess of York each with a pair of rich gloves.
Then their majesties rode forward to receive the welcome of
the mayor and corporation. Here Charles was presented with
a richly embroidered silk purse containing £300, " which the
King took with his left hand and put in his pocket." Some-
body else, no doubt, was carrying the Bible.

The other royalties received presents of more rich gloves
and the Duke of Monmouth was incorporated M.A. Anthony
Wood gives us a fairly full account of the events of those
crowded days.[11] No doubt Crewe as senior proctor was
present at all the functions, but his great day was when on
Monday the 28th, at about four in the afternoon, the King
visited the University Library. There was a *contretemps* to
begin with. The doctors, proctors and masters were mar-
shalled in the street to receive him, but they waited in the

[9] *Memoirs*, p. 6, and Clark's notes.
[10] Wood, *Life and Times*, I, p. 490.
[11] *Life and Times*, I, pp. 490–9.

wrong street, for the King came another way " and deceived
them all." One can imagine the ruffled dignity and anxiety
with which they hastened back to the library. Crewe,
kneeling near the globes—the terrestrial and celestial globes
were a prominent feature in most old libraries—made a witty
Latin speech of welcome. Charles listened to many speeches
during his visit, and he still had to listen to Mr. Thomas
Ireland, who next day spake " 116 English verses on his
knees " and to several other persons who made orations in
prose and verse, but he seemed particularly pleased with
Crewe's address. This was Crewe's first introduction to the
King and under very favourable circumstances, " for as no
man understood good speaking and address better than King
Charles, so no man spoke better and addressed with greater
advantage than Mr. Crewe." The King wished to confer
knighthood upon him, but he begged to be excused, and
according to one of his biographers he was supported by the
heads of the university in this. The reasons given were that
he purposed to take holy orders and that being the son of a
peer knighthood was unnecessary for him.[12] Henceforward,
however, Crewe had Court influence behind him. Not only
had he gained the King's favour but Lady Castlemaine's :
and he became a *persona grata* with the Duke of York. A
young man of thirty, of good position, agreeable personal
appearance, attractive manners, and a thorough courtier, from
this time his future career was assured.

But life is not all applause and smiles, even for the fortu-
nate. Three days later Crewe found himself in trouble in
the university. On Thursday, October 1st, Convocation was
held to confer degrees of Doctor of Divinity, and there was
considerable opposition to the candidates proposed. Five
had been nominated by the chancellor; Robert Powell of
All Souls, on condition that he gave a guarantee that he would
perform the exercises required for the degree, James Sessions,
B.D. and Thomas Barton, M.A., both of Magdalen Hall,
John Clegg, M.A. and Robert South, M.A., a distinguished
preacher and chaplain to the chancellor. There was great

[12] *Memoirs,* pp. 6, 7.

opposition to Powell and South : indeed, there were protests
against all of them, and Convocation demanded that the
protests should be registered. The vice-chancellor proposed
all the names together, but the masters opposed this, and
" Crewe, the perfidious proctor," proposed that the graces for
the degrees should be taken separately, though it is difficult
to see what was " perfidious " about that. There was very
great opposition to Powell. The doctors, however, generally
consented ; but the masters generally voted *non-placet*. Then
there should have been a *scrutinium*, that is the proctors
should have conducted a formal election and taken the votes :
but the senior proctor pronounced him *virtute juramenti sui*
passed by the majority. The same thing happened with
Sessions and Barton and Clegg ; though there seems some doubt
as to whether Clegg appeared at all. Finally, there came the
question of Robert South. In his case the opposition was the
most violent. He was most unpopular, largely because of the
rapidity with which he had changed his views at the Restoration. There seemed no doubt that the *non-placets* had it ; a
scrutiny was demanded, and the house was in a tumult.
The doctors, who were generally in favour of the proposal,
even went down among the masters to try to persuade various
individuals to consent. Their efforts proving vain, the
scrutiny was proceeded with and the senior proctor,
apparently taking the vote orally, declared " with his usual
perfidy which he frequently exercised in his office, for he was
born and bred a presbyterian," that South had a majority.
This being done, Powell and South were presented by
Dr. John Wallis, and admitted by the vice-chancellor *ad
lectionem alicuius epistolarum Divi Pauli,* that is to the degree
of B.D. Next Powell was presented, and admitted to the
degree of D.D. *necnon suffragandum in domo utraque,* and
Sessions and South were admitted *ad incipiendum.* Nothing
is said about Barton proceeding to the degree that day. The
opposition was largely voiced by Ralph Rawson of Brasenose
and Robert Hawkins of Balliol ; and the first at any rate
afterwards spoke strongly about the proceedings in his sermons.[13] Party feeling was intense and the accusations were

[13] Wood, *Life and Times,* pp. 500–2, with Clark's notes.

made against Crewe by bitter partisans.[14] Many churchmen
detested those presbyterians who had changed sides at the
Restoration and complained that they had received more
honours than the loyal men. For long this complaint was
dragged into everything, in academic disputes no less than
others. Certainly there was an attempt to confer degrees on
persons of insufficient standing, but they had been nominated
by the chancellor and they had considerable support, and
there seems no real reason for blaming the senior proctor.

At Convocation on April 20th, 1664 Crewe laid down his
proctorship. Delivering up the *Liber Niger Procuratorum,*
which was always kept in the care of the senior proctor and
contained a record of the severer penalties which it had been
necessary to award, he was able to say, " *Ne vel una macula
nigrior.*" There was a general hum of applause at this which
may have been " a public testimony of their great satisfaction
at his conduct,"[15] or " a proof of his popularity,"[16] or
approval of his speech. Wood, however, said that he made " a
light, vain, silly speech not befitting his place, but rather a
Terræ filius." He picked out two statements: that in
Oliver's day the times were stagnant, but now they ran clear
with a free course, and that though Mr. Gilbert was not he
that wrote *De Magnete,* yet he had a magnet in his house, a
handsome daughter, who was married to Mr. Sproston.[17] We
do not know enough of Crewe's speech to pass any judgment.
Probably the reference to Gilbert and Sproston occurred in
some remarks about events during his year of office, while
what he said about Oliver was quite sufficient to make Wood
snarl at " this fellow that ran with the times " and " was afterwards preferred because his father had been a notorious
rebel." Not everyone thought like Wood : Thomas Tomkyns

[14] MS. Bodl. 594, p. 46. MS. Rawl. D. olim 1290, quoted by A. Clark.
Wood, *Life and Times,* II, p. 16.
[15] *Memoirs.*
[16] *Examination.*
[17] Mr. Gilbert was probably Thomas Gilbert, B.D., ejected from the
vicarage of Edgemond, Shropshire, and living in retirement for many
years in St. Ebb's parish. Palmer, *Nonc. Mem.,* III, p. 145. The
author of *De Magnete* was William Gilbert. This book was published
in 1600.

of All Souls, who had made his speech in St. Mary's on April 2nd, 1664 commended his fellow proctor, and said that as Lord Brooke desired that his epitaph should be that he was " a friend to Sir Philip Sidney," so he himself desired that over his grave it should be inscribed that he had been the colleague of Crewe in the proctorship.[18] In the maintenance of discipline in the college Crewe acted " with a decision with which the college had long been a stranger." In July 1664 a servitor named Ward behaved with insolence towards Mr. William Adams, one of the fellows. Crewe at once expelled him, and it was only after an abject submission, the intercession of Mr. Adams himself, and a public apology made by the offender on his bended knees, that he was allowed to return.[19]

By the foundation of John Crosby, one of the fellows of Lincoln College was to be a student of canon law, and Crewe had been elected to the canonist fellowship on March 22nd, 1659. It was one of the statutes of the college that every fellow should graduate in divinity except this one fellow, who formerly had been required to take the degrees in canon law. Such a degree was no longer given : it had never been abolished, but since the canon law was no longer studied in Oxford the degree had fallen into desuetude. So the college ordered Crewe to graduate in civil law instead and he was to do so before July 1663. He had, however, deferred taking the bachelor's degree owing to the work which the proctorship had entailed. As a special favour he was allowed to take his doctor's degree by accumulation. On July 2nd, 1664 a letter from the Chancellor, Lord Clarendon, was read in Convocation, in which he spoke warmly of Crewe " who deserves no less to be valued for his parts and learning than for the condition of his birth, and who did so well acquit himself in that part of the King's reception which fell to his share that His Majesty was pleased to take particular notice of him." He desired, if Convocation approved, and Crewe himself were willing, to confer the degree of Doctor of Laws

[18] Wood, *Life and Times*, II, pp. 8–11.
[19] A. Clark, *Lincoln*, p. 140.

upon him, " provided he would be willing to answer the doctors *in Comitiis* and standing in the Act." Convocation agreed and Crewe answered the doctors " in the public Act for the exercise according to the statutes." Sir Lionel Jenkyns was Moderator, and the question Crewe disputed upon was " *An solius Principis sit leges interpretari* " ; the doctors evidently approved, and he was admitted to the degree of Doctor of Laws that very day.[20] The disputation can hardly have been a very long one, and some students in these days might envy the facility with which so high a degree was attained. Wood, who says Crewe was admitted a Doctor of the Civil and Canon Law, comments characteristically by throwing doubts on Crewe's parts and learning, and saying that " as for his birth his father was but an ordinary gentleman, and a grand rebel and presbyterian, and made a baron but a little more than three years agone." [21] Wood continually drags up the past. One cannot but feel that there was a great deal of jealousy in this poor, shy and embittered man. In 1665 he asked permission to peruse the registers, muniments and records of Lincoln College. The permit was signed on June 8th by Nathaniel Crewe, as sub-rector, and Henry Foulis, one of the fellows. On the eighth of March in the following year we have a glimpse of Wood perusing the old register of the college in Crewe's chamber.[22] It must have galled him to be in any way beholden to a man he disliked so much, whom he seldom or never mentioned without scornful comments.

After the legal disputation in Convocation Dr. Pierce, President of Magdalen College, remarked upon the accuracy with which Crewe had defended his position, and in offering his congratulations urged him to take holy orders. The conditions of his fellowship demanded that he should do so, but Crewe seems to have hesitated for some time. On January 21st, 1662 the college gave him a dispensation from ordination till July 1663. Still he remained a layman and on May

[20] Wood, *Life and Times,* II, pp. 15, 16.
[21] Wood, *Life and Times,* II, p. 16.
[22] *Ibid.,* II, p. 121.

6th, 1664 he had received a second dispensation granting him permission to postpone once more until the Lent Ember Week in 1665. He explained to Dr. Pierce the reasons for his delay : he was apprehensive that certain persons might entertain unjust and groundless opinions of him on account of his early history, and he was unwilling to take the office of a clergyman while there was any suspicion that he was not thoroughly well affected to the service of the Church.[23] Whether his scruples were overcome, or whether because, as one of his biographers said, "these jealousies were vanished," [24] or whether the college regulations could no longer be evaded, he took holy orders in 1665. Archbishop Sheldon granted him a faculty to be ordained deacon and priest on the same day, probably in order that there should be no further delay in obeying the statutes. Dr. George Morley, Bishop of Winchester, who was also Dean of the Chapel Royal, ordained him. Dr. John Dolben, Dean of Westminster, Clerk of the Closet and Archdeacon of London, presented Crewe and another candidate whose name is not given. The Ordination Service requires the bishop to say :

> "Take heed that the persons whom ye present unto us, be apt and meet, for their learning and godly conversation, to exercise their ministry duly, to the honour of God, and the edifying of His Church."

To which the archdeacon shall answer :

> "I have enquired of them and also examined them, and think them so to be."

Dolben therefore told Crewe that he would have to examine him. So he asked him to turn into Latin : "I have examined them and find them qualified," to which Crewe replied immediately, "*Satis exploratos habui, eosque idoneos judico ut in sacros ordines initeantur.*" "Oh," said the Archdeacon, "I'll examine you no further." We are not told what happened to the other candidate, or whether the one answer did for the two of them, but as we do not hear that he was

[23] *Memoirs*, pp. 7–8.
[24] *Memoirs*, p. 8.

C

rejected we may assume that he was ordained also. It was a perfunctory affair but for long afterwards the idea that a graduate with a good reputation for scholarship was sufficiently qualified for the priesthood still held. The wonder was that the Anglican Church had any influence amongst the laity when her clergy were expected to know so little about their business. The fact that so many of them pursued their theological studies of their own volition and that the more eminent divines of the time were really remarkable for their sacred learning explains a good deal.

After the ordination Morley introduced Crewe to the King, who promised to take care of him and said he was glad to find a *gentleman* undertaking the service of the Church. It certainly was not a common thing. Crewe is believed to have been the first bishop who came of a noble family since the Reformation, and Compton the second. From the end of September 1665 to the end of January the Court was at Oxford because of the plague. The King and Queen were there, the Duke and Duchess of York, the Duke and Duchess of Monmouth and Lady Castlemaine and her two sons, the Duke of Southampton and the Duke of Grafton. These two lodged in the same house with Anthony Wood and the Duchess gave birth to another son in December while she was living in Merton College. On October 9th Parliament was gathered in Oxford; the Lords met in the Geometry School, the Commons in the Convocation House, while the Divinity School was used for committees. On September 26th the vice-chancellor, proctors and doctors appeared in full scarlet before the King. Dr. Robert South, the Public Orator, made a speech of welcome and they all kissed hands. On subsequent occasions, with similar formalities, they welcomed the Queen, the Duke of York and the Duchess of York, though in the last case there were many who disapproved. Lady Castlemaine was very unpopular and signs of this were not difficult to see. No doubt Crewe as a doctor was present at these functions, but generally speaking there was a marked line of division between the Court and the university. " The greater sort of the courtiers were high, proud, insolent, and looked upon scholars no more than pedants, or pedagogical persons : the lower sort also made no more of them than the greater, not suffering them to see the King or Queen at dinner or supper or scarce at cards or at mass. . . . The townsmen, who were gainers by the Court, grew rich and proud, and cared not for scholars : but when the court was gone they sneaked to them again." [25] Altogether Oxford was better when they went. Charles' promise of patronage was soon fulfilled, for on November 5th, 1666 Crewe was sworn in by the Lord Chamberlain, the Earl of Manchester, as one of the King's Chaplains in Ordinary.[26] On his appointment as chaplain Lord Manchester told him that by virtue of his oath he was to pay duty to him, and commanded his immediate attendance. When he officiated the King took notice of him and said, " He has an honest countenance." In 1667 the King gave Crewe a sinecure in Lincolnshire, the rectory of Gedney which was without cure of souls. The *Examination* says that the mandate under the Broad Seal mistakenly described him as a Doctor of Divinity, so that he had to go to the trouble of taking that degree and paying the necessary fees, the expense of which greatly reduced the profits of his sinecure. The catalogue of Oxford graduates mentions the D.C.L., and says nothing about D.D., though it is true that it makes no mention of M.A. either.[27]

When Lord Clarendon was dismissed from the chancellorship in that year several prominent ecclesiastics lost their positions and influence at Court, Archbishop Sheldon, Bishop Morley and Dean Dolben amongst them. Dr. Croft, Bishop of Hereford, became Dean of the Chapel Royal, and Dr. Blandford, Warden of Wadham College, Oxford, became Clerk to the Closet with Crewe as his Deputy Clerk. Crewe was getting on fast : he had birth, position and prospects : he was handsome and took some pride in his personal appear-

---

[25] Wood, *Life and Times*, p. 68.

[26] The *Memoirs* say 1666, but the *Examination* says " Dr. Outram was to be chaplain in turn, but on account of the sickness was excused." If the sickness was the Plague the date is more likely to have been 1665.

[27] *A Catalogue of all Graduates in the University of Oxford*, 1659–1850, Oxford, 1851.

ance, but when his friend Bishop Croft told him that his curled hair looked unbecoming to a divine he had it cut shorter next day, and his mentor was greatly pleased with his submissive behaviour. Bishop Croft did not remain Clerk of the Closet long. He was a little too outspoken to the King about his mistresses, and even dared to say that the King's conduct in certain matters was not what might be expected from one who received the Holy Sacrament. Charles received the rebuke coldly, the bishop asked leave to retire and Crewe was appointed in his place. His conduct towards the King won him increased favour. It was remarked that whereas Dolben, while Dean of the Closet, had been in the habit of using familiarities with Charles, such as playing with his Majesty's band-strings and such like, Crewe, though he was assiduous in his attentions, behaved always with the exact courtesy of a gentleman.

He was appointed Lent preacher at Court in 1668.[28] It would be somewhat of an ordeal for a man not very long in orders and with very little experience in preaching, and so he asked Dr. Fell, Dean of Christ Church, to look over his first sermon. His critic suggested the removal of " some smart strokes " : perhaps he was showing a little too much of the clever young man : but at any rate the offending passages were removed. The modern Invocation before the sermon was then unknown : the Puritan ministers generally poured forth a long extempore prayer ; the Anglican-minded usually said a collect. This is why it is recorded for us that Crewe prefaced his discourse with the petition from the Litany " Remember not, O Lord, our offences nor the offences of our forefathers," etc. The text of the sermon was, " If we say that we have no sin we deceive ourselves and the truth is not in us, but if we confess our sins He is faithful and just to forgive us our sins and to cleanse us from all unrighteousness." The King was not a good listener when it came to sermons. Sometimes he slept, sometimes he talked : on this occasion he stood up all the while, which was sufficiently disconcerting for the unfortunate divine, who was

[28] The *Examination* says 1666.

" a little abashed." But the Duke of York, who with all his faults had more regard for religion than his brother, spoke to him kindly and appreciatively afterwards and said that he wished his father, meaning King Charles I, had heard him.

Samuel Pepys was a friend of old Lord Crewe. Before the latter was raised to the peerage he even borrowed money from him.[29] The diary records a number of times (about thirty) in which Pepys dined with him, and Lord Crewe seemed pleased with his visits. In company with Lady Sandwich and Mrs. Sanderson he met Nathaniel Crewe at the Wardrobe. Nathaniel was accompanied by a friend and fellow student of his of a good family, Mr. Knightley, whom Lady Sandwich looked upon as a possible husband for her daughter Jemima.[30] In 1666 we come across several references to Nathaniel Crewe :

"Thence to my Lord Crewe's, and there dined, and mightily made of, having not, to my shame, been there in eight months before. Here my Lord and Sir Thomas Crewe, Mr. John (younger son of the first Lord Crewe) and Dr. Crewe, and two strangers. The best family in the world for goodness and sobriety. Here beyond my expectation I met my Lord Hinchingbroke, who is come to town two days since from Hinchingbroke, and brought his sister and brother Carteret with him, who are at Sir G. Carteret's. After dinner I and Sir Thomas Crewe went aside to discourse of public matters. . . . After dinner and this discourse I took coach, and at the same time find my Lord Hinchingbroke and Mr. John Crewe and the Doctor going out to see the ruins of the city ; so I took the Doctor into my hackney coach (and he is a very fine sober gentleman), and so through the city. But Lord ! what pretty and sober observations he made of the city and its desolation ; till anon we come to my house, and there I took them upon Tower Hill to shew them what houses were pulled down there since the fire, and then to my house, where I treated them with good wine of several sorts, and they took it mighty respectfully, and a fine company of

[29] *Diary,* Jan. 10th, 1660.
[30] *Ibid.,* May 17th, 1662.

gentlemen they are. Here I got them to appoint Wednesday come se'nnight to dine here at my house and so we broke up and all took coach again and I carried the Doctor to Chancery Lane and thence I went to Whitehall." [31]

On April 3rd, 1667 Pepys was at Whitehall, and went to service in the chapel. He heard that Dr. Crewe was to preach; so he went up into the organ loft, where he found Mr. Carteret and my Lady Jemima, and Sir Thomas Crewe's two daughters, " and Dr. Crewe did make a very pretty, neat, sober, honest sermon : and delivered it very readily, decently and gravely, beyond his years; [32] so as I was exceedingly taken with it, and I believe the whole chapel, he being but young; but his manner of his delivery I do like exceedingly. His text was ' But seek ye first the kingdom of God and his righteousness and all these things shall be added unto you.' " [33] Pepys was very critical of sermons, so his testimony here is all the stronger.

There is abundant evidence that the revulsion of feeling caused by the Restoration was not for the good of Oxford morals and behaviour. We hear much of gambling, drunkenness, immorality and bad language; discipline was slack, the undergraduates were rowdy, and if we were to believe all we are told, learning was disgracefully neglected. The wickedness of the period has become almost proverbial, but it has been exaggerated, for there still existed throughout the land the great multitude of decent folk who were not the observed of the reporter and the diarist. There were in Oxford, even at such periods of temptation as when the Court stayed there during the plague time, numbers of men whose love of learning, inquisitive desire for new knowledge and thirst for genuine culture were the chief characteristics. Such a man was Crewe whom we find taking lessons, amongst other things, in science.

In Oxford there had been from 1659 to 1664 a German teacher of chemistry, Peter Sthael of Strasburg who had been

---

[31] *Diary*, November 6th, 1666.
[32] He was then thirty-four years of age.
[33] *Diary*, April 3rd, 1667.

brought to the university by Robert Boyle. He lived first in a house called Deep Hall on the west side of University College, then in a house belonging to an apothecary, close by, and finally established himself and furnished a laboratory in the Ram Inn in High Street, formerly a hostel. His lecture room was " an old hall or refectory." He went away to London in 1664 to conduct researches for the Royal Society, but while he was in Oxford some notable people came to him as pupils, Joseph Williamson, John Wallis, John Locke, Christopher Wren and Francis Turner, afterwards Bishop of Ely.[34] Crewe was another and his pursuit of this new branch of learning shows him to have had an inquiring mind and broad interests. He was a member of a musical society which had been established in 1656 and had included in its early days among its members such people as Sir Kenelm Digby, and the future Bishop Ken, then an undergraduate at New College. The members met in Broad Street, at the house of William Ellis, formerly organist of St. John's College, and his wife, the daughter of the Lincoln cook. The house was a sort of tavern, and at each meeting each member was expected to spend sixpence on drink for the good of the house.[35] At these weekly meetings there came together the chief performers in Oxford. The Musical Club still meets on Tuesdays as of old.[36] Crewe had the reputation of being a good judge of music and a good performer on more than one instrument, and one of his biographers gravely informs us that his mother, a little before his birth, dreamed of a fine concert of music in the rookery. Heavenly harmony from a rookery would, no doubt, be surprising, but perhaps our author goes too far in thinking this dream an important prenatal influence. Anthony Wood, who sometimes was present at the club, admitted Crewe to be a performer, but said that he had not a good ear for music and always played out of tune.[37] The King was a good judge of the arts and it says something at least for Crewe's musical knowledge and taste that

[34] Wood, *Life and Times*, I, pp. 290, 472–3.
[35] Clark, *Lincoln*, p. 125.
[36] Mrs. M. C. N. Munro, *Oxford Mag.*, June 10th, 1937.
[37] Wood, *Life and Times*, I, p. 274.

Charles generally approved of Crewe's choice of music for the chapel, and sometimes deferred to it, and Crewe improved the musical part of the services by bringing Dr. Turner and Mr. Gosling into the choir.

On August 2nd, 1668 Dr. Paul Hood, Rector of Lincoln College, died at the age of eighty-two. He had ruled the college for over forty-seven years and perhaps he had his long reign in mind when he recommended Crewe to seek the rectorship, for then he would have a long life. Hood had been nearly blind for some years, and the sub-rector had really ruled the house.[38] The fellows unanimously invited Crewe to succeed him and sent the invitation to London by the hands of one of the Bible clerks. He was on duty at the Chapel Royal and leave of absence had to be requested of the King, which was done through the Lord Chamberlain. On Monday August 10th he left London and arrived in Oxford by noon on Tuesday. Then as sub-rector he summoned a meeting of the fellows and was unanimously elected on the 12th. He returned to London and on the Friday morning officiated before the King in the chapel. Charles seems to have been surprised at his quick return, but it was one of Crewe's sayings that " it is better to be an hour too soon than a minute too late." On September 8th he was in Lincoln, whither he had gone to be instituted to his sinecure, and to be admitted rector by the visitor, Bishop Fuller, who issued a mandate for his installation, and on the 17th, " sitting in the chiefest seat of the choir " of All Saints' Church, Oxford, he was duly installed after the second lesson at Morning Prayer. Mr. Foulis prophesied that if he lived another seven years he would be a bishop. This came true in less time than that.

He held the rectorship of Lincoln College for four years, during which time a great deal was done for the benefit of the college. The finances were put on a sound footing, among other ways by benefactions: the buildings were repaired and made more comfortable. His father in 1656 had fitted up the old chapel as a library and turned the old library into

[38] Clark, *Lincoln*, p. 140.

a fine set of rooms at a cost of about £200.[39] Nathaniel also contributed liberally to various needs. The fellows were in the habit of letting the attics above their rooms to students. Crewe was insistent that these rooms should be kept in fit condition for habitation. The new chapel, consecrated in 1631, was redecorated and the Anglican services were steadily maintained. He was responsible for improvement in the work of the undergraduates, who were made to write dissertations, and for their benefit two Greek lectures were provided every week. Discipline was not forgotten. Lincoln had suffered like other colleges from the prevailing depravation of manners during the past few years. Bad conduct, bad language and brawling were put down with a firm hand, disorderly behaviour in the college was stopped, and altogether there was a real reformation, so that Lincoln became one of the quietest and best-behaved colleges in Oxford, and in a far higher position than it had held before.[40] Consequently the numbers of students showed a steady increase. It was surprising that he did so much in such a short time, seeing how much of his time was spent at Court. The high standard which he set up was maintained by his successors.[41] Nor were the fellows unmindful of what their rector had done. Even after he had resigned his office he kept up regular intercourse with the college and his advice was frequently sought, especially in the election of new fellows.

Crewe's polished manners and good looks made him very acceptable to the King, who was determined to promote him. In 1668 Dr. Reeves, the Dean of Windsor, was said to be dying, and Prince Rupert asked the King whom he had in mind for the appointment. Charles declared his intention of giving it to Crewe and Prince Rupert was very pleased. Dr. Reeves, however, got better. The King nominated Crewe to the archdeaconry of Canterbury, being under the impression that the patronage lay in his hands. The appointment

[39] Wood, *Hist. Univ. Oxf.*, ed. by John Gulch, 1786, pp. 248–9.
[40] Clark, *Lincoln*, p. 142.
[41] Malet, *Hist. Univ. Oxf.*, I, pp. 360–1. S. A. Warner, *Lincoln College, Oxford*, 1908, p. 16.

had actually appeared in the public prints when it was discovered that the gift lay with the Archbishop. Even then, so Dean Dolben said, Crewe might have had it by asking Sheldon, but he declined to do so. In the following spring the deanery of Chichester fell vacant, and the King said that if it were worth Crewe's acceptance he should have it. The precentorship, also in the King's gift, was vacant at the same time, so Crewe was collated to the latter office on April 28th and installed dean on the following day. The chapter of Chichester then elected him a member of their body, so that he became entitled to the common dividend from the chapter property. Some time after his installation an impropriation held by lease from the dean and chapter fell in; for its renewal the fine was set at £1,000. The dean, however, proposed and carried a resolution in chapter that half of this sum should be applied to the augmentation of the vicarage and the rest divided among the members of the chapter, who otherwise would have shared out the whole sum. Crewe remained Dean of Chichester for two years. He was invited in 1669 to accept the vice-chancellorship of the University of Oxford. The invitation came from the Heads of Houses. The writer of the *Memoirs* referring to the question of the vice-chancellorship said that Sheldon who was then chancellor declined to act. This somewhat ambiguous statement might be taken as meaning a slight to Crewe, but it was not that. Though Sheldon had been elected in 1667 he had never been installed and so the powers of the chancellor seem to have been exercised either by Convocation or by the Heads of Houses. Sheldon resigned on July 31st, 1669 so the offer to Crewe must have been made before that date. The latter declined the vice-chancellorship on account of his obligation to attend at Court.[42]

Crewe's enemies constantly raked up against him that he had once been a Presbyterian: but he seems to have become a High Churchman of the Anglo-Catholic school. Perhaps that word may seem an anachronism, and Laudian more fitting; but there was a strong body of Anglican divines who

[42] Clark, *Lincoln*, p. 142.

maintained that the Church of England was still a part of the Catholic Church, and held all the doctrines of the Catholic Church which could fall under the Vincentian canon : *quod semper, quod ubique, quod ab omnibus.* Crewe's development may explain to some extent his later conduct, and is illustrated by some of his sayings. Thus, in one of his Lenten courses he had to preach on Lady Day and, referring to our Lady, he spoke to this effect : " Nowadays, some are so far from doing her honour that they won't so much allow her the respect due to her, Lord Savile and others having publicly and shamefully cast reproaches at her." This, though some people thought it a very seasonable rebuke, of course gave great offence, among other people to Crewe's own father. Old Lord Crewe not only feared that Nathaniel would do himself harm by such sayings, but was afraid that he was in danger from superstition as well as from ambition.[43]

While the King and Court were at Dover in 1670 Crewe obtained leave from the King to accompany the English ambassador who was going over with complimentary messages to Louis who had just returned from Holland. The French King was at Calais, so that Crewe was able to see him and his Court " in all their grandeur." A kinsman, Sir Harry Jones, Captain of the Band of Pensioners, acted as cicerone and showed him all that it was possible to see in a few days. Discussing his journey with the Duchess of York, he told her that he much admired the pictures in the chapel at Calais and thought they were very fine, if put to a good use ; to which the Duchess, already leaning towards Rome, replied " Put to a good use." [44]

In 1671 the bishopric of Worcester fell vacant and the Duke of Buckingham tried to get it for Dr. Wilkins. The Duke of Ormond, however, obtained it for Dr. Walter Blandford, Bishop of Oxford since 1665, and Crewe was then nominated by the King as his successor. Henshaw, Bishop of Salisbury, used to say that it was " Crewe's interest that pushed Blandford up to Worcester." Crewe gave up his

[43] *Examination.*
[44] Wood, *Life and Times*, II, p. 221. *Memoirs*, p. 11.

Lincolnshire sinecure, for in May the Rev. Gregory Hascard petitioned for the rectory of Gedney, about to become void by the promotion of Dr. Nathaniel Crewe to Oxford,[45] but on May 22nd the rectory was granted to Dr. James Gardiner.[46] In July, however, it was given to Robert Mapletoft, Dean of Ely.[47] On May 25th a warrant was issued to the Clerk of the Signet for the presentation of Dr. Crewe to the rectory of Witney in Oxfordshire, void by the promotion of Dr. Blandford.[48] On June 13th Crewe applied for a *Commendam* to enable him to hold the rectory in plurality.[49] This was granted under the Broad Seal on June 19th.[50] This living, which was given to him by the King at the request of the Archbishop was worth £47 a year [51] and he was collated to it before his consecration. Anthony Wood refers angrily to his promotion to the episcopate, " of which function, if you consider his learning, real honesty and religion, which I myself do know full well is altogether unworthy : but presbyterians for their money must be served while the royal party put off with inconsiderable nothings." [52] Crewe's religion would be suspect to Wood because he had once been a presbyterian. If you throw enough mud some of it will stick, and the mud-throwing of Wood, Burnet and White Kennet has caused a great deal to stick right down to the present day.

He was elected on June 16th and confirmed in the Savoy Chapel on the 27th. Bishop Cosin who officiated told him that if he were but old enough he believed he would be his successor at Durham, another prophecy that came true. Cosin told Dean Dolben that he knew he was hoping some day to be Bishop of Durham, but that he would find himself mistaken. This also came true for Dolben became Archbishop

[45] *Calendar of State Papers Domestic* 290, No. 27.
[46] *C.S.P.D.* Entry Book 35B, f. 15.
[47] *C.S.P.D.* Docquets, Vol. 25, No. 33.
[48] *C.S.P.D.* 290, No. 46.
[49] *C.S.P.D.* 290, No. 210.
[50] *C.S.P.D.* Entry Book 25B, f. 14.
[51] The *Memoirs* say £600. But Ecton's official valuation in 1711 was £47 9s. 4½d. *Liber Valorum et Decimarum,* 1711.
[52] Wood, *Life and Times,* I, pp. 332–3.

of York instead. The royal assent to the election was given on June 30th [53] and Crewe was consecrated at Lambeth on the second Sunday after Trinity, July 2nd, by Archbishop Sheldon, Humphrey Bishop of London, Benjamin Bishop of Ely, Walter Bishop of Worcester, John Bishop of Rochester and William Bishop of Lincoln.[54] The temporalities of the see were restored to him in July.[55] He was enthroned in Christ Church Cathedral, Oxford, three days later. On the day of his consecration, with his usual magnificence, he gave a noble feast, which the Archbishop of Canterbury described as the finest that he ever saw. The Duke of Ormond was present and so was the Earl of Sandwich, who said it was the most joyful day he had ever seen. Sandwich was Crewe's brother-in-law. At the age of seventeen Edward Montagu, as he was then, had married Jemima Crewe, daughter of John Crewe of Steane. She was only ten days older than her husband. She was an excellent wife and mother, and Pepys, a poor cousin of Montagu and at first his secretary, had a profound admiration and affection for her. She treated him " with extraordinary love and kindness," [56] and he said of her " so good and discreet a woman I know not in the world." [57]

The see of Oxford was not a large or a wealthy one. Comparatively small, cut out of the diocese of Lincoln in the days of Henry VIII, it contained the hundred and sixty-nine parishes which made up the old archdeaconry of Oxford, and forty years later was said to be worth £381 11s. 0½d.[58] The former church of St. Frideswide's Abbey was now both the cathedral for the diocese and chapel for the college of Christ Church. From the foundation of the see down to the time of Bishop Bancroft there was no official residence provided, but the last named bishop had built a palace at Cuddesdon for the purpose. This was burnt down by Colonel Legge in 1644, and though Dr. William Paul

[53] *C.S.P.D.* Docquets, Vol. 25, No. 89.
[54] Sheldon Reg. 83, 90. Hist. MSS. Com. Alan Geo. Finch MSS. II, p. 20.
[55] *C.S.P.D.* Docquets, Vol. 25, No. 97.
[56] *Diary*, Oct. 13th, 1660.
[57] *Ibid.,* Oct. 25th, 1661.
[58] J. Ecton, *Liber Valorum,* 1711, p. 334.

prepared timber for the rebuilding, the shortness of his episcopate (1663–5) prevented anything being done!

In addition to his see and the living of Witney, Crewe had
leave to hold the rectorship of Lincoln College *in commendam*. This was of particular advantage to him as there
was no episcopal residence, and Oxford was conveniently
situated for his diocesan work. Moreover, the college statutes
permitted the headship to be held *cum quocumque beneficio
ecclesiastico*. Dean Fell told him it was improper to hold the
two together, but evidently changed his mind later in life
when he showed no qualms of conscience in holding the
deanery and bishopric of Oxford together from 1676 to 1686.
Crewe did not retain the deanery of Chichester: he was
succeeded in that office by Dr. George Stradling.

Academic life is ordinarily quiet and has no history. The
only event which ruffled the calm of the rector during his last
year was what one of his biographers called " a tempest in a
bason," or as we should say, a storm in a teacup, over the
nomination of a new fellow. Crewe dismissed two of his
chaplains for opposing him in the matter, Thomas Pargiter,
a Lincoln College man [59] and George Hickes, who was afterwards the non-juring Dean of Worcester.[60] " Thus early did
ingratitude appear within those walls." [61] Crewe used to
say that he would continue master while he was within the
walls, so we may be sure he got his own way over the
appointment. His hospitality was lavish and his " handsome
entertainments " were talked about. For some reason he only
retained the rectorship for a year after his promotion to the
episcopate. His departure was a trifle dramatic. He stayed
in the college for a few days in October 1672 and entertained
the society in " the handsomest and most generous manner."
On the eighteenth all the fellows accompanied his carriage
to the gates. We can picture the deep and reverent salutes,
the dignified and affable condescension of his lordship, who
as soon as he was outside the gates handed in his resignation.

[59] Thomas Pargiter, B.A. 1663, D.D. 1676.
[60] George Hickes, B.A. Magd. 1662, M.A. Linc. 1665, B.D. 1675,
D.D. 1679.
[61] *Examination*, p. 26.

So he kept his determination to be master as long as he was within those walls. He never forgot his beloved college and remained its generous friend. He was succeeded by Dr. Marshall, an old acquaintance of his father, who was elected through " Dr. Crewe's influence."

Crewe was not long enough in the diocese of Oxford to make any mark, and very little information remains to us, for the diocesan records for the period are very deficient. The volume of Institutions and Ordinations 1660–1702 gives an account of three ordinations which he held. The first was in the cathedral on St. Thomas' Day, 1673, when he ordained thirty-five deacons and thirty-one priests. Next day, December 22nd, he ordained one deacon and two priests in Lincoln College chapel. The deacon was John Massey, B.A., who is given as of Magdalen College. If this was the future Dean of Christ Church in the days of James II his college seems to have been given wrongly, for Wood says that he was of University College and later of Merton : otherwise the identification fits. Dean Massey took his M.A. in 1675. At the September ordination of 1674, held in the cathedral, forty-one persons were admitted to the diaconate and twenty-seven to the priesthood.[62] In the accounts of the vice-chancellor for 1673–4 appears the following entry : " To a French gentleman recommended by the Bishop of Oxford and Rochester, by consent of the Heads of Houses, £2." It is fairly safe to say that the bishop performed the usual round of visitation and confirmation. His diligence in that respect was remarked upon in his second diocese. We know too that he must have spent some time at Court.

In 1672 it was noticed that James Duke of York had absented himself from the Church of England services on Good Friday, Easter Eve and Easter Day and this was causing some alarm. Crewe probably had as much influence as anybody at Court, and he felt it was his duty to act the part of a candid friend. So on Easter Tuesday he went in his episcopal habit and lawn sleeves to James' apartments in the

[62] Information from Mr. E. A. Bacon, Assistant Registrar, and Miss E. G. Parker.

palace and asked leave to speak with him. Permission being
granted he told the Duke that he was sorry to see that he had
not attended service lately, to which James replied that he
could not dissemble with God and man any longer and that
he should come no more. Crewe boldly told him that whoever advised him to take that line was no true friend, and the
Duke, who had a great liking for him, replied, " My Lord,
I shall take nothing ill that you say." No doubt the bishop's
stately courtesy and deference took the sting out of his plain
speaking and so gave no cause for resentment. The conversation took place in the bed-chamber and behind the great bed,
where they would be free from eavesdroppers. Crewe on one
occasion, Dr. Smith says it was about the time of the Popish
Plot, discussed Catholicism with the King, giving it as his
opinion that the Jesuits had done great mischief to the nation
at large, and expressing his belief that no Roman Catholic
was his own master, to which Charles replied, " The truth is,
they are an odd sort of people." Dr. Smith comments on all
this by saying : " We cannot but take notice of his watch-
fulness against the influences of the papists, or any the least
deviation in the King or Duke from the Established Church,
and consequently the injustice of those who would reproach
his lordship with having been a favourer of popery." Few
men remain absolutely constant and without wavering in their
religious views all their life long. In 1672 Crewe no doubt
saw the danger to the monarchy if James left the Church of
England. At the time of the Popish Plot most people were
carried away by the tempest of Protestant passion aroused
by Oates and his fellow rascals. At a later date his High
Anglicanism seems to have produced some leanings towards
Rome on his part, and he refused on one occasion to introduce
Simon Patrick to the King because of the dean's zeal against
popery.[63] It may have been, of course, that he felt that
Patrick would not be acceptable to the King, and his affection
for the King made him very considerate for the latter's feelings.

While Crewe was Bishop of Oxford he suffered several

[63] Birch, *Life of Tillotson,* 1753, I, p. 99.

bereavements—not his first, for his younger brother Samuel, who had been at Lincoln College with him and had taken his degree at the same time as Nathaniel, had died of the spotted fever on July 2nd, 1661. In May 1672 his brother-in-law, the Earl of Sandwich had gone down with his ship at the battle of Southwold Bay. The King condoled with him on his loss and he replied that " since he was lost he rejoiced that it was in His Majesty's service." On January 17th, 1673 Crewe's secretary, Thomas Law, M.A., sometime scholar of Corpus and fellow of Lincoln, died and was buried the next day in the chancel of St. Michael's Church, Oxford, by the grave of Henry Foulis, B.D., sub-rector of Lincoln, who had died in 1669. In 1674 Jemima Lady Sandwich died. She had lost her daughter-in-law, Lady Hinchingbroke, in 1671 and her husband in the following year, two blows from which she never really recovered.

In 1673 Henry Mordaunt (second) Earl of Peterborough had been sent to Italy to secure as a bride for James, Mary Beatrice Eleanora, the daughter of the Duchess of Modena. There were many difficulties in the way. The young lady herself was one. She was fourteen and he was forty, moreover she wanted to give her life to the Church. She was persuaded, however, that she might be the means of restoring the Catholic faith in England and so she gave way. James had resigned his offices on the passing of the Test Act, and he had not communicated at Anglican altars for a long time. Everybody believed he was a Roman Catholic, but it had not been officially announced and would not be if King Charles could prevent it. The Pope was not satisfied with this and was insisting that Mary should have full liberty to exercise her religion : Charles was afraid to give open and public sanction to a Catholic chapel in Whitehall. There was need for hurry—Parliament would be summoned soon and Parliament would oppose the match violently. The Bishop of Modena dared not risk offending the Pope, for threats of excommunication were flying about. At last, on the last day of September 1673 Mary Beatrice was married to the Duke of York, the Earl of Peterborough acting as proxy. To per-

D

form the service a priest was found about the court who had nothing to lose, " and on whom the terror of excommunication did not so much prevail." Peterborough was conducted to a chamber near the chapel where he reposed himself " till so much of the service was done as seemed obnoxious to the religion he did profess." After that he was led into the chapel and the actual marriage ceremony took place. Then they set out on the journey through Italy and France and, crossing from Calais, arrived at Dover.

When the rumour got about that the heir to the throne was about to marry an Italian Roman Catholic the House of Commons on October 20th presented an address to the King urging him to forbid the proposed nuptials. They had asked the Upper House to join in the protest but the Lords refused. A second remonstrance stated that such a marriage would lessen the people's affections for his Royal Highness and since the princess had so many relations at the Court of Rome " this marriage would furnish them with the means to pene-trate into His Majesty's most secret councils." This too was ineffectual. James told Crewe that he intended him to per-form the marriage service and bade him go to Lambeth and ask the Archbishop of Canterbury about his procedure when he married the King to Catherine of Braganza. Shaftesbury advised Crewe that if he did perform the ceremony he would be wise to take out a licence to do so under the Broad Seal. Shaftesbury was Lord Chancellor until November 9th that year, and would probably have refused it. James, however, told Crewe : " My Lord, in that you may be safe in what you do, the King will empower you under his signet." This was done and the warrant from the King ran as follows : " Whereas at the Duke of York's request we have appointed you to assist and attend him in the performance of all those rites and ceremonies which shall be requisite to the com-pleting of his marriage with the Princess Maria d'Este, we warrant you hereby for your discharge in so doing." [64]

At Dover on November 21st, 1673 James met his new bride. " After she had reposed herself, his Royal Highness,

[64] *C.S.P.D.* Entry Book 31, f. 21.

that had provided so to confirm the matter . . . that the
malice of any age to come, should have no pretence to call
it in question, led out his duchess into the great room before
his bed-chamber and there, in the presence of all the lords who
attended him from London, of all the country gentlemen who
were come to see him, and what it could contain of the citizens
of Dover, he married again his wife, after the form of the
Church of England, by the hands of Dr. Nathaniel Crewe." [65]
It was perhaps a bold thing on the part of Dr. Crewe, but
his action has been described by his enemies as servile compliance. Now James had been married by proxy according
to Catholic rites and for the satisfaction of the English people
he was married again according to the Anglican rite. Who
was to perform the ceremony? Not necessarily the Archbishop of Canterbury. And if not, then some other Anglican
bishop. The duke had the right of all bridegrooms to ask a
friend to marry him, and Crewe did so. Though we are not
actually told so he would use none other than the marriage
service of the Prayer Book. If he had used, say, the Roman
rite to please his patron and friend, there might have been
some ground for accusations of servility. Sir Peter Wyche
wrote to Sir Joseph Williamson : " The Duchess had a very
pleasant passage from Calais to Dover and was declared by
the Bishop of Oxford that evening." [66] By " declared "
presumably is meant that in the course of the marriage service
he used the usual words from the Book of Common Prayer, " I
pronounce that they be man and wife together." The Anglican form would be of little import to James and his bride, but
the fact that it was he who performed the additional ceremony
was an additional reason for their friendly feeling towards
Crewe. There is no doubt whatever that the bishop was
devoted to the Duke of York. Shaftesbury said to Crewe one
day in the Court of Chancery, " Pray have you been at the
duke's levée ? " and was answered " No indeed, I am highly
to blame for I have not been there to-day."

[65] David Jones, *Life of James II*, 2nd edn., 1703, supplement,
pp. 38–41.
[66] *C.S.P.D.* 338, No. 43.

On one occasion James warned Crewe that he had many enemies, to which the latter replied that he valued them not as long as his Royal Highness was his friend. " My lord," said the duke, " I promise you I'll stick by you." When on one occasion Lord Danby spoke against Crewe in the House of Lords, the Duke of York said pointedly that the bishop was his friend :[67] he seems, indeed, to have said this on more than one occasion in reply to criticism of the bishop. Crewe constantly believed that the duke increased the number of his own enemies by his steady kindness to himself, and it is equally true that Crewe incurred enmity because of his loyalty to James. Amongst those who were particularly hostile to him were Shaftesbury, Buckingham, Danby, Lauderdale, Archbishop Sheldon, the Secretary Coventry and the Lord Keeper Finch. Crewe spoke boldly against the first three on one occasion in the House of Lords and a good deal of notice was taken of it. On another occasion his father rebuked him at home for speaking too severely about the " late troubles " in the House of Lords, and said, " Son, you had better have been sick in your bed," to which he replied, " Pray let me have my health whatever I suffer beside." It would not be pleasant for Lord Crewe to hear his son attack the deeds and policy in which he had had a share, and he is said never to have entered the House of Lords after his son entered it. " The bishop had exhibited principles so different to those of his father that the father was obliged to withdraw himself." [68] But Lord Crewe practically retired from public life after he was admitted to the peerage, and was seventy-three years old when Nathaniel entered the Upper House, so that political antagonism, if it existed, could not have been of great importance. The bishop seems to have sat in the House with great frequency. Bishop Reynolds, who had Puritan sympathies, on one occasion left his proxy with him, and Crewe told this to several of the lords and said he would make him vote right, which suggests that the vote when given might not be on the side Reynolds intended.

[67] *Examination*, p. 32.
[68] *Examination*, p. 31 n.

Besides political foes he had ecclesiastical rivals as well, Compton and Dolben among them. He was looked on in certain quarters as a pushing young man " on the make " as a modern vulgarism has it. His wealth, his rapid rise, his early history and that of his family, were all used against him. What counted more with him was that he had friends in the highest quarters, the Duke and Duchess, Prince Robert (as the English people preferred to call Rupert) who on one occasion presented him with some coins from the Bishop of Durham's mint, dating from the reign of Henry VI, and best of all the King and Queen.

After the Duke of York returned to town the Duke said in his drawing room the next morning that he would be ready to do the bishop any kindness and so would the Duchess. About a week after this Crewe waited upon him and was encouraged by him to ask some favour. The bishop replied that there was but one thing vacant in the Church, but it was so great a preferment that he dared not mention it. Asked what it was he replied that it was the bishopric of Durham, whereupon the Duke said he would speak to the King about it immediately and would exercise all his influence on his behalf. Bishop Cosin of Durham had died as far back as January 15th, 1672, and there had been a long delay in the appointment of a successor and Lauderdale had been heard to remark that he should eat a peck of salt before the see was filled. A newsletter, dated February 6th 1672, said that no one would be named until the King had appointed a commission to inquire into the government of the county palatine and to revise its revenues.[69] This was not done but some encroachments were made on the rights of the bishopric during the vacancy. Many rumours were going about, the most absurd being that there was a project, on the part of whom it was not stated, to make the Duke of Monmouth King of Scotland and to annex the bishopric to his kingdom. It appears, however, that the Duke of Monmouth was receiving at least part of the revenues of the see during the vacancy.[70]

[69] *Hist. MSS. Com.*, S. H. le Fleming MSS., p. 88.
[70] Hutchinson, *Hist. Durh.*, 1817–23, I, p. 688.

Several people were anxious to be promoted to Durham. Dean Dolben's claims were urged, and he was told publicly by Shaftesbury at a dinner in Lambeth to get his boots and spurs on, for he was to go to Durham.[71] Compton tried to gain the Duke of York's interest, and magnified his own family's loyalty and sufferings for the royal cause, while at the same time he took the opportunity to depreciate both Crewe and his family. James, however, was not to be drawn, and said that Durham would be given to a bishop on translation and put Compton off that way. Seth Ward was actually offered the bishopric of Durham, but he refused it because he did not like the conditions. Dr. Walter Pope said that he met the Bishop of Durham at Reading, where Pope happened to be at the time in company with Ward, then Bishop of Salisbury. Pope knew Crewe ever since his first admission to Lincoln College and took the opportunity to felicitate him on his promotion to Durham. He replied, " 'Twas proffered to your bishop (Salisbury) but he did not think fit to accept it." [72] Crewe definitely asked for Durham through the Duke of York, and his father advised him to do so. As early as April 1674 he had private intimation that it was going to be given to him, but that the King would take his own time. Someone made the objection to the King that he was too young for that important see, to which Charles answered that that was a fault that would mend every day. Dr. Croft, Bishop of Hereford, waited on the King and inquired why he did not order the *congé d'élire* to be issued for the election of the Bishop to Durham. All that Charles would say was " My lord, he shall be sure of it."

" He liked not the conditions." The following story told by Richard Earl of Scarborough in 1715, if true, explains this utterance. " After Bishop Crewe had got a promise of the bishopric of Durham, it was long before he could get possession, though he diligently solicited matters : but still something hindered which he could not find out, till he applied to Lord Lumley (afterwards Earl of Scarborough).

[71] *Examination*, p. 33.
[72] W. Pope, *Life of Seth Ward*, 1697, pp. 90, 91.

My lord discovered that the King had promised a sum to be paid to Mrs. Eleanor Gwyn out of this bishopric, and without agreeing with her, nothing could be done. Whereupon the bishop by his agent applied to her and agreed to pay £5,000 or £6,000. One Arden was bound with the bishop for the money, and thereupon he got into possession. The money was duly paid and the bishop made Arden his steward." [73] The writer of the *Examination* says : " Concerning a negotiation of that nature, we could not expect an explicit memorandum : there was an unaccountable delay, and the practice of ingrafting, so well known, we should not presume was without existence in so corrupt and vicious a reign. Indeed we find no cause of impeachment on this head in the manuscript before us [74] and are inclined to exculpate the prelate of so corrupt a dealing, whatever Mr. Arden might do under the rose." This was not the first time the see had been plundered for the sake of a king's mistress, by this new method of royal-papal provision : Anne Boleyn had £1,000 a year from it to keep up her dignity as Marchioness of Pembroke. A scurrilous pamphlet published in 1675 said that Crewe was made Bishop of Durham " at the first word of the Duchess of Portsmouth," but this production said the same about Dr. Brideoak, Bishop of Chichester.[75] How much was mere lying gossip it would be difficult to say. There seems no reason for the Duchess of Portsmouth having anything to do with the appointment. But she was believed to represent both the French and papist interest and she was blamed for most things of which anyone disapproved. Crewe had no doubt that it was to the Duke of York that he owed his promotion. The story of the payment to Nell Gwyn, if it is true, is a disgraceful one. Her biographer, Peter Cunningham, in his *Story of Nell Gwyn* does not mention it. It was disgraceful that the money of the Church should be misappropriated by the Crown for a King's bastard and a King's mistress. The royal supremacy, which had been thrust on the Church by

[73] W. Hutchinson, *Hist. Durham,* 1817, I, p. 688. The story is taken from MSS. notes of " Counsellor Gray of Newcastle-on-Tyne."
[74] *Examination,* see Preface.
[75] *A Libel Counterfeiting a Speech of the King's,* 1675.

Henry VIII, had been accepted abjectly by Anglicans. The King was the head of the Church : whatever the King did must not be resisted : so the hot-heads for divine right urged. They urged it till James II took their word for it, which was one of the causes of his own downfall. If Crewe had refused the bishopric there were others ready to take it and it would be hard to prove that the other candidates were better qualified. A composition was better than an annual payment, and it might be considered in the light of a settlement of outstanding claims, and that is all that can be said. But the evidence that it happened is not decisive. What we do know is this, that one day in 1674 Crewe was seated at the chaplain's table while the King was at dinner, and that Charles sent for him and then and there gave him the bishopric of Durham. In his courtly way he replied that as His Majesty had given him the best preferment in his gift he would try to live answerably. Little Queen Catherine, Catholic as she was, expressed her pleasure at the appointment : which brought a cheerful jest from Charles, " What will the Pope think when I make bishops of such as please you ? "

Not every one was pleased. The story was told that his father was ashamed of the means by which the promotion had been obtained. If there is anything at all in this it must refer to the payment to Nelly. Compton was offended at being passed over for one whom he afterwards called " the spawn of a puritan turned papist." Lord Keeper Finch, who was far from being a friend, when he passed the seals for the appointment said, " Sure this will stop your mouth for one twenty years." The Duke of York's adversaries, now increasing in number, naturally disliked the rapid advance of James' friend, but little was said against his personal fitness for the office. That was left for Burnet, who in after years admitted his good birth, pointed to his early puritanism, and described him as " an ignorant, worthless, vain and abject man, without any one good quality." [76] As a set-off to this let us hear Denis Granville, Archdeacon of Durham. At his Michaelmas visitation of his archdeaconry he told the clergy that it was no small

[76] Burnet, *James II*, Oxford 1852, p. 121.

testimony of the Divine goodness that "a pastor of such worthy qualifications" had been provided for them: "a person so capable (in a multitude of respects) to do God and this church service." He added "We may justly promise ourselves all possible encouragement in the comfortable discharge of our offices from the temper and qualities of our bishop." He had taken upon himself to represent to his lordship when he was looking towards Durham "this diocese as one of the most orderly in England." [77]

On August 12th, 1674 the warrant was issued for the *congé d'élire* to be sent to the dean and chapter of Durham to elect a bishop, and for the letter missive recommending Nathaniel Bishop of Oxford and Clerk of the Closet for election.[78] He was elected by the chapter on August 18th, the chapter signed a certificate of the election on August 26th,[79] and two days later appointed Sancroft and five others as their proctors to notify the election to the King.[80] The warrant for the royal assent and confirmation was issued on September 7th.[81]

By Crewe's promotion to Durham the rectory of Witney became vacant, and the Clerk of the Signet was directed to enter a *caveat* with the Archbishop of Canterbury that no institution or induction should be given until it had been decided at law whether the presentation lay with the King or the Bishop of Winchester.[82]

The temporalities of the see were restored on November 12th,[83] and shortly afterwards he took the oath of homage.[84] On the 20th he was enthroned by proxy in his cathedral. Richard Potts, writing from Stockton to Williamson, expressed the great satisfaction of the inhabitants of the county palatine, who had suffered great losses and inconvenience during the

[77] *Remains of Denis Granville*, Pt. II, Surtees Soc., p. 16.
[78] *C.S.P.D.* Entry Book 35B, f. 31.
[79] *C.S.P.D.* Car. II, Case F, No. 59.
[80] *Ibid.*, No. 60.
[81] *C.S.P.D.* Entry Book 35B, f. 31.
[82] *C.S.P.D.* Entry Book 45, p. 2.
[83] *C.S.P.D.* Entry Book 47, p. 1.
[84] *C.S.P.D.* Case F, No. 64.

long vacancy, particularly persons whose leases for lives or years had nearly run out.

Now all was complete except paying for the promotion. There were fees to Mr. Secretary Williamson's office, £5 for the warrant for the lieutenancy, £5 for the restitution of the temporalities,[85] and doubtless more fees. Every lawyer or other official who had the slightest thing to do in connection with the translation would demand his fee. These, however, were small matters compared with the Crown's pickings : the sum of £1,638 19s. 3½d. had to be paid as first fruits, in four equal yearly portions, the first falling due in Michaelmas, 1675.[86]

Crewe was now Bishop of Durham, and was succeeded by his rival, Henry Compton, in the see of Oxford, but for some unknown reason he did not go to his new see for months. He was certainly at Court part of the time.

[85] *C.S.P.D.* 1673–5, pp. 510–11.
[86] *C.S.P.D.* Entry Book 47, p. 2.

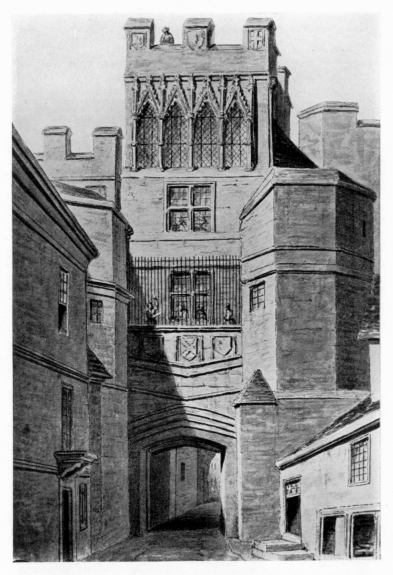

THE OLD NORTH GATE, DURHAM.

Facing page 47.

CHAPTER III

THE DIOCESE OF DURHAM IN 1674

MACAULAY has reminded us that if a vision of England as it was during the latter part of the seventeenth century could be unrolled before our eyes we should not know one landscape in a hundred or one building in ten thousand. This would be especially true of the counties of Durham and Northumberland. The new bishop found himself the shepherd of a wide spreading and thinly populated diocese, with a few small towns, many scattered villages, large regions quite uncultivated, with here and there some nascent industrial centres. The city of Durham itself was in general lay-out much as it is at present. The streets were much the same as to-day and many of them bore the same names. Celia Fiennes thus described it : " I must say of the whole city of Durham it's the noblest—clean and pleasant buildings, streets large, well-pitched." [1] It would be too much to say that the local gentry went to Durham as those elsewhere went to London, to the court of the reigning sovereign, but they frequented the city regularly, especially when the bishop was there. The dominating architectural features of the city were the cathedral, the castle, and the great prison which extended from the North Gate (destroyed in 1820) to Elvet Bridge. Portions of the old city walls still remained. The low-lying parts of the city suffered badly from floods. There was a great flood on April 26th and 27th, 1682; and on August 3rd in the following year there was such an inundation that the judges of assize had to enter the city by Gilesgate.

The county of Durham boasted of eight market towns—Auckland, Sunderland, Stockton, Darlington, Hartlepool, Staindrop, Barnard Castle and Wolsingham. Ecclesiastically there were eighty cures of souls, consisting of thirty rectories, twenty-two vicarages and twenty-eight chapelries.

[1] Celia Fiennes, *Through England on a Side-Saddle*, 1888, pp. 179–81.

Gateshead had a population estimated at seven thousand. It was too much overshadowed by Newcastle to be of great importance. In the Tolbooth the Bishops of Durham held their manor courts. Further down the Tyne was Shields. There ships were laden with coal for London and other places, and coals were taken up the river to Newcastle in barges and lighters. The harbour was the centre of a great fishing industry. On both banks of the river were many convenient houses " for the entertainment of seamen and dwellings for colliers." [2] To guide ships at night there was a lighthouse in which a large coal fire was kept constantly burning. Glass making began at South Shields in the middle of the eighteenth century, and a great impetus was given to it here and in other places on Tyneside by the influx of foreign Protestants. The salt works were famous and at the end of the seventeenth century there were a hundred and forty-three salt pans, some of them the largest used anywhere in Great Britain. " Here," said Marmaduke Rawdon, " they boil salt water and make great quantities of white salt, but it causeth such a smoke that one would think the town were on fire." Sunderland was a seaport greatly enriched by the coal trade. It was one of the four corporate boroughs in the county of Durham, but unlike the other three, Durham, Stockton and Hartlepool, it had no mayor.[3] Hartlepool possessed a harbour of some importance as a place of refuge for the Newcastle coal ships in bad weather, but the town generally speaking was declining : even its weekly market had decayed. Stockton was proving in many respects a successful rival, and in October 1680 the principal offices of the customs were moved thither from Hartlepool. Stockton had a considerable trade in lead, butter and beer. At Darlington, which Defoe at the beginning of the eighteenth century thought a dirty place, there was a weekly market for cattle and corn. The town was noted for the bleaching of linen which was even brought from Scotland to be bleached there. Before the century was out a vigorous linen manufacture was established in the town.

[2] Cox, *Magna Britannia*, 1720.
[3] Cox, *Magna Britannia*.

Barnard Castle consisted of one long street, with divers lanes branching out from it. It was well known for its tanners, leather dressers, glovers and stocking-makers.[4]

Ralph Thoresby complained of the unpleasantness of a journey from Chester-le-Street to Newcastle, but in Northumberland communication was much more difficult than in Durham. Packhorses carried goods along the road from Newcastle to Carlisle, the middle part of the journey, which took four days, being generally along the line of the Roman road. In the more remote districts the people were in a low state of civilization. Even in the eighteenth century a traveller saw near Kielder Castle a scene like a Red Indian war dance—half naked women singing a wild measure while the men danced and brandished daggers.[5] The old moss-troopers were gone but in their stead there were bands of robbers who plundered houses and raided sheep and cattle. Some of these robbers, known as Bedlamers, knocked people on the head at the slightest provocation. The King's judges travelling from Newcastle to Carlisle, attended by the barristers and their clerks and servants, were escorted by guards provided by the sheriffs. Various statutes of Charles II[6] gave authority to the magistrates on the English side of the border to raise armed forces to keep order and defend property, and the expense of this was to be met by local taxation.[7] The free-booters had secret paths and hiding places amongst the hills and up the valleys and it was by no means easy to track them. Border justice when administered was swift, and inspired by hatred and fear, and so strongly did people feel about cattle stealing that in the criminal courts " a violent suspicion there was next to conviction."[8]

Newcastle was the largest town in the whole diocese, with a population estimated in the reign of Anne as 18,000.[9] It was still a walled town, in spite of the destruction of the

[4] Thoresby, *Diary*, 1830, I, p. 279.   Surtees, *Hist. Durham*, IV, p. 86.
[5] Lockhart, *Life of Scott*.
[6] 14 Car. II, c. 22.   18 & 19 Car. II, c. 33.   29 & 30 Car. II, c. 2.
[7] Nicholson and Bourne, *Hist. of Westmorland and Cumberland*, Chaps. I and II, Discourses of the Ancient State of the Border.
[8] R. North, *Lives of the Norths*, ed. by A. Jessopp, 1890, I, pp. 175–91.
[9] *Archaeologia Aeliana*, 2nd series, III, p. 64.

civil wars, for in 1667 the Common Council had ordered the immediate repair of the walls, gates and drawbridges. The old postern gate on the Castle Garth Stairs is still one of the oldest bits of Newcastle. The Water Gate at the bottom of the Sandhill, the Sandgate, the Pandon Gate, the West Gate, sometimes used as a prison, and the Pilgrim Gate at the head of Pilgrim Street, which was described in 1649 as "the longest and fairest street in the town " [10] were all in existence then, as were the towers—Heber Tower, Morden Tower, Carliol Tower and the rest.

To enter the town from the south the traveller had to cross the old Tyne Bridge, a large and stately bridge on seven arches, which Defoe described as "rather stronger than the arches of London Bridge." It had on it houses and shops, three towers and an old chapel. Below the battlement of the south front of the central tower was a slab bearing the arms of Newcastle with the civic motto *Fortiter defendit triumphans* and the date 1645. On the bridge itself, but nearer the south than the north end, was a blue stone which marked the division between Gateshead and Newcastle and between the counties of Durham and Northumberland. At the north end of the bridge was a very fine city gate known as the Magazine Gate. The old castle was in ruins and at the end of the century all that a visitor noticed was that some of the walls were "built up in houses." There was little as yet in the way of noteworthy buildings. The house erected in the sixteenth century by Robert Anderson on the site of the Grey Friars attracted attention,[11] as did Barber Surgeons' Hall which had been erected in the Manors by permission of the Corporation given in 1648. Near the spot where the present railway station stands was Westmorland Place, the great mansion of the Nevilles. There were the churches of St. Nicholas, St. John and St. Andrew, and the chapel of St. Thomas near the end of the Tyne Bridge. There was also a church of All Hallows, a long aisled building with a square tower and south porch. At a later date it was pulled down and on the

[10] William Gray, *Chorographia,* 1649.
[11] It was destroyed when Grey Street was built.

OLD NEWCASTLE.

Facing page 50.

site was built the ugly erection now called All Saints. On the Sandhill was the Hospital of St. Catherine, commonly known as the Maison de Dieu and in the Manors the old square tower of the Austin Friars still remained.

The town walls ran parallel with the river and the space between was " wharfed up " and faced with free stone for such a distance that Newcastle could claim the longest quay in England except Yarmouth. Ships of more than three hundred tons burden could not come right up to it, owing to the shallowness of the river. The trade of the town consisted mostly of coals, iron and salt, and the revenue arising therefrom was very considerable. There were in the town a corn market and a hay market, the Bigg market or barley market and a cloth market, beside the regular Saturday general market. Hardware, wrought iron and glass were manufactured and the coal fires of the various works made it a smoky place even then. Ships were built and naval stores were on sale in abundance. Provisions were plentiful and cheap. Altogether it was a wealthy town, the most flourishing in the north of England, with revenues considerable enough to enable it to allow its mayor £700 a year with an extra allowance for entertaining the King's judges. When Francis, Lord Guildford, visited the north on his judicial circuit the magistrates took him for a trip on the river in the town barge, and provided a pleasant picnic on one of the islands.[12]

When Nathaniel Crewe began his long reign over his northern see the counties of Durham and Northumberland were even then entering upon conditions of industrial and commercial prosperity which were to continue right down to very recent years. Coal-mining was, of course, the principal industry : there were mines of lead and iron, and some marble quarries, but these products were in no request in comparison with coal. Coal went to London by sea since land carriage was too expensive, but the Newcastle merchants also had considerable trade with the north of Europe. During the next forty years the commercial north would see great developments, Ambrose Crowley's great iron works at Winlaton and

[12] North, *Lives of the Norths,* ed. Jessopp 1890, I, p. 175.

Swalwell, Sir William Blackett's mining operations in
Northumberland, the use of waggon ways by Thomas Allan
of Newcastle, Sir Ralph Delaval's construction of the Seaton
sluice, then looked upon as a wonderful engineering feat, and
the commencement of stage coach communication between
Newcastle and London.

Except Newcastle there were no towns of importance in
Northumberland. Tynemouth had a fort and a garrison, but
a fairly inefficient garrison. Morpeth, on the Wansbeck,
seemed to be declining. Alnwick consisted chiefly of a cluster
of small and miserable houses round the castle. Bamburgh
Castle was in ruins. There was a little group of houses and
a garrison on Holy Island. Berwick was a small town
defended by walls and trenches and not far away was the
castle of Norham, which was once the property of the bishops
of Durham but in the possession of the Crown since the
Reformation.

The Bishop of Durham was not only the ecclesiastical ruler
over a large diocese, consisting of the counties of Durham
and Northumberland, but over a great part of it he had down
to the sixteenth century powers which, saving his homage to
the King, were those of royalty. This palatinate jurisdiction
extended over the county of Durham and the earldom of
Sadberge, which latter the Bishop of Durham held by barony,
and north of the Tyne over the three districts known as
Norhamshire, Islandshire and Bedlingtonshire.

Sadberge, near Haughton-le-Skerne, was granted by
Richard I to Hugh de Puiset, Bishop of Durham, and he and
his successors were Earls of Sadberge until the end of the
palatinate jurisdiction when the earldom passed to the Crown.
The powers of the bishops were exercised by sheriffs,
escheators, coroners and other officials, distinct from those of
the county of Durham. Ralph Flambard, Bishop of Durham,
built Norham Castle and Norham was more or less the capital,
not only of Norhamshire, but of the whole of the northern
portion of the palatinate. Islandshire included Lindisfarne,
Tweedmouth and the parts adjacent. Bedlington was a
manor belonging to the see of Durham and the liberties of

this manor received the name of shire. The district was bounded by the Wansbeck on the north and the Blyth on the south. Down to the time of Henry VIII these three Northumberland districts had their own officials and courts of justice, acting by the bishop's commission. The three "shires" were not annexed to the county of Northumberland until 1844. The Bishop of Durham also had jurisdiction over parts of Yorkshire. The manor of Crayke, twelve miles from York, remained as an outlying part of the county of Durham and was so marked in old maps until 1844, when parliament incorporated it with Yorkshire : the manor had already been sold by Van Mildert, the last of the prince bishops, as we still incorrectly speak of them, who died in 1836. After Henry VIII, down to the abolition of the palatinate jurisdiction, the inhabitants of all the four districts mentioned resorted to Durham for justice in all matters of law and civil jurisdiction. The peculiar of Northallertonshire was one of the districts described by Hutchinson as "outbranches" of the palatinate. William Rufus gave the manor of Northallerton to the church of Durham, and down to the nineteenth century the bishop had ecclesiastical jurisdiction over all the "shire," and also kept his manorial courts there twice a year. The castle was built by Bishop Geoffrey Rufus and the bishops had a manor house there. The peculiar of Howdenshire, on the river Ouse, twenty-two miles from Hull, was given by William Rufus to Bishop William of St. Calais. In the Middle Ages the bishops of Durham held at Howden not only a manorial court and a criminal court, but also a forest court for their rights in the forests of Ouse and Derwent.[13] The manor of Howden and its privileges belonged to the see of Durham until the nineteenth century. Some parts of the palace still remain.

The palatinate territory then consisted of Durham, the three shires of Northumberland and the manor of Crayke. People talked of "going into the Bishopric," "living in the Bishopric" and so on, where we would talk of Durham and Northumberland. In addition the bishop had manorial

[13] *Yorks Arch. Journ.*, IX, pp. 384-93.

rights and jurisdiction in Northallertonshire and Howdenshire. His ecclesiastical authority included all these, the parish of Alston in Cumberland, and most of the remaining portions of Northumberland, with the exception of Hexhamshire which was under the ecclesiastical jurisdiction of the Archbishop of York.

Under Henry VIII the palatinate power had been considerably lessened. Neglect on the part of the Elizabethan bishops had weakened it still more. Still in Crewe's day, the bishop had by Statute 27, Hen. VIII, c. 24, his own Court of Chancery. The sheriff, the under-sheriff, the county clerk, the gaoler, the clerk of the crown, the protonotary or clerk of the civil pleas and assizes, the clerk of the peace, the cursitor or clerk of the Latin chancery and emoluments, and other officials, were appointed by a patent from the bishop. The bishop was Custos Rotulorum. His sheriff was not obliged to account to the royal exchequer but made his audit to the bishop. The bishop's temporal courts included a Court of Pleas, and fines and recoveries in the Court of Common Pleas at Westminster of lands within the palatinate were void. He received composition money upon fines, levies and recoveries suffered in his Court of Pleas and on all the original writs issued out of his courts when the debt or damages exceeded £40. Forfeited recognizances, fines and amercements also fell to him, as did escheats, deodands and treasure-trove. The bishop and his temporal chancellor were both justices of the peace and the former could preside in any of his own courts of judicature. He had powers for the preservation of the peace and the punishment of malefactors.[14] He could appoint commissions out of his chancery to inquire into the estates of idiots and lunatics within his jurisdiction. One example will suffice. In Crewe's time, by this process, the custody of William Harrison, a lunatic, was given to George Harrison of Sunderland.

From time out of mind the bishops of Durham had enjoyed a royal jurisdiction of admiralty, and therefore had all the privileges, forfeitures and profits incident thereto, as

[14] Cox, *Magna Britannia*, 1720.

counts palatine, which the Kings of England had outside the palatinate; wrecks, duties on ships, anchorage, moorage, rights over royal fish, and so on. They appointed by patent vice-admirals and judges of their court of admiralty. Thus, in 1662 Bishop Cosin granted a new lease to Robert Adamson, of the borough and port of Sunderland, and of all the anchorage, beaconage, wharfage, ballast-shores, etc. there for twenty-one years, at an annual rent of £10. This lease was surrendered in 1676, and renewed by Crewe to Edward Arden, George Forster and Robert Adamson for twenty-one years. In 1682 it was again surrendered and renewed to George French for twenty-one years at the same rent.[15] Various examples of the bishop's claims to rights over wrecks may be seen in Cosin's correspondence:[16] but here is an example from Crewe's reign:[17]

> "May y° 27. 1676 upon y° view and taking into custody y° shipwreck, now near Shields, I do hereby undertake to clear Nicholas Conyers Esq, now Sheriff of Durham, and Mr. John Spearman, Under-sheriff, of all charges, wages, and other demands which may accrue by y° salving and getting off and bringing of y° same.
>
> Thomas Burdon."

The legal and judicial system still remained largely distinct from the legal and judicial system of the rest of England. The King's judges now held their assizes within the bounds of the bishopric; but in order to practise as an attorney in the palatinate courts application had to be made to the chancellor. Thus, Robert Adamson, " of the city of Durham, gentleman," in the year 1703 made application in the form of a petition " to the right worshipful Robert Dormer, Esq., Chancellor of the county palatine of Durham and Sadberge," setting forth that for four years past he had served as a clerk to Mr. Ralph Gowland, an attorney in the temporal courts of the county palatine, and he prayed that the chancellor " would be pleased to admit him an attorney in the

---

[15] Spearman, Enquiry, p. 34.
[16] Cosin, Correspondence, Surtees Soc., I, pp. 274–5, 277, 282.
[17] Hodgson, South Shields, 1903, p. 113.

said courts." The petition was countersigned by Ralph Gowland and by John Spearman, the deputy-registrar, who certified the claim in the petition to be true; and at the foot was
written: " The 2 of Aug. 1703. The petitioner having taken
the usual oaths before me: he is admitted an attorney as
desired. Robert Dormer." [18]

The bishop possessed and drew revenues from various
ferries over the rivers. Thus, as lord of the manor of Stockton
he owned the ferryboat which was the only means of crossing
the Tees. For the use of this, fees were paid to him by the
inhabitants of Stockton and Thornaby twice a year, on Easter
Monday and on St. Stephen's Day. When, in 1771, a bridge
across the Tees was opened it was agreed that the trustees
of the bridge should pay the bishop £90 a year as an
indemnity.[19] " My lord of Durham " enjoyed divers markets
and fairs. At Howden King John had granted by charter
a fair held annually on the vigil and day of St. Maurice.
On December 11th, 1678 a royal warrant was issued for a
grant to the Bishop of Durham and his successors of three fairs
to be held at Howden, on the second Tuesday in January, the
Tuesday before March 25th, and the second Tuesday in July,
as also of a fortnightly fair on every second Saturday, yearly
for ever.[20]

The bishop's authority and influence were exercised in
many ways. Christopher Hunter, the historian and antiquary, took his M.B. degree at St. John's College, Cambridge
in 1698 and began medical practice at Stockton-on-Tees in
that year. He received a licence, dated October 7th, 1701,
from Dr. Brooksbank, the spiritual chancellor, to practise
physic throughout the diocese. The Durham race meeting,
which lasted until comparatively recent times, began in the
seventeenth century. One would hardly have connected
the bishop with it: but a sessions order signed by George
Morland, mayor of Durham, and nine other justices, dated
January 14th, 1695 runs, " Resolved by the justices in open

[18] There is a bundle of similar documents in the Record Office.
[19] Brewster, *Stockton-upon-Tees,* 1796, p. 92.
[20] *C.S.P.D.* 408, No. 114.

court that from henceforth their wages go and be employed for and towards the procuring of a plate or plates to be run for on Durham moor. And that it be recommended to Mr. Mayor of Durham, chairman at this sessions, to communicate the same to the Bishop of Durham. And that the same continue until further resolution of the justices of the peace of this country."

The bishops of Durham had rights over certain boroughs, and could grant charters of incorporation, which they had done more than once in the case of the city of Durham. The mayor, aldermen, and commonalty could, by their recorder and town clerk, hold a court leet and a court baron under the style of " The Court of the Right Rev. Father in God, N. Lord Bishop of Durham and his Successors, held before A.B., Mayor, and C.D., Recorder of the City of Durham." The corporation on fair days held a Court of Pie Powder for the city, for which they paid about £20 a year to the bishop or to whomsoever he might devise it by a lease for three lives.[21] When the bishop visited Durham it seems to have been the custom that the mayor and corporation waited on him and he signed their minute book.[22] There must have been a considerable number of officials in the small city of Durham in the seventeenth century, with their offices and courts round about the cathedral and castle. The bishop lived in the latter building only occasionally. It was in the charge of the constable of Durham castle, and there was also a keeper of the wardrobe there. Celia Fiennes, who visited it in the days of William III saw " very stately good rooms, parlours, drawing rooms and a noble hall, but the furniture was not very fine, the best being taken down in the absence of my Lord Crewe. . . . He comes sometimes thither, but for the most part lives at another castle which is a noble seat about twelve miles off, which is very well furnished." [23] This, of course, was at Bishop Auckland. Both castles had suffered damage during the Commonwealth times and Bishop Cosin

---

[21] Cox, *Magna Britannia*.
[22] Information from Mr. G. A. Carpenter, Recorder of Durham.
[23] *Through England in a Side-Saddle in the days of William and Mary,* London, 1888, pp. 179–81.

had spent large sums on repairs. Sir Arthur Heselrige had destroyed the chapels at Auckland and used the materials to build additional rooms. Bishop Cosin pulled down these and had built a new chapel. There was an episcopal manor house at Darlington and Crewe is believed to have been the last of the bishops to occupy it. The Yorkshire houses belonging to the see were all in ruins.

John Spearman, who was under-sheriff for thirty-two years, and deputy registrar of the Court of Chancery for forty-two, was asked by Dr. Nicolson, afterwards Bishop of Carlisle, to give a summary of the ancient state of the palatinate. He completed a short historical survey in the year 1697. In 1729 his son, Gilbert, published at Edinburgh, *An Enquiry into the Ancient and Present State of the County Palatine of Durham*. The first portion of the work was his father's account; the rest contained an attack on the whole palatinate jurisdiction : " the oppressions which attend the subjects of this county by the maladministration of the present ministers and officers," and urged the " freeholders, leaseholders and copy-holders to consider ways and means to remedy the said abuses, or entirely to take away the said county palatine, and the bishop's temporal power and jurisdiction therein." Gilbert was the leader of a strong party in the bishopric, and it is hardly a matter of surprise, therefore, that he was not appointed to his father's office.

Spearman objected both to the general principle of the independent jurisdiction of the bishop and the means taken to preserve it. Much of his work seems vitiated by personal feeling against Bishop Talbot (1721–30), who had abolished the office of under-sheriff,[24] and he never misses an opportunity of a personal attack. After reading his book it is plain to see that the judicial system of the palatinate had serious deficiencies; but he tended to spoil his case by over-statement. Thus, he attacked a somewhat complicated process for the attachment of goods before judgment in the Court of Common Pleas, though in a footnote he admitted that he had misread a statute of 1728.[25] He gave as one of the incon-

[24] Spearman, pp. 102–3.
[25] *Ibid.*, pp. 53–4.

veniences of the system the provision that foreign attorneys
were not allowed to practise in the palatinate, and that others
were required to take an oath not to carry any suit outside
the jurisdiction when it was possible to have it determined
therein.   He seemed certainly to be going too far when he
said that it was doubtful whether the Habeas Corpus and
other beneficial acts extended to Durham.[26]   The Court of
Chancery, he complained, was still a court of exchequer for
the bishop's revenue, and determined matters between him
and his tenants.   It was held only once a year, and never sat
more than three or four days at a time.   It was dilatory.
Its jurisdiction could not be enforced outside the county.   The
bishop heard and determined all appeals, though without any
evidence of right, and there was no appeal to parliament.[27]
In making this last statement Spearman seems to have been
unaware that in 1689 Serjeant Tremayne, counsel for the
King, said that an appeal lay from Durham to the House of
Lords, but not from Durham, or any other such court (e.g.
Chester, Lancaster, Ludlow) to Westminster Hall.[28]   What
was a serious evil was that prosecutions in criminal cases were
conducted by the bishop's officers, not *ex officio* but at the
expense of the prosecution.   Offices were bought and sold.   In
1691 Dr. John Brooksbank bought the spiritual chancellorship from James Montagu for a thousand guineas.   David
Hilton was seneschal to Crewe and five of his successors, and
was steward of the Halmote Court for forty-eight years.
According to Spearman he bought the office of cursitor for a
sum of between £600 and £700.[29]   Episcopal favour counted
for a great deal.   Ralph Trotter, on September 2nd, 1768
signed the instrument of the consecration of St. Anne's, Newcastle, as a witness, and added, " now above sixty years
registrar of the diocese."   He must have been appointed to
his post of principal registrar of the spiritual court at the age
of twenty.   He had formerly been page to Lady Crewe, and
that probably accounts for it.   Spearman's chief complaint

[26] Spearman, p. 55.
[27] *Ibid.*, pp. 55, 56.
[28] Hist. MSS. Com., House of Lords MSS., 1689–90, p. 107.
[29] Spearman, pp. 101–3.

was against the persons who held office : some of the members of the palatinate bench were clergymen, and tradesmen ignorant of the law. In the later years of Crewe there seems to have been some deterioration in the system. " In the time of Sheriff Spearman, who had a patent for life, there was never a bad verdict nor a bad jury at the Durham Assizes." The Earl of Scarborough told Crewe when Spearman died that the bishop had lost the best officer he ever had. " That sheriff was not to be influenced by the bishop, but to do that bishop's memory justice, it is believed he never attempted it." [30]

The see of Durham was one of the wealthiest in England, and it was commonly stated that the income was over £6,000 a year. Whatever it may have been before the civil wars, it had suffered great diminution. At the beginning of Cosin's episcopate the gross revenue was estimated at £3,915 8s. 3d.; but various deductions and expenses reduced it to £1,693 16s. 8¼d.[31] In 1720 the value was given as £1,821 1s. 5¾d.[32] The Act of Parliament which at the Restoration had abolished feudal tenures *in capite* was said to have been responsible for a deduction of £2,000 a year. Since the days of Queen Elizabeth a yearly rent of £880 had been paid to the Crown : Elizabeth had promised to make this good by a grant of impropriations, a promise which was never performed. In consideration of the bishops' heavy losses in feudal dues they had been released from this annual burden by patent under the Great Seal. The bishop paid £340 per annum to various officers of the palatinate, the expenses of assizes and sessions fell on him, and he was liable to repair certain river banks in Howdenshire, as well as the houses belonging to the see. Some of the rents had been improved by Cosin to the extent of £400, and it was calculated that from 1670 onwards the annual revenue of the bishopric would be £3,280.[33] John Ecton of the First Fruits Office, however, published a work, *Liber Valorum et Deci-*

[30] Spearman, p. 94.
[31] Cosin, *Correspondence,* II, pp. 91–4.
[32] Cox, *Magna Britannia,* 1720.
[33] Lapsley, *County Palatine,* 1900, p. 201. Chamberlayne, *Angliæ Notitiæ,* 1690, p. 205.

marum, in which he gave the value of the various benefices in England and Wales; and in the edition of 1711, which he claimed to be more correct than anything of the kind hitherto printed, stated that the income of the see of Durham was £1,821 2s. 3d. If this is so, there must have been a great loss of income somewhere during this period; even Cosin's estimate seems remarkably low when we remember that between 1660 and 1668 he spent £41,000, over £5,000 a year, on buildings and charities.[34] But the bishop had sources of income which did not come within Ecton's survey.

Money came to the Bishop of Durham from curious sources. Thus, in the books of the Company of Barber Surgeons, Waxmakers, Ropers and Stringers of Durham we find the following rules made at this time :

> Feb. 6th, 1679. No member shall take any apprentice above the age of twenty years on pain of a fine of £10 to go to the bishop or mayor of this city and another £10 for the use of the trade.
>
> May 6th, 1680. For keeping a person more than a month on trial the fine was to be 39s. 11d. to the bishop or mayor and 39s. 11d. to the Company.
>
> Nov. 17th, 1684. If a barber or his apprentice or servants shaved a customer or cut his hair, or trimmed any person on a Sunday the master barber should pay 6s. 8d. to the bishop and 6s. 8d. to the trade for every offence.
>
> Nov. 2nd, 1685. For absence from the head meeting (that is, the annual meeting) 6s. 8d., from a quarterly meeting 3s. 4d., from a bye meeting 12 pence to the bishop or mayor and an equal sum to the trade.

Some of the other guilds had similar rules.

The diocese in 1720 contained 185 parishes, of which 87 were impropriate.[35] The value of some of the livings was as much exaggerated as the value of the see. Defoe was told by some unknown persons (" they told me ") that the Bishop of Durham had thirteen livings in his gift, from £500 a year

---

[34] Cosin, *Correspondence,* II, p. 171.
[35] Cox, *Magna Britannia,* 1720.

to £1,300 a year : and that the living of Sedgefield was worth £1,200 a year, beside the small tithes, " which maintain a curate, or might do so." [36]   According to Ecton's almost contemporary list of a hundred and twelve benefices in the diocese, only five were worth more than £60 per annum : Houghton-le-Spring £124, Sedgefield £73 18s. 1½d., Bishop-wearmouth £89 18s. 1½d., Brancepeth £60 10s. 5d. and Stanhope £67 6s. 8d.   Spearman, however, asserted that Sedgefield was worth £800 a year.[37]

From the accounts of several visitors to Durham we gather that the ancient Catholic tradition had not entirely disappeared.   On September 15th, 1680 Ralph Thoresby " went to see the Abbey : viewed the exceedingly rich copes and robes . . . tapers, basins and richly embroidered I H S upon the high altar, with the picture of God the Father, like an old man, the Son as a young man, richly embroidered upon their copes." [38]   If there was such a cope then it does not exist now, though some of the old copes have been preserved for us by subsequent disuse.   Thoresby visited Durham again in November, 1682 and noted " St Cuthbert and his cow (cut in stone upon the Minster) and Venerable Bede who lies interred under a stately blue marble, but without inscription, save this, handsomely chalked round the edge : *Hac sunt in fossa Bedae Venerabilis ossa.*" [39]   Celia Fiennes, some dozen or so years later, visited the cathedral : " The abbey or the cathedral is very large, the choir is good but nothing extraordinary, some good painting in the glass of the windows and wood carving.   There is over the altar a painting of a large Catherine wheel which encompasses the whole window and fills it up.   The bishop's seat has several steps up. It's called the throne, with a cloth of gold carpet before it. The seat was King Charles the first's of crimson damask.   A good organ and a fine clock in which is the signs, with chimes, and

[36] Defoe, *Tour through the Whole Island of Great Britain,* ed. Cole, 1927, II, p. 657.
[37] *Enquiry,* p. 119.
[38] Thoresby, *Diary,* I, p. 61.
[39] *Ibid.,* p. 140.

finely carved with four pyramidy spires on each corner, a much
larger and higher one in the middle well carved and painted.
The font is of marble, the top was carved wood very high,
and terminates in a point and resembles the picture of the
building of Babel—it's not painted. . . . The chapel called
St. Mary's now used for to keep their spiritual courts, and in
the vestry I saw several fine embroidered copes, three or four.
I saw one above the rest was so richly embroidered with the
whole description of Christ's nativity, life, death and ascension : this is put on the Dean's shoulders at the administration
of the Lord's Supper, here is the only place that they use
such things in England, and several more ceremonies and rites
retained from the times of popery." [40]   Joseph Taylor of the
Inner Temple visited Durham in 1705, and tells us : " I must
not omit taking notice of the seven copes of velvet and silk,
which are used there in divine service at the altar; they are
so curiously wrought, and express the several histories of the
Bible, and other particular passages relating to our Saviour,
all in needlework.   In these habits the priests look like
monarchs triumphant, and since we are so happy to have
reformed from Romish idolatry, I could not forbear calling
these relics of their pride, rich rags of the Whore of Babylon."
" After sermon we went about the cathedral and observed
. . . the font, and clock, which tells the age of the moon, the
day of the week and the hour of the day, and the altar piece
of stone are very fine."

" . . . After we had viewed the whole city we returned to our
inns, and sent for one of the singing boys to entertain us with
some songs who, amongst the rest, sung a catch upon the
Queen set by the organist of Durham." [41]   The organist
referred to was William Gregg who was organist of the
cathedral from 1685 to 1710. He was the son of John
Gregg, a gentleman from York who had been a sufferer for
King Charles I. William, who was buried in St. Mary-the-
Less, is not known to have published any musical works. He

[40] *Celia Fiennes*, pp. 179–81.
[41] Joseph Taylor, *A Journey to Edinburgh in Scotland*, ed. by
Wm. Cowan, Edinburgh, 1903, pp. 78–89.

was succeeded by James Heseltine who seems to have been the cathedral organist for over fifty years.

Durham cathedral had a dean and twelve prebendaries. Each stall was separately endowed with property in the diocese and elsewhere, and so the stipends varied considerably. The statutes, dating from the reign of Philip and Mary, provided for twelve petty-canons, one of whom was Epistoler and another Gospeller, ten singing clerks, a master of the choristers or organist,[42] ten choristers, two sub-sacrists or vergers, two bell-ringers, who were also keepers of the clock, two porters, two butlers and two cooks. Also connected with the cathedral were the master and usher of the grammar school with their eighteen scholars.[43]

The chapter of Durham contained some very distinguished churchmen. The dean was Dr. John Sudbury, a Cambridge man, formerly a prebendary of Westminster. He had been installed in 1661 and remained in Durham till his death in 1684. He it was who restored the refectory to provide a room for a library. Dr. Thomas Smith, formerly fellow and tutor of Queen's College, Oxford, who held the first stall from 1668 to 1684, was Dean and afterwards Bishop of Carlisle, to which see he was consecrated in 1684, whereupon he resigned his stall.

Perhaps the most noteworthy of the prebendaries at the time of Crewe's arrival, and indeed for a long time after, was Dr. Denis Granville. He was the third son of Sir Bevil Granville, who was killed at Lansdown fight, and brother of the Earl of Bath. Ordained by Bishop Sanderson in 1661 he became rector of Kilkhampton in Cornwall, though he never resided there. In 1662, when he had been one year in holy orders, he was made prebendary of the first stall in Durham Cathedral, archdeacon of Durham, rector of Easington and rector of Elwick. In 1668 he exchanged the first for the second, a more lucrative stall, and was made rector of Sedgefield in addition to his other preferments, giving up Elwick

---

[42] The organist at the time of Crewe's arrival was John Forster, who held the office from 1661–77, and was buried in the cathedral.

[43] *Misc. Granville Letters*, Surtees Soc., p. 252.

however. He was also chaplain-in-ordinary to the King. In spite of several sources of income he was frequently in debt, and on July 8th, 1674, as he was coming from a funeral which had been attended by some of the principal gentry of the country, he was arrested in the cloisters by three bailiffs and carried off to gaol in his canonical habit. It was a dreadful scandal, but the persons responsible had exceeded their authority, perhaps actuated by spite, and were summoned before the King's Council and threatened with prosecution for daring to arrest one of the King's chaplains. Mr. Richard Neile was dismissed from his office as under-sheriff, but made submission and apology and, it is believed, was reinstated at a later time. It was a severe lesson to Granville and after that he was more careful about his expenditure. He did not get on well with his wife, Anne, the youngest daughter of Bishop Cosin, who seems to have suffered from hysteria and melancholia, and at times was scarcely sane, though Cosin refused to believe it.[44] This explains in part why Granville was not in favour with his stern father-in-law, who was also annoyed at his extravagance and his frequent absences in Oxford and London. In spite of all his faults Granville was a good and pious man who laboured earnestly for the welfare of the diocese and the cathedral. Isaac Basire the younger wrote to the Earl of Bath on St. Stephen's Day, 1674 giving a good report of the archdeacon, his preaching and his recent economies, and added " I write this to do right to a person who has been severely misrepresented and injured without colourable grounds, partly because of the envy of his brethren."

Dr. John Neile had been appointed to the third stall since 1635. He was also a prebendary of York, a prebendary of Southwell, vicar of Northallerton and vicar of Sigston, near Northallerton. In 1674 he was made Dean of Ripon, but he died in the following year.

Dr. John Durell, a Jersey man, entered Merton College, Oxford in 1640; but owing to the troubles went abroad, and graduated at the Sylvanian College at Caen in 1644. He

[44] *Granville's Letters,* II, Surtees Soc., pp. 7, 10.

became the first minister of the French episcopal chapel in the Savoy in 1660, was made chaplain to Charles II in 1662, prebendary of Salisbury in 1663 and of Windsor in 1664. He was appointed to the fourth stall in Durham in 1668, and retained it till his death in 1683. He held the living of Witney, in Oxfordshire, and was made Dean of Windsor and of Wolverhampton in 1677. He was a learned man, and translated the Book of Common Prayer into French for the use of the Huguenots in England; and he also helped Sancroft in the final revision of the Latin translation of the Prayer Book. He published *The Liturgy of the Church of England asserted in a Sermon Preached at the Chapel of the Savoy* in 1662 and, in the same year, *A View of the Government and Public Worship of God in the Reformed Churches beyond the Seas,* in which he attempted to prove a real unity in faith and worship between the Anglican and foreign Protestant churches. His *Sanctae Ecclesiae Anglicanae . . . Vindiciae* appeared in 1669.

Dr. Thomas Cartwright, one of the King's chaplains, held the fifth stall as one of his numerous preferments. He became Dean of Ripon and later Bishop of Chester. Burnet said he was " a man of good capacity and had made some progress in learning, ambitious and servile, cruel and boisterous, and by the great liberties he allowed himself he fell under much scandal of the worst sort." But Burnet was a spiteful and malicious gossip, who seldom had a good word to say of any of his brethren and never if they were on the opposite side in politics. Cartwright's diary during the time he was Bishop of Chester gives a very different impression.[45]

Richard Wrench, B.D. had been ejected from a fellowship at St. John's College, Cambridge. Bishop Morton collated him to the sixth stall in 1645 but the civil troubles prevented his installation until the return of the King. He died in 1675. On his return to Cambridge he found a worthy man in his place and refused to disturb him : but he found his compensations at Durham where he was earnest in the encouragement of learning and took a great interest in the

[45] Cartwright, *Diary,* Camden Series, 1843.

grammar school.[46]   He was vicar of Heighington from 1661 to 1665 and rector of Boldon from 1665 to 1675.

Isaac Basire held the seventh stall, to which he had been collated in 1643. Educated at Rotterdam and Leyden, he had settled in England in 1628, was ordained by Morton, Bishop of Lichfield, received the degree of D.D. at Cambridge by mandate from the King, and had incorporated at Oxford and received the same degree there. He became rector of Egglescliffe in 1636, chaplain-extraordinary to the King in 1646, archdeacon of Northumberland in 1644 and rector of Stanhope in 1646. In that year, however, he was driven out of England by the success of the parliamentary party. He was for a time in Italy, after which he travelled for three or four years in the East, and at last was made professor of divinity at Weissemburg in Transylvania. During this time his wife was living a harassed and poverty-stricken life at Egglescliffe. In 1660 he was restored to his prebend, his archdeaconry and his two livings. During his wanderings abroad he made a special study of the confessions of faith of the different eastern churches. He was a learned theologian, and the author of many pamphlets and discourses on religious subjects: the most interesting is his little book on Bishop Cosin, containing the funeral sermon he himself preached after the bishop's death, and a short life of that prelate. It was published under the title of *The Dead Man's Real Speech*. Basire died on October 12th, 1676, aged sixty-nine years.

Robert Grey, brother of the first Lord Grey of Wark, was born in 1610 and was educated at Northallerton Grammar School and Christ's College, Cambridge. In 1652 he became rector of Bishopwearmouth. He had been collated to the eighth stall in 1643, but was not installed till 1660. He was admitted B.D. in July and D.D. in September 1660 by royal mandamus. He had the reputation of being a learned and conscientious man who constantly resided at his rectory or prebendal house by turns and daily performed his office till the last week of his life, and he lived to be ninety-four. He

<hr/>

[46] *Life of John P. Barwick,* 1724, p. 306.

was strict in the assertion of his rights and tithes and yet a generous man. The story is told of him that having won a lawsuit about some glebe land he first made his opponent pay and then returned him a great part of the money. Where the parties were poor he took the tithe in kind, but generally restored it with as much money as its value, and if he retained it gave the tithepayer double the value. On one occasion when his curate rebuked some poor people for coming for assistance two days running, Grey reminded him that *he* asked for his daily bread every day.[47]

At the time Crewe was appointed, William Sancroft who held the ninth stall had resigned it, just two years before he was made Archbishop of Canterbury.

Dr. Daniel Brevin, or Brevint as the English people called him, was a Jersey man who after an education in France became a fellow of Jesus College, Oxford, from which he was ejected by the parliamentary commissioners. While in exile abroad he was chaplain for some time to Turenne. In 1660 he was appointed to the tenth stall. He became rector of Brancepeth in 1662, and prebendary and Dean of Lincoln in 1681, retaining all his appointments till his death in 1695. He was the author of some devotional and polemical works. Of the latter type was *Missale Romanum, or the Depth and Mystery of the Roman Mass laid open and Explained.*[48] A Catholic giving the initials R.F. replied with *Missale Vindicatum, or a Vindication of the Roman Mass,* to which Brevint replied in 1674 with *Saul and Samuel at Endor, or the New Ways of Salvation and Service.* Copies of this work are now rare.

Dr. Thomas Wood, rector of Whickham from 1635 to 1671, who was presented to the eleventh stall in July 1660, became Dean of Lichfield in 1671. A dispensation was issued for him to hold his prebend (with its £300 a year) for life, together with his bishopric. He was in high favour with the Duchess of Cleveland, whose son, Charles Fitzroy, Duke of Southampton, married his wealthy niece and ward.[49] She

[47] Raine, *North Durham,* 1852, pp. 330–2.
[48] Oxford 1672.
[49] *C.S.P.D.* Car. II. 291, No. 34. Entry Bk. B. 13.

was the daughter and heiress of his elder brother, Sir Henry Wood. He had to be forced by decree in Chancery in 1685 to pay over £30,000 as part of her fortune.[50] Bishop Hacket, who did so much to rebuild the cathedral after the damage it had received in the civil wars, and who was told by the " phrenetique dean " that he was doing more harm than good, wrote to the Archbishop of Canterbury on December 14th, 1668, " My most humble request (and in great earnest) to your grace is, to entreat with my Lord Bishop of Durham to call our most untractable and filthy natured dean from hence, and to command him to his benefice, or his prebend at Durham. He is a professed favourer of non-conformists. His wife seldom comes to sermons (as to Dr. Boilston) but not above twice in three months to cathedral prayers. I rebuked the dean for keeping company with puritans altogether. He answered me scornfully he did do so and he would do so. For the sake of the welfare of a poor church, and for God's sake, at least carry him away to Durham. He hath kept his residence to his full days, and his brethren the residentiaries will praise God for his absence." [51] Later, when he was Bishop of Lichfield, Wood was suspended by Archbishop Sancroft in 1684 for gross neglect of duty. He died in 1692.

Dr. Guy Carleton had been presented to the twelfth stall by the King in 1669 *sede vacante*. The presentation was a reward for his valour and sufferings during the civil war and he was allowed to hold with his prebend *in commendam* the deanery of Carlisle. He resigned the latter office in 1671 when he received the bishopric of Bristol, and on account of the smallness of the revenues of that see he was allowed to retain his prebend as well, together with the rectory of Wolsingham. Later he became Bishop of Chichester, still holding Wolsingham *in commendam*.[52]

The prebendaries of Durham were good, worthy men, some of them of good family, scholars most of them. They did their best according to their lights : but the system of plurali-

---

[50] Hutchinson, *Hist. Durham*, 1817–23, II, p. 274 n.
[51] *Miscell.*, Surtees Soc., xxxvii, pp. xiv, xv.
[52] *C.S.P.D.* Entry Book 53, pp. 3, 4.

ties and non-residence was bad, and the Church suffered from it for a long time to come. When the canons of a cathedral only appeared on duty for a short time in the year or, as the citizens of Durham bitterly expressed it, when they came as rent-gatherers [53] and everything was left to be done by the minor canons, who had not the real responsibility, a bad example of slackness and neglect was set to the lesser clergy, and a fruitful cause of discontent was given to the laity.

Whatever other faults could be found with the prebendaries of the cathedral, lack of hospitality was not one of them. Dean Granville noted down a list of his hospitalities during his residence from Saturday, October 1st, to Friday, October 21st, in 1687. He entertained on different days bedesmen, prebendaries, petty canons and their wives, singing men and their wives, justices of the peace, bell-ringers and other servants of the cathedral, ecclesiastical officers and attorneys, county gentry, tradesmen, poor widows and neighbouring citizens, tenants in the Elvet, shopkeepers and workmen, the master of the school and the King's scholars, the organist and choristers and their kindred. An Act of Chapter dealt with the residence and hospitality of the prebends. After saying that hospitality since the Reformation had tended to become excessive, it laid down that no dean or prebend, during his residence of twenty-one days, except on one day a week, should invite more than six persons, except such strangers as he might accidentally meet. Every time this rule was broken, unless it were on some extraordinary occasion specially approved by the chapter, £5 should be deducted from the offender's salary and given to the poor.[54]

Sir George Wheler, in his *Protestant Monastery*,[55] said, " The noblest remains of this English, and I think I may say Christian, hospitality is the residential entertainments of the cathedral church of Durham, where each prebendary in his turn entertains with great liberality the poor and rich neighbours and strangers with generous welcome, Christian free-

[53] Spearman, p. 117.
[54] *Denis Granville*, II, pp. 139–40.
[55] *The Protestant Monastery, or Christian Economics, containing Directions for the Religious Conduct of a Family*, 1698, p. 175.

dom, modest deportment, good and plentiful cheer, moderate eating and sober drinking. They give God thanks, read a chapter in the midst between the courses, during which all men reverently uncover their heads: and after grace again, there is seldom more drank than the *Poculum Charitatis,* or the Love Cup, and the King's good health, and then every one to his home, business and studies."

Church life in the diocese seems to have been in a very low state. The duty of preaching was lightly regarded, and catechizing neglected, except perhaps in Lent. Many of the clergy degraded their calling by secular employments and unsuitable recreations. In most of the churches Holy Communion was only celebrated three or four times in the year. Baptism was carelessly administered, oftener on weekdays than on Sundays, and when a child was baptized at home no attempt was made to bring it to church to be publicly received into Christ's flock. The office for the Visitation of the Sick was often read in part before the congregation instead of at the house of the sick person. The churching of women was commonly performed at home. The festivals of the Church were scandalously neglected, and services were sometimes put off for such things as horse races.[56]

During a vacancy in the see of Durham the King exercised numerous rights within the palatinate. He presented to all vacant livings which were normally in the gift of the bishop and he had the disposal of vacant prebends, and claimed to appoint some of the officials of the palatinate. On August 26th, 1673 a royal warrant was issued for the appointment of Sir John Otway, Vice-Chancellor of the county palatine of Lancaster, to be Keeper of the Great Seal of the bishopric and county palatine of Durham *sede vacante.*[57] This made him the temporal chancellor of the palatinate for the time being.

Dr. Thomas Burrell, or Burwell, the spiritual chancellor and vicar-general from 1631, having died in 1673, a grant of the office was made by the King, in April of that year, to

[56] Granville, *Letters,* II, pp. 11–13, 15, 17, 20, 23, 24.
[57] *C.S.P.D.* Entry Book 40, p. 99.

Thomas Ireland, M.A., LL.B., of Christ Church, Oxford.[58] Anthony Wood says of him, " His father was verger of Westminster and I suppose he was born there." [59] The chapter, having charge of the see during the vacancy, had appointed two members of the chapter as commissioners. A somewhat acrimonious correspondence ensued. The King wrote that he had granted the office, as of right he might during the vacancy, to Thomas Ireland for life. He did not expect that they would use any power of their own to bring in any other person as commissary; and he judged the persons appointed to be improper, and ordered them to resign and Ireland to be admitted.[60] On June 27th the dean wrote to Lord Arlington asking him to inform the King that if Ireland had given His Majesty the information on which his last letter was based, he had misrepresented the position. There was no such office as chancellor of the diocese of Durham: he was the bishop's chancellor, and when there was no bishop there was no chancellor. When the King saw fit to nominate a bishop it was, of course, in his power to signify his pleasure that Ireland should be his chancellor; but if Ireland should take upon him to act as chancellor in any other name than that of the bishop, or by any other patent than that received from the bishop, all his acts would be null. The bishop's ecclesiastical jurisdiction lay *sede vacante* in the hands of the guardian of the spiritualities, who exercised that jurisdiction by his commissary which the bishop did by his chancellor. When the dean and chapter of Durham were guardians of the spiritualities, they were bound by law to appoint a commissary to exercise the jurisdiction under them within eight days from the vacancy of the see; otherwise their power devolved on the archbishop of the province. The dean and chapter of Durham, like other deans and chapters, when guardians of the spiritualities, usually exercised the jurisdiction by one or more of themselves and not by him who had been chancellor. Though in this last vacancy they had made

[58] *C.S.P.D.* Docquets, Vol. 25, No. 324.
[59] Wood, *Life and Times,* II, p. 362.
[60] *C.S.P.D.* Entry Book 35, 13, f. 29. The King to the dean and chapter of Durham, June 17th, 1673.

Dr. Burwell their commissary, it was not because he had been chancellor to the late bishop, but for other reasons. On Burwell's death the dean was in London; but he wrote with all speed to the chapter to propose fit persons to succeed him (declining the office himself). They commended two of their body, the dean sent to the chapter to seal a commission to them, and all this before any of them had any knowledge of Mr. Ireland; nor could they imagine he had any design on the place of commissary when he applied to the King for the office of chancellor. The dean was anxious that no one should suspect him of desiring any advantage to himself in the disposal of the office. He had had a great deal of trouble in asserting the rights of the church of Durham in the recent suit with the Archbishop of York about the jurisdiction; but not for any private ends of his own. As for the King's command that the commissaries should resign, both of them expressed themselves willing to go up to London to do so at once; but inasmuch as they were required by a late Act to take the oaths of allegiance and supremacy at the next quarter sessions, they desired that this necessary postponement should not be taken as representing any unwillingness on their part.[61]

Ireland replied to the dean's letter. Granted that they had the guardianship of the spiritualities *sede vacante,* why did they not allow the King's recommendation of himself to be their commissary, when the King had constituted him to be chancellor when there should be a bishop? They chose the last bishop's chancellor to be commissary: why, then, did they not choose the King's? "They say that they are bound to choose a commissary within eight days, and they did so before anything was known of my appointment as chancellor. But the dean had notice of it at the burial of Dr. Burrell and again three or four days later. If, as the dean says, he had to send notice of the vacancy to the chapter, which would take three or four days by post, then they must have a meeting to propose persons to him which would ask the same time to return, and then his consent must be forwarded, certainly he might have prevented the effects of his first letter. It seems

[61] *C.S.P.D.* 336, No. 54.

from his first letter they would have chosen me had they known of it. To say they did not imagine when I asked to be chancellor I meant to be commissary is to suppose I moved the King for an uncertainty. I did not know, indeed, that there was such a thing to be asked, nor that their statutes obliged them to so quick a choice. As soon as I did, I made all civil application for it, with a letter to the dean from Lord Arlington, and have not been guilty of the least disrespect. The dean told me he was sorry it was out of his power, but if the King's letter came they knew not how to oppose it, which was the ground for seeking a mandate which was accompanied by a most obliging letter from Lord Arlington, to both of which the above was the answer. I must insist they are under their promise of resigning at the King's feet; the delay of their immediate obedience has been dispensed with in order to do it, and now it is what is desired and expected of them. As to my aspersing the dean, I meant only, what I had heard from his own mouth, that having been at great expense in a suit with the archbishop they thought to exercise this office by some of themselves." [62]

With this document in the Record Office are two others which were probably enclosed : a statement of the case as to the chancellorship of Durham with arguments against the contention of the dean and chapter, and a copy of the statute 37 Hen. viii. c. 17, empowering chancellors to exercise ecclesiastical jurisdiction.[63] An undated paper by the Dean of Durham, possibly written in July, shortly stated the facts about Mr. Ireland, and inquired whether this chancellor, by virtue of his patent from the King, could act as judge in the ecclesiastical court, so that acts done by him in virtue thereof were valid, and whether on appeal they would not be made nullities as being acts done *coram non judice*.[64] Possibly the copy of the statute is a reply to this.

On September 12th the dean received a letter from the King. "Pursuant to the King's letter of June 17th, your

[62] *C.S.P.D.* 336, No. 193.
[63] *C.S.P.D.* 336, No. 193. I. and No. 193 II.
[64] *C.S.P.D.* 336, No. 194.

commission of the first of April for the execution of your commissaries has been delivered by Dr. Thomas Cartwright, a prebendary and one of the commissaries, with submission to our pleasure for constituting the said Ireland, whom we have chosen for the chancellorship of the diocese as soon as a bishop shall succeed, to be your commissary *sede vacante,* and finding on better information the reason on which your first election of your said commissaries, and your delays in suspending hitherto your compliance with our pleasure, was solely grounded on your desire to assert your own title to the disposal of that office, we hereby express our entire satisfaction in that your compliance. Without more difficulty or delay you will, on receipt of these letters, issue your commission to Thomas Ireland with mention of the revocation of the before mentioned commission, appointing him your commissary *sede vacante.*" [65]

So Ireland was appointed, and the bishop had no choice. There was no doubt about the headship of the Church of England as by law established. The method of appointment would hardly conduct to amenity. Crewe admitted him as his chancellor in 1675; but he did not live long to enjoy the office, for he died in London in the following year. On May 17th, 1674 the clerkship of the County Court Office in Durham was confirmed to Thomas Burwell, M.D., by royal order, in consideration of the services of, himself and of his father, Thomas Burwell, deceased. [66]

While the see was empty great efforts were made to induce the King to appoint a sheriff at Durham, but this was opposed by the Duke of York who said it was hard if the bishop could not appoint his own sheriff and the King agreed. But there was a far greater innovation than anything of that kind. Hitherto, as an exempt jurisdiction the bishopric of Durham sent no members to the King's parliament at Westminster. There was an assembly of the palatinate which Mr. Lapsley compared in some measure with the Manx Tynwald and there was the bishop's council which had adminis-

[65] *C.S.P.D.* Entry Book 31, f. 117.
[66] *C.S.P.D.* Entry Book 21, p. 136, and 40, p. 192.

trative functions.[67] Under the Commonwealth the people of
the palatinate had received parliamentary privileges which
they were not anxious to lose. On October 3rd, 1666 the
grand jury at the general quarter sessions at Durham had
petitioned on behalf of the freeholders of the county for the
" privilege of sending members to parliament as all other
counties of the kingdom do." Bishop Cosin had sturdily
opposed. But now there was no bishop, so in 1673 there was
passed at Westminster " An Act to enable the County Palatine
of Durham to send Knights and Burgesses to Parliament," [68]
empowering the freeholders of the county to elect two knights
and the mayor, aldermen and freemen of the city of Durham
to elect two burgesses to represent them as county and city
members respectively. The Act stated that these members
were to be elected by virtue of the King's writ, directed by
the Lord Chancellor or Keeper of the Great Seal in that
behalf, to the Bishop of Durham or his temporal chancellor,
and then the bishop or his chancellor should issue a precept
thereon to the sheriff of the county.

The first election for parliament for the county (excluding
the three elections during the Commonwealth) was held in
June 1675. There were three candidates: Sir James
Clavering, Bart., of Axwell Park, an old royalist; John
Tempest of the Isle and of Old Durham, another old cavalier,
described in a pamphlet published two years later as " a
papist, a pensioner and a court-dinner man " ; [69] and Thomas
Vane, eldest surviving son of Sir Henry Vane of Raby.
Tempest and Vane were elected. But Vane died the morning
after the poll was declared, so a new writ was issued in
October, and Christopher Vane, his younger brother, was
nominated. The Vanes were powerful in the lordship of
Raby and Barnard Castle and had many tenants in their
houses and on their farms. Christopher Sanderson of Eggles-
tone, writing to Sir Joseph Williamson, said that the election
of Vane had caused all the sectaries to prick up their ears,

[67] Lapsley, *County Palatine of Durham*, 1900, pp. 112, 149–51.
[68] 25 Car. II. 1673.
[69] A Seasonable Argument to persuade all Grand Juries to Petition for
a New Parliament, Amsterdam 1677.

and that after Thomas Vane had been made a justice of the peace in the preceding year the fanatics were constantly resorting to him.[70]   On the other hand, when Christopher Vane was put up, William Christian, sheriff of Newcastle, expressed the opinion that the Bishop of Durham and most of the gentry would be on his side.[71]   However this may have been, Christopher Vane was elected unopposed.

Even the prebendaries' residence might come under the regard of the King. On March 17th, 1674 Charles wrote to the dean and chapter rebuking them for their treatment of Dr. Carleton, whom they had " defalked . . . of his quotidians and other profits " on account of his non-residence. In future he was to receive all his profits as though actually resident, since he had been granted a dispensation for non-residence.[72]   Three months later, June 20th, 1674, the King complained again, this time about the way they had treated Dr. Durell. He had been informed that in the previous year no allowance had been made for Dr. Durell's attendance as chaplain-in-ordinary for the month of July nor for the time necessary for his journey to London, and that he had been " defalked of his quotidians " for that time, contrary to his privileges, allowed by their statutes, as the King's servant in ordinary. This had been done under the pretence that July was not the month for his waiting on the King. He commanded them to pay Durell his quotidians for the same month and for one month more, as a reasonable period for his journeys, and he forbade them in future to make any such attempt against him or any other chaplain-in-ordinary. As canon of Windsor and chaplain to the Order of the Garter, Dr. Durell was bound to be at Windsor on all solemn installations, and to attend there as long as the King resided there. Therefore the King ordered that the whole time since the King's pleasure was made known of having an installation at Windsor, until the day of his removing thence, should be allowed Dr. Durell for his residence at Durham as though

[70] C.S.P.D. June 28th, 1675, 371, No. 142.
[71] C.S.P.D. 373, No. 100.
[72] C.S.P.D. Entry Book 27, f. 59.

he had actually been present there. Furthermore he must
be allowed to keep his twenty-one days residence at any time
of the year.[73] The dean of the Chapel Royal, Windsor, died
a few months later and Durell was made dean.[74]

On September 10th, 1674, before Crewe had been
enthroned, the King wrote to him " effectually recommending " him to grant to Humphrey Wharton a lease of the lott
ore of his own lead mines in the parishes of Stanhope and
Wolsingham, of which he had been possessed by virtue of
several leases from the late bishop, and by the King's grant
sede vacante for twenty-one years at least, at the rate of £60
reserved by their former lease, over and above £150, an
increase added by Act of Parliament.[75] John How and
Humphrey Wharton had petitioned the King for the renewal
of this lease, and the matter had been referred to Sir John
Otway, the temporal chancellor of Durham.[76] Before the
end of September, however, the letter of the 10th was revoked,
and the King ordered that the lease of the lott ore should be
granted to John Wickliffe, to whom the King had made a
previous promise, at the same rent at which Wharton had
held the lease.[77]

[73] *C.S.P.D.* Entry Book 31, f. 133.
[74] Oct. 10th, 1674. *C.S.P.D.* Entry Book 27, f. 61.
[75] *C.S.P.D.* Entry Book 31, f. 142.
[76] *C.S.P.D.* 338, No. 55, 1673.
[77] *C.S.P.D.* Entry Book 42, p. 1.

CHAPTER IV

THE Bishop of Durham, amongst other ecclesiastical offices in his gift, had the right of appointment to the prebends in the cathedral. During the vacancy of the see the King appointed, and as far back as July 1673 a warrant had been issued for a grant to Thomas Musgrave of one of the stalls.[1] They were all occupied at the time, but the King was making the best of his opportunities : moreover, Musgrave was a son of Sir Philip Musgrave of Hartley Castle and it was one way of showing a little kindness to a faithful old cavalier. Nicholas Salvin of Durham, who had received instructions to acquaint Sir Christopher Musgrave with the first vacancy in a Durham prebend, wrote on January 5th, 1675 to say that Dr. John Neile, who held the third stall and had in the previous March been made Dean of Ripon, was lying ill at Ripon and could not " continue long." [2] Of course now that there was a Bishop of Durham the appointment no longer lay in the King's hands, but Crewe was not the kind of person to stand in the way of a royal promise. There was another appointment to be made by the King. When prebendary Thomas Cartwright, as one of the two commissaries of the chancellorship, had been made by the King to give up that office because Charles wished to appoint Thomas Ireland, he was promised as a *solatium* that he should have the deanery of Ripon. Caveats had been entered accordingly, and Arlington had undertaken to see the King's promise made effectual. Arlington being away from the court at the time, the prudent Cartwright, fearing lest Neile should die before he returned, wrote to Sir Joseph Williamson about the matter and urged, as an additional reason why he should have the deanery, that the chapter of Durham intended to present

[1] *C.S.P.D.* Entry Book 35B, f. 29.
[2] *C.S.P.D.* 367, No. 25.

him to the living of Northallerton when the Dean of Ripon died, and as Northallerton lay midway between Durham and Ripon he would be able " to draw all his concerns into the north." [3]   On the evening of the 11th the news of Neile's death arrived in London, and Crewe wrote from Leicester Fields to Williamson : " You know very well how necessary despatch in things of this nature is, and therefore I submit the person recommended for it to your care and favour." [4]   The deanery, however, was given to Dr. Thomas Tully.   Some promise or other had been made to him, for on January 16th he wrote to Williamson thanking him warmly for his kindness " in the business of Ripon " which he hoped was " past danger."   However, he had to wait in anxiety for he was not appointed till April.   Crewe was waiting on the King one day at dinner, and he recommended Dr. Tully, who had been long a chaplain, and was a very learned man, to the deanery, and the King immediately consented, and gave orders to Sir Joseph Williamson to draw up the warrant.[5]   Even then he held it only for a short time, for he died the following January and then Cartwright got his desire.   Thomas Holdsworth, Dean of Middleham, in Yorkshire was collated to the ninth stall in May 1675, on the presentation of King Charles, under the pretence that the temporalities of the see were still in his hands.[6]

The King was concerned about the growth of Catholicism, or perhaps about the rising tide of public feeling against it. In January 1675 he desired that as many as possible of the bishops should meet together to consider how best to protect the Church from the growing danger of popery, and to give him their advice thereon.   A document by way of reply was presented to the King on behalf of the bishops.   They thankfully acknowledged his great sense of, and care for, religion and his condescension in recommending to their consideration so important a work as the maintenance of the blessed and glorious Reformation.   Atheism and profaneness abounded,

[3] C.S.P.D. 367, No. 3, Jan. 1st, 1675.
[4] C.S.P.D. 367, No. 51.
[5] Memoirs, p. 20.
[6] Hutchinson, Hist. Durham, II, p. 264.

and there were many defections on the one hand to Rome, and on the other to " the pernicious and destructive novelties of the various sects raised in the worst of times." Only a few members of the episcopal bench had been able to meet; but these met several times, and had come to the following conclusions : Nothing was more necessary than to suppress the prevalent atheism, profaneness and open wickedness. Their unanimous opinion was that the existing laws were sufficient for the suppression of popery and the preservation of the Church of England; but they urged that the King should issue orders that the laws be duly put in force, and that obstructions to the execution should be removed. They urged that upholders and enforcers of the law should be supported, and those who obstructed the enforcement of it should be discountenanced, and especially such persons as pretended to any licence or encouragement to violate the laws. This document was signed by the Archbishop of Canterbury and seven other bishops, of whom Crewe was one.[7]

At the beginning of 1675 the Bishop of Durham baptized Katherine Laura, the daughter of the Duke and Duchess of York. Born on January 16th and baptized on the 30th, she lived scarcely nine months. On March 18th Crewe officiated at a wedding which would be quite impossible nowadays. Sir Ralph Verney wrote : " A young wedding between Lady Grace Grenville and Sir George Cartwright's grandson which was consummated on Tuesday by the Bishop of Durham ; she is six years old and he is a little above eight years old, therefore questionless they will carry themselves very gravely and love dearly." It was not uncommon in aristocratic families thus to make alliances. About the same time the Earl of Lichfield, aged twelve, was married to the Duchess of Cleveland's daughter, aged eleven.[8] Such weddings seem disgraceful to us and even then provoked unfavourable comment in certain quarters.

A sidelight on Crewe's office as Clerk of the Closet is seen in a warrant issued by the King at Westminster, June

---

[7] *C.S.P.D.* 367, No. 131.
[8] *Memoirs of the Verney Family*, 1889, IV, p. 225.

24th, 1675, to Ralph Montagu, Master of the Great Wardrobe, to deliver to the Bishop of Durham as Clerk of the Closet the following, for the service of the King's Closet:

Two palls of cloth of gold of two breadths apiece and 5 yards each in length, lined with fustian and fringed with gold and silk and sewed with silk, for the Communion Tables.

Two long and one short cushions of the like cloth of gold for the King's own seat, fringed and tasselled with gold.

A dozen small cushions of crimson velvet to kneel on. 16 ells of fine diaper for 4 cloths for the Communion. 20 ells of fine Holland for 4 cloths more for the Communion Table.

13 ells of fine diaper for 2 Communion towels. 4 surplices of fine holland gathered.

2 great and 2 lesser Bibles for the King's own use, bound accordingly.

1 dozen of service books and 2 other service books richly bound accordingly.

This order was repeated on June 24th, 1678, with the following additions:

One traverse of crimson taffety, containing 10 breadths and 5 yards deep, with lyors of thread, ribbons of silk, and copper rings to it and sewed with silk.

One demy carpet and two small carpets of Turkey work for the King's own seat.

12 yards of green cloth to lay between three pair of fronts, each front containing 2 yards.

One bare hide of ox-leather.

2 standards bound with iron, with locks and keys to them.

2 trussing coffers and another coffer.

2,000 hooks, one great fire shovel, one pair tongs, one perfuming pan, 2 great hammers and two brushes.[9]

In Cosin's Library, Durham are a Bible and Prayer

---

[9] *C.S.P.D.* State Paper, Signet Office. IX, pp. 249, 322.

Book which had been presented to the bishop by Charles II. They came from the Chapel Royal. Both volumes are in royal red binding, probably by Mearns, bearing the royal monogram of two interlaced Cs with the crown. They also have heraldic fore-edge painting—the arms of England, Scotland, the monogram as above, France and Ireland. In University College Chapel, Durham is a similar Prayer Book. The two in Cosin's Library have each a note : " This Book belonged to King Charles the Second when Dr. Nathaniel Crewe was Clerk of the Closet to His Majesty and was afterwards consecrated Bishop of Oxford An. 1671, and from Thence was Translated to the Bishoprick of Durham An. 1674. And then Gave This Book to this Library which was Erected by Bishop Cosin for the use of his Successors in that See."

Crewe was not likely to undervalue his great position and he set out in 1675 on his first journey to his new diocese in great state.   He entered the Bishopric on June 9th, a remarkably hot day, with quite a cavalcade.   There were two coaches each drawn by six horses, twelve led horses besides, and a great number of running footmen and mounted servants.   Six gentlemen attended him.   On his arrival at the crossing of the Tees he would be presented by the Lord of Sockburn or his representative with the Conyers falchion. This was presented to Cosin in 1661 *in* the Tees, which was at the time very shallow.   We have an account of its presentation to Van Mildert, the last Bishop of Durham with palatine powers.   The person who presented it said it was the falchion wherewith the Conyers long ago slew the worm or dragon which was the terror of the countryside, in memory of which deed the then reigning king gave him the manor of Sockburn to hold by this tenure, that on the first entrance of every Bishop of Durham into the county the falchion should be presented to him.   The falchion was in the seventeenth century kept at the manor house of Sockburn.   On one side of the pommel were the arms of the Plantagenet Kings of England ; on the other " the eagle of Morcar, Earl of Northumberland." [10]

[10] Surtees, *Hist. Durham,* III, p. 244. *Monthly Chronicle of Lore and Legend,* V, p. 290.

On November 4th, 1674 Crewe had been granted the office of Lord Lieutenant of the county palatine of Durham.[11] After the troubles of 1536 Tunstal was made president of the Council of the North, and later became Lord Lieutenant of the county. The latter office was of less importance because military affairs were as a rule under the jurisdiction of the council. Tunstal's case was not a precedent. From the establishment of the office till the eighteenth century it was held only four times by the bishop.[12] Cosin was Lord Lieutenant in 1666. Crewe's tenure of the office was renewed on March 5th, 1685.[13] In August 1675 in his capacity as Lord Lieutenant he held near the city of Durham a general muster of all the trainbands of the county. The gentry, to his infinite satisfaction, attended the function in great numbers, and when it was all over he rode back proudly to the city at the head of the whole force, and attended, like a general with his staff, by all the deputy-lieutenants.[14] He was very proud of his position as Lord Lieutenant, and it was a great grief to him when in later years he was deprived of it. One can imagine him riding a gaily caparisoned steed that day, he himself clad in purple and conscious that he was the successor of Anthony Bec, the lord Anthony, as men called him, Patriarch of Jerusalem, King of Man and Bishop of Durham, who led the army of the palatinate to the Scottish wars, and of Thomas Hatfield, another ecclesiastical warrior bishop, who fought at the head of the soldiers from the diocese at the siege of Calais.

From Durham the bishop passed to Sunderland. On September 14th he made his first appearance there. His appointment to the see had given " great satisfaction to the inhabitants of the county palatine," and by this time the Sunderland people had heard a great deal about him. So a crowd went out to meet him and he found them waiting for him two miles along the road. They expected the Bishop of

[11] C.S.P.D. Entry Book 44, p. 2.
[12] Lapsley, *County Palatine*, p. 309. Surtees, *Hist. Durham*, I, p. cxlvii.
[13] *Patent Roll*, I Jac. II, Pt. I, No. 3.
[14] C.S.P.D. 372, No. 219.

Durham to behave as a man of high rank and importance, though they liked him of course to be condescending and affable, yet maintaining his dignity all the time. At last the running footmen and the mounted servants appeared and then the lumbering coach and six. The salutations and cheering over, the crowd turned and accompanied their new lord to the sea shore. He came out of his carriage, and they saw him properly for the first time. Tall, good looking, and certainly condescending, he fully came up to their expectations, though of course there would be some fault finders. The new bishop gazed with interest on something he had never seen before; a fleet of Newcastle colliers going south, and there would be many to tell him that day all about the north country coal trade. Then, to the great joy of the sightseers, his lordship walked back into the town, where he was entertained with great honour by the quality and, finally, having honoured Captain Conyers by dining with him, he returned that same evening to Durham.[15] He must have been reminded more than once that day that he held the high and honourable office of Admiral of Sunderland, though the work of that office throughout his long reign in Durham was mostly in the hands of his successive vice-admirals, William Blakeston, Charles Montagu and William Lambton.[16]

One of Crewe's earliest acts as Bishop of Durham was to collate Thomas Musgrave, the King's nominee, to the third stall on July 12th.[17] At last the bishop found himself able to make an appointment: Richard Knightley, fellow of Lincoln College, and one of Crewe's personal friends, was promoted to the sixth stall, and was installed by proxy on November 17th.[18]

The new bishop soon found that all was not peace at

[15] *C.S.P.D.* 373, No. 132.
[16] Spearman, p. 222.
[17] Thomas Musgrave, M.A., Queen's Coll., Oxford, D.D. 1685. Preb. of Carlisle 1669–76. Rector of Whitburn 1675. Preb. of Chichester 1681. Dean of Carlisle 1684. Died at the age of 47 and was buried in Durham Cathedral March 28th, 1686.
[18] He had the livings of Charwelton and Aston. He gave up the second in 1688 when he succeeded to his father's living of Byfield. He died in 1695.

G

Durham. Archdeacon Granville wrote to him, probably in 1675, perhaps before Crewe came to Durham, an undated letter in which he said, "If your lordship do not find me an honest, faithful (though a poor and inconsiderable) humble servant, and a true hearty lover and honourer of you, let me be eternally branded and proclaimed for as great a villain as I, or any of my friends, have been represented by my enemies, whose envy and malice is still rampant against me and all that own me." He then referred to "their late malicious impudence of disturbing even your lordship with a notorious untruth concerning my brother-in-law." This was Isaac Basire, Official of the Archdeaconry of Northumberland, son of the prebendary of the same name and son-in-law of Bishop Cosin. Thomas Wright, captain of a trainband, and Proto-notary of the Court of Common Pleas,[19] "a notorious sot," had created a scene in Isaac Basire's chambers, had been turned out and had caused a drunken brawl in the street outside. He was a friend of Neile the under-sheriff and Miles Stapleton, formerly secretary to Bishop Cosin, the two who had arrested the archdeacon for debt, and they were all three very angry at the way Granville had been defended, and at the rebuke Neile and Stapleton had received before the Privy Council. Isaac Basire himself wrote to the bishop, "I should not have troubled your lordship but I am well informed of the false suggestions of revengeful persons at this juncture, occasioned by my assisting . . . the just cause of the Church and my brother Grenville at the Council Board against the malicious attempts of those that were engaged therein." He wished to explain that among his other offices he was Keeper of Frankland Wood, near Durham, which he had obtained by patent for life on the death of his stepson who had also held it on the same terms. His purpose in getting the patent from the King had been to frustrate Neile who had clandestinely procured a royal warrant to deprive him of the post. Since that time he had built a new house at his own expense, the former house being a total ruin,[20] another example of how

[19] Surtees, *Hist. Durham*, IV, p. 153.
[20] *Miscellanea, Granville Letters*, Surtees Soc., pp. 155–7.

things had gone to ruin in "the late times" as people called them.

Archdeacon Granville had a number of warm friends who stood by him well in his troubles. On the whole he was not popular with the clergy of the diocese. Perhaps he lectured and scolded them too much, and incidentally they knew something of his weaknesses. In November he wrote to the Archdeacon of Northumberland complaining that he had been accused of being quarrelsome and of writing untruths to the bishop.[21]

We hear very little about Crewe's relatives. Of course the family scattered as the children grew up. A few words of Lord Crewe to his son the bishop have come down to us. No letters between members of the family have been preserved, but then very few letters to or from Nathaniel Crewe are still extant. On October 14th, 1675 he lost his mother, Lady Jemima Crewe, who died in London at the age of seventy-three. According to Sir Symonds D'Ewes she had not got on well with her husband or, as he puts it, "there was no great contentment between them." But Sir Symonds had been the rejected suitor and no doubt felt that the "gracious mistress Jemima" would have been much happier with himself. Pepys twice mentions the kindness he had received from her, but described her as "the same weak, silly lady as ever, asking such saintly questions";[22] it must be admitted, a somewhat wearing type to live with. The Bishop of Durham was with his mother at the last and at his father's request read the service for the Visitation of the Sick and the commendation of the departing soul at her bedside.

On April 23rd, 1676 he was sworn as a privy councillor, and he had no doubt that he owed the honour to James, for he waited till the latter had left the royal presence, and then kissed his hand and thanked him for it. He was on such good terms with the King that he could dare to speak to him very freely, and at a later date when fierce attacks were being made on James in Parliament he happened to be with Charles and

[21] *Ibid.*, p. 147.
[22] Pepys, *Diary*, Jan. 17th, 1665.

the duke in the Red Chamber. He took the opportunity to
tell the King that the purpose of the King's enemies was to
make a rift between him and his brother. Whoever wished
to do that was not the King's friend, and who could be so
entirely the King's friend as his own brother? He always
had a ready answer. Somewhere about 1677 Charles, looking at the bishop's list of persons proposed as deputy-
lieutenants, said " My lord, I don't like that name of Frank
Bowes." " Sire," was the reply, " the name is a good one
if you will put William instead of Frank." There was an
implication in this which was understood by the King and
those round him, so much so that Lord Radnor spoke approv-
ingly of the answer at a council meeting.

In 1676 the Bishop of Durham made a visitation throughout his diocese with much pomp. The post-reformation
bishops had taken over the pomp of their predecessors, whatever else they had changed, and this was one of the reasons
which made many of the laity dislike them. Crewe felt that
it was necessary, in order to keep up the dignity of the Church,
and there is no doubt that he liked it: it went with his
temperament. Pepys, who was not a lover of prelates, when
he visited Durham noted that the bishop lived " more like
a prince of this than a preacher of the other world." In the
course of his visitation the bishop came to Newcastle. He
preached in St. Nicholas' Church, the mayor, Sir William
Blackett, and " all the aldermen in their scarlet attending on
his lordship." At Alnwick the clergy were summoned to meet
him and the next day he went on to Berwick. There the
governor, the Duke of Newcastle's eldest son, had given orders
to receive the bishop with the same honours as they showed
to himself. So the whole garrison, five hundred strong, were
turned out, the mayor conducted the bishop to his lodgings
over which two sentinels stood on guard, and the bishop
was requested to give the password for each night that he was
there. He stayed in Berwick three or four days and confirmed
most of the garrison besides a great number of other persons.
Presbyterianism was strong in Berwick and the mayor and
some of the aldermen, after conducting him to the parish

church door for the confirmation, desired him to excuse them
from proceeding any further because they were of different
principles from the Church of England. Next day the bishop
was escorted round the defences of the town. The mayor
was particularly anxious for him to see the great bridge which
every traveller admired, built at great expense by James I,
and when they came to the middle of it the mayor laid down
his white staff and said, " Your lordship is now in your own
country," meaning that Scotland lay on the other side of the
staff.

There was a little unpleasantness during the visitation of the
cathedral : the names of the chapter were called out, the dean
answered his name and then sat down. People stood in a
bishop's presence. Dr. Sudbury was described as " a morose
man," and what followed was hardly improving to the
temper. " Mr. dean," said the bishop reprovingly, " your
posture does not become you." " Your predecessor, my lord,"
said Sudbury, " always bade us sit down." " Yes," was the
reply, " when I *bid* you sit down, sit down." [23]

The mastership of Christ's Hospital in Sherburn was in
the gift of the Bishop of Durham. It had a fair income, there
was a demesne called Byersgarth and Garmondsway which
in the time of Bishop Cosin was farmed at about £400 per
annum, while other rents and small fines brought in something over £80 a year. The brethren who lived in the hospital received twenty shillings a year each and certain small
allowances, and there were a number of out-brethren, each
in receipt of an annual sum of forty shillings.[24] The master
was John Machon, M.A., who had been put in by Bishop
Morton in 1636. An inventory taken at that time showed
the hospital then to be possessed of cattle, horses, sheep and
pigs to the value of £370 and a large quantity of household
furniture, but during the rebellion the master had been
turned out, the hospital plundered, and all the muniments
destroyed or taken away. The master appears to have
received what was left after the necessary expenses of main-

[23] *Examination*, p. 39.
[24] Cosin, *Correspondence*, II, pp. 124–7.

tenance, upkeep and pensions had been paid, and there was practically nothing for him to do. In the summer of 1676 it was thought that there would soon be a vacancy, as Machon was getting old, and the eagles were gathering together before the carcase was quite ready. The Reverend John Mason was expecting the reversion. Crewe, after his accession to Durham, had promised it to Dr. Trevor, but he had recently died.[25] The King had been got at during the vacancy of the see, and had promised the reversion to a relative of Sir Gilbert Talbot, but the post had not fallen vacant while the King had the power of appointment. Sir John Talbot wrote to Williamson,[26] " It was the greatest mortification I ever received to have it forced away after passing the palatine seal. I hope your brother secretary will think it reasonable if Trevor be dead that I might have the benefit of the King's promise, for I fear the bishop will deny His Majesty the disposal of it, unless he lay his positive commands that he do it in performance of his royal promise made before he was in his intentions for bishop of that diocese. You judged rightly that the concern was Sir Gilbert's, if he outlived Machon the present master and John Mason, clerk, my nominal master in trust likewise living." The last clause is illuminating as to the position of Mason in the matter. Sir Gilbert Talbot also wrote to Williamson begging him to remind the King of his promise made during the vacancy of the bishopric, of a reversionary grant to his (Sir Gilbert's) nephew's son. Trevor had taken this reversion from the Talbot family by a subsequent grant from the bishop. Perhaps the King could be induced to recommend the Talbot claim to the bishop now that Trevor was dead. The present possessor was " a very aged man and of a disorderly diet." Lest he should be putting too much on the secretary, Sir Gilbert had asked Bernard Granville to approach the King on the subject, and he desired Williamson to second him.[27] On September 13th Crewe visited the hospital and ordered that on account of his suffer-

[25] Richard Trevor, M.D. *Padua,* Fellow of Merton College, Oxford, died July 17th, 1676.
[26] *C.S.P.D.* 338, No. 157, July 24th, 1676.
[27] *C.S.P.D.* 384, No. 79, Aug. 2nd, 1676.

ings, losses and loyalty, Machon should only be required to
leave to his successor the sum of £220 in stock and plate.[28]
In spite of the anxiety of others to take possession of his
place, Machon lived on, his " disorderly diet " notwithstanding, until 1679, and then Crewe collated to the mastership
his nephew, the Hon. John Montagu, afterwards Dean of
Durham, and he retained it for nearly fifty years.

The bishop must have had a lot of trouble about the
appointments in his gift. King Charles was determined to lose
none of his ecclesiastical powers if he could help it, and Crewe
was not the man to resist him as a rule, though occasionally he had to do so. On April 27th, 1676 Lord Frescheville wrote to the Rev. Thomas Comber, afterwards Dean of
Durham, but then at Stonegrave in Yorkshire, that the Lord
Treasurer Danby had just told him that the King had
promised he should have the first prebend in Durham that
fell vacant. Danby had undertaken " to acquaint the Bishop
of Durham with his majesty's gracious promise, to the end
that it may not be forgotten." On May 23rd Frescheville
wrote again to say that the Bishop of Durham had greatly
opposed the execution of the King's promise " on pretence of
other engagements." However, the Archbishop of York
intended to give him the vacant prebend of Holme in York
minster, but advised him to be in no haste to be installed, as
a better was intended for him if any should fall vacant in a
short time.[29] He was, however, installed prebendary of Holme
on July 5th, 1677.

In September Dr. Isaac Basire, chaplain-in-ordinary to the
King, lay dying. Charles II heard of it and wrote to the
Bishop of Durham recounting how Basire had suffered sixteen
years' banishment for loyalty, and how he had spent large
sums in building and repairing the ruined houses and chancels
of his benefices, and in paying off the debts contracted during
his exile ; and so was unable to provide for his two children.
The King recommended that Basire's younger son, Charles,
should succeed his father in the rectory of Egglescliffe, the

[28] *Collections relating to Sherburn Hospital* 1771, p. 198.
[29] Comber, *Life of T. Comber*, 1799, pp. 90, 91.

least of all his preferments.[30] This, however, was not done. Charles Basire had been appointed to Boldon in 1675, and remained there until his death in 1691. Prebendary Basire died on October 12th. A few days later Sir Christopher Musgrave, writing from Edenhall to Secretary Williamson, told him how his brother, Thomas Musgrave, had resigned his prebend in Carlisle Cathedral in favour of John Ardrey, and intended to have been present at his friend's installation, " but their lordly bishop has summoned him to Durham." The reason was, however, he admits, that the bishop desired to dispose of Dr. Basire's prebend before he went to Court again, to anticipate any applications from that quarter.[31] There was more than this to fear. On November 18th, 1676 Secretary Coventry wrote informing the bishop that the King had ordered the issue of a *Quare impedit* to settle the question whether the right of disposing of prebends at Durham lay with the bishop or the King. He promised that all diligence would be used in clearing the question up; but meanwhile, if any vacancy should arise the bishop was not to make any presentations, and so the matter dragged on until March. The Attorney General was consulted, and must have given his decision in favour of the bishop, for the Lord Treasurer was ordered to withdraw the prohibition, and the bishop was informed of the fact by Coventry.[32]

This was not the only way in which the royal hand fell heavily on Durham at this time. On August 29th, 1676 the King wrote to the dean and chapter dispensing Denis Granville from residence for two years, as he was by the King's command repairing beyond the seas and during that time he was to enjoy his full emoluments.[33] In 1678 this dispensation was extended for another year.[34]

Prebendary Richard Knightley applied to the King on November 13th for a dispensation for absence from the next general chapter, to be held on November 20th, which he was bound to attend by statute, he being hindered by some extra-ordinary sad occasions in his family; and having been admitted a prebendary for twelve months, and having kept his residence there, he further asked that the dean and chapter might allow him a full dividend from the time of his admission to the end of the approaching audit.[35] On the same day the King granted the dispensation requested.[36]

There was more trouble at Durham about Dr. Durell's absences in 1678. On September 28th in that year the King wrote to the dean and chapter dispensing with the residence at Durham of that prebendary, who was now Dean of Windsor and Registrar of the Order of the Garter, by reason of which dignity he was bound to give attendance on the King on all "sudden and emergent occasions." By the statutes some defalcation had to be made of his profits when he was non-resident: the King required that Dr. Durell should receive all his emoluments, both for present and future years, except the £50 a year usually granted to prebends for their necessary twenty-one days' residence and hospitality. That sum he was only to receive when resident. He was also to see that his courses of preaching should be constantly supplied by fit persons, approved by the dean.[37]

The Bishop of Durham held a high position and knew it, and was apt to take a high line in manifesting his wishes, as a matter of course. On one occasion he found himself opposed by Sir John Reresby, who noted in his memoirs: "The post-master of Doncaster having disobliged me (one Hunt) I endeavoured to put him out: but finding greater opposition than I expected from the Bishop of Durham, Duke Lauderdale and several other persons of quality that used to be at his house, I could not effect it, till, speaking twice myself to the Duke of York, he granted my request, and gave it to my quarter-master of a militia troop that kept an inn there."[38] The words "used to be at his house" suggest that Hunt had convenient lodgings for the bishop on his journeys to and

---

[35] *C.S.P.D.* 386, No. 230, Nov. 13th, 1676.
[36] *C.S.P.D.* Entry Book 47, f. 40.
[37] *C.S.P.D.* Entry Book 27, f. 119.
[38] Reresby, *Memoirs*, May 6th, 1677.

from the north.　He might defend Hunt, but he would not oppose James or James' protégé.

On November 7th, 1677 the Duchess of York was delivered of a son, Charles Duke of Cambridge, the fifth of the infant sons of James who bore this title and his first son by Mary of Modena.　It was christened the following evening at St. James', Crewe being the officiant.　The King and the Prince of Orange were godfathers, and Lady Frances Villiers acted as proxy for the Princess Isabella, the second daughter of James and Mary Beatrice.　But the child in whom such great hopes were set only lived a little over a month, dying of smallpox on December 12th, and his little godmother only lived till March 1681.[39]　Mary of Modena said in after years : "I only knew happiness in England from the age of fifteen to twenty, but during those five years I was always having children, and lost them all, so judge of that happiness."

In November 1677 Archbishop Sheldon died.　Ralph Montagu urged Crewe to become a candidate for St. Augustine's chair, and he would have had the support of the Montagu family.　Compton was also a candidate and would have been backed by his own relatives.　The Duke of York was a supporter of Crewe, Danby of Compton.　On the whole less offence would be given if a third party were made archbishop and on December 30th Dr. Sancroft was appointed. It is said that it was through the interest of Lord Belasyse and others of the Roman Catholic nobility, who thought he would never be obnoxious to the Catholic party even though when he was at Cambridge he had taken the Covenant, and though his promotion was supported by Lord Falconberg, who married Cromwell's daughter.[40]　On the day of Sancroft's appointment the Earl of Thomond met the bishops of London and Durham as they came from chapel and said, "very pleasantly, ' My lords, you have been shown a Newmarket trick, but you see God Almighty's rule doth often hold : He putteth down the mighty from their seat, and exalteth them of low degree.' " [41]　Lord Crewe, we are told, prayed earnestly

[39] *Diary of Edward Lake,* Camden Miscell., 1847, p. 7.
[40] *Memoirs,* p. 17.
[41] *Diary of Dr. Edward Lake,* Camden Ser., p. 21.

that his son might not be appointed, and told him so. " Son, I prayed that you might not be removed," he said, for he feared whither his son's ambitious spirit might lead him, and Nathaniel used to say that he only lost the archbishopric through his father's prayers. Considering all the difficulties which would confront an Archbishop of Canterbury in the near future, he may have learnt to look on the disappointment as a blessing in disguise. He would have liked to go to Canterbury and it is said that this was the only time in which he failed to attain his wish in the whole course of his life. The bishop's father had not got rid of his early puritanism as his son had, and he disliked his type of churchmanship. He objected to his bowing to the altar, and said, " Son, you give me offence," and he used to pray that Nathaniel might be delivered from ambition and superstition.

Though the first parliamentary election for the county of Durham was held in 1675, doubts regarding the person who should issue the writ postponed the first election for the city until 1678. The Committee of Elections reported to the House of Commons on February 25th, 1678 that they were not clear on the matter, and recommended that the matter should be left for further consideration. However, a writ was ordered to be issued immediately. The high sheriff issued a precept to the mayor of Durham on March 22nd, 1678 stating that he had received a *mandamus* under the seal of the palatinate from the chancery of Durham made and awarded to the Bishop of Durham, grounded on His Majesty's writ issued out of the High Court of Chancery directed to the bishop, whereby he is commanded to cause to be elected within the city of Durham two sufficient and discreet burgesses. The process seemed to be this : the High Court of Chancery issued a writ to the Bishop of Durham ; at the bishop's command the bishop's chancellor issued a *mandamus* or precept to the high sheriff ; the sheriff then issued a precept to the mayor. The mayor would then summon the aldermen and freemen, and proceed to the election, and certify the result to the high sheriff. The voters were the freemen of the guilds of which there were then sixteen. The various trade-guilds of Durham have a history reaching back to the Middle Ages. The custom grew up of electing the bishop an honorary member of one of them. Crewe and Edward Arden, his secretary, were both enrolled in the mercers' guild on October 16th, 1676 and the bishop was thus able to record his vote at the parliamentary elections for the city.[42] At the 1678 election for Durham city, no freeman of the goldsmiths', plumbers' and potters' guild seems to have voted. In all there polled 838 voters, though on a scrutiny it was found that 27 voters were not freemen, six were under age, and three polled twice over. The successful candidates were Sir Ralph Cole of Brancepeth castle and John Parkhurst of Catesby, Northants, the bishop's secretary.

The years 1678 and 1679 were troubled years in the diocese of Durham; the northern part especially had its share in the troubles. In the old moss-trooping days refugees from one side of the border could always find safety and protection on the other. From 1662 onwards Presbyterians and Covenanters found shelter in Northumberland, where the people were largely sympathetic and the authorities were slack. Three of the fiercest men of the Pentland rising were to be found there. Gabriel Semple took up his abode near Ford and, while James Scott was rector, preached in the church there until 1677 when a new incumbent refused him permission. Semple returned to Scotland in 1690 but his influence lived after him. John Welsh was frequently in Northumberland when things were too hot for him in Scotland: and William Veitch, *alias* George Johnstone, settled down after Rullion Green at Stanton, near Morpeth. In 1676 it was reported that great conventicles were being held in the north of Northumberland. Often, like the Covenanters' meetings in Scotland, they were simply gatherings of armed men who denied all authority and condemned all worship other than their own. The justices of the peace were too timid to do anything and disregarded instructions from headquarters bidding them enforce the law.[43]

[42] Surtees, *Hist. Durham*, I, App. clxiii–clxv.
[43] *C.S.P.D.*, Nov. 24th, 1676, 387, No. 41.

Matters became so serious that the Government determined at the beginning of 1678 to send two troops of Lord Oxford's regiment, and to call up a thousand of the Northumberland militia. These were all to gather at Alnwick; but though there might be accommodation there for the two troops of horse, there certainly would not be for the militia. It was doubtful whether half the required number of militia could be got together at that time of year (February), to say nothing of the fact that many of them would at heart sympathize with the conventiclers. Things drifted on during the summer, the Covenanters were becoming more and more dangerous in southern Scotland. In September orders were issued to the Duke of Newcastle as Lord Lieutenant of Northumberland to suppress all field conventicles, to arrest all religious teachers and others who were disturbing the peace, and all Scottish fugitives. The Duke of Monmouth, as General of the Forces, received similar instructions, and he was to give the Duke of Newcastle all the assistance necessary.[44] George Hume of Graden, a Berwickshire laird, was captured, and a party of Covenanters determined to rescue him. The result was an affray at Crookham, a few miles south-east of Cornhill. About fourteen or fifteen armed and mounted Covenanters fell in with Colonel Strother, one of the deputy-lieutenants of Northumberland, and three companions. On the King's side Robert Mailey was killed, and on the rebel side Thomas Ker and several of the combatants were wounded.[45]

On September 19th Captain Ralph Widdrington, in a letter to Sir Joseph Williamson, said the offenders were sheltered and countenanced in all the towns near the borders, and a story had been set about that " these rogues were set upon by the gentlemen on the King's highway, being all drunk, for which there is no manner of truth." The " town " of Crookham belonged to Justice Black, and was a disloyal place. Before the fight the Covenanters had been entertained in one of the houses there, for which the owner had been sent

[44] C.S.P.D. 366, p. 583. Entry Book 42, p. 46. Entry Book 43, p. 216. Entry Book 41, pp. 158, 159.
[45] R. A. Bosanquet, The Crookham Affray. Arch. Ael., 4th series, Vol. IX, pp. 1–49. C.S.P.D. 366, p. 571. 405, No. 161.

to prison; and many of the people there had climbed to the houses and stacks, had given no help to the weaker party, and had refused to join in the hue and cry when the fight was over.[46]

The Government was alarmed. The King wrote to the mayor and aldermen of Newcastle warning them that certain seditious persons, formerly ministers and teachers in several counties of the north, were in Newcastle, and were carrying on dangerous correspondence and practices against the peace of the Church and State, and filling weak minds with a dislike of government. They were to put in force effectually the Act against seditious conventicles.[47] Colonel Strother received from Whitehall an expression of the King's approval of his diligence. Further forces were to be sent to his assistance, and the King had ordered that he should receive 20s. a day while on this service.[48] The Duke of Newcastle was commanded to urge all officers of the militia and justices of the peace to greater energy in suppressing riotous conduct, and in arresting the leaders.[49] Major Binns, commanding the government troops in Northumberland, received orders from the Duke of Monmouth that he was, if necessary, to pursue fleeing rebels into Scotland, and he was to be prepared to assist any troops from over the border who might pursue fugitives into England.[50] More troops were being sent, and Binns and other regular officers were to give every assistance to Colonel Strother.[51] Renewed exhortations to activity were sent to the Duke of Newcastle (who all this time seems to have remained at Welbeck passing on instructions express to his subordinates) and to the mayor of Newcastle.[52] The Duke urged upon Sir Joseph Williamson that three of the disaffected Northumberland justices ought to be put out of the commission of the peace.[53] Matthew Jeffreyson, mayor of New-

[46] C.S.P.D. 406, No. 151.
[47] C.S.P.D. Entry Book 42, p. 52, Sept. 25th, 1678.
[48] C.S.P.D. Entry Book 41, p. 160, Sept. 26th, 1678.
[49] C.S.P.D. Entry Book 42, p. 53, Sept. 25th, 1678.
[50] C.S.P.D. Entry Book 41, p. 164, Sept. 26th, 1678.
[51] C.S.P.D. Entry Book 41, pp. 165, 166, Sept. 26th, 1678.
[52] C.S.P.D. Entry Book 46, pp. 219, 220, Sept. 26th, 1678.
[53] C.S.P.D. 406, No. 183, Sept. 29th, 1678.

castle, and eight aldermen, wrote to Williamson saying they would most readily comply with the King's commands for putting the laws in execution against the nonconformists. Three days later the mayor and three aldermen reported that they had given orders to the churchwardens to make diligent search for conventicles, and that warrants would be issued against ministers who refused to take the oaths required by law.[54] " George Johnstone," had been seized and imprisoned in Morpeth gaol by a *mittimus* from Colonel Strother. Orders were issued in January that he should be delivered to the sheriff of Berwickshire to be conveyed before the Privy Council at Edinburgh.[55]

Local feeling of independence, pride in the ancient government of the palatinate and respect for the bishop may account for the following. In November 1678 there was a man in Durham gaol calling himself David Constable and suspected of being a popish priest. The mayor, William Blakeston, had refused when requested to send an account of the man to a secretary of state; they had a Lord Lieutenant in Durham, he said (meaning the bishop) to whom they gave account. Secretary Coventry wrote on November 21st saying that " without the least derogation to the Lord Lieutenant, whose authority we own, and whose person we honour," the King expected and required a speedy and particular account of the prisoner through the hands of one of the secretaries of state.[56]

The manuscript lives of Crewe tell of a visit by the Duke and Duchess of Lauderdale to Durham, but the only evidence of its date is that it occurred when he was High Commissioner to Scotland. As the visit is mentioned in juxtaposition with the visits of Monmouth and the Duke and Duchess of York who were in Durham in 1679, and as the last occasion on which Lauderdale went north as High Commissioner was 1678, probably it was during the latter year. The bishop had sent two of his gentlemen as far as Berwick inviting important

[54] *C.S.P.D.* 406, Nos. 222 and 233, Oct. 1st and Oct. 4th, 1678.
[55] *C.S.P.D.* 411, No. 53, Jan. 25th, 1679.
[56] *C.S.P.D.* Entry Book 51, f. 84.

people to meet the duke. During dinner Lauderdale looked round the table and said, " My lord, the major part of the nobility of Scotland are now at your lordship's table "—a humorous exaggeration no doubt, but a testimony to the largeness of the episcopal hospitality. When the duke spoke apologetically of the size of the train he had brought with him, as though fearing that it would be a burden on the bishop, one of the latter's officials replied courteously, " The greater the number, your grace, the more welcome they will be to my lord." Partly because he was away from Court a long time and partly because he had entertained Lauderdale, Crewe was thought to have lost ground at Court. There were many backbiters, of course : Secretary Coventry said that he had heard that the Scots had come even to Durham, and there were little insinuations flying about that as Lord Lieutenant he was not really ruling well.

The Popish Plot had some slight connection with the diocese of Durham. One of the witnesses in the trials of Wakeman and Lord Stafford in 1679 was Robert Jenison of Gray's Inn, the younger brother of Thomas Jenison, a Catholic priest, who had been thrown into Newgate towards the end of 1678 and died there the following September. Their father, John Jenison, a wealthy man, lived at Walworth Castle, near Darlington, and the family till recently had all been Catholics. With them lived a relative, a priest named John Smith, who acted as chaplain to the household, but towards the end of 1678 the father, his son Robert, and John Smith, had all joined the Church of England. John Jenison journeyed to London in December 1678 to visit Thomas Jenison in prison. The Bishop of Durham reported this to the House of Lords and said that the father was trying to induce his son to make " discoveries " of the plot. On the 19th he informed the House that Jenison the elder was at the door. Smith was with him, and the Lords took favourable notice of their zeal and gave permission for them to have free access to Newgate. All that they could report after interviewing the prisoner was that he was mad and could not give an account of anything. John Jenison took the opportunity while in the House of Lords to beg that Smith might be permitted to officiate in the Church of England, and testified that he had abandoned the Church of Rome and had taken the oaths of allegiance and supremacy. Their lordships ordered that he should wait upon the Lord Bishop of Durham and satisfy him as to the reality of his conversion and his abilities. On the bishop's report the House would consider what directions to give therein.[57] Crewe would not be likely to treat the request very sympathetically, and whatever the result of the interview may have been Smith was never curate or incumbent in the diocese of Durham. He had been for a time a member of the Jesuit College at Rome, though he never entered the Society, returned to England in 1676 and went to live at Walworth. According to Robert Jenison's story, private knowledge of the plot came to the family and so they all turned Protestant. Robert Jenison and Smith also turned informers. The former was anxious that it should be believed that his conversion and his informing were not due to any private ends directed towards the possession of the family estate.[58] A gentleman of sensitive honour, but it did not prevent him from swearing away an innocent man's life. Smith did not attempt any very outrageous stories. In September 1679 he made a sworn deposition before Mr. Justice Warcup in London in the course of which he said that since the Restoration the papists had taken advantage of their interest at Court. He had heard the Jesuits preach the Pope's right to dethrone and kill heretical princes, and he told how he had heard in 1676 that large sums of money were being raised for the repair of the Catholic college at Douai, more than was necessary in fact, implying of course that the surplus would be used to the danger of England.[59] He was very soon one of the regular informers and was nicknamed " Narrative Smith."

Robert Bolron was another local product. He was a native

---

[57] The Whole Series of all that hath been Transacted in the House of Lords Concerning the Popish Plot, London 1681, pp. 153, 156-7, 161.
[58] History of the Damnable Popish Plot, 1680, pp. 279, 310-16.
[59] The Narrative of Mr. John Smith, London 1679.

of Newcastle who had been apprenticed to a jeweller in London. Running away from that he soon found himself a soldier in Tynemouth castle. Sent on board the *Rainbow* to fight against the Dutch he deserted. Next he was found in the service of Sir Thomas Gascoigne of Barnbrough, near Leeds, and was by him made inspector of one of his coalmines near Newcastle. Found guilty of gross peculation he was dismissed, and became a discoverer of popish plots, one of his first victims being his old benefactor Gascoigne who was, however, acquitted. On November 14th, 1679, "Robert Bolron of Newcastle-upon-Tyne, milliner" (on November 27th he was a "gentleman") made deposition at York that a Catholic priest, Robert Killingbeck, was at a general consultation at Barnbrough where it was determined to kill the King and all Protestants who would not turn Catholic. Thomas Riddell, Esq. of Fenham, Northumberland, had promised to contribute liberally to the design and Sir Thomas Haggerston of Haggerston was also in the plot.[60] Riddell was acquitted by the magistrates, but since Dom Robert Killingbeck, O.S.B., was his chaplain from 1677–9, he remained under suspicion, and in 1681 was convicted of high treason for sending his son Mark to be educated abroad. He remained in gaol for a long time.

The Popish Plot stories had caused a wave of hysteria throughout the whole nation. In the eyes of most Englishmen the Duke of York was deeply committed to it. Victims of the informers were being put to death. Danby was attacked. Five Catholic lords were sent to the Tower. Fresh informers came forward with stories as time went on. It was an anxious time for the Bishop of Durham for his great friend was in danger. The Long Parliament of the Restoration came to an end in 1678 and a new Parliament was to be elected.

Northallerton being part of his jurisdiction, Crewe was anxious that in the February elections of 1679 members favourable to the Government should be chosen. Thomas Lascelles wrote to Sir William Frankland on February 3rd:

---

[60] *Depositions from York Castle,* Surtees Soc., 1861, pp. 245–6.

" I have communicated yours about the election of knights of the shire to several freeholders hereabouts and have not failed to make Sir Gilbert Gerard's and Sir Henry Calverley's interest as strong as I am." I hope they will carry it "though Mr. Marwood, by his brother Metcalfe's interest, puts in to give us some trouble. My lord of Durham also hath recommended his elder brother with some earnestness, and a kind of little threatening, but obstinate tempers will not be wrought upon by any impressions but such as they like." In the end Marwood withdrew and Gerard and Calverley were elected.[61]

In April 1679 Anthony Wood learned from letters sent from London that five bishops had been impeached for complicity in the Popish Plot, Crewe of Durham, Gunning of Ely, Mews of Bath and Wells, Pritchett of Gloucester and Barrow of St. Asaph, on the ground that in the last parliament they had been in favour of the Catholic lords sitting in the Upper House.[62] The story was, of course, quite untrue, but there was much wild talk on the subject going about. What may have had something to do with the rumour is to be found in a letter dated April 24th, 1679, written by Ruisshe Wentworth to John Wentworth, giving a list of former privy councillors who had been left out of the new council, Sir William Temple's large new Council of Thirty, established on April 21st.[63] Crewe was one of those whose names had been omitted from the list, although he had been a member of the Privy Council ever since April 1671. It is easy to see how a rumour might be started that he had fallen out of favour and that worse was coming to him. Titus Oates was once at dinner in the chaplains' room at Whitehall when Crewe was present as Clerk of the Closet, and the latter asked him who was to have been Bishop of Durham if the plot had succeeded. Oates, who was never at a loss for a lie, named a certain lord. It was a wise question on the part of the bishop, and the question was put and the answer given in the presence of wit-

[61] *Hist. MSS. Com.*, MSS. Frankland-Russell-Astley, pp. 38, 41.
[62] Wood, *Life and Times*, II, p. 447.
[63] *Hist. MSS. Com.*, Various Collections, II, p. 394. MSS. of Mrs. Wentworth.

nesses. It was quite likely that if he had not been present and someone else had asked the question the reply would have been that the Catholics intended Crewe to continue.   There were many attempts about this time to blacken the bishop's character because he was a friend of the King's brother whom they hoped to pull down.   Dr. Stillingfleet, apropos of this little scene in the chaplains' room, said that " my lord was a cunning man."   The word may mean no more than clever, but the commentator in the *Examination*[64] asked " if the bishop was innocent what need of policy? "   Innocence saved no man from Oates, Bedloe, Dangerfield and the rest.   Any person whom they chose as a victim was in great danger, and Crewe was clever enough to stop Oates' lying mouth from one story at least.

During the first week of May 1679 there was a quarrel between the two Houses of Parliament on the subject of jurisdiction.   The Earl of Danby was under impeachment, and five Roman Catholic lords were due for trial as implicated in the Popish Plot.   The bishops claimed the right to sit during the preliminary stages of a capital charge but to leave before the sentence was declared.   The House of Lords agreed with this position, which had the sanction of constitutional custom, though Shaftesbury, Halifax and their followers protested.   On the 6th the Lords debated whether the bishops could vote on the question of the validity of Danby's pardon, which might really be a decision of life or death, inasmuch as if the pardon did not hold good, an attainder was presumed to follow.   The discussion was continued on the following day, the preponderance of the speeches being on the side of the bishops' claims.[65]   The Commons, however, when the matter was discussed in their House, declared that as the bishops were incapable of giving judgment they were incapable of sitting during the early stages of the trial.   They even objected to the presence of the bishops in the Lords while the validity of the pardon was being discussed.   The real objection to the bishops was that their votes had hitherto seemed to favour

[64] *Examination*, p. 44.
[65] *Hist. MSS. Com.*, Ormond MSS., V, pp. 86–8.

Danby.[66] The Lords had decided that Danby should be tried
on the 13th, and they asked the King to appoint a Lord High
Steward for the purpose. To this the Commons objected that
a Lord High Steward was unnecessary in the case of an
impeachment. There was another deadlock. The Commons
proposed that a committee should be appointed consisting of
representatives of both Houses to discuss all matters relating
to the trials of the accused lords, but the Lords replied that
this was unnecessary.

Algernon Sidney in a letter to Henry Savile dated May
12th, 1679 said, " Several proposals have been made by the
Commons of conferring with them upon all the points in
question, or appointing a committee of both Houses, which,
meeting together, might adjust all those that might be
occasion of difference ; but their lordships disdaining to
confer upon points that as they did suppose depended wholly
upon their will, on Friday last did vote that they would have
no such committee, which vote was carried only by two
voices, the one side having 54, the other 52. Of eighteen
bishops there were present, sixteen were on the victorious side,
and only Durham and Carlisle were so humble as to join with
the vanquished. Of those 52, one and fifty the next day protested and I think only laziness hindered the Earl of Leicester,
who was the other, not to protest, as well as the others with
whom he had voted." [67]

In the House of Lords the Bishop of Durham supported the
attack on the Earl of Danby. When the question was debated
whether Danby should be committed to the Tower, Crewe
walked out of the House and two other bishops who were his
friends followed him. He would not vote for him, and
neither would he vote against him, but it is said that those
three votes would have saved him from going to the Tower on
April 16th, though it is probable that his enemies would have
returned to the attack even if he had temporarily escaped
them. Sancroft asked Crewe what made him so hostile to the

[66] Ormond MSS., IV, p. 510.
[67] Letters of Algernon Sidney to Henry Savile, London 1742.

fallen minister, to which he replied, " Because he is an enemy
to the Duke of York, my principal friend."

The Government had reason to be alarmed at the state of
the Border in 1679. In April the Duke of Monmouth sent a
circular to all the governors of castles, including the Duke of
Newcastle as Governor of Berwick, asking for a full account
of the present condition of the garrisons, stores and so on.[68]
In June the rebellion broke out in Scotland. It was necessary
to keep Berwick safe from fear of surprise or open attack, and
the Lord Lieutenant was commanded by the King to put five
hundred men of the Northumberland militia into it at once.[69]
But the King was not unmindful of what had happened in the
previous year. He wrote to the Bishop of Durham, enclosing
a copy of his letter to the Duke of Newcastle, and saying that
he understood that the militia of Northumberland hardly
amounted to five hundred; and so Crewe was to order some
of his deputy-lieutenants to raise and march to Berwick such
companies of the Bishopric militia as were in that neighbourhood, and thus provide for its defence till other provision
could be made.[70] Lord Sunderland, however, informed the
Duke of Newcastle that the King was quite satisfied with his
measures for raising the militia and defending Berwick. If it
had been found necessary to raise any considerable number of
troops His Majesty would have accepted the duke's offer of
personal service.[71] But the rebellion collapsed, and speedy
orders were issued to dismiss the militia.[72] When the Duke of
Monmouth was sent north in command of the army, Crewe
had been sent off in haste to his diocese to raise the Bishopric
militia. Setting out from London on Monday he arrived at
Auckland at midday on Friday, which was swift travelling for
those days, and met all his deputy-lieutenants who had already
been summoned. While they were at dinner an express came
with a special order from the council to raise at once that part
of the militia which was near Berwick. Monmouth was enter-

[68] C.S.P.D. Entry Book 58, p. 11, April 23rd, 1679.
[69] C.S.P.D. Entry Book 164, p. 13, June 10th, 1679.
[70] C.S.P.D. Entry Book 164, p. 17, June 11th, 1679.
[71] C.S.P.D. Entry Book 56, p. 6, June 21st, 1679.
[72] C.S.P.D. Entry Book 56, p. 9, July 15th, 1679.

NATHANIEL LORD CREWE.
From the portrait in University College, Durham.

Facing page 107.

tained very lavishly by the bishop both on his journey north and on his return after his victory at Bothwell Bridge. He congratulated the bishop on the militia of the Bishopric which he considered, he said, the most regular and the best disciplined that he had ever seen. After dinner at Durham castle he declared his intention of riding post to Darlington, but Crewe offered to lend him his coach, saying that it would carry him faster than any posthorse would. The duke accepted the offer, reached Darlington in two hours, and said he had never travelled so fast even in the King's coaches. He probably was as excited about it as any modern young man who wants to see what his new motor can do.

In November 1679 the Duke and Duchess of York, on their way to Scotland where the duke was going as High Commissioner, stayed for two or three days at Durham castle as the guests of the bishop. Crewe had set out for London and was five days journey on his way thither when he heard that the duke was going by land, so he hastened back to Durham to be in time to receive him.[73] His horses' speed must have been well tested again. With his own coaches and accompanied by the coaches of the county magnates and a great number of horsemen, he proceeded to Piercebridge to meet the royal party. A company of militia had been turned out to receive the duke. On the way to Durham an unfortunate *contretemps* occurred. A Mr. Smith, a loyal Roman Catholic, offered wine to the duke and duchess, but unfortunately the person who actually handed it to them was his brother, who was none other than the odious " Narrative Smith." They both received a glass from him with royal courtesy, not knowing in the least who the man was. When they found out later they were naturally angry, and the duchess said that if she had known sooner she would have thrown the glass in his face. In Durham Crewe received his royal guests on the steps leading to the castle hall and it was noted that James kissed him, which was a very particular mark of favour. " No Popery " was being shouted everywhere, exclusion was being

[73] Ormonde MSS., V, p. 235.

agitated in parliament, and the duke had been sent to Scotland to keep him out of sight till the excitement died down. Everything he did and said would be noted and talked about. Very wisely therefore he allowed a private intimation to go forth that no Roman Catholics should come to the castle while he was staying at Durham. The bishop entertained his visitors sumptuously, all the rarities that could be procured were provided, and those of their numerous retinue for whom there was no room in the castle were accommodated with lodgings in the city at the bishop's charges. This was going far beyond what it was necessary to do, and James " who had had no great entertainment at York " [74] was much struck by this mark of attention : indeed he often referred to it afterwards with admiration. In the octagon room in Durham castle there hang two portraits, one of James by Sir Godfrey Kneller and the other of Mary Beatrice by Sir Peter Lely. They may be mementoes of this visit. In this year, 1679, the Bishop of Durham was referred to as one of the duke's " twelve disciples," others being the Archbishop of Canterbury, Lord Chancellor Finch, the Lord Treasurer Danby, the Duke of Lauderdale, the Marquess of Worcester and the Earl of Peterborough.[75] There was no doubt about Crewe's devotion. While the debates on the Exclusion Bill were going on the King complained to him that Mr. Parkhurst, the bishop's steward and a member for Durham, had voted for the bill. " Sire," said Crewe, " I'll turn him off to-morrow," and so he did.

Two letters written to the Archbishop of Canterbury by Crewe during 1679 are chiefly concerned with appointments. " Mr. Sorsby," mentioned in the first, was Martin Soresby or Sowersby, whose appointment to the rectory of Ryton is here referred to. He remained there until his death in 1706.

May it please your Grace.

On Thursday night I received your Grace's commands concerning Ritson, on Friday I obeyed them in conferring that

---

[74] *Hist. MSS. Com.,* Rep. VII, Verney MSS. 7/495.
[75] *C.S.P.D.* 417, No. 71, Feb. 3rd, 1679.

place on Mr. Sorsby whose Qualifications questionless are good when recomended by your Grace. The month of October this yeere has much lost its credditt; however your Grace's advice to hasten up prepared me for a sudden journey, which now shall not be altered, (God willing) notwithstanding the news of another prorogation. Travelling in January will be worse. I shall not interrupt your Grace any longer; but wish long life and happinesse may attend yr Grace the prosperity of the church being concerned therein.

I ever remain

Your Grace's faithfull humble servant
N. Duresme.

Durham Castle Octob 20th, 1679.[76]

The other letter was a recommendation of Sir Richard Lloyd to the post of Master of the Faculty Office in place of Sir John Birkenhead who had just died.[77] The office was not given to Lloyd in spite of Crewe's request, although he desired to be his Grace's obliged servant.

May it please your Grace.

I am credibly informed this morning that Sir John Birkenhead is dead; I doe most humbly and earnestly renew my request to your Grace in the behalfe of Sr Richard Lloyd who I am sure will be a faithful servant to your Grace and to the Church: His Majesty and his Royall Highnesse have a particular kindnesse for him. Your Grace's favour herein will further oblige one who really is and always desires to be.

Yr Grace's

Obliged humble servant
N. Duresme.

Saturday, December 6th 1679.[78]

Crewe lost his father this year. He died on December 12th at the ripe age of eighty-one. Looking back on life he seems to have regretted the days when he was a rebel, for he gave

[76] Tanner MS., Bodleian, 38 f. 92.
[77] Sir Richard Lloyd, Fellow of All Souls, Oxford, LL.D. 1662. Chancellor of Llandaff. Spiritual Chancellor of Durham.
[78] *Ibid.*, I, lrd, f. 104.

this advice to his children : " Beware of projects. Have no hand in changes of government. Had I the world to begin again I would never be concerned about them." He was succeeded in the title by his son Thomas, who had been knighted at Whitehall in December 1660. He had sat in parliament as member for Northamptonshire in 1656, and for Brackley from 1660–79. In May 1650 he married Mary, the eldest daughter of Sir Roger Townshend of Raynham, Norfolk, by whom he had four children, John who died in 1669 at the age of fifteen and would have succeeded to the barony had he lived, Anne who married John Jolliffe of Coston, Staffordshire and died childless in 1696, Temperance who married first Sir Roland Aston who died in 1697, and secondly Sir John Wostenholme, whom she outlived nearly twenty years, dying in 1728, and Jemima who married Henry eleventh Duke of Kent. Mary Crewe died in 1668, and six years later Thomas Crewe married the second time, his bride being Anne daughter of Sir William Armine and widow of Sir Thomas Wodehouse of Kimberley. In succession to his father Thomas Lord Crewe and his wife now came into possession of Steane.[79]

In July 1680 Bishop Crewe was able, without any royal interference as far as is known, to appoint a prebendary to the ninth stall in succession to Thomas Holdsworth. This was Dr. Henry Bagshaw, some time student of Christ Church, Oxford and Rector of Houghton-le-Spring. He was described as a quarrelsome person, but the only evidence is in a letter written in the throes of the Revolution in November 1688, and it is easy to conjecture that there was political feeling at work. On his monument in Houghton-le-Spring he was described as a scholar, " a famous London preacher who shone . . . by his earnest search after piety and his agreeableness of manner." Making all allowance for the fulsomeness of eighteenth century epitaphs, this suggests anything but a turbulent man, and one thing that we do know about him is that he was extremely kind and generous to Granville after the latter's banishment.

[79] Gibbs and Doubleday, *Complete Peerage*, III, pp. 533–4.

Granville himself was active in trying to improve the religious condition of the diocese, about which he had made many complaints in his visitation in 1674.[80] Unhappily, like many others of his brethren, he tried to make use of the strong arm of the law. He was desirous of reviving the statute of the first year of Elizabeth which ordered a fine of twelve pence per Sunday for absence from church. Sir Edward Atkins, Baron of the Exchequer, told him in the presence of the bishop that any justice of the peace could proceed under this statute, and that if the churchwardens did not do their duty in presenting offenders, they ought to be summoned to do so by a justice of the peace and punished if they refused. Atkins also said that though it was the King's pleasure (so he conceived) to proceed more especially against the papists, yet if other recusants were notoriously refractory, they also should be dealt with according to law. Armed with this judicial opinion a meeting of the county justices was held at Durham castle on August 14th and the Bishop of Durham, instigated by his archdeacon ("This day I prevailed with my Lord of Durham to stir up the justices of the peace" are Granville's actual words), tried to rouse the justices, one of whom was Bishop Wood, to the performance of their duty, and all those present, seventeen in number, promised obedience.[81]

That same year the archdeacon drew up a list of some of the grievances and abuses which vexed the Church and to which he believed the decay of religion was largely due. The door of ordination had been made too wide, not so much by the Church herself as by churchmen. Convocation and diocesan synods had been allowed to fall into contempt, partly by the fact that if they did attend there was no business for them. The non-residence of deans and prebendaries was another stumbling block. The poverty of the clergy, the miserable salaries allowed them by impropriators and others, and the way in which gentlemen treated their chaplains as servants, all tended to bring the clerical office into contempt and conduced to the increase of papists and sectaries.[82]

[80] Granville, II, pp. 11–13.
[81] Granville, *Letters,* I, p. 51.
[82] *Ibid.,* p. 45.

In Granville's mind one of the greatest causes of the decay of religion lay in the neglect of the sacraments, especially that of the altar. The reformers of the sixteenth century, in trying to increase communions, had ordered that every churchman should communicate three times in the year, and they had insisted that there should be no celebration without communicants. The practical result had been that in most parishes three or at the most four communion services had become the maximum instead of the minimum. Leeds parish church was remarkable for a monthly celebration.[83] In 1680 the archdeacon began a vigorous effort to establish a weekly celebration in Durham cathedral. He expected opposition from the dean and prebendaries, and especially from his " boisterous brother Cartwright " and his expectations were fulfilled. Cartwright said it was not prudent to begin such innovations at that time, and the general opinion seemed to be that it would be a reflection on other cathedrals. Granville wrote letters to various eminent divines asking their opinion. The Bishop of Oxford (Dr. Fell) agreed that weekly communion was a plain duty. Barnabas Oley, canon of Worcester, who had persuaded the authorities of that cathedral to have a weekly celebration, Dr. Allestree, Dr. Peter Samways, Dr. Beveridge and Dr. Comber all wrote agreeing with the archdeacon's contentions, but for all that a letter which he wrote to the chapter in the November of the following year was quite unsuccessful, and he had to possess his soul in patience for some time to come.[84]

In September 1680 we hear of the appearance in Durham of one Dalton who claimed to be a converted Catholic priest and had come from Ireland by way of Edinburgh. Before the Bishop of Durham and three justices he declared that he knew nothing of the Popish Plot but he accused the Earl of Tyrone who, he said, was a professed papist, of saying that there was nothing he wished for more than the destruction of the King, and that the King of France would be more

---

[83] R. Thoresby, *Letters,* 1832, I, p. 326.
[84] *Granville,* II, pp. 48, 50, 90.

faithful in his promises than the King of England.[85]   The
Popish Plot had produced a crop of Irish informers—informing was such a profitable business—and quite a number came
over to England in rags and returned in velvet.   Any information was acceptable to the nervous authorities, so Crewe wrote
off immediately to Sir Leoline Jenkins the Secretary, who laid
the matter before a committee of Council, who expressed
their approval of the bishop's action.   A full meeting of the
Council was held.   They considered the matter of very great
importance and ordered the Earl of Tyrone to be committed
and further inquiries to be made.   The bishop was to send
Dalton to London, to Lord Sunderland or Sir Leoline
Jenkins, as soon as possible, and since he was " in so low a
condition " he was to be provided with a " viaticum " not
exceeding £10.[86]   Crewe wrote from Auckland castle on
September 28th that Dalton had that day begun his journey,
and since his information seemed so important to the Council,
and he had never been in England before, he had sent one of
his servants with him.[87]   A few days later Dalton appeared
before the Council and charged Tyrone with talking treason.[88]

In November Crewe received a letter from the Archbishop
of Canterbury inviting him to preach before the King on
December 22nd.   He asked for time to consider and said,
" I am well assured of your real respects and favours to me
and therefore am obliged to consider this intimation from
your grace, though very unfit for such an undertaking.   I
hope a day's deliberation will be no disappointment, whatever my resolution may be." [89]   He may well have hesitated
for, as John Evelyn expresses it, December 22nd was set apart
as " a solemn public fast that God would prevent all popish
plots, avert His judgments, and give a blessing to the proceedings of parliament now assembled, and which struck at the

[85] C.S.P.D. Entry Book 62, p. 79.   Secretary Jenkins to Sidney
Godolphin, Sept. 20th, 1680.
[86] C.S.P.D. Entry Book 51, f. 371.   62 f. 91.   S.P. Ireland, c. II, 340,
p. 16.
[87] C.S.P.D. 414, No. 107.
[88] Sec. Jenkins to Sidney Godolphin.   C.S.P.D. Entry Book 62, p. 111.
[89] Tanner MSS. 37, f. 208.

succession of the Duke of York." [90]   The Bishop of Durham
made up his mind and wrote to Sancroft from Covent Garden
on the first day of the month.

May it please your Grace.

Being yesterday surprised with your commands, it will I
hope excuse my not returning a present answer then, which
now attends your Grace, and submitts to that which I must
count a Task, having never engaged before on the like subject.
My inclinations have alwayse beene averse to appeare in
publicke, especially before soe great a presence on such a
solemne sudden occasion, and I assure your Grace that nothing
but my presuming on the reality of your friendship to me in
this suggestion more than on my owne abilityes could have
prevailed with me for such an undertaking.   I can now say I
have chosen a text, and must beg your prayers to Almighty
God for his Assistance and Blessing upon the endeavours of
Your Grace's
most obedient faithfull servant
N. DURESME. [91]

In March 1681 Charles II called his last Parliament at
Oxford.   The Whigs came to Oxford armed, the King's
guards patrolled the roads and civil war seemed not unlikely.
It was the last struggle over the exclusion of James from the
throne.   Crewe was there as a member of the House of Lords
and on Sunday, March 20th, he preached before the King in
the cathedral, and " gave great content." [92]   After the dissolu-
tion of the parliament the King issued a declaration in which
he set forth his reasons for his action and promised to govern
according to the laws of the kingdom and to protect it against
popery and other dangers.   Applauding addresses were sent
to Charles from all parts of the kingdom, the signatories
offering to support him with their lives and fortunes.   The
grand jury at the July assizes in Durham voted such an
address.   It was signed in court by the members of the jury,
the bishop, and the rest of the bench with two exceptions,

[90] *Diary*, Dec. 22nd, 1680.
[91] Tanner MSS. 37, f. 209.
[92] Wood, *Life*, II, p. 531.

Sir Gilbert Gerard, who was the constable of Durham castle, and Mr. Parkhurst, of whose refractory ways we have already heard. There was another address from the lieutenancy of the county and the officers of the militia saying that those who signed it rejoiced that the King held command of the militia and they trusted he would always keep it, remembering the fate of his father when he was deprived of it. The Bishop of Durham himself sent the two addresses with a covering letter to Sir Leoline Jenkins, who duly presented them, and told Crewe in reply that King Charles had received them very graciously, and took especial note of the bishop's name at the head of the militia. The King sent his hearty thanks to the subscribers and desired the secretary to assure them that the appearance of the civil and military power hand in hand was very acceptable to him, and that his full purpose was by the grace of God to stand by the Church and govern by the laws. A third address was sent up in August from the county palatine through the bishop and received a similar gracious answer, and there were others.[93] In March in the following year another address, this time against Shaftesbury's Association scheme, was sent up to the King, who ordered such acknowledgment to the bishop and the rest of the gentry as might be more acceptable to them, and gave permission for the address to be printed.[94]

In spite of these loyal addresses there was a considerable amount of disaffection, especially in the northern part of the diocese at this time. It was looked upon as disaffection by the Government, but in reality it was a sturdy resistance on the part of nonconformists to the laws which forbade their meetings. Early in the year the authorities heard of a great meeting of about two thousand people, English and Scottish, at Downham in Northumberland. Strict orders were issued for the suppression of such gatherings; the deputy lieutenants and justices were to be vigilant, but all the same a conventicle attended by some two hundred persons was held at Crookham

[93] *C.S.P.D.* Entry Book 62, pp. 210, 217, 274. Luttrell, *Brief Relation of State Affairs,* 1857, I, p. 103.
[94] *C.S.P.D.* 418, No. 149.

a few weeks after.[95] In April these meetings were being held in or near Berwick. The magistrates were ordered to put the law in motion against offenders and in particular the Five Mile Act was to be enforced in the case of the preachers.[96] Against persons in authority were hurled many accusations of disaffection, disloyalty and lack of zeal in the King's business. At the Christmas sessions of 1682 the grand jury laid information before the bench of a dangerous conventicle meeting weekly, most of the men armed. Dr. Isaac Basire complained bitterly of the party spirit and the violent and litigious behaviour that distracted Northumberland.[97]

An incident occurred in 1681, unimportant in itself, but interesting as showing ideas which were held in some quarters with regard to the church service. Be it remembered that after Matins and Litany it was the custom to read the Communion Service as far as the Nicene Creed and then stop. Now one Sunday in February 1681 Archdeacon Granville was conducting morning service at Easington in the usual way. After the Nicene Creed he gave out the notices, urged the congregation to keep Lent well, and then proceeded to give them advice concerning the election to the Oxford Parliament, recommending them to vote for Bowes and Featherstone because they were well affected to the Church. In the congregation was Mr. William Mitford, who was not well affected to the Church, in fact he had been indicted at the last assizes for non-conformity but had managed to get off. He jumped up angrily and interrupted the archdeacon three times and proceeded to give his views on Bowes and Featherstone, who according to him were not good Protestants since they were not sufficiently hostile to popery. He was prosecuted for brawling in church and the case came on at the July assizes before Baron Gregory. It was stated that Dr. Granville had said in giving out the notices that he had finished with spiritual matters and would now turn to

[95] *C.S.P.D.* Entry Book 62, p. 127, Jan. 6th, 1681. *C.S.P.D.* 415, No. 7, Jan. 13th. No. 19, Jan. 26th.
[96] *C.S.P.D.* 415, Nos. 125, 126, April 13th, 1681.
[97] *C.S.P.D.* 422, No. 103, Feb. 26th, 1683, and 422, Nos. 129–31, March 6th, 1683.

temporal. The judge delivered his decision. As Granville's remarks had been made *after* the Nicene Creed, at the time appointed for the notices, and as Mitford had not replied during divine service, therefore he was not guilty under the statute against brawling in church.[98] The archdeacon told Sir Leoline Jenkins that as there was no redress elsewhere he had presented Mitford in the ecclesiastical court,[99] but the secretary replied that as Granville himself was one of the persons who had bound Mitford over, and as he had chosen to prosecute him before a lay tribunal, he could not proceed against him in the ecclesiastical courts after that.[100] The archdeacon was very dissatisfied and two years later was questioning various authorities about Gregory's ruling. Sir Robert Sawyer, the Attorney-General, said the judge was right. Sir Leoline Jenkins, however, said that if the disturbance happened between two services the brawling was during divine service, and Sir Thomas Exton, vicar-general to the Archbishop of Canterbury, expressed the same view.[101]

Hopes of a prebend at Durham had been held out to Dr. Comber, as we have seen, in 1676. He was now anxious to exchange his prebend at York for one in Durham, and on July 6th, 1681 he wrote as follows to Sancroft:

"Your Grace's many and weighty cares forbid me to trouble you but on great occasion, and when that offers itself your wonted goodness invites me to beg your favour. I gratefully remember and own the honour your Grace did me in first making me known (with special marks of your Grace's kindness) to my Lord of Durham, who may in a short time do me that kindness which your Grace was pleased to think the most proper for me being fixed in the North, there are like to be four Prebends of Durham void in a short time : and Dr. Brevint, Dr. Greenvile and some others have expressed great desires of my advancement into their Body :

[98] Roger Granville, *Life of Denis Granville*, Exeter 1902, pp. 243-6. *C.S.P.D.* Newsletter Greenwich Hosp., I, p. 117. There is a very biased account of the trial in Janeway's *Impartial Prot. Mercury*, No. 30.

[99] *C.S.P.D.*, Sept. 9th, 1681, 461, No. 146.

[100] *C.S.P.D.* Entry Book 62, p. 303, Sept. 20th, 1681.

[101] R. Granville, *Life of Granville*, pp. 291, 296, 309.

I

and some of them have offered to engage some of their great friends to move my Lord of Durham in that affair with respect to me: Now if your Grace would so far honour me as to write a few lines to my Lord of Durham, though but in general to give me a fair character to that Bishop, I doubt not but it will be a great means to obtain his Lordship's good opinion of me, and wonderfully promote this courteous design of my other friends: Your Grace's constant respects to me is my only apology for this presumption, which I hope your Grace will pardon, and if your Grace will please to do me so singular a favour: I shall ever be obliged to pray for your spiritual, temporal and eternal happiness." [102]

On the day after this letter was written Granville sent to Comber a copy of a letter he had written to his brother, the Earl of Bath, warning him that Lord Frescheville and some considerable friends of Danby would probably write to ask the earl's influence on behalf of Comber. Danby was his patron but Danby was now under a cloud. The Archbishop of Canterbury had a great regard for Comber and Granville thought, though here he was probably mistaken, that the Bishop of Durham had too. As it turned out the bishop was already " deeply engaged for several vacancies which were expected to happen in a short time." The King, before Danby applied to him on Comber's behalf, had promised not to interfere in the preferments in Durham cathedral, so Comber had to wait a few years longer.[103]

In 1681 John Crewe, the bishop's brother died, and left to him his estate of Newbold Verdon in Leicestershire. It was described as " well wooded and watered with a fine park and all the conveniences and ornaments of a good seat " and worth between £500 and £600 a year. He wished, he said, to leave his property to " one who would make the chimney smoke," and there was no doubt that Nathaniel's generous hospitality would do that. The house itself would make a very convenient halting place for the bishop on his journeys to and from the north. It has long since been pulled down.

[102] Letter in the writer's possession—a copy in Comber's hand of the letter to the Archbishop.
[103] Comber, *Life of T. Comber*, pp. 141–7.

In the latter half of 1681 a change was gradually coming over the country. People were beginning to be ashamed of the Popish Plot, the Government, with its hand on the reviving pulse of loyalty in the nation, began to turn on its enemies. " A scene of tyranny and blood was opened, to the terror and amazement of the whole Protestant world," said John Old-mixon,[104] who apparently saw nothing to be amazed at in the terror and bloodshed of the three preceding years. Shaftesbury was tried for treason and escaped because the grand jury brought in a verdict of *Ignoramus,* but his bow was shot, and till he went abroad towards the end of the following year he carried much less weight than hitherto in the counsels of the Whig party. In the north we may be sure that all the influence which the bishop and dean could exercise would be on the side of loyalty in Church and State. In Durham city the King's birthday was kept in 1682 with great demonstrations of enthusiasm, and in particular they burnt copies of Shaftesbury's *Association* and of Robert Ferguson's *No Protestant Plot,* which had been published in two parts in the previous October and November.[105] In June the news reached Durham that the King was ill and likely to die, and a number of the " fanatics " gathered at the house of a man called Racket, who lived in Durham and was looked upon as a leader of the disaffected party. The story that the King was dead or dying was spread by interested persons, but the news soon arrived that he was better, and whatever the restless ones may have had in mind, the mayor was able to report that both the city and the county were loyal and in a good condition of defence.[106]

Through all the excitements and troubles Crewe continued regularly to attend to his Court duties, and there is extant a curious memorandum by him, dated December 23rd, 1682, dealing with the occasions on which the King had " touched for the evil " during the six months July 4th, 1682 to December 23rd in the same year. On twenty-four occasions

[104] Oldmixon, *Reign of the Stuarts,* 1730, p. 665.
[105] Luttrell, I, p. 193.
[106] *C.S.P.D.* 419, Nos. 79, 84, June 6th and 8th, 1682.

the ceremony had taken place—a religious service which included the touching of the scrofulous persons by the King, who gave to each a medal. During the period mentioned a total of 3,535 afflicted persons had been touched, and the same number of medals presented to them. The summary is set out by months, each month's totals being signed by J. Pearse, the maker of the memorandum, and the whole document by " N. Duresme, Clerk of the Closet." [107] How great was the belief in the healing touch of the King at this time is shown by the numbers who sought it. George I discontinued a practice which had lasted since the time of Edward the Confessor. The Jacobites, of course, said the reason was obvious.

The year 1683 was a troubled year, the year of the Rye House plot, the attempt of some angry Whigs to push Charles from his throne, to prevent the accession of James and to ensure the establishment on the throne of a Protestant king. Party feeling was fierce. Every trumpery thing was gravely reported to the Government. Two horse-thieves were in Durham gaol and thought to make matters easier for themselves by accusing two Roman Catholic debtors of saying they hoped to see the King die like his father, to kiss the Pope's hand in England, to have as much power as the Bishop of Durham, and to lead a troop of horse in Durham in the service of the Pope. Three magistrates, John Hutchinson, John Morland and Miles Stapleton, gravely reported this nonsense to Jenkins the secretary. [108]

Letters from Sir Leoline Jenkins to Bishop Crewe said that Richard Goodenough and Richard Nelthorpe were to be searched for, as it was believed they were making their way northward, and the Duke of Monmouth and Lord Grey of Wark were to be arrested if they came that way. [109] Crewe wrote from Durham castle on July 2nd to Jenkins: " I have little more since my last, only a servant of Lord Grey was

[107] Hist. MSS. Com. 9th Rep. MSS. of Alfred Morison, p. 457.
[108] C.S.P.D. 420, No. 50, II.
[109] C.S.P.D. Entry Book 54, p. 172. Book 68, pp. 298, 305. June 26th and 27th, 1683.

going towards London with two very good horses for him, but they were stopped in this county and are here. We are very watchful and have made diligent search for arms and for the persons mentioned in your letters. For better securing the peace I desired the justices for several, whose affections to the Government are justly suspected, to find sureties for their good behaviour." [110]   On the 14th he wrote again : " In obedience to His Majesty's commands I shall with all speed send a list of those whose houses have been searched and their arms seized. I doubt that we have been more strict than either to allow swords or fowling pieces, but I hope this is an error on the right hand. I continue a search for arms. The militia is daily on duty, but without extraordinary charge or trouble, the horse as well as foot being mustered in small parcels and relieved every two days. I hope the two addresses from this place are safely arrived." [111]   The grand jury and the justices of the peace at the general quarter sessions at Durham forwarded through the bishop an address of loyalty to the King, who sent his thanks to Crewe, and ordered the address to be printed, but since many other addresses had come in, the bishop was told through Jenkins that this particular one would have to wait its turn. [112]   The inventory of weapons seized was forwarded by the bishop on the 16th. [113]   Early in July the deputy-lieutenants of the North Riding had written to Crewe asking him to send any intelligence which might have come from northward. [114]   William Bowes of Greta Bridge was as active as any man in the Bishopric and in September received a letter of thanks from Jenkins, who promised to mention him with especial commendation to the bishop. [115]   Crewe, too, was told that his diligence and that of his justices had been very acceptable to the King and this no doubt spurred him to further efforts. [116]   There were complaints, however, that some

[110] C.S.P.D. 427, No. 17a, July 2nd.   427, No. 107, July 6th.
[111] C.S.P.D. 428, No. 155.
[112] C.S.P.D. 428, No. 115, July 3rd, 1683.   Entry Book 68, p. 332, July 14th.
[113] C.S.P.D. 428, No. 192.
[114] Hist. MSS. Com., Various Collections, II, p. 169.   Wombwell MSS.
[115] C.S.P.D. Entry Book 64, p. 107, Sept. 29th, 1683.
[116] C.S.P.D. Entry Book 68, p. 318, July 7th.

of the magistrates had been very lax, especially when papists had been arrested.[117] None of the principal fugitives for whom watch was kept had been captured: it was known later that none of them had fled northward. Richard Nelthorpe, one of the conspirators, had property in the Bishopric, and in May 1684 it was granted by the King to Edward Arden, the bishop's secretary.[118] Careful observation had been made of all strangers passing through Berwick and a hunt had been made after Scottish ministers who were suspected of treasonable practices and had left some books of a fierce covenanting type behind them at the house of John Mann in Newcastle. Twenty Scottish pedlars were arrested on suspicion at Darlington and were sent to Durham to be examined by the bishop. No cause of suspicion was found on them, and at the command of the King they were set free.[119]

The chief of the Rye House plotters suffered the penalty of the law and all was quiet in the northern diocese again except for the perpetual trouble about church and dissent. Captain Ralph Widdrington, Governor of Berwick, complained to Sir Leoline Jenkins at the end of September that a new mayor and several new bailiffs had been elected in Berwick the day before, but the mayor and several of the bailiffs were under sentence of excommunication at Durham, and that according to what he had heard, the mayor had never received the sacrament and was therefore incapable of executing the office.[120]

In the autumn of 1683 there was talk in the county of Durham that another parliament was shortly to be summoned, so Crewe arranged that a meeting should be held on October 4th to consider a choice of fit and proper persons. But on September 29th Mr. Secretary Jenkins wrote to him to contradict the rumour. He added that if there had been anything in it the bishop was one of the first persons whom he would have personally informed, both on account of the

[117] C.S.P.D. 424, Nos. 155, 156, July 8th, 1683. 425, No. 97, June 27th.
[118] Newsletter, Adm. Greenwich Hos., 2, No. 81, May 6th, 1684.
[119] C.S.P.D. 427, Nos. 42, 43.
[120] C.S.P.D. 433, No. 14.

bishop's zeal and loyalty, and because Jenkins' particular friends, Sir Richard Lloyd and Mr. Bowes, had received the bishop's countenance and protection on such occasions. If it was now necessary to hold the meeting Crewe would know exactly what ought to be done to prevent any unreasonable expectations which might lead to " heats and disquiets." [121]

It is pleasant to turn from the strife and politics of the time to Granville's efforts to improve religious observance within the diocese, though he complained that his efforts, continued for twenty years, had produced very little effect. In 1682 we find him issuing an injunction to the minister of St. Nicholas', Durham, ordering him to obey the Prayer Book in such matters as the recital of the daily offices and catechizing on Sundays and holy days. [122] He continued striving for more frequent celebrations of the Holy Communion. In 1683 he was in Oxford. In a conversation on Friday, June 15th, Bishop Fell asked him how his efforts were succeeding in regard to Durham cathedral, adding that he could not see any validity in the objection made by the dean and prebends that there would not be a sufficient number of communicants to keep up the dignity of the Holy Mysteries. He thought, moreover, that arguments about desuetude and innovation were weak and frivolous, and suggested that Granville should stir up the devout churchpeople to demand a weekly celebration. Other people in Oxford were thinking in the same way at that time. Dr. Arthur Bury, the author of *The Constant Communicant,* a work which urged the indispensable duty of frequent reception, talked with Granville daily during this visit, and expressed the view that there should be a celebration on feast days as well as Sundays. Henry Dodwell, afterwards Camden professor of history, with whom Granville discussed the subject, was in favour of a weekly celebration.

After this Granville became as zealous for the weekly Eucharist as he had always been for the daily matins and evensong. He told Sancroft that within his jurisdiction he had got daily prayers and a monthly sacrament in the most

[121] *C.S.P.D.* Entry Book 64, p. 108, Sept. 29th, 1683.
[122] Granville, *Letters,* II, p. 100.

important places, and would have done in others had not the
cathedral set a bad example in not having the Holy Communion every week. He asked Sancroft either to use his
influence with the dean, or else to persuade the Archbishop of
York to have a weekly celebration in the minster. He thought
the latter course the most likely to influence the dean, as one
of the excuses made throughout the province was that it was
not done at York.

On October 20th, 1683 Archbishop Dolben wrote to
Sancroft saying that he had the subject in mind and that
Comber would be on his side. On November 3rd Granville
said in a letter to Sir William Dugdale that the Archbishops
of Canterbury and York were determined to establish a weekly
communion (hitherto existing in no cathedral except Christ
Church, Ely, and Worcester), and were urging other bishops
to do the same. His opponents were saying that it was bringing back the Mass. " I have had a very hard game to play
these twenty years in maintaining the exact order which
Bishop Cosin set on foot here." [123] Dr. Comber, as it turned
out, was not keen. In a letter to Granville, dated June 23rd,
1684 he said he would not oppose the weekly sacrament, but
would rather promote it " as soon as I see our great ones
encourage the thing. . . . In the mean time you must think
of *bene* as well as *saepe,* or else religion will rather lose than
gain by reviving this long sleeping rubric." [124]

In February 1684 Dr. Isaac Basire, Official of the archdeaconry of Northumberland, issued a mandate to the clergy
of that county in which he ordered them to observe the
rubrics of the baptismal service. He said that owing to the
great neglect of the clergy most of the children born in Newcastle had been baptized privately. Even when they were
brought to the church for the purpose they were frequently
brought after the congregation had gone, or were even
brought when Holy Communion was to be administered, thus
causing great disorder.[125] Such was the slackness and neglect

[123] Granville, I, pp. 171–9.
[124] *Ibid.,* pp. 181–3. A weekly celebration began in Canterbury in
November 1683, and at York in April 1685.
[125] Granville, II, pp. 130, 131.

in many parts of the diocese in the administration of the sacraments that it is not surprising that Granville sometimes despaired of obtaining any results from all his work. He could appreciate the efforts of a man like Basire, and he wrote to Sir Leoline Jenkins saying that sundry loyal people in the county were dissatisfied with the recorder of Berwick, and that he joined with others in desiring his removal and his supersession by Isaac Basire, the eldest son of the prebendary of that name, a barrister, a justice of the peace and a Bachelor of Civil Law.[126]

When Dr. Richard Sterne, Archbishop of York, died in 1683, the see had been offered to Bishop Crewe. If he had been the ambitious and self-seeking prelate his enemies depicted him we might have expected him to grasp at it, but he refused it, as he did a second time at a later date, and in consequence it went to Dr. John Dolben, who had been his rival for Durham. Dolben was translated to York from Rochester, of which he had been bishop for seventeen years. Cartwright from his prebend at Durham and his deanery of Ripon had hoped for York and when that failed for Rochester. Then he looked with longing eyes towards St. Davids, which had become vacant through the translation of Dr. William Thomas to Worcester. On July 28th, 1683 Crewe wrote from Durham castle to the Archbishop of Canterbury about it, but not quite in the way Cartwright would have wished :
" May it please your Grace.

'Tis confidently reported here that Dr. Cartwright, who has lately missed the archbishoprick of York, and since that the bishoprick of Rochester, is now very likely by his great importunityes to succeed in St. Davids ; not to hinder his journey thither I shall only desire he may not hold his Durham prebend with a bishoprick especially soe remote. My Lord, your Grace knows, there are two bishops already that are now prebendaryes here, and soe many non-residents will be prejudicial to the service of this place. Your Grace having been formerly of this church cannot but wish as well to it as I do."

[126] *C.S.P.D.* 437, No. 83, April 4th, 1684.

Dr. Lawrence Womack was appointed to St. Davids.

On June 21st, 1684 Archdeacon Nicolson of Carlisle went to Durham and he noted in his diary that after dinner he was with the bishop in his library and new gardens. What the new gardens were we cannot be certain. There was already in existence the garden entered from the castle courtyard, known in Cosin's day as " my lord's privy garden," so that this can hardly be the new garden. Cosin however had terraced the mound on which the keep stands, and it seems a reasonable suggestion that Crewe laid out either one or more of the terraces as a garden, or else the flat piece of ground behind the wall which faces the Palace Green. Crewe is an elusive person; we hear as little of his recreations as of his relationships with his family. Nor does he appear ever to have taken a prominent part in the affairs of the Church outside his diocese. On June 29th, 1684 Dr. Thomas Smith was consecrated Bishop of Carlisle in York minster, the consecrators being the Archbishop of York, the Bishop of Durham and the Bishop of Sodor and Man. This was the fourth consecration at which Crewe had officiated, the previous ones being those of Guy Carleton to Bristol in 1672, Pearson to Chester and Mews to Bath and Wells in 1673, Turner to Rochester and Womack to St. Davids in 1683. He was one of the consecrators three times during the reign of James II, at the consecrations of Ken to Bath and Wells in 1685, Trelawney to Bristol in 1685, and Lloyd, Parker and Cartwright to St. Davids, Oxford and Chester respectively in 1686. After the last he never took part in another. During his long episcopate there were sixty-seven consecrations, and he only had a share in seven of them.

In 1684 there was a renewal of the rumours that a parliament was to be called shortly. A circular letter was sent from the King to the lords-lieutenant of the counties to the effect that His Majesty would summon parliament when requisite and before he did so would let them know. In the meantime they were to use all possible means to prevent his subjects from being misled by these rumours, and to discourage tumultuous and seditious petitions for a parliament, which some people were designing to promote. The Bishop of Durham, of course, received one of these letters, and three days later there came another saying that arms had been seized from dangerous and disaffected persons. After such seizures the deputy-lieutenants were to choose those weapons which were suitable and use them for the militia. The bishop was to see that any others seized in the county were to be stored at Tynemouth fort. In Northumberland the Duke of Northumberland as lord-lieutenant was also to store such weapons at Tynemouth.[127]

On June 13th, 1684 by virtue of a commission under the Great Seal of England issued on July 26th in the previous year and directed for the due execution of the statute passed on October 20th in the forty-sixth year of Elizabeth, entitled "An Act to Redress the misemployment of lands, goods and stocks of money heretofore given to charitable uses," an inquisition was taken in Durham. The same thing, of course, was being done elsewhere. The Durham commissioners were the bishop, Thomas Musgrave, prebendary, John Hutchinson, mayor of Durham, Miles Stapleton, John Duck, James Mickleton, John Sedgwick and Marmaduke Allenson. There was a jury of fourteen "honest and lawful men of the county duly returned: impanelled and sworn." Nine were described as gentlemen and beside these were a grocer, two tanners, a barber and a cordwainer. The jury gave sworn information of ten cases of such misemployment of trust property for charity. Here are examples:

Gabriel Clark, D.D., by will dated May 8th, 1660, left £5 to increase the stock of the poor at Greatham and £60 to buy a lease worth £10 a year, which £10 was to be paid to the schoolmaster at Easington. Dr. Clark's daughter and executor, Sybilla Clark, married Thomas Cradock, Esq. of Durham and he promptly intermeddled with Dr. Clark's property. Sybilla died, the widower held the money and had paid nothing.

Richard Todd of Newcastle had in his hands £10 10s. belonging to the poor stock of the chapelry of Escomb and

[127] *C.S.P.D.* Entry Book 56, pp. 101, 102, 103, May 16th and 20th, 1684.

had paid interest on it; but was now three years in arrears. He had a copyhold estate in Escomb and the jurors thought it might be made liable for his debt.

John Cornforth of Blackwell, near Darlington, by will dated March 1st, 1625, bequeathed £40 to trustees and their heirs to buy land, of which the profits should be distributed annually among the poor of Blackwell. Cornforth's brother, Whayer Fawcett, was his executor. He entered on the estate and paid nothing to the trustees.

Michael Newton in 1671 left by will the sum of forty shillings for the poor of Egglescliffe. His wife and executor married again, her second husband being Richard Case, a Yorkshireman. Though he knew of the bequest he never paid it. The jury held that he ought not only to pay the forty shillings, but also thirteen years' interest.

The jury also declared that John Sheppard of Bishopwearmouth ought to pay an ancient charge on lands that he held in the chapelry of St. Margaret, Durham.

It all showed how easily charitable bequests could be lost sight of and how lax, very often, the people were who were supposed to be in charge of them.

The medieval priors of Durham held the manor house of Beaurepaire, a name corrupted in later times to Bearpark. For about three hundred years it was one of their summer residences. An inquest of the possessions of the deanery, taken in 1684 said " There are or were the following " . . . " a hall, two passages near the hall, one large kitchen and oven in it, a back room adjoining on the west end of the kitchen, a dining room, a great room leading to the chapel called the dormitory, some arches and two rooms above the arches, a chapel and a room under it, three rooms, or two at least, called the prior's chamber, and the western room thereof called the prior's lodgings, a little room adjoining the prior's chamber, a staircase and vaults under all and every the lower or floor rooms of the said mansion house, excepting the hall and kitchen and the room aforesaid adjoining the kitchen. And at Bearpark aforesaid there formerly have been belonging to the said manor house several courts and gardens that were walled about, and also sundry outhouses now wholly dilapidated." When Dean Sudbury died in 1684 there was a proposal to bring an action against his executors for the sum of £2,500 which would be needed for repairs to the buildings, on the ground that he had neglected them. The description given above seems rather to represent what had been formerly than what really was in 1684, for William Wilson, afterwards spiritual chancellor of the diocese, said that all the old men he had asked could only remember a large useless hall and dining-room with three or four mean rooms in which Dean Hunt (1620–38), the last dean to make use of it, spent a few nights in the summer time. He further said that the Scots had demolished it in the civil wars, leaving only some old walls, and Dean Sudbury had considered himself discharged from the needless expense of rebuilding. The Bearpark estate was worth from £285 to £300 a year.[128]

In 1684 there was a general attack on the existing charters of the corporate towns throughout the county. Newcastle was a somewhat refractory town, not unaffected by the covenanting spirit from the Border, and nonconformity was strong there. Early in the year its charter was surrendered at the King's demand, though the surrender was not enrolled. A new charter was then granted in which power was reserved to the King to grant or confirm the appointment of the mayor, sheriff, town-clerk and aldermen, or to remove any one of them at pleasure. This charter only arrived in Newcastle a week after the death of King Charles. The charter of Durham was a different matter. The city was governed under a charter granted by Bishop Matthew in 1602. The mayor and a majority of the aldermen and councillors surrendered this charter to Bishop Crewe on August 25th. A month before that date the Earl of Sunderland wrote to tell him that the King had heard that the surrender had actually been made, and His Majesty thought it requisite before a new charter should be granted, or the old one confirmed, that the bishop should send him an account of the state of the corporation, and

[128] Surtees, *Hist. Durham*, II, pp. 373–4. Hunter MSS.

inform him what alterations it would be well to make. He desired to be told of any suggestions the bishop might offer for the better regulation of the city in the future.[129] In the following March Crewe granted a new charter, we may suppose after some kind of consultation with the King, but it was the bishop who granted it. In it he reserved to himself the power of approving and confirming the mayor, recorder, aldermen and councillors. " O tempora! " said Luttrell[130] when recording this in his diary. Some informality, however, was discovered in the new charter and it was afterwards claimed that the surrender had been invalid, so the old charter was revived and remained in force till 1768.

The ill-health of Dean Sudbury in 1684 caused a flutter in Durham circles: who should succeed him? The Earl of Bath wanted the deanery for Denis Granville, the Bishop of Durham wanted it for his nephew, Dr. Montagu. On May 24th Crewe wrote to Sir Richard Lloyd, the chancellor of the diocese, and told him that he had suggested to the Earl of Bath, who seemed to agree, that it would be better for Granville to resign his claims to the deanery in favour of Montagu. Sherburn hospital would then become vacant: it was free from trouble and attendance, lay between Durham and Easington, was worth more than £300 a year, besides " casualities of fines," and with all his preferments Granville would be better off than if he held the deanery alone.[131] In a second letter to Lloyd, dated from Auckland castle on June 26th, the bishop said, " If the Earl of Bath and the archdeacon shall be pleased to promote my nephew's being Dean of Durham I shall most willingly be kind to their nephew, Sir George Wheler, in assuring him of Dr. Grey's prebend, whenever it falls into my disposal. Further I shall as readily give the archdeacon an opportunity of pleasuring any friend with Dr. Grey's living of Wearmouth, reputed commonly about £200 a year. Grey is of great age and often

[129] C.S.P.D. Entry Book 56, p. 118, July 24th, 1684. Entry Book 71, pp. 35, 37, 45, Nov. 3rd, 1684.
[130] Luttrell, I, p. 314. Sykes, Local Records, I, p. 119.
[131] Hunter MSS. xxxvi, 13.

infirmities. Upon my nephew's being made dean I shall substitute Dr. Grenville to attend the Closet in my absence *sometimes*. This I confess may be a very great step to his future preferment and will much lessen his expenses, e.g. there is diet for chaplains to the Clerk of the Closet, the use of my apartment, and he will be near his relations. If this does not turn out I shall be satisfied with Grenville to be dean, Easington and Sedgefield thereby voided to Montagu, who shall hand over Sherburn to his younger brother James, youngest son of the Earl of Sandwich."

Crewe then set forth the advantages of the mastership of Sherburn hospital in detail. The present manager of the hospital, Mr. Delaval, was prepared to rent it of Dr. Montagu for seven years at £340 per annum, providing all things necessary for the poor brethren, except repairs, which according to the bishop's injunctions, must be " made substantial " by the master. The goods and chattels of the house were valued at £200. The casual fines, which in the previous year had been considerable, belonged to the master. There were no tenths or first-fruits to pay, there was no residence required and no duty: the master nominated a chaplain for the last, and he was maintained by the house. Not only so, the master was patron of Bishopton, Grindon, Sockburn and Ebbchester (and Granville would be able to nominate his friends to the curacies of Easington and Sedgefield) and was as great an almoner as the dean, seeing that the hospital provided for sixteen inmates and sixteen out-pensioners.

On the other hand, the deanery was not worth more than £1,300 a year, and was likely to be less. The rents had decayed, and there was heavy expense for a new and costly organ (the " Father Smith " organ of which a part is still in the chapel of University College, Durham), and for constant repairs, in all which charges the dean paid a double share. The dean had to live in a costly way and had great expenses for hospitality. The charges in passing the Great Seal for the patent and the fees and expenses of installation would amount to at least £100. If the old dean died soon after Michaelmas the whole year's revenue until the following Michaelmas would belong to his executors and not to his successor. It was a small mark of favour to exchange the title of archdeacon for that of dean, and Granville might reasonably expect something better. Lastly, he pointed out that the dean's office was not altogether an easy one. His veto was questionable in many ways, and to get the chapter's consent sometimes meant troublesome disputes, and might occasion lapse of livings. It was a good case of special pleading, but the dean was not dead yet. Crewe had to admit that though Sudbury had a lame leg he was " recovering and very hearty."[132] As for Prebendary Grey, he did not die for another twenty years.

Granville was calculating differently. He wanted the deanery with the archdeaconry and his livings as well, and he wrote to the Archbishop of Canterbury,[133] who was averse to this, and pleaded that if this were allowed he would be in a position of greater authority. He admitted that in the past he had not been a good manager, but as long as he was in debt he was anxious not to part with anything which he could honestly keep, and he pleaded naïvely that he was twenty-four years older than when Sancroft knew him first. The story is told that the archbishop disapproved of Granville altogether. " He said to my lord that Granville was not worthy of the least stall in Durham church. My lord replied, ' He rather chose a gentleman than a silly fellow who knew nothing but books.' Says the archbishop, ' I beshrew thee.' "[134] " Sancroft did not think that because a man was a good churchman and a gentleman he should therefore be overloaded with preferments, to the exclusion of others who were of much greater mark." [135] Isaac Basire wrote to Thomas Cradock, a former attorney-general of the diocese,[136] and said that the King was determined that Granville should be dean and that he should hold the office together with his archdeaconry and his living of Sedgefield.[137] Sudbury died on November 29th.

[132] Granville, I, pp. 183–7.
[133] Nov. 26th, 1684.
[134] *Examination*, p. 51.
[135] Overton, *The Nonjurors*, 1902, p. 164.
[136] M.P. for Richmond 1678, 1679, 1685. Died 1689.
[137] Granville, I, pp. 183–90.

Granville was presented to the deanery [138] and allowed to keep his livings.

Dr. Comber was still hankering after a Durham prebend. In the summer June 23rd, 1684 he had written to Granville, " I will not complain that while you are at London the commissioners gave away a prebend of your church, and you did not speak a word for a man you used to wish were your near neighbour, for it is now too late, and that person is content, only he makes some remarks of his friend's vigilance." The new prebendary was Dr. William Graham, the son of Sir George Graham of Netherby, and the younger brother of Viscount Preston. Though the holder of two successive deaneries, and a living, he kept his stall until his death. Granville, in the letter already quoted,[139] said, " Please use what arguments you can with the bishop to bestow a prebend on Dr. Comber. . . . But I perceive his lordship is fixed on his chaplains or Lincoln College men. If so I wish he would think of Sir George Wheler."

As soon as Granville was nominated dean Judge Jeffreys got the promise of the vacant stall. Lord Bath warned his brother, who promptly told Crewe, who persuaded Granville to resign his prebend while the patent for the deanery was passing the Great Seal. The Duke of York, too, used his influence with the bishop, through Lord Peterborough as intermediary, in favour of Wheler, and the bishop put Wheler into the stall forthwith. Granville wrote to Comber, " I discern there is no standing for Cambridge men against an Oxford man of Lincoln College, which gained his point more than his interest, though it is very considerable, or the intercession of his friends, which are not a few, he being a person of great merit and piety. I named you before him, and used but little zeal for him, knowing that he was sure enough to carry a prebend hereafter, and might very well stay a little longer, having an estate and being a very young priest, though I should be unjust to him if I styled him a young man. My lord of Canterbury and lord of London, though much your

[138] C.S.P.D. Entry Book 57, p. 102, Dec. 6th, 1684.
[139] Nov. 26th, 1684.

K

friends, discerning the nail would go, have thought fit not much to appear for you." [140]

George Wheler was the son of Colonel Charles Wheler and was born at Breda during the exile of his parents for their loyalty to the King. He went to Lincoln College in 1667, but before taking his degree he spent some time travelling in Greece and Asia Minor in company with Dr. Jacques Spon of Lyons. He published an account of this in 1682 under the title of *A Journey into Greece* in a folio in six books with many archæological and scientific notes. The book was dedicated to the King, to whom he presented a copy and as a reward was knighted. Wheler married Grace, daughter of Sir Thomas Higgons. His wife's mother was Bridget, sister of the Earl of Bath and the new Dean of Durham. In 1683 he took holy orders and became vicar of Basingstoke, a preferment which he held for many years. John Evelyn met him at dinner at Lambeth palace, and after evening prayers walked over the ice with him to Horse-ferry, the Thames being frozen at the time. [141] Wheler was a High Churchman, and took a great interest in ecclesiastical antiquity, as shown in his *Account of the Churches or Places of Assembly of the Primitive Christians Described by Eusebius; and Ocular Observations of several very Ancient Edifices of those Churches yet extant in those parts, with a Seasonable Application,* published in 1689. He was a learned man with wide interests; " the ingenious Sir George Wheler " Ralph Thoresby the antiquary called him, and there is still preserved in the cathedral library a cabinet of Greek coins and medals which he bequeathed to the dean and chapter. His little work *Officium Eucharisticum: or Directions to Devout Communicants in Times of Celebration* [142] shows him to have been a man of piety.

On March 21st, 1685 Dean Granville wrote to Mr. William Wilson to tell him that Sir George was setting out in the York coach for Durham on the following Monday and asked him

[140] Comber, *Life of T. Comber,* pp. 200, 201. Thomas Zouch, *Works,* York 1820, II, p. 158.
[141] Evelyn, *Diary,* Jan. 9th, 1684.
[142] Newcastle-on-Tyne, 46 pp. 1720.

SIR GEORGE WHELER.

Facing page 134.

to get a woman to clean the prebendal house—a homely touch. He desired Wilson to give the new prebendary all the help he could and said that Mr. John Smith (the minor canon) had known Sir George in the south and would do his best for him.

The Trotter MS., referring to Granville's accession to the deanery, says " Thus the Bath family was encouraged and Jeffreys was balked." [143] If there is anything in the story that Jeffreys asked for a prebend, that is, the patronage of one, it is difficult to see how he comes on the scene, except that he was on the northern circuit in July 1684 with Sir Richard Holloway. It was on this circuit he received the charters of a number of towns. The puritan alderman, Ambrose Barnes, complained of his railleries and jests and said he went to bed drunk every night, though how he knew the last it would be hard to say. It is reported that he said in court that he had " a black list of damned fanatics and was resolved to scour them." A number of young men who had banded themselves together in a religious society were charged with conspiracy and high treason. According to Barnes John Rumney, the sheriff, had a packed jury ready. There were about thirty of these young men and one of them had turned informer, which suggests that he might have had something to inform. Jeffreys questioned one of them, Thomas Venner by name. " Can you read, sirrah?" " Yes, my lord." The judge said to the clerk, " Reach him the book," whereupon the clerk gave Venner a Latin Testament. He seems to have chosen a passage for himself and read " *Ne judicate, ne judicemini* " (Matt. vii. 1, 2). " Construe it sirrah," and the young man replied, " Judge not, that ye be not judged," which after all was what any schoolboy would recognize as " polite cheek." According to their own story the puritans always confounded their adversaries and so we are told that Jeffreys remained in silence for a time. They were all remanded to gaol, bailed out the following February and set free entirely at the assizes in 1686, the judge then saying " Go and sin no more lest a worse thing befall ye." [144]

[143] *Examination*, p. 51.
[144] *Life of Ambrose Barnes*, Surtees Soc., pp. 196–8, 425.

On the northern circuit Jeffreys and Holloway came to Durham. At Durham Jeffreys fined Baddiley, the coroner, five pounds for not standing up when his name was called, telling him that he would make him pay for his laziness. After dinner that night the offender was admitted into the presence of the Lord Chief Justice who had dined in the castle with the bishop. " How now," said Jeffreys, " I suppose you are come to beg off your fine." " No, my lord," intervened the bishop, " nothing of the sort can be done : you have laid it, but nobody can take it off but myself," which put the Lord Chief Justice somewhat out of countenance. He had forgotten that all fines and amercements were always excepted out of the King's commission of assize for Durham as of right belonging to the see. On one occasion Crewe had refused to allow Lord Chief Justice Sir Thomas Jones to read the common assize commission there which he read in other places.[145] There is a portrait of Jeffreys in Durham castle ; there is, or was, another in Lambton castle, and a third, painted by Kneller and representing him in his robes as Lord Chancellor, at Chillingham castle. He seems not to have been without some admirers in the north.

There was almost as much intriguing for livings as for deaneries. Take, for example, this letter written from London by Alexander Davison, vicar of Norham, on January 27th, 1685 : " I received a letter from my father upon this day eight days of the death of my dear friend Mr. Horsburgh of Wooler [146] upon which I wrote to Sir Richard Lloyd, and he went immediately to the Bishop of Durham for it for me, that so he might have made friends to my Lord Dartmouth for Lewisham for his friend : but Captain Witherington (Widdrington) had the day before been with his lordship in behalf of Mr. Werge of Kirknewton [147] and promised that Colonel

[145] The *Memoirs* give the date 1685 for this. Jeffreys was certainly on the northern circuit in 1684, but there seems no other evidence that he returned in 1685.

[146] John Horsbrough, vicar of Wooler 1663–95.

[147] John Werge, vicar of Kirknewton 1681–1732.

Struther (Strother) should present Mr. Chisim [148] to whom my lord had promised Wooler when his lordship came first down to Durham, to Kirknewton, upon Mr. Werge's institution to Wooler : so that I think he will have it, unless my Lord Dartmouth who is gone about it, do prevail; but of this, as it offers, you shall know without fail. Mr. Philbridge [149] is come up post, and I presume that he will endeavour by the Duchess of Portsmouth to get the King's presentation and so tray title with the bishop." [150] But Mr. Horsbrough was not dead : he lived another ten years, after which Mr. Chisholm succeeded to the living.

The Bishop of Durham was very assiduous in his duties as Clerk of the Closet. One day he was absent when the King went to chapel, and on his return he humbly begged His Majesty's pardon, explaining that he had been engaged in marrying a couple. Charles replied, " My lord, I hope you asked *their* pardon before you did it." But now the time was drawing near when King Charles' jests would be heard no more. Early in 1685 an ominous missive came from the Earl of Sunderland to all the lords-lieutenant, Crewe among them, informing them that the Council thought it necessary that more than ordinary care should be taken by the lieutenancy and the militia officers for the preservation of the peace. [151] The King had been taken ill that day. The manner of Charles' dying is too well known to need description here, better known than that of any other King of England who died in his bed. Crewe had attended upon him at chapel on the Sunday before, and for five days and nights was not absent from him for more than two hours. It must then have been during those two hours that Fr. Huddleston was smuggled in. Charles died on February 6th. The Clerk of the Closet had lost a friend but a still greater friend had succeeded to the throne.

[148] John Chisholm who became vicar of Wooler in 1695 and continued there thirty years.
[149] Adam Felbridge, vicar of Carham 1679–1701 and Chatton 1681–1700.
[150] Raine, *North Durham*, pp. 334–5.
[151] *C.S.P.D.* Entry Book 56, p. 161, Feb. 2nd, 1685.

CHAPTER V

· THE KING'S FRIEND

WHEN James came to the throne there was much loyal rejoicing throughout the kingdom. Gateshead expended on the coronation day, April 23rd, £6 for two barrels of gunpowder, £2 for a hogshead of ale, for " bringing up and carrying down " nine great guns £1 0s. 4d., and for " nine tar barrels and labourers " 11s. They paid the gunners and their mate 15s. and it cost 2s. 6d. to mend the churchyard wall which was pulled down for the guns. Minor expenses came to 5s. 9d.[1] Addresses expressing congratulation on his accession, and condolence on the death of his brother, were forwarded from the town of Newcastle and the city of Durham.[2]

The Earl of Argyle landed in Scotland in May and the Duke of Monmouth at Lyme Regis on June 11th, and immediately there were great hurryings to and fro. Some of Crewe's enemies at court whispered in the King's ear that the Bishop of Durham was a great friend of the rebellious duke and had entertained him at Durham with great splendour. Would it be wise, they asked, to leave the militia in such uncertain hands? " He was therefore not thought so proper a person, to be trusted as Lord Lieutenant, in raising the militia on that occasion." Accordingly Sir John Fenwick was put in command of the forces of the palatinate, while they were kept under arms for the space of fourteen days. When it was all over Fenwick told the King that the militia of Durham were the most regular and best disciplined of any in the kingdom, and the King was pleased to repeat this to the bishop. " This was said to soften my lord upon Sir John's being put over him." [3] This is Dr. John Smith's story and he is usually pretty accurate. It seems difficult to believe that

[1] Surtees, *Hist. Durham*, II, p. 124.
[2] Luttrell, I, p. 333.
[3] *Memoirs*, p. 22.

James would be suspicious of one of his most loyal friends. The bishop, lord-lieutenant though he was, would not be expected to lead the county militia in actual fighting. It was the most natural thing in the world that a layman should be put in command when the necessity for fighting was possible, if not actually probable. No doubt some people whispered to the King, and there is equal likelihood that others whispered to the bishop, and we know how sensitive Crewe was in the matter of his palatine and episcopal rights.

It would seem that Crewe had been carefully considering the question of weekly communion and had at last made up his mind. To Granville's great joy he received a letter from his bishop, who wrote from his house in Covent Garden on April 7th, 1685.

" This comes not so much by way of Injunction, as of Advice to you, Mr. Dean and the Prebendarys, of Durham, that you would Consult the Rubrick in the Communion Service, concerning the weekly Receiving the holy Sacrament of the Lord's Supper in the Cathedrall Churches, which Laudable and Statutable Practice, according to the Liturgy (though too much Disused in many places) is now received in Several Cathedralls; the Neglect of which I think not Justifiable, especially when there is a Convenient Number of Communicants, which can never be wanting, if you and the Prebendarys would contrive so to serve your Parish Churches, as by Turns to Attend this most Holy Duty in the Cathedrall. I am sure your own Inclinations to this Devoc̄on are such as might save me the Labour of Enforcing what the Law Requires, and however I commend this matter to your Care, and shall Expect that after next Easter the holy Comunion be duly administered every Sunday in the Cathedrall and I Question not but that you will find by this a great Encrease of piety which will be not only an advantage to the Receivers but also a Satisfaction to those, who attend God's Altar in this Sacred Administration. You have the Prayers and Blessing of
Your very affectionate Diocesan
N. DURESME." [4]

[4] MS. Rawlinson, D. 850, f. 47.

The bishop's wishes were further set forth in a statement of the matters decided upon at his visitation of the chapter held in the chapter house on September 19th, 1685 when the following matters were decided :—

That the lease of the house in the Church yard being expired it shall be taken down according to King Charles the First his Letter.

That all possible care be taken to preserve the Timber in Bear Parke and that exact Tallyes be made and given into the Dean and Chapter every year at their Audit of the Number of Trees cut down and for what use according to the Statute Cap. de Silvis etc. and exhibited to the Bpp. in his visitations.

That the Quantityes of Firewood used by the Dean and Chapter shall be Limited to a certain Number of Loads (30) to the Dean and each Prebendarye (5).

That Bpp. Cosin's Injunctions given in his Visitations be registered.

That the Prebendall houses shall be yearly Repaired by the Treasurer according to the Statutes.

That the Number of Minor Canons (which by the Statutes ought to be twelve) be immediately increased from the Number of Six (which are at present) to eight.

That no Persons shall be suffered to drye Linnen in the Church Yard nor Horses to Graze there.

That the Times of Residence which fall between Michaelmas and the Grand Chapter in November be Chosen and settled at the Grand Chapter in July.

That the Treasurer's Booke after every Audit shall be left in the Treasury and the Treasurer shall have a discharge under the Chapter Seale.

That there shall be Sermons in the Cathedrall every Wednesday and Friday in Advent and Lent.

That the weekly Communion be continued with jubilation.[5]

Dean Granville had gained his point in securing the weekly celebration in the cathedral, but he had to endure the angry

[5] MS. Rawlinson, D. 851, f. 50.

resentment of his defeated opponents in the chapter. Cartwright, Dean of Ripon, was one of these and Granville had to
endure long controversial letters from him, to which he
replied he says in a " curt and resolute manner." In writing
to his friend Dr. Basire, Granville had made some indiscreet
references to the Bishop of Durham, the Archbishop of York
and other bishops, complaining of their slackness in enforcing
the use of the Bidding Prayer before the sermon instead of the
long extempore prayers beloved by the puritan-minded clergy.
One of his enemies got hold of one of these letters and sent it
up maliciously to the Bishop of Durham in the hope of making
a breach between them. Granville wrote a letter, dated
Easter Eve 1685, to Sancroft about it : " Though I am well
persuaded my Lord of Durham is so wise and good a man
that whatever use he makes of the treason (pretended to be
discovered in my late intercepted letter) he will not fail at
least to hang the traitor, yet I am so jealous of misrepresenta-
tions to my Lord the Archbishop of York and some other
bishops (which were meant though not named in my letter)
that I have ventured . . . to inclose herein a protestation of my
innocency." What he had written, he said, he had written
out of the loyalty of his heart. In the protest enclosed in the
letter he said he had not intended any dishonour to the Bishop
of Durham or to support Dr. Basire against him, particularly
as the bishop's practice was to use the Bidding Prayer. But he
was opposing an irregular and dangerous practice of the
vicar of Newcastle, which was in contempt of his diocesan,
the chapter of Durham, the whole of the clergy of the
bishoprick, and the greater, elder and wiser part of his own
brethren of Newcastle. Granville admitted that he had used
an unwary expression in saying that the Bishop of Durham
" would in a short while become a good rubric man," but all
he meant was that the bishop, after reading Sir George
Wheler's manuscript on the rubrics, and Dr. Beveridge's about
the Bidding Prayer (both of which were in the hands of the
bishop at the time), would be so satisfied that he would give
no countenance to the vicar of Newcastle.[6]

[6] Granville, I, pp. 201–10.

On October 17th he wrote again to the archbishop and told him that the evil designs of his enemies in intercepting his letter had been of none effect: " My lord, after a thorough inquisition and view of the worst of me, discovered me to be no other than an honest man and his lordship's humble servant. Whereto I have great obligations, having received extraordinary expressions of favour from my lord since my arrival, as well as mighty satisfaction in his visitation, which his lordship has managed hugely to his honour and the edifica-tion of us all." Moreover the bishop had strictly enjoined the chapter to continue the weekly celebration (fallen into disuse since Cosin's death) and the sermons on Wednesdays and Fridays in Lent and Advent, according to the present practice of York and the ancient practice of Durham and probably all cathedral and collegiate churches.[7]

The dean preached the first of these sermons on the first Wednesday in Advent[8] and afterwards published it with a dedicatory epistle to the bishop, in which he declared that " the magistrates and people of the best quality in this city " had shown by their attendance their appreciation of this new step. In the following Advent the mayor and aldermen absented themselves, and Granville wrote to the mayor saying that he hoped that the next Lent would see them present again or at least represented, " which will be not only pleasing to my lord of Durham, who enjoined me to be very diligent in keeping up this ancient and excellent order, and myself and chapter in particular, but much to the edification of the whole city." [9]

Granville was not the only member of the chapter who had trouble with his brethren. Sir George Wheler had not been very long in Durham before he found himself in a heated controversy with Prebendary John Morton. The latter had been collated to the seventh stall in 1676, and had in the same year, to please Crewe who wanted the seventh stall for his friend Richard Knightley, exchanged it for the less

[7] Granville, I, pp. 210–11.
[8] Dec. 2nd, 1685.
[9] Roger Granville, *Life of Denis Granville*, p. 360.

remunerative sixth.[10] In 1685 he exchanged once more; this time he removed to the twelfth stall. Wheler, who had been collated to the second stall in the previous December claimed precedence, the question being whether seniority was counted from a first installation or from admission to a new stall. Crewe, as visitor, decreed that seniority in the chapter was to be counted from the first installation and that a prebendary did not lose his seniority by changing from one stall to another. The decree was written in Latin and began in the time-honoured way: " Nathaniel providentia divina Dunelm Episcopus." [11] The bishops of Durham hold their office " by divine providence " (so runs their official formula) and not, as other bishops, " by divine permission." The episcopal throne in Durham cathedral is said to be the most lofty in Christendom. But that is only a coincidence.

Crewe also had trouble with Morton. At his visitation the latter did not appear and said he was exempted from visitations by being an archdeacon. For this he was suspended and removed from his office as chaplain to the bishop. " An obstinate fellow, advanced by my lord from the lowest degree to a high station. . . . This man, when my lord's castle was by some accidental means deprived of water, and all the prebendaries had desired my lord to convey some from their fountain, he obstinately refused his consent. My lord, in his speech to the chapter, told them he was sorry to be denied water where he had given bread." [12] " But," says one of the biographers, " so great was the bishop's goodness towards him, in forgiving his offence, and in testifying the true spirit of a Christian, he afterwards removed him from a lesser prebend to one of the best in the church and from a small parsonage to the very best in the diocese." [13]

On April 23rd, 1685 James and his consort were crowned. The Bishop of Durham supported the King on his right hand

[10] John Morton, B.D. 1674, D.D. 1692. Fellow of Lincoln College, Rector of Egglescliffe 1676–1711, Sedgefield 1711–22. Archdeacon of Northumberland 1685–1722.
[11] Jefferson Hogg MSS. Library Univ. Durham, II, p. 2.
[12] *Examination*, pp. 65–6.
[13] *Memoirs*, pp. 23–4.

and the Bishop of Bath and Wells on the left. Crewe was much at Court, and during James II's reign lived a great part of his time in his London house, No. 43 King Street, Covent Garden. This house had been occupied successively by Sir Thomas Killigrew, Sir Harry Vane and Sir Kenelm Digby. When the bishop lived there it was a great social centre, but it had a curious distinction and a rather unwelcome one we should imagine—it was the custom of the parish to lay all the foundlings on the doorstep. In Thackeray's day the house was Evans' Hotel, famous for its suppers and singers, and frequently used in that writer's novels. After that it was the home of the National Sporting Club, and in 1933 it was a fruit warehouse.[14]

James II, on December 29th, made Crewe Dean of the Chapel Royal. In this office he succeeded Compton, Bishop of London, whom the King disliked. When the deanery was offered him Crewe asked James whether Compton had offended him, to which James replied, " My lord, I am determined he shall not be there." The Bishop of Durham then said, " As your Majesty is resolved on it, and finding the Church is so unhappy as not to have you, since I cannot be so near your person as I was to your royal brother, I shall most humbly accept of your goodness." As a member of the Church of England Crewe could not be the King's chaplain, but he retained his favour, and had a good deal of influence. It was largely through him that Sir Jonathan Trelawney was promoted in 1685 to the see of Bristol. But he found more constraint than pleasure in the office. The Bishop of Rochester succeeded him as Clerk of the Closet and was sworn in on the same day as Crewe took the oath as dean.[15] There was some ill-feeling about both appointments. Sir John Bramston wrote that Crewe's father " had been of the long rebellious parliament and continued there until Cromwell garbled the House of the Presbyterians. And the Earl of Northampton lost his life in defence of the Crown in that rebellion : so did some of

[14] *Yorkshire Post*, April 8th, 1933.
[15] Dec. 29th. Wood, *Life and Times*, III, p. 173. Hist. MSS. Com., Downshire MSS., I, p. 83.

his sons : all were in arms for the King and stoutly defended his cause." [16] The old story was never forgotten. There were people who said that both the bishops must be leaning towards the King's religion or they would never have received such preferment, and when in the following January the Bishop of Durham was sworn a member of the Privy Council the gossips thought they had an additional reason for accusing him of popery.[17]

On May 12th the Princess Anne of Denmark was safely delivered of a daughter, who was baptized the same night by the Bishop of Durham and was named Anne Sophia. The Earl of Feversham was godfather, the Countess of Roscommon and Lady Churchill godmothers.

On June 28th, 1686 Sir Richard Lloyd, spiritual chancellor of the diocese, died in Doctors' Commons.[18] On July 1st Crewe wrote from Durham castle to the Archbishop of Canterbury.

" Yesterday by the post I received a request from my Lord Chancellor that I would not dispose of my Chancellor's place, which was likely too soone to be void till I heard from his Lordship. The Answer I sent to him I hope will not be an indecent return to your Grace's com̄ands, which was that I have been too apprehensive of worthy Sir R. Lloyd's dangerous condition almost this week and thereupon thought it necessary for preventing all importunityes to fix my Resolution in case of soe sad an occasion. I question not the qualifications of Dr. Hedges, nor of many others in Drs. Com̄ons, but what I chiefly aimed at is, to be my owne chancellor as much as I can by having a person who will be directed and governed by me. This, my Lord, I think will be the great concernment of every Bishop in England upon like circumstances ; the exorbitancy of such patents having beene more mischievous to the

---

[16] *Autobiography of Sir John Bramston,* Camden Series, 1845, p. 217.
[17] *Revolution Politics,* 1733, Pt. II, pp. 15, 17.
[18] Sir Richard Lloyd. Fellow of All Souls ; Doctor of Law 1662. Advocate in the Court of Arches, Chancellor of Llandaff. Became Chancellor of Durham 1676. Official of the Court of Arches 1684 and then Dean of Peculiars. Succeeded Sir L. Jenkins as Judge of the Admiralty Court. M.P. for Durham City since 1679.

Church than any one thing belonging to it; because the bishops oftentimes though they cannot help it, must bear the blame which their spiritual officers in their courts are guilty of. I need not tell your Grace, how sorry I am for this irreparable losse, partly that the whole profession is much impaired by it, and I am sure your Grace in particular will hardly find a fitter person, for Learning, Loyalty and Integrity, to succeed in your Court of Arches. Your news of his Decease being the first and the hasty returne of the bearer cannot but put me into some confusion which is the best excuse I can make at present for

Your Grace's most obedient humble servant
N. Duresme." [19]

When there was a vacancy in one of the chief offices at Durham influence was generally brought to bear by important people on behalf of their friends, and the bishop usually had to make up his mind very quickly. The vacancy at Doctors' Commons was filled by Sir Thomas Exton, who hoped that his friend Dr. Hedges might succeed Lloyd at Durham.[20] In August it was expected that the bishop would " put it into civil hands, for Natty Lloyd," his godson.[21] The person to whom Crewe actually gave the post was Charles Montagu, son of the Earl of Sandwich, who however did not retain it long, for three years later he sold it to Mr. William Wilson, registrar to the dean and chapter.

On June 17th, 1686 the King announced the appointment of seven Lords Commissioners for Ecclesiastical Affairs for executing and exercising all ecclesiastical jurisdiction. The setting up of such a body was first proposed in the Privy Council. Since James, though officially Supreme Governor of the Church of England, was a Roman Catholic, it was thought to be only fair that a body of churchmen should exercise his authority. Archbishop Sancroft assented to the scheme: eleven out of twelve judges said it was legal, the only dissentient being Baron Atkins. There was much to be said for

---

[19] Tanner MS. 30, f. 68.
[20] Hist. MSS. Com., Downshire MSS., I, p. 192.
[21] *Ibid.*, p. 210.

such a scheme if it had been worked with moderation and not
used chiefly as an ecclesiastical law court, whose object was
to punish those who opposed the King. But it had to exercise
the royal jurisdiction as James understood it. The first members were Sancroft, Crewe, Sprat, Bishop of Rochester;
Lord Chancellor Jeffreys, Sunderland, the Lord President of
the Council; Rochester, the Lord Treasurer; and Lord Chief
Justice Herbert. The Lord Chancellor with any two other
members were to form a quorum. Crewe was at Durham at
the time of the establishment of the commission and seems to
have been appointed without being consulted. The announce-
ment was made and he received orders to attend the first
meeting and that was all. He considered, however, that as the
scheme had been approved by the Council and the judges no
objection could be made. He was a commissioner until the
abolition of the commission in October 1688. According to
Burnet he was proud of his membership and declared his
name would be recorded in history, and when some of his
friends pointed out the danger of acting in a court so illegally
constituted he said he could not live if he should lose the
King's gracious smile.[22]

It was said that the commissioners had ecclesiastical jurisdiction " in the largest extent that had been known in England." [23] This is incorrect. The old High Commission Court
had power to fine and imprison; these commissioners could
do neither. But they had a power of excommunication, and
since the Lord Chancellor and two other members formed a
quorum, this could mean putting the power of excommunication into the hands of three laymen, a thing unheard of.
Anthony Wood's comment was, " Though every one understood that the design of this was to introduce a Roman
hierarchy which assumes a power over the temporal . . . yet
here this Commission grants the temporal power a power of
excommunication, which is a pure spiritual act." [24] It must
be said that no sentence of excommunication was issued.

[22] Burnet, *James II*, p. 121. Hist. MSS. Com., Rep. V, p. 186.
[23] Eachard, *Hist. Eng.*, 1720, p. 1078. Kennet, *Hist. Eng.*, 1719, III,
p. 594.
[24] Wood, *Life and Times*, III, pp. 193-4.

The Ecclesiastical Commissioners opened their commission at Whitehall on August 3rd, 1686 and sat the following day in the prince's chamber. The Archbishop of Canterbury did not appear at the first meeting, so a messenger was sent to tell him of the second meeting, but he would not come. Crewe went to Lambeth and told him that his appearing to consent at first and then refusing to attend " appeared a design to abuse the others that remained." This gave the archbishop great uneasiness and caused him some sleepless nights, but he still refused to appear. The King himself arranged to meet him at Colebrook and there discussed the matter with him— Sancroft was apologetic, begged James' pardon, but still said that on second thoughts he would not come. Thus the Primate refused to have anything to do with the commission, the Archbishop of York was dying or dead, and Compton, Bishop of London, was always opposed to the King, so it was left for Crewe to be the leading ecclesiastic on the commission and later to bear much of the odium. He may have been the leading ecclesiastic, but he seems to have taken a far from prominent share in what went on.

The first business of the commissioners was with Compton, who had not complied with the King's order to suspend Dr. Sharp for preaching seditiously against the Government : in other words, for preaching against Roman Catholicism. Compton appeared before the commissioners four times— August 9th, 16th, 31st and September 6th. He protested against the jurisdiction of the commissioners, claimed the right to be tried by his metropolitan, and further questioned whether he could be called to account for anything he had done before the date of the establishment of the commission. Finally he was suspended from all ecclesiastical functions during the King's pleasure, under pain of deprivation.[25] The Bishop of Durham seems to have been present on all occasions mentioned above. It was he who desired that Compton should be suspended

<hr>

[25] *A True Narrative of the Proceedings against the Lord Bishop of London in the Council Chamber at Whitehall*, London 1688. *An Exact Account of the Whole Proceedings against the Bishop of London*, London 1688.

during the King's pleasure, and Jeffreys supported him, but the Earl and Bishop of Rochester and Lord Chief Justice Herbert were against this. Ranke, on the evidence of Barillon, gives a slightly different account. He says that Sunderland expressed his opinion in favour of the suspension of Compton and that Crewe sided with him (Barillon does not actually mention Crewe). In the presence of this difference of opinion among the commissioners Sunderland advised having recourse to the King himself.[26] It was Crewe who proposed that the suspension should be merely *ab officio* and not from the income of the see. Immediately after the suspension three commissioners, the bishops of Rochester (Sprat), Peterborough (White) and Durham, were appointed to exercise ecclesiastical jurisdiction in the diocese of London. They tried to make matters as easy as they could for Compton, for when preferments in his gift fell vacant they allowed him to nominate and his wishes were complied with.

While Crewe was one of the commissioners for the diocese of London he was present, in 1687, at the examination of that learned young man Henry Wharton for holy orders, and so much admired the readiness of his answers that he promised to make him one of his chaplains, which promise for some reason or other was not kept. Because of this Wharton, in his MS. diary, referred to the bishop as " *levis iste ac versipellis episcopus,*" and spoke scornfully of his perfidy.[27] Wharton became Sancroft's chaplain, though unlike his master, he accepted the revolution and remained in his benefice. He had little with which to rebuke the Bishop of Durham on that score; the cause of offence then seems to be that the chaplaincy was not immediately forthcoming. Thus are good and bad reputations sometimes made.

The Ecclesiastical Commission issued an order that no marriage was to take place without a licence, or after due publication of banns. Another order required bishops to send in a certified list of all hospitals in their respective dioceses.

[26] Ranke, *Hist. Eng.,* 1875, IV, p. 301.
[27] *Biog. Brit.,* 2nd edn., IV, p. 440. Birch, *Life of Tillotson,* London 1752, p. 149.

The customary practice with royal orders was that they were sent to the Archbishop of Canterbury, who then requested the Bishop of London to disperse copies of the orders throughout the province. The Bishop of London not being available, Sancroft sent the usual letter to the three episcopal commissioners for the diocese, but through an oversight omitted to sign it. The Bishop of Durham took this as an intentional slight to their commission. It is probable that the feelings between the archbishop and the other three bishops was rather strained. Sancroft had pleaded poor health as an excuse for not appearing at the meetings of the Ecclesiastical Commission, but it was obvious that he disapproved of it and its doings. Hearing, however, that his oversight had been misunderstood, he caused another letter to be written, which he signed and forwarded with apologies for the previous omission, at the same time asking that the unsigned letter might be returned to him. Crewe refused to be placated or to return the letter. On the contrary, he kept it "intending to make use of it as occasion should be offered, and hath done the archbishop's errand to the King, who before was not at all pleased with the archbishop for not attending the commission." This story is Sir John Bramston's, but he gives us no hint how he came to know all this.[28]

Prebendary Cartwright was in London during October 1686 and was consecrated Bishop of Chester at Lambeth on the 17th of that month. Lloyd was consecrated to St. Davids and Parker to Oxford at the same time. The consecrators were the Archbishop of Canterbury and the bishops of Durham, Norwich, Ely and Rochester. He noted in his diary on the 4th, "I was kindly entertained at dinner with my son at the Bishop of Durham's": ten days later he dined with Crewe again. On the 19th he visited Bishop Leyburn, at that time the only Roman Catholic bishop in England. Cartwright and he seem to have been good friends and there are many references to him in the Bishop of Chester's diary. This friendship was no doubt one of the reasons why, like Parker,

---

[28] *Autobiography of Sir John Bramston,* Camden Series, pp. 265–6.

THOMAS CARTWRIGHT, BISHOP OF CHESTER.

Facing page 151.

he was accused of being a Roman Catholic. The Protestant faction asserted that they had both turned papist for the sake of a bishopric.[29] On October 25th Cartwright visited Crewe once more and wrote, " I took leave of my lord of Durham who received me with great expressions of kindness." The two had much in common in their political and religious opinions, yet one of Crewe's biographers says : " Certain it was he (Cartwright) was my lord's great enemy." [30] From London Cartwright proceeded to Durham. On November 15th he was met at Farewell Hall, just outside Durham, by some prebendaries and others of the gentry, and so conducted into the city where he was " welcomed by the dean, prebends and aldermen and many other gentlemen." On the following day he dined with the dean and supped with Alderman Duck, a famous local worthy. Let the diary tell its own story of the two following days :

17. " I received twenty guineas of the Dean and Chapter for my books relating to the state of the College : delivered up my treasury books and received a release under seal. Dined with Dr. Bagshaw, then in residence, and supped at the castle with Mr. High Sheriff and his lady and Dr. Montague, Mr. Basire and others."

18. " I was at morning prayer and took my leave of Mr. Dean and Dr. Grey and gave institution to Gabriel Blakeston, Master of Arts, to the rectory of Danby Wiske . . . and had Sir William Blakeston the patron's bond to save me harmless, after which I went to Piercebridge accompanied by Sir Ralph Cole and others to Sunderland Bridge, and met at my inn by Sir Robert Eden and Mr. Brass." The new Bishop of Chester had resigned his canonry of Durham in which he was succeeded by Constantine Jessopp.

The Rev. Samuel Johnson was tried in Trinity term 1686 before Chief Justice Herbert for two scandalous and seditious libels intended to incite the King's subjects to rebellion. He

[29] Aug. 22nd, 1686. " This day it was affirmed that Cartwright and Parker had turned Roman Catholic." *Revolution Politics*, 1733, Pt. II, p. 47.
[30] *Examination*, p. 55.

was a zealous Protestant, had been chaplain to William, Lord Russell, and had in 1682 attacked James, then Duke of York, in a work entitled *Julian the Apostate*. He followed this up in 1683 with *Julian's Arts to Extirpate and Undermine Christianity*. For the former he was fined and imprisoned. Now he produced *An address to the English Protestants in King James' Army*, and a similar appeal to the Navy. In the following term he was sentenced to stand in the pillory three times, at Westminster, Charing Cross and the Royal Exchange respectively, to pay a fine of five hundred marks, and to be whipped from Newgate to Tyburn. Out of respect to his cloth the court ordered him to be degraded from holy orders before the more humiliating punishments were inflicted. Johnson was an aggressive person who asked for trouble and got it, but no civil court had the power to make such an order as the last, and the three commissioners for the diocese of London should have ignored it. No cleric could be degraded from holy orders except after trial and sentence in an ecclesiastical court. The three bishops, though joined with certain clerical assessors, were not a canonical court, and yet took upon themselves at the behest of the King's Bench to declare Johnson to be henceforth a layman. The ceremony of degradation took place in the chapter house of St. Paul's on November 20th. Crewe, Sprat and White were all present. Dean Stillingfleet refused to have anything to do with the business, but eight other divines acted as assessors to the bishops and signed with them the sentence; the Dean of Windsor, Drs. Holder, Grove, Scott, Sherlock, Cave, Bridge and Dove. Johnson protested against the commissioners' jurisdiction saying that he saw three bishops present and he hoped they were Protestants, but he did not see his own diocesan the Bishop of London, who was his ordinary, and according to the canon law he ought to be tried by him. If however Dr. Compton was sequestered, as he heard he was, then the jurisdiction of course lay with the metropolitan, the Archbishop of Canterbury. The bishops replied that they had sufficient authority by the King's commission, during the suspension of the Bishop of London, to execute all eccle-

siastical jurisdiction in the diocese. Crewe seems to have been
the chief spokesman of the bishops throughout. He told the
prisoner they proceeded against him in order to the execution
of the sentence pronounced against him by the King's Bench.
Johnson answered he hoped they would try him themselves
and not be only the echo to the other court, and they might
very well believe all sentences given in that court had not been
found to be always just when they had been afterwards
removed to another court. He told them also that their lordships might consider that preaching against popery, or many
sorts of speeches, might by inuendoes and interpretations be
made sedition and treason : and that what he had written was
the opinion of all the bishops in Queen Elizabeth's days. The
Bishop of Rochester replied that that was the most malicious
thing he could say of the Church of England. To whom
Johnson replied, "But 'tis true, my lord." The prisoner further
told them that the sentence against him, viz. the whipping, was
the punishment of a dog, and that he had rather have been
hanged at Westminster, and that his orders and gown were
dearer to him than his life. After the sentence was passed the
Bishop of Durham ordered the officer to deliver a Bible into
Johnson's hands, which having been done, he was commanded
to take it from him. After that a square cap was set upon his
head, and the officer ordered to take it off. Then the officer
took off his gown, and after that his girdle, and when he was
about to take off his cassock too, the bishop said it was enough,
he might leave that. Finally the bishop told him he delivered
him over to the secular power as a mere layman. Johnson
protested and appealed to the King's delegates in Chancery,
but he was carried back to Newgate to undergo later his
punishments of the pillory and whipping. After the execution
of the sentence the King presented Johnson's Essex living
to another clergyman who made application to the three
episcopal commissioners for institution. They said he should
have it if he could get two common lawyers and two civilians
to certify that Johnson was legally degraded and therefore
deprived. This he failed to do, and they made him give them
a bond of £500 to indemnify them before they would grant

institution. So violent however was the opposition of the parishioners that he never got possession.[31]

The omission to take his cassock from him, small a matter as it seemed, was sufficient at a later date for the lawyers to find the degradation of Johnson technically incomplete, and so he was able to regain possession of his living.[32] Dr. John Smith has recorded that the Bishop of Durham, two years before the revolution, ordered £500 to be paid to Johnson in consideration of his sufferings, by yearly payments of £100 a year for five years, if Crewe should continue so long in possession of the see.[33] Another story is that he voluntarily gave him £300. Luttrell said that Crewe gave Johnson a present of £200, and promised to allow him £100 a year for three years and to give him the first good living of which he had the presentation.[34] The enemy story is this: " His giving the money was at a distant day when it was necessary to him to still the clamours of the injured; when under the revolution he was afraid for his bishopric and was in jeopardy of the wrath of the Court. This was his voluntary giving, in the language of the Jesuit: it was not compelled by fine or amercement: it was an oblation." All that we are told in the memoir of Johnson, attached to the volume of his collected works, is that about the time of the meeting of William's first parliament " the Bishop of Durham gave Mr. Johnson and his lawyer a meeting and made his peace with him to their mutual satisfaction." [35]

In December Dean Brevint wrote from Lincoln to Bernard Granville, the second surviving son of Sir Bevil: " I am so sorry to hear of too much ferment between the Bishop and the Dean of Durham." Six weeks later Bernard Granville referred in a letter to " the late unhappy dispute between the dean and the bishop." [36] Unfortunately we know only one side of this dispute: we have the long letters of Granville to

[31] *The Works of Samuel Johnson,* 1710, p. xiii.
[32] *The History of King James' Ecclesiastical Commission,* 1711, p. 21.
[33] *Memoirs,* p. 22.
[34] Luttrell, II, p. 17, March 10th, 1690. *Examination,* p. 63.
[35] *Works of Samuel Johnson,* p. xiv.
[36] Granville, I, pp. 219–22, Dec. 11th, 1686; Jan. 27th, 1687.

Crewe but not the replies. The dean was full of protests. He
wished the bishop to see " the very bottom of his soul " as he
had done on the occasion when he met with such treacherous
dealings at Newcastle. He admitted that at that time he had
acted with some unwariness and indiscretion, but this time he
was not ashamed of anything he had done nor the way in
which he had done it, nor would the bishop have been displeased if he had been present. Even if he had known the
bishop would disapprove, his conscience would have forced
him to act in the same way, indeed he had believed that what
he was doing was his real duty to his lordship. The bishop
had recently made a public declaration of his good opinion of
the dean, and Granville hoped to retain that good opinion in
spite of opponents and detractors, inasmuch as he had been
actuated solely and simply by a desire for the welfare of the
cathedral church. He was much disturbed at the thought of
a breach in the happy relations which had always existed
between himself and his diocesan, since such a breach must
needs be a manifest injury to the service of God and the King.
He hoped that God would strengthen the bishop's heart to
resist the temptation to allow a division between them " as
wisely, christianly and honorably as you did in reference to
the other wicked and malicious attempt the last year." Not
very tactful the last sentence, perhaps, but the impulsive
Granville was not overburdened with tact, and consequently
was often in hot water. But he was fighting for obedience to
the cathedral statutes and trying to enforce the residence of
the prebendaries.

The statutes of the cathedral ordered that at least one-third
of the prebendaries should be continually present. A prebendary could be away from Durham eighty days in the year :
moreover, if he were employed in the service of the King or
Queen, or on any business of the Church, or in attendance on
parliament, or on convocation, or if he were absent through
sickness, the periods thus employed would not be counted as
part of the eighty days. It was taken for granted that he
would have other benefices. Consequently any prebendary
could be absent for a very considerable proportion of the year,

and it sometimes happened at the cathedral services that all the prebendal stalls were empty. With a view to remedy this an order had recently been made in chapter, largely it would seem through the dean's urgent insistence, that every prebendary should reside at least four months in the year or else lose a proportion of his revenues. Certain members of the chapter were very angry. They preferred to live at one or the other of their additional benefices and to perform the minimum of their cathedral duties. These malcontents had appealed to the bishop, who disapproved of this new rule and its infliction of fines. He was annoyed at not having been consulted beforehand and complained that it showed contempt of his authority, or at least a lack of trust in him, a complaint which the dean earnestly deprecated. By the fortieth chapter of the statutes of Philip and Mary no new statutes conflicting with the old might be made, and it was the duty of the bishop as visitor to see that this was not done. If there was any question of doubt or ambiguity in the statutes the dean and chapter had to seek the visitor's interpretation and abide by it.[37]

Granville protested that there was no one who would so heartily labour to assist the bishop in all his " worthy designs to support the crown and mitre with the highest pomp and grandeur " than himself. He added : " In reference to which my notions do so well agree with those which I have heard your lordship sometime declare yourself to have, that were it not for some few different ones which are now rooted in my nature, and which I have sucked in from my two deceased masters, Bishop Cosin and Bishop Gunning, in spurring on some of my brethren . . . to a right and thorough-paced conformity . . . we two in our very makes, circumstances and interests, are so composed that there may be the firmest union that there ever was between dean and bishop." Granville was as surprised that the bishop should listen to the tales of the malcontents as that he should seem lukewarm in the cause of suppressing absenteeism. He urged that all the members of

---

[37] *Durham Cathedral Statutes,* Surtees Soc., 1929.

the chapter who were present had voted for the new rule, and since the dean and prebendaries were without all peradventure the bishop's council, he still hoped that Crewe would look on the affair in that light.[38] Crewe, however, seems to have abided by a strictly legal interpretation of the statutes. A fortnight later the dean wrote again. To manifest himself the bishop's humble servant he had consented to lay aside the late order made by the chapter, and instead his brethren and he had sent an address to the bishop, in which they left it to his wisdom and care to see that a sufficient number of prebendaries should always be in residence.[39] Crewe, as visitor, had expressed himself very firmly in a letter to the dean, and had demanded that his letter should be registered among the chapter proceedings. The dean demurred and stated his reasons. It was without precedent that such a letter, written on the occasion of such a dispute, should be registered. It made the prebendaries liable to expulsion if they admitted his lordship's accusation that they were attempting to make new statutes. It would dishonour both bishop and chapter to put on record the cause of the contention. Moreover, the offending regulation had been withdrawn.[40] In his next letter he told the bishop that he had sent for all the ecclesiastical officers " to confer with them altogether, that I might understand from them the utmost extent of your lordship's inhibitions, that if I have made any false steps or unwary orders during this visitation I may undo and rectify them. . . . I am more than sorry . . . that you should so greatly mistake your dean that he would on any such account contend with his bishop." [41] So the matter might have ended. The bishop had issued some orders about residence and had desired that Mr. Knightley, Dr. Montagu and Sir George Wheler should stay a month longer. When informed of this, Mr. Knightley broke into a passion and said that he would not stay more than three months from his livings for the lord of Durham or

[38] Rawlinson MSS. D, f. 206, Nov. 5th, 1686.
[39] Rawlinson MSS. D, f. 215, Nov. 19th, 1686.
[40] Ibid., f. 218, Nov. 26th.
[41] Ibid., f. 220, Dec. 4th, 1686.

any other lord, and that he would part with his prebend first, and he had then left Durham without permission. The dean complained that Knightley had been the chief cause of the late dispute, just as it had been prebendary Morton who had called for the recent extraordinary episcopal visitation, without any real grounds for it.[42] These men had constantly mis-represented him to the bishop, and he urged that his lordship should make a thorough enquiry into what was going on, or else the Church would be continually torn with these quarrels.[43] Crewe replied, and apparently laid great insistence on the statute which commanded sufficient residence. In answer to this the dean said, " The care and zeal which your lordship therein discovers for that statute . . . would render us unpardonable, if either dean or brethren should ever more make new orders of the like nature during a visitation without consulting our visitor, which I am sorry I did ever do." [44] On Christmas Day the bishop wrote again bidding the dean desire Dr. Montagu, Mr. Knightley and Sir George Wheler to remain in residence a month longer, in order to be present at chapter on January 22nd. Sir George's wife had meanwhile been confined, so that Granville had not ventured to detain him any longer. The dean replied that he hoped the others would remain, but Mr. Knightley had expressed great resent-ment and desired him to communicate it to the bishop. He was still anxious that the bishop should enquire into the causes of " the late clashing " and the mischief makers who were responsible for it.[45]

During the reign of James II Crewe made three appoint-ments to canonries in the cathedral. Dr. FitzHerbert Adams, one of the bishop's chaplains, became prebendary of the sixth stall in 1685.[46] In May that same year he was elected Rector of Lincoln College and Wood described his entry into Oxford

[42] By the statutes the Bishop was bound to hold a triennial visitation, but by request he might hold a special visitation, such as he had recently made in order to enquire into the quarrel about residence.
[43] Rawlinson MSS. D, f. 221.
[44] Ibid., f. 225, Dec. 11th, 1686.
[45] Ibid., f. 226.
[46] Lincoln Coll. B.D. 1682, D.D. 1685. Rector of Washington 1683. Removed to tenth stall 1685 and to eleventh in 1711. Died 1719.

attended by about forty people of his own house. He spent
money lavishly in beautifying the college chapel and the
rector's lodgings and was vice-chancellor in 1695. The second
was John Cave, also a fellow of Lincoln, who was collated to
the third stall in 1686.[47] Constantine Jessop, prebendary of
the fifth stall, was appointed in 1686.[48] Writing to Crewe
early in 1687, Granville thanked him for securing two prebendaries against the next chapter, at which there would be
business of some importance. He had written to Cave with
some importunity urging him to be present. " Mr. Morton
writ to him not to come till after Christmas, though I had
writ to him positively to be here in November, which I conceive very ill done of Mr. Morton, and I have told him so,
once or twice in chapter. Had Mr. Cave followed my first
counsel in coming down last summer in July, he might have
so understood the state of affairs and his own interests as to
have proof against such a snare." Now he was three or four
score pounds out of pocket.[49]

The Ecclesiastical Commissioners had power over the
universities as church institutions. Dr. Peachell, the vice-
chancellor of Cambridge, and eight delegates appeared before
them at Whitehall on April 21st, 1687 to explain why they
had refused to admit the Benedictine Alban Francis to the
degree of M.A. at the request of the King. They said they
could not admit him unless he took the oaths. Degrees were
frequently granted at the command of the King, and a little
while previously they had conferred an honorary degree on a
Mohammedan without demanding the oaths, though of course
the case was somewhat different, inasmuch as he was not one
of the King's subjects. The defendants protested that the
commission was an illegal court and that they were forbidden
by their statutes to do what was required of them. Dr. Peachell
was deprived of his offices in the university. Crewe seems to

[47] Rector of Gateshead 1679–83, then of Nailston and of Cole Orton
in Leicestershire. Died 1690.
[48] M.A., D.D. Magdalen, Oxford. Rector of Brinton, Northants,
where he died 1695.
[49] Rawlinson MS., Bodleian D, f. 226.

have been present at the meetings of the commission which dealt with this case.[50]

The President of Magdalen College, Oxford, died in March 1687 and early in April the fellows received a royal mandate to elect Anthony Farmer, who by the college statutes was ineligible, and moreover was unsuitable in every way. On April 10th, 1687 Dr. Thomas Smith wrote to the vice-president of the college, Dr. Aldworth, to say that Mr. Francis Bagshaw went with him to Whitehall to interview the Lord President and to ask him to deliver to the King the petition of the college against appointing Anthony Farmer. " I thought it proper for us to go to my lord of Durham who was then in the chapel at prayers, after which we attended him in his apartment and humbly moved him to represent the case to the King, but we could not obtain this favour from him, he making several difficulties, as that the King had never consulted or so much as spake one word to him about it : then at least that he would be our friend with the Earl of Sunderland and my Lord Chancellor : but my lord was pleased to refuse to intermeddle at all and, in short, told me that he was of opinion that the King's resolution was unalterable." [51] On April 15th, the last legal day according to the statutes, they elected John Hough as president. Crewe was present at a meeting of the Ecclesiastical Commission on May 28th in the council chamber at Hampton Court, where a citation was ordered against the vice-president and fellows of the college or such fellows as should be empowered to appear.[52] On June 6th Dr. Aldworth and the deputies appointed by the fellows appeared before the commissions at the council chamber at Whitehall in answer to the citation.[53] Again, a week later the vice-president and deputies attended with their answer signed by the vice-president and four fellows. Crewe was present on both occasions and at further meetings of the commission on October 17th and November 3rd.[54] Three

[50] *The Cambridge Case,* 1689.
[51] Bloxham, *Magdalen Coll. and James II,* Ox. Hist. Soc., 1886, p. 18.
[52] *Ibid.,* p. 50.
[53] *Ibid.,* p. 53.
[54] *Ibid.,* pp. 108, 178.

commissioners visited the college on October 21st. Cartwright, in his opening speech, rebuked the fellows' disingenuousness, " their disobliging and petulant humour, and their obstinate and unreasonable stiffness." He told them that the Church of England taught unconditional and unlimited obedience and asked them, why, if they were so particular about their statutes, they did not say Mass as the statutes directed. Finally the commission expelled them from the college. At the meeting in the council chamber at Whitehall on November 28th the Lord President moved that the expelled fellows should be incapacitated from all ecclesiastical promotion by sentence of that court. Lord Chief Justice Herbert gave it as his opinion that Dr. Hough's election had been regular, and therefore could not give his assent. The Bishop of Rochester said the same. Lord Chief Justice Wright thought they ought to proceed further. The Bishop of Durham expressed his view that those who had preferments already ought not to be deprived, but that those who had not should be incapacitated. On the face of it this seemed an unfair distinction, but probably he meant that the former should be incapacitated from any further promotion. Finally the Lord Chancellor, the Lord President, Lord Chief Justice Wright and the bishops of Durham and Chester agreed that the expelled fellows ought to be incapacitated from receiving any ecclesiastical preferment for the future if that court could do it.[55] Crewe was present again on November 29th [56] and on December 8th. Four lawyers, the Solicitor-General, Sir Robert Baldock, Sir Thomas Pinfold and Dr. Hedges, on the latter occasion gave answer to questions which had been referred to them on the 28th, and there was a debate among the commissioners on the question " whether there is matter enough before the court for it without further process." The Bishop of Durham voted for the affirmative, that is, for proceeding to judgment at once, but the Lord Chancellor held that there should be further proceedings first.[57] The debate was resumed on the 10th and on that day

[55] *Ibid.*, p. 219.
[56] *Ibid.*, p. 220.
[57] *Ibid.*, p. 221.

Dr. Hough and the expelled fellows were declared incapable henceforth of ecclesiastical dignity, benefice or promotion.[58] Lastly, on the 12th the order for incapacitating them was read and approved, and it was decided that a copy of the order should be sent to every archbishop and bishop.[59] Crewe was present at all these meetings, but he was not a member of the special commission of three sent down to Oxford in October. He does not seem to have taken a very vigorous part even in the meetings he did attend. Nevertheless, he was by some unjustly called the " Grand Inquisitor." [60]

On April 4th, 1687 James issued his first Declaration of Indulgence. A large number of addresses expressing thanks and loyalty came in from all parts of the kingdom. " The nonconformists presented addresses of thanks so high and extravagant that some of them were thought offensive to the very ears of the King." During the summer the *Gazette* was full of such effusions.[61] Some of them were couched in the most flattering language, e.g. those from the dean and chapter of Durham in May, and from the city of Durham in June.[62] The bishops of Chester, Rochester and Peterborough dined at Crewe's house in London on April 10th, and it is no great stress of imagination to think that they discussed the declaration very seriously. On the 20th Cartwright tells us in his diary: " I met my Lord President and the Bishops of Durham, Rochester, Peterborough and Oxon, at my Lord Chancellor's, where he and my Lord President, before dinner, acquainted us that His Majesty expected thanks from us for the care he had of us, and the gracious promises he hath made to protect us in his late gracious declaration: of which I penned the form, and with the Bishop of Oxon subscribed it before dinner, and carried it down to my Lord Chancellor, who after dinner asked the other three to do it, two of which, Rochester

---

[58] Bloxham, *Magdalen Coll. and James II*, Ox. Hist. Soc., 1886, pp. 221–2.

[59] *Ibid.*, p. 222.

[60] *Examination*, p. 67. *Hist. King James Eccl. Com.*, 1711, pp. 30–53. *Autob. Sir John Bramston*, p. 302, which says the Commissioners were " very much divided."

[61] Eachard, II, pp. 1084, 1085.

[62] Luttrell, I, pp. 404, 405.

and Peterborough, refused till the form of it were somewhat
altered, which being done, Durham, Rochester and I subscribed it; Peterborough desired to deliberate till to-morrow,
and we were ordered to meet there again at four in the afternoon for that purpose." Rochester and Peterborough had
doubts about the genuineness of the King's zeal for toleration.
After this meeting on the 20th Crewe and Cartwright went to
visit Bishop Leyburn. Next day the Lord President told
Cartwright that the King "liked well of our subscriptions,"
but by that time the Bishop of Peterborough had made up his
mind and utterly refused to join with them. On the 25th
Cartwright tells us that he met the Lord President and the
bishops of Durham and Rochester at the Lord Chancellor's
and subscribed an address to the King, which he sent on to
the bishops of Lichfield and Lincoln and the deans of York
and Lincoln. The Bishop of Lincoln wrote expressing his
approval, and Cartwright dining at Lambeth on the 30th
showed his letter to Crewe, the archbishop and others.

Crewe and Cartwright seem to have been on very friendly
terms at this time. No doubt public affairs and common
principles brought them together. They were both in London
during May and June 1687. Crewe visited Cartwright on
May 7th and June 21st. Cartwright visited Crewe on
May 19th and June 20th, dined with him on May 30th and
June 13th (when the Dean of Durham was also present), and
supped with him at the Dean of Windsor's on July 2nd. On
the last occasion Fr. Graham was present. Similarly Cartwright
was visited by Dean Granville on June 5th. The dean and
Dr. Basire dined with him on the 10th and 17th, the dean
supped with him on the 16th and Cartwright dined with the
dean on the 18th. They all seemed friendly enough. While
Granville was in London he was received very kindly by
Crewe who invited him to dinner the following day. In a
letter to Mr. Cradock, his Official, he tells how at York and
other places on his journey down he had been attacked by
people urging that no addresses of thanks should be sent to
the King, but he says "I held my own very stoutly and convinced most that, at least in my case, coming from my lawful

superior, it ought to be done." He expressed himself anxious to know how it was that the London clergy " should not only be for twenty years more deficient in conformity than we in the bishopric of Durham, but now also in point of gratitude to the King." [63]

In May Ferdinand Count d'Ada had been consecrated titular Archbishop of Amasia in the chapel at Whitehall by Bishop Leyburn the vicar apostolic, and two Irish bishops. The church was thronged : Crewe, Cartwright and Massey were there, according to Wood, out of curiosity.[64] On Sunday, July 3rd, for the first time for many a long year, a papal nuncio went in state to be received by a King of England at Windsor. The little town was crowded : it was difficult to get food or accommodation, and many of those who came to the spectacle had to remain in their coaches for a great part of the day. The ceremony was expected to take place at noon but it was between five and six o'clock before the nuncio arrived. First came one of the Knight Marshal's men on horseback and two others on foot, followed by the nuncio's twelve footmen in dark grey coats trimmed with white and purple lace. Then with two pages walking on each side came the royal state coach, in which sat the nuncio robed in purple with a gold crucifix at his breast, and riding in the same coach were Sir Charles Cotterel, Master of the Ceremonies, and the Duke of Grafton. Three other coaches followed, one of them, the nuncio's own, being empty ; in the other two were ten priests. Then to the indignation of the Protestants followed in order the Lord Chancellor's coach, two coaches of the Lord President, the Lord Privy Seal's coach, the Lord Chamberlain's coach, and eighteen coaches more, each drawn by six horses, and among them the coaches of the bishops of Durham and Chester. The procession arrived at the castle, and the nuncio went up to St. George's Hall, where the King and Queen waited for him under a canopy. He made a speech, their majesties severally replied,

[63] Granville, I, pp. 225–6.
[64] Wood, Life and Times, III, p. 219.

and the nuncio then returned to his lodgings.[65] The story was told that John Coventry, Crewe's coachman, refused to drive his master that day. If it were so Crewe must have forgiven him for he left a bequest to him in his will. There seems good evidence however that if the bishop's carriage was there the bishop was not. Sir John Bramston was told " by one that did see the company " that he was not, and Dr. Smith wrote : " The story of the bishop's meeting the Pope's nuncio was entirely false." [66]

In August of that same year Bishop Leyburn visited Durham. The Venetian envoy in London reported that he and his attendants " received courtesies from all the gentry of the places along the road." On entering the city he was met by the magistrates and received an invitation from the bishop to dine with him at the castle, which he did, and was treated magnificently. In the county of Durham he is said to have confirmed over a thousand persons.[67] During his stay in the city he is believed to have lived at 16 Old Elvet. Strype, referring to d'Ada in 1719 said : " By report he is now Archbishop of Milan and has shown great civilities to English strangers, and always enquires after his brother the Bishop of Durham and drinks his health." [68] The story scarcely rings true. It is not likely that the Archbishop of Milan would look on Crewe as a *brother* or even as a bishop. But to the Protestants it would tell against Crewe and that was sufficient.

People believed that Crewe had definitely become a Roman Catholic. Wood noted it in his diary on April 3rd, 1687.[69] Confidence in the rumour was strengthened by his having been at Whitehall " to observe some of the popish ceremonies." His loyalty to the King probably took him further than he intended to go. He was known to have urged the clergy and others to send loyal addresses to the throne. He was con-

---

[65] *A Full and True Relation of his Excellency the Pope's Nuncio making his Public Entry at Windsor*, London 1687.
[66] *Memoirs*, p. 24. *Autobiography of Sir John Bramston*, p. 280.
[67] Newsletter, Aug. 18th, 1687. Downshire MSS., I, p. 258. Venetian Transcripts, B.M. Add. MSS.
[68] Kennet, *Hist. Eng.*, III, p. 494. Strype's note.
[69] Cf. *Evelyn Diary*, April 10th, 1686. Luttrell, I, p. 399.

M

stantly being spied on. " In King James's reign three well-dressed gentlemen came to my lord's house about nine at night and asked the porter where the bishop was. The porter replied that he was in bed, and for aught he knew was asleep. Nevertheless they vehemently affirmed that he was at the popish Mass." The ferocity of Protestantism at the time was only equalled by its ignorance. Mass at nine at night! Crewe always refused to hold conversations with strangers who came wishing to talk to him privately and always kept two or three servants in the room. People frequently said, " My lord, I have private affairs with you," to which he always replied, " Sir, I have none with you, nor do I know of aught you cannot speak before this company." [70]

What one of his fellow bishops thought of him is shown in a letter written in June by the Bishop of Ely to the Archbishop of Canterbury :

" I am really in pain for your Grace when I consider what unwelcome guests you must endure on the day of the new bishop's consecration.[71] And I cannot help humbly advertising and representing to you, my lord, that the weak, vain man of Durham makes but ill use of all your condescending goodness at those meetings. Your treating him with so much particularity and respect he interprets standing in awe of him. Were I to attend there (as I thank God I am not) I would entertain his friend Chester with more and greater regards, on purpose to show how much I slighted a High Commissioner." [72]

In November 1687 Fr. Petre, who had a greater influence over the King than anyone else, was sworn a member of the Privy Council. After that the Bishop of Durham, who had not known of it and was surprised when he saw him there, ceased to attend the council, and Lord Preston, by the King's order, wrote to him to say that His Majesty had noticed that he had not attended council for a month. So the bishop went

[70] *Examination,* p. 77.
[71] This was Thomas Watson, who was consecrated Bishop of St. Davids at Lambeth on June 26th by Archbishop Sancroft and the Bishops of Rochester and Chester. Stubbs, *Registrum Sacrum Anglicanum,* p. 129.
[72] Tanner MSS. 29, f. 34, June 6th, 1687.

to see the King, who said, " My lord, you abandon me,"
words which cut Crewe very deeply, but he replied that he
could not come to council while Father Petre was there.
Crewe's biographers say James replied that if that was the
reason Fr. Petre should attend no more. James could ill brook
opposition of any sort. " He that is not with me is against
me " he told the council, and some of his oldest friends soon
realized how quickly they could fall out of favour. Crewe
retained his friendship longer than many of them. The Earl
of Sunderland was another of the King's evil counsellors, and
though he used to say to Crewe " We must all be of a piece,"
he opposed him whenever it suited his own purposes. Thus
when the Bishop of Durham recommended one of the
Montagu family to the King, Sunderland, when he heard of
it, said to James, " Sir, did you ever see a Montagu who was
an honest man ? "

Towards the end of the year some of the Anglican preachers
were declaiming vigorously against Rome. On Sunday,
November 13th, Dr. William Jane preached at Whitehall
before the Princess Anne. Crewe was present, and so were
Bishop Watson of St. Davids, and Bishop Cartwright. By
his references to the massacre of St. Bartholomew the preacher
gave great offence and was forbidden to preach at court
again.[73] Crewe is said to have severely rebuked Dr. Simon
Patrick for his fierce tirades against popery and to have
refused to introduce him to the King.[74]

We have two glimpses of Crewe as one of the commissioners
of the diocese of London during this year. One is a letter to
the Reverend James Fynney, Vicar of Kirklington and chaplain to Lord Burlington, dated May 8th :

" You are appointed to preach your Paulscross Sermon
before the Lord Mayor in the Chappel at Guildhall London
on the 25th of June next being Sunday. These are therefore
to desire you not to fail at the time appointed but to send your
answer of acceptance to Mr. Henry Parker at Londonhouse
in Aldersgate St., and not to exceed an hour & a quarter in

[73] Luttrell, I, p. 422.
[74] *Biog. Brit.*, ed. 1789, IV, p. 439.

both Prayer and Sermon—& also to give notice of your being in Town on the Thursday before to M^r· Benjamin Took, Bookseller, in St. Paul's Church yard.

Your most assured friends and Brethren

N. DURESME.

THO: ROFFEN.

THO: PETRIBURGENS." [75]

When it was announced that the Queen was expecting to be a mother again the King took the unusual step of ordering a public thanksgiving throughout the nation, to be kept in London on January 15th and in the provinces a fortnight later. For the Church of England the three bishops in charge of the diocese of London, Nathaniel of Durham, Thomas of Rochester and Thomas of Peterborough published " A Form or Order of Thanksgiving and Prayers to be used in London, and Ten Miles round it, on Sunday the 15th of this instant January; and throughout England the 29th of the same month by all Parsons, Vicars, Curates &c., in their respective Parish Churches and Chapels, in behalf of the King, the Queen, the Royal Family, upon the occasion of the Queen's being with Child." It was issued by special command of the King and was simple enough. There were special psalms and lessons, a special collect, epistle and gospel, a prayer to be added at the end of the litany, and a prayer to be added after the prayer for the Church Militant. The last contained a sentence which, in the light of events which occurred barely twelve months afterwards, seem now almost ironical : " And do Thou so graciously bless and multiply the whole Royal Family, that the ages to come may evermore rejoice under the government of our Sovereign and His posterity."

Never probably had there been so much talk, gossip and slander before the birth of a prince as there was before the birth of the unfortunate son of James II. All the Queen's children so far had died and a feeling seems to have prevailed that she would have no more. In 1683 it had been announced that she was an expectant mother, and even then there had

<hr>

[75] Hunter MSS., Durham Cath. Lib. *Letters,* Vol. I, No. 175. Mr. Fynney afterwards became a prebendary of Durham.

been rumours of imposture and scurrilous songs and lies.[76]
There was no antecedent improbability that she might have
another child : she had had several already, was even then
not over thirty years of age and she had another child four
years later. The Catholics talked foolishly and perhaps sometimes provocatively about an expected miracle, and this roused
a growing volume of hoarse and angry Protestant laughter :
laughter which was in scorn of popish miracles, anger which
had its source in fear. Every foul thing that could be
imagined about " old mother East," the innocent queen, was
imagined and said. A number of violent lampoons came out :
the following which appeared in December is a specimen :

> Two Toms and a Nat
> Together sat,
> To rig out a Thanksgiving,
> Or a dainty fine Prayer,
> For a Son and Heir,
> That's neither dead nor living.
>
> Old Mother East,
> As 'tis exprest
> All in her last Epistle,
> Devoted the Baby
> Unto our Lady
> With Coral, Bells and Whistle.
>
> As soon as e'er
> The Queen of Prayer
> Had received the Diamond Bodkin,
> Our Queen had leave
> For to conceive,
> And was not that an odd Thing?
>
> Here's a health in Ale
> To the Prince of Wale,
> And most are of Opinion
> That when he comes out,
> A double Clout
> Will cover his Dominion.[77]

There were others of the same character, even more irreverent
and too disgusting to quote.

[76] Clarke, *James II*, 1816, p. 192.
[77] *Revolution Politics*, Pt. IV, pp. 44–6.

Some interesting details have come down to us about clerical appointments in the diocese of Durham at this time. The following were the rules about the chapter patronage : Members of the chapter were first to be provided for, then the curates of the dean and the various prebends, and thirdly the vicars within the chapter's own jurisdiction. The dean wished that these rules were better known. It might prevent many applications and, as things were, the livings in the gift of the chapter were " too few and too mean " for their own dependents.[78]

There were not many curates or, more properly, assistant curates in the diocese at this time, but we have some details about the conditions of appointment in two cases. On November 3rd, 1687 Mr James Hope became curate to the Dean of Durham at Easington. His salary was to be £50 a year, and he was to hand over the surplice fees to his employer. When Granville or his wife happened to be living in Easington he might have board and lodging in the rectory. If Hope went to Durham, and the dean happened to have a spare bed, which would not be often, he might sleep there as a favour but not as a right. Otherwise he had to provide for himself. He was not to have the command of the dean's stable as Dr. Davis, one of his predecessors, had ; but if the dean could spare a horse Hope might, with his permission or that of his steward, borrow it for his journeys within the Bishopric. A year's notice might be given on either side. It may be remarked that part of Hope's salary and his other perquisites were due to the fact that he was the dean's amanuensis. His fellow-curate, Marshall, received only £30 a year, and he received so much because he was a priest and not a deacon. His other privileges were that when the dean was at Easington Marshall might eat at his table and he was further permitted to make use of certain rooms in the rectory for reading, writing or devotion.[79]

Not all the patronage was in the hands of the superior clergy. The Rev. John March, vicar of Newcastle, thought

[78] Granville, I, p. 227.
[79] Granville, II, pp. 140, 142.

he had the right of appointing the morning lecturer at All Saints' in that town, and on November 2nd, 1686 he gave it to Nathaniel Ellison. The corporation had no objection to the nominee, but as they paid his salary they claimed the right to nominate the lecturer. Apparently offence was taken at the vicar's claim, and when March died on December 3rd, 1692 the corporation met the next day and decided to stop their contribution of £90 a year towards the vicar of Newcastle's stipend, and they further agreed " not to pay it to any future vicar upon any pretence or account whatsoever." During the two years in which Leonard Welstead was vicar they kept to their determination, but when Nathaniel Ellison was appointed to the living in November 1694 they not only renewed their grant, but also undertook to repair the chancel of St. Nicholas church and to beautify the altar.

The town of Newcastle was loyal enough, but several things had occurred during the reign of James to shake that loyalty considerably. A certain Sir William Creagh, an Irishman, and a zealous Roman Catholic, was in such high favour with the King that the latter actually sent some of his mandates to the local authorities through him. In March 1686 James sent a mandate to the Merchants' and Hostmen's Company of Newcastle to admit him as a brother of the company, which was done on May 4th, but not so fully as the King intended, so a year later another mandate ordered him to be admitted as a freeman of Newcastle with all the rights and privileges of a freeman. This also was done on June 30th.[80] Similar orders were sent to enfranchise John and Thomas Errington and these were complied with. The rulers of the city were docile enough and on September 20th, 1687 they presented an address to James, thanking him for his grace and bounty and for his care for the Church of England. That Michaelmas the town chose John Squire as mayor and William Ramsey as sheriff. Both were churchmen and so were the deputy-recorder and some new aldermen. On Christmas Eve, however, a *mandamus* from the King displaced the

[80] By order the Common Council Sept. 23rd, 1689 his freedom was made void.

mayor, sheriff, deputy-recorder, six aldermen and fifteen counsellors. In their place they were to elect Creagh as mayor, Samuel Gill, a nonconformist, as sheriff, Joseph Barnes, the son of the well-known nonconformist Ambrose of that name, four other dissenters and two Catholics as aldermen. This reduced the Anglican representation on the corporation to four aldermen and nine counsellors. As the electors did not do as they were told, the changes were made by royal order on January 3rd.

On January 10th a very fulsome (according to the Whigs), loyal (according to the Tories) address was signed by the new mayor and the Catholic, and some of the nonconformist, members of the corporation and magistracy, though the violent opposition of the other members was effectual in preventing its presentation to the King. On January 29th the mayor and corporation went in state to the Catholic chapel, where Father Philip Metcalfe, a Jesuit, preached a sermon, afterwards published with a dedication to Sir William Creagh, in which the preacher referred to the King as " James the Just." The corporation was no longer an Anglican preserve, indeed it was remarked that when that body officially attended service, the cap, mace and sword were one day carried to the church, another day to the Catholic chapel, and a third to the dissenting meeting house. The last was the one on the east side of the Tuthill Stairs, and within it were affixed to the old pews two hands for holding the sword and mace of the corporation.[81]

Crewe went to his diocese in the spring of 1688 to do his utmost to promote the King's policy of a general toleration and the abolition of the penal laws. It is probable that some of the clergy were already shaken in their loyalty: the Dean of Durham noted in March that Mr. Woodmas (afterwards vicar of Bedlington) had begun to have odd notions of a limited supremacy.[82] Crewe was said to have put certain questions to the clergy on the subject and to have threatened

[81] *Life of Ambrose Barnes,* Surtees Soc., p. 177.
[82] Granville, I, p. 229.

with suspension those who replied unfavourably.[83]   There is
no doubt that such a paper was sent round and a copy was
forwarded to the Bishop of Chichester.   The questions were :

1. Whether or no a subject is bound in Conscience to
   Comply with the Coṁands or reasonable Intimations
   of the Pleasure of his Prince in all cases where he is not
   bound in Conscience to the Contrary.

2. Whether a Man may not Comply with his Prince in
   many things which are very inexpedient, nay preiudiciall
   to the well being of his Church (provided the being of
   it be secured) if the King do presse thereunto, and he
   have no way to avoyd that Coṁand but by being dis-
   obedient to it.

3. Whether the Reformed Church of England was not an
   Establisht Church before the Enacting of the Penal
   laws and whether a man may not with a Good Conscience consent to the abrogating them rather than
   provoke the King (on whose favour next under God we
   now depend) since It may tend to the destruction of its
   being.[84]

A set of answers is still extant,[85] and it certainly would not
have satisfied the bishop if he had set the questions.   The
Bishop of Carlisle, however, wrote to Sir Daniel Fleming
saying that the Bishop of Durham was much annoyed at the
report, which everyone believed, that he had put questions
to the clergy.   It was quite untrue.   " But the dean, it seems,
having framed them and sent them to his friend Sir Roger
L'Estrange, with whom he hath long held an intimate correspondence, merely for the satisfaction of his own private conscience, these idle questions of his were by mistake generally
believed to have proceeded from the bishop, who utterly
disclaims them, and the dean, I suppose, by this time is much
ashamed of them, having thereby given occasion of no little

[83] Hist. MSS. Com., Kenyon MSS., p. 189.   Letter from William
Bankes to Roger Kenyon.   Hist. MSS. Com., XI, App. vii, Leeds MSS.,
p. 30.
[84] Tanner MSS., Bodl. 29, f. 23.
[85] Rawlinson MSS., D. 850, f. 87.

disturbance to the whole nation." [86] This was the true story. The dean set it all down in a paper which he entitled " A Short Relation of the Queries maliciously Dispersed up and down under the Notion of the Bishop of Durham's Queries." The King had ordered the lord lieutenants to ask all their deputy lieutenants and justices whether they would be in favour of abolishing all penal laws and tests in religious matters, whether they would assist the election of persons as favoured such an abolition, and whether they would support the King's Declaration for Liberty of Conscience by endeavouring to live at peace with persons of all persuasions. The dean had been much censured for complying with the King's expectations when he had been asked the questions by his bishop as lord lieutenant. He had therefore drawn up his own three questions and had asked Sir Roger l'Estrange's opinion on them. He had also communicated them to some of the younger clergy who depended on him, since he saw them beginning to run counter to his own principles. By treachery or by someone's imprudence these queries had been made public, but much varied in expression. He was not ashamed of them, nay he would answer them in the affirmative, but he declared that neither the bishop nor he himself ever intended they should be made public. Some unknown person had been dispersing copies in London and in the universities, without doubt in the hope of making a division between the bishop and the dean.[87] A newsletter of June 9th repeated the story about the bishop's questions in a different form, that the Bishop of Durham had offered a paper to be subscribed by the vintners and victuallers, and that about a hundred of these had refused and lost their licences.[88] Crewe was certainly actively supporting the King's plans for a general toleration. In February 1688 a paper stating that the subscribers would give their vote and interest to elect such members of parliament as the King should recommend, they being members of the Church of England, " was offered to the burgesses of

[86] May 14th, 1688. S. H. le Fleming MSS., p. 210.
[87] Rawlinson MSS., D. 851, f. 52.
[88] Hist. MSS. Com., Welbeck Abbey MSS., III, p. 409.

Newcastle, and by the Bishop of Durham to the freemen in Durham; an engine used to repeal the penal laws that support the Church established," but only six persons signed. On February 10th a *quo warranto* had been issued against the Newcastle corporation charter, and on March 8th a surrender of the charter was sealed under the common seal and signed by the mayor, sheriff, eight aldermen and fourteen councillors. On March 17th four aldermen were turned out and four others were put in; Ralph Widdrington, Ralph Brandling, Henry Jenison and Ralph Elstob, who were named in the additional charter given to the town by James II.[89] There was certainly a ruthless combing out of all opposition. Important names were removed from the commission of the peace: Sir Christopher Musgrave, Sir Robert Eden, Mr. Henry Lambton, Mr. Cuthbert Carr, Mr. Byerley and Mr. George Morland. The Bishop of Carlisle wrote to Sir Daniel Fleming: " The old gentleman, Mr. Lambton, I hear, made his exit very pleasantly: he was sitting upon the Bench when the commission was read, and observing that his name was left out, he rose up, made a bow to the bishop and so made way to be gone. The bishop called to him and desired him to keep his place. ' No, my lord,' said he, ' I find you have left no place for me here, so God be with you all gentlemen,' and away he went." [90]

On April 27th there was issued James's second Declaration of Indulgence, more generous in its offers than its predecessor. A week later the King made the mistake of ordering it to be read in all churches and chapels. It was not a surprising mistake: other royal orders had been published, and the Anglican clergy had loudly proclaimed their unconditional obedience, as their opponents were not slow in reminding them.[91] But there was a growing alarm among them, and it seemed to them that toleration meant destruction. The days of publication were to be May 20th and 27th in London

[89] *Mark Browell's Diary,* Surtees Soc., No. 124, pp. 183–4.
[90] MSS. of S. H. le Fleming, p. 210.
[91] *Vox Cleri pro Rege: Or the Rights of the Imperial Sovereignty of the Crown of England,* 1688—is a single example out of many.

and the neighbourhood, and June 3rd and 10th in the provinces.

There is a well-known story of a conversation between Crewe and two of his prebendaries, Dr. Grey and Dr. Morton, whom he had summoned to discuss the question of reading the King's declaration. They were men of importance in the diocese; Grey was rector of Bishopwearmouth, and Morton was rector of Boldon and archdeacon of Northumberland. In spite of the bishop's exhortations they flatly refused to read the declaration and argued warmly against doing so. Crewe angrily told Grey that age made him dote; he had forgotten his learning; to which the other briskly replied that he had forgotten more learning than his lordship ever had. " Well," said the bishop, " I'll forgive you and reverence you, but cannot pardon that blackhead Morton, whom I raised from nothing." They then took their leave and the bishop politely escorted them to the castle gate. The porter threw open the wicket and the bishop said, " Sirrah, why don't you open the great gates? " " No," said Dr. Grey, " my lord, we'll leave the broad way to your lordship, the strait way will serve us."

In a copy of Granville's *Remains* which belonged originally to Thomas Baker, the non-juror, there is a note : " When the King's declaration was appointed to be read the most condescending thing the bishop ever did with me was coming to my chamber, remote from his, to prevail with me to read it in his chapel at Auckland; which I could not do, having wrote to my curate not to read it in my living at Long Newton. But he did prevail with the curate at Auckland to read it in his church where the bishop was present to countenance the performance. When all was over the bishop, as penance, I presume, ordered me to go to the dean, as archdeacon, and require him to make a return to Court of the names of all such as had not read it, which I did, though I was one of the number." [92]

Seven of the bishops had in May presented their petition to the King asking that the clergy might be relieved of the duty of reading the petition. On June 2nd the Bishop of

[92] R. S. Rait, *Episcopal Palaces of York,* London 1911, pp. 84–6.

Carlisle expressed his resolve to concur with his brethren in the matter of the petition and said it was believed that they could reckon on sixteen or seventeen of the bishops out of twenty-four. Lincoln and Hereford were looked on as doubtful, " the remaining five, Durham, Rochester, Chester, St. Davids and Lichfield they despair of." [93] Crewe does not seem to have been consulted at all.

The Declaration was read in the cathedral, in St. Mary-the-Less, Durham, in the South Church, Auckland, and eighteen other churches in the county. No canon read it. John Cock of St. Oswald's, Durham and the rest of the clergy of the city refused, in spite of the bishop's injunctions and personal exhortations.[94] Dr. Morton not only refused to read it, but in the suffrages in the cathedral changed the words " O Lord save the King " to " O Lord save the people." One of Crewe's biographers believed that the bishop himself was present.[95] The bishop summoned all the clergy of Northumberland to meet him at his visitation in Newcastle on June 28th, 1688. They were asked if they had received and read the King's declaration in their churches. They replied that they had received it, but it appeared that none of them had read it except " the refuse of the clergy." His lordship returned home the same day " with little sign of respect from either the clergy or the laity." There were only five clergy at the visitation dinner, only two aldermen, Edward Widdrington, a Roman Catholic and Thomas Partis a nonconformist, Barnes the recorder and Gill the sheriff.[96]

Now comes another of the stories spread about the bishop. He was reported to have suspended thirty of his clergy, including Dr. Morton, for refusing to read the declaration.[97] Early in August it was said that the Bishop of Durham was expected shortly at Court to give an account of these suspensions.[98] The story spread widely. Luttrell heard of it.[99]

[93] S. H. le Fleming MSS., p. 210.
[94] Granville, II, p. 147.
[95] Examination, p. 65.
[96] Mark Browell's Diary, Surtees Soc., p. 186.
[97] Ellis Correspondence, 1829, II, p. 63. Clarke, James II, 1816, II, p. 167.
[98] Ibid., p. 105.
[99] Luttrell, I, p. 451.

John Wittie wrote in the following year, " For the Jesuits and Priests of Baal Anti-Christ, did now feed on the best of the Flock, and devour the Fruit of our land, while many able Ministers of the Gospel had scarce Bread left for to put in their mouths (I mean those that were suspended by the Bishop of Durham)." [100]   In *The Memorial of the English Protestants to the Prince and Princess of Orange,* a pamphlet published in the same year, it was stated still more falsely that the number of the suspended in the county of Durham alone was two hundred. The story was altogether untrue.[101] Morton was said to have been one of those suspended, but as already noted he was suspended a long time before, for quite a different reason.

Sir Thomas Haggerston, one of the chief Roman Catholics of Northumberland, was passing through Durham and inquired whether the bishop had read the declaration. He was told that he had not, to which Sir Thomas replied, " But if he does not, care may be taken to have a bishop that will." [102] The story is confused, but it shows that rising assertiveness which was doing harm to the Catholic cause. The nation had not got over the Popish Plot panic : there were thousands who still believed it. The mere rumour that the King was going to give the ruins of St. Mary-le-Bow church in Durham to the Catholics set the church people hastily restoring it in 1685. The Catholics, harassed and persecuted as they had been for over a hundred years, and now dazzled by their new freedom and the royal favour, talked too much about their approaching triumph and domination. It was not surprising—it was only a few years since the Popish Plot terror. It was unwise, no doubt, but it was very natural and very human. On one occasion Prebendary Grey was riding on horseback to Durham from Bishopwearmouth. Mr. Lamb, a Roman Catholic justice of the peace, overtook him and told him that he wondered that he should ride so fine a palfrey when his

[100] *An Exact Diary of the Late Expedition of His Illustrious Highness the Prince of Orange.* By John Wittie, London 1689, p. 8.

[101] *Eachard,* II, p. 1107.   *Memoirs,* p. 23.

[102] *Memoirs,* p. 24.

Saviour was content to ride a colt, the foal of an ass. Grey replied, " 'Tis true, sir, but the King has made so many asses justices of the peace that he has not left me one to ride on."

When the unhappy Prince of Wales was born an address of congratulation was sent up by the city of Durham. In it the signatories " most humbly offer up their public praises and thanksgivings to Almighty God for the happy birth of the young prince, the greatest of blessings that could possibly descend upon these kingdoms : they pray that their Majesties may be blessed with more children and more sons." The signatories of a similar address from the county palatine of Durham " held themselves obliged to give public thanksgiving to Heaven, to congratulate their Majesties in the most joyful news of the birth of a young prince." [103] But the lie about the spurious birth was spread in Durham. " 1688. June 16th. The supposed Prince of Wales was born, being Sunday" wrote Jacob Bee in his diary. The bishop was at Durham at the time of the child's birth and did not see him for three months afterwards. But he never believed the slander. Dr. Smith, however, got hold of a story that when Crewe saw the child it seemed to him to be eight months old,[104] which would only prove that the bachelor bishop was a bad judge of babies.

When the day of thanksgiving for the child's birth came the bishop gave what Thomas Baker, his chaplain, described as the greatest and most splendid entertainment he had ever seen in Durham, and the bishop himself preached " a very excellent sermon exhorting all to loyalty and obedience to the King." So the *Gazette*.[105] Baker thought the account had been sent to the *Gazette* by Peters, the bishop's secretary, but Peters said it had been sent up by the bishop himself. Baker said, " Many other instances I would add, for he (the bishop) was really troublesome and I sometimes weary, with his recounting his great and many obligations to the duke and

[103] *Revolution Politics,* V, p. 46.
[104] *Memoirs,* p. 25.
[105] July 5th to July 9th, 1688.

after to the King.[106]   Crewe was devoted to the King, was grieved at being somewhat under a cloud for his plain speaking about Petre, and was perhaps calling attention to his loyalty.

[106] Note on the flyleaf of Granville's *Resigned and Resolved Christian* in the Bodleian and in the British Museum.

DIONYSIUS GRANVILLE DECANUS DUNELMENSIS MDCLXXIV

D. Logonette pinxit

G. F. Edelinck Sculp.

Impensis Thomæ Hacquet

Rotomagensis hospitis sui anno Dom. 1693.

Serenissimum Dominum Jacobum Secundum Magnæ Britaniæ Regem secutus est in Galliam Anno 1688.

Propter fidelitatem Suam Domino Regi Principe Arausiacensi Coronam Angliæ Usurpante, deprivatus fuit Anno 1691.

DEAN GRANVILLE.

Facing page 181.

CHAPTER VI

THE REVOLUTION

Now everything was changing. The King, when it was too late, realized that he had gone too far and everything he had done was to be undone. On October 5th the High Commission Court was dissolved, and pardons were issued to the Bishop of Durham and the Bishop of Chester that same month to cover them from attacks for any illegality they might be accused of having committed.[1] New charters which had been issued to corporations were withdrawn, so in Newcastle where the new charter had only been received in August, everything went back to the old state of affairs. Even the October elections were void, and on November 5th a new set of officials was chosen.[2]

Up till the summer of 1688 Durham had been what the King was accustomed to call " his loyal county of Durham," but from Dean Granville we get a detailed account of the growth of distrust of the King there. In a letter to his brother the Earl of Bath, he said that about the end of September, on the first intelligence of the Dutch invasion, he had used his utmost endeavours to keep his people at Sedgefield and Easington firm in their allegiance. He repaired to Durham, gathered the prebendaries in the chapter house and urged them to support James with their purses as well as their prayers. All present agreed and all the absent members except one expressed agreement by letter. An Act of Chapter was passed that the dean should advance £100 and every prebend (except one) £50 for the King's service and for raising horse and foot if necessary. He summoned the clergy of his archdeaconry (the bishop had gone to London) and at their meeting on October 15th he urged them to secure their

[1] Hist. MSS. Com., House of Lords, 1689–90, p. 308. Lindsey MSS., p. 448.
[2] *London Gazette*, August 13th. *Mark Browell's Diary*, p. 186. Sykes, *Local Records*, I, p. 121.

N

flocks from being seduced from their allegiance. Next he tried to get the chapter and "my brethren of the Bench" to join in an address of loyalty to the King, but the first and all but two of the second refused. In spite of all the protestations of loyalty and passive obedience with which the Anglican pulpits had rung for years, James was beginning to be disabused. The declaration of the Prince of Orange came into his hands wherein he read that William had been invited by, among others of the English nation, a great many of the lords both spiritual and temporal. On Thursday, November 1st he questioned Compton, Bishop of London, about it and that ingenious divine replied that he was confident the rest of the bishops would as readily answer in the negative as himself. It is difficult to distinguish this evasion from a lie. He was one of the seven who signed the invitation. Next morning all the bishops who could be hastily gathered together were summoned to Whitehall. There were present the Archbishop of Canterbury and the bishops of London, Durham, Chester and St. Davids. They were called into the King's closet and James told them that he had seized a person who had been dispersing the Prince's declarations in the city. He himself had received five or six copies from different persons to whom they had been sent among the penny-post letters, and he had thrown them into the fire, except one which Lord Preston, who was standing by the King, had in his hand. He then directed the secretary to read an extract, pointing out to him the places where he wished him to begin and end. It was, of course, the passage about the invitation.

James then said that he did not believe a word of it, but he thought they should know of this and therefore had sent for them to acquaint them with it. The archbishop thanked the King for his good opinion and said that he had taken the oaths of supremacy and allegiance and could have but one King, and that as His Majesty well knew, he never worshipped the rising sun, nor made court to any but his King. As for the charge of inviting the Prince of Orange and his own share in it, it was utterly false and he did not know, nor could he believe, that any of his brethren had ever given the Prince any

such invitation. Compton cunningly said that he had given
the King his answer the day before. Crewe said " I am sure
I am none of them. I shall be the last man in England that
shall be guilty of that."

The King repeated that he believed that the charge was
nothing but a groundless aspersion, but he thought that for
their own sakes and for his service they ought to publish an
official denial. He commanded the archbishop to call as many
of the bishops as were at hand and to consult with them what
would be the best way of vindicating themselves. Sancroft
replied that he thought that all those in town were present
except the Bishop of Rochester to whom he would send that
night. The Bishop of St. Davids was able to add the information that the Bishop of Peterborough had recently arrived in
London. King James then said that if they agreed on some
sort of defence or denial the archbishop should bring it to
him, or rather, not to endanger Sancroft's health, should send
it to him. After the King had received it and approved it, it
could be sent to the other bishops for their concurrence.

James wished them to say not merely that they had not
invited the invader but that they disapproved of his coming.
To this, however, " neither the archbishop, nor the Bishop of
London, nor any of the other three, as far as it is remembered,
returned one word." It would have been a very awkward
thing for Compton at any rate to sign.[3] Luttrell, repeating
the gossip of the day, says they were pressed to sign a paper
ready drawn declaring abhorrence of the Prince's declaration,
but since they were not allowed to peruse the whole document
they refused to sign abhorrence of they knew not what.[4]

On Saturday, November 10th Henry Earl of Clarendon
went to call on the Bishop of Ely who had sent him word that
he had arrived in town on the previous evening. They went
together to Lambeth and there dined. " We found there the
bishops of Durham and Peterborough, which I was a little
startled at. The archbishop told me that Durham had made
many professions to him, and that he was perfectly come

[3] Henry Earl of Clarendon. *Diary,* 1828, II, pp. 494-5.
[4] *Luttrell,* I, p. 472.

into our sentiments." [5] " As he was servile, so was he abject :
he threw himself in the way of the Archbishop of Canterbury,
to tell him he was sorry for having so long concurred with the
Court and he begged to be reconciled with the archbishop and
other bishops." [6] This is the unfriendly version. In the eyes
of his enemies whatever Crewe did, if it was not bad in itself,
was inspired by a bad motive. Though he had been somewhat under a cloud for refusing to sit in council with unqualified persons, nevertheless he was sometimes admitted to the
royal presence. On November 14th he took the opportunity
of presenting to James a paper entitled " The Humble and
Faithful Advice of your Majesty's ever Dutiful Subject and
Servant the Bishop of Durham." In it he made the following
recommendations :

" That your Majesty would be pleased to withdraw your
protection of those Romish chapels which are daily made the
occasion of so much disturbance and mischief here, and if
continued any longer, I fear, will unavoidably endanger the
peace and safety of this your great city and consequently of
your whole kingdom.

" That the archbishopric of York, which your Majesty
hath been pleased to offer me, may be filled with some other
more deserving person : and that your Majesty would be
pleased to make another dean of Christ Church in Oxford,
instead of Mr. Massey who is utterly incapable thereof by law :
that the fellows of Sidney College in Cambridge, for whom I
have so often moved your Majesty, may have leave to elect a
new Master, in the place of Mr. Bassett (he being also unqualified on the same account) to proceed on all other affairs
relating to that society, according to their original statutes
and constitution.

" That your Majesty would be pleased to call a free parliament so soon as may be, this being the only probable means
for preserving your sacred person, for preventing the effusion
of Christian blood, and for establishing your throne and

---

[5] *Clarendon Diary*, II, p. 201.
[6] Wood, *Ath.*, II, 1177. *Examination*, p. 68 n.

government, both in church and state, upon sure and lasting foundations."

The only part of the advice which the King followed was that which concerned the archbishopric of York, to which he appointed the Bishop of Exeter, who was himself to be succeeded by the Bishop of Bristol.[7] Anthony Wood heard a rumour of the Bishop of Durham's petition to the King. "Abominable falseness. Very like him, if true," was his characteristic comment.[8]

Even if the King had attempted to follow Crewe's advice it would have been too late. His enemies were now taking possession of the country. On November 27th Dean Granville despatched a letter containing his own personal assurance of fidelity to James, but this was intercepted by Lord Danby, Lord Lumley and other lords at York. As a civil magistrate he tried a few days later, but in vain, to get the justices of the peace and deputy-lieutenants to meet him to take measures of defence against William's supporters, who were advancing northward with the intention of seizing York and Newcastle. Granville then sent an express to the King with a duplicate of the papers which had been intercepted, and a despairing letter setting forth the hopeless condition of the King's affairs in the north.

On Wednesday, December 5th, 1688 Lord Lumley entered the city of Durham with a party of about fifty horse and a number of the gentlemen of the counties of Durham and York, on behalf of the Prince of Orange. He sent Captain Ireton with ten troopers to the deanery to demand the surrender of the dean's arms and horses. Dr. Granville refused to deliver them, or to attend upon Lumley, and was kept more or less a prisoner in his own house till the rebels had gone. Next day Lumley read the Prince of Orange's declaration at the castle in the presence of the deputy-lieutenants, justices and other principal gentry who flocked to him. Encouraged by their compliant mood he sent to New-

---

[7] Mickleton MSS. Durham, XLVI, f. 237. S. M. le Fleming MSS., p. 219. Magrath, *Flemings in Oxford,* Oxf. Hist. Soc., II, p. 238.
[8] Wood, *Life and Times,* III, p. 285.

castle to demand admittance there, but the magistrates of that town refused him entrance; so on the Saturday he again read the Prince's declaration, this time at the Durham market cross, in the presence of a large number of the gentry and of the county troop, and then set off again with his followers to York. He had "no horses or men of mine," said the dean, and "I preached a sermon on loyalty next day." [9]

The Declaration of the Lords Spiritual and Temporal of December 11th was signed by Lord Crewe, the bishop's brother, and two days later the gentlemen of the Bishopric signed a petition for a free parliament.[10] On the 15th King James returned to London after his ill-advised flight. "My lord received him and knelt down to kiss his hand, and he kindly took my lord by the hand and squeezed it, with some delight to see him." [11] The King had been received in London with "such bonfires, ringing of bells and all imaginable marks of love and esteem," [12] that he thought all would now go as before, and so at meals a Jesuit said grace as usual. Yet in two days the unhappy man was once more in flight, never to see his country again. William marched into London a few hours later, and on the 18th Roger Kenyon wrote to the Earl of Derby to tell him that the Bishop of London had been made Clerk of the Closet and the Bishop of Durham turned out.[13] In Durham Dean Granville preached two farewell sermons in the cathedral, one on the 5th and the other on the 9th of December, both of them from the text Gen. xliii. 14: "If I be bereaved of my children I am bereaved." These, with certain letters and a speech delivered at his archidiaconal visitation in Bow Church on November 15th, were subsequently printed under the title of *The Resigned and Resolved Christian and Faithful and Undaunted Royalist,* of which only twenty copies were printed.[14] In his visitation speech he

[9] *The Dean of Durham's Reasons for his Withdrawing into France,* 1689, pp. 4, 5.
[10] Hist. MSS. Com., Rydal Hall MSS., p. 228.
[11] *Memoirs,* p. 26. *Examination,* p. 77.
[12] Clarke, *James II,* II, p. 262.
[13] Kenyon MSS., p. 211. He means Dean of the Chapel Royal.
[14] The work was subsequently reprinted in the Granville volumes of the Surtees Society.

had said "If the Prince of Orange landing with 14,000 traitors (or supporters and abettors of treason) at his heels will not convince men that there was such a thing as an evil intended invasion . . . then he should give them up for lost, for men void of common sense." The English people were murmurers like the Israelites and the result was that "one of the freest and most happy nations of Europe" truckled "to an upstart commonwealth and an anti-monarchical generation, who by their continued sheltering, encouraging and assisting of traitors, proclaim their enmity to the very name of king." Loyal he had always been, loyal he would remain. At midnight on December 11th, with the help of two faithful servants, he set off for Hexham. Then by way of Carlisle and Berwick he reached Edinburgh, where he found a ship and after a long and tedious voyage landed in France and made his way to Rouen, where he arrived on March 25th. In exile he remained, snubbed and cold-shouldered by James' Catholic entourage, pursued by invitations to return and threats of deprivation if he did not, yet he kept his loyalty in the spirit of his sermon " If I be bereaved of my preferment I am bereaved." Careless of his money, impulsive and hot-tempered, yet he was a faithful, God-fearing and lovable soul.

There were some public disturbances in the palatinate as well as in other parts of the country. In Durham in the Old Elvet there had been a Catholic mission at least since 1590. In 1685 Fr. Pearson of the Society of Jesus became the priest-in-charge there. He built a chapel, opened a seminary and soon collected a large number of scholars. When the news came that William had entered London a Durham mob destroyed the chapel and publicly burnt a cross, while the principal Roman Catholics had their houses pillaged and burnt, and the clergy had to flee for their lives. In Sunderland on December 20th certain masters and mariners, with certain fitters and a rabble, broke open the Quaker meeting-house in that town (the copyhold property of William Maud) and between 1 a.m. and 8 a.m. utterly demolished and burnt the house and its furniture. Then they marched through the streets and did much damage to the houses of several other Quakers.[15] Probably this ruffianism was induced by the story so frequently told that the Quakers were a society founded and inspired by the Jesuits.

During the revolution an association was formed by a number of peers, bishops and other leading persons of the kingdom binding the subscribers to stand by one another until a free Parliament should secure their liberties and privileges. It was signed by thousands. Archbishop Sancroft was one of the signatories, but Crewe when pressed to sign it in the House of Lords declined to do so. " No," said he, " when it is law, I will sign it, not before." The unknown commentator on the Trotter MS. said scornfully, " We see the Bishop of Durham in full character : he would not sign the Association till it was law : when it was law his signature would have been as insignificant as his refusal was." [16]

When Father Petre absconded the Bishop of Durham was one of the members of the council who signed a warrant for his apprehension, but the messenger sent after him failed to find him and he got safely away. Feversham in accordance with the King's orders had dismissed the royal army and the soldiers were scattered about the countryside without officers to command them and without food. Crewe was one of those who signed the order bringing them back to discipline again.[17] On Tuesday, January 29th the House of Lords was busy on the question of the future government of the country. Nottingham, Clarendon and Rochester led the debate in favour of a regency and the Bishop of Durham voted on their side.[18] The motion was lost by 51 to 49. On January 31st they agreed that the throne had been deserted. On February 2nd they declared that the throne was not vacant, that is to say, they agreed on the word "deserted" and wished the words in the Commons' resolution " and that the throne is thereby vacant " to be left out. Finally on February 6th they gave

[15] Sykes, *Local Records*, I, p. 124.
[16] *Examination*, p. 76 n.
[17] *Examination*, p. 76.
[18] Clarendon, *Diary*, II, p.256 and note.

way to the Commons and agreed to their formula.[19] The resolution was carried by 65 to 48. Out of eighteen bishops only two voted for it, and these were Compton and Crewe, " to the wonder of all," said Wood, who added " Oh! false-ness! he that ran with the humour of King James now for-sakes him to cringe to the Prince of Orange in hopes to keep his bishopric." [20] Muddiman's newsletters say that Crewe was the only one who voted for abdication and that Compton voted on the other side. The printed lists say that only eleven bishops voted against the abdication clause. Clarendon's account is that on Wednesday, February 6th " the Bishop of Durham, who had been at the House but twice before, came to-day to give his vote against the King who had raised him." [21]

Aylesbury has another story about the voting in the House of Lords on the subject of the King's abdication : " We were about sixty that were against the vote that the King had abdicated, but some very few there were that did not enter their protest. On the first question we carried it by one voice or two, on which Lord Mordaunt, after Earl of Monmouth and Peterborough, made a great noise according to custom and gave out as if the militia should be placed in the Palace Yard, which intimidated some weak hearts that did not appear when the main question was put. I cannot charge my memory, but as I remember, we lost the main question but by one voice, and at numbering the House with another lord of the prevailing party, I understand by one that the Earl of Falconberg and Crewe, Bishop of Durham, retired between the hanging and the door next to the bishops' room." [22]

There is yet another story. On May 18th, 1694 Lord Montagu wrote to King William asking for a dukedom. He protested his long service to William and his friends and, amongst other things, he claimed that in the face of the great opposition of the Jacobites he had induced Lord Huntingdon, the Bishop of Durham and Lord Ashley to vote against the

[19] *Eachard*, II, p. 1142.
[20] Wood, *Life and Times*, III, p. 298.
[21] Clarendon, *Diary*, II, p. 261.
[22] *Memoirs of Thomas, Earl of Aylesbury*, London 1890, I, p. 230.

regency and for the offer of the crown to William : " which
was carried but by those three votes and my own." [23] Since,
however, some of the other claims which he put forward in
this letter rested on a doubtful basis, it may be the same with
this.

When all is said there is no doubt that Crewe did vote
against James. He had more than once taken upon him to
remonstrate with the King and probably by this time he had
come to the conclusion that there would be nothing but confusion and strife in the country as long as he remained on the
throne. After all Clarendon had little ground for reproaching
Crewe.

Crewe took the precaution towards the end of 1688 of
taking out a pardon for his share in the High Commission
Court. Jeffreys, Sir Nicholas Butler and the Bishop of
Chester, and some twenty others, took out their pardons on the
same day, November 1st.[24] The possession of this pardon was
a safeguard to him when his troubles began. There were
some who would gladly have seen him deprived of his
bishopric. Burnet, for example, drew up a paper on ecclesiastical matters which he presented to the King. In it he
specially recommended nine of the clergy to him, and warned
him against three, of whom Crewe was one, the others being
Hall, Bishop of Oxford and Watson, Bishop of St. Davids.[25]
Crewe felt it wiser to be out of the way for a time, so in
February, accompanied by his nephew, James Montagu, and
his servant, Harry Carter, he went to Holland. Montagu
could speak French well, and Carter had some knowledge of
Dutch so that languages were not likely to prove a difficulty.
With them went John Turner, fellow of King's College,
Cambridge, described as " a facetious pleasant man." They
embarked on a new yacht, which he hired, and which had a
crew of four, but they were tossed about in a violent storm for
five days. We are told that the sailors lost their reckoning

[23] *C.S.P.D.*, Will. and Mary, 1694–5, p. 15. King William's Chest 15,
No. 15. Printed in full in Dalrymple, App. to Book VI, Vol. II,
p. 257.
[24] *Eachard*, II, p. 1116.
[25] Clarke and Foxcroft, *Life of Burnet*, 1907, pp. 257–8.

and that Crewe, on Saturday evening at 6 p.m., took the compass and steered the vessel into the Brill.[26] This seems hard to believe seeing that as far as our knowledge goes the bishop had never had any experience of navigation in his life. The *Memoirs* say, "They steered the vessel into Brill." Though the wind dropped the tide was contrary and it was not till one o'clock on Sunday that they arrived in Rotterdam. It was February 22nd and on that day the 105th Psalm is read in the Anglican service, a very suitable psalm for that particular day and ever afterwards one of his favourites, reminding him how he came safe that day from perils of the sea. They landed and after refreshing themselves they walked about to see the churches and other sights of the town. They stayed in Rotterdam about three weeks and attended the Protestant services, and in after years Crewe used to imitate the gestures of the Dutch preachers with great amusement. This is a new light on the bishop: we should hardly have thought of that rather severe looking figure as a mimic. Next they went to Leyden where they met Crewe's old tutor, Hickman, who had given up the living of Brackley at the time of the Restoration. When he heard that oaths of loyalty to the new government were to be exacted he said, "Alack! Alack! Are they come to that again? That is poor doing indeed." From Leyden Crewe and his party went on to Brussels and Antwerp: altogether they were abroad five months, and he greatly enjoyed the trip, and often said he would not have missed it on any consideration. He travelled in mufti as the clergy say to-day, and he wore a wig and sword. People thought he was some great man in disguise. Some believed him to be the Earl of Northumberland, *un homme fort sçavant*. While he was abroad William and Mary were crowned. His faithful biographer says, "My lord had letters kindly written to invite his attendance to assist, and large promises of favour and welcome reception, but he would not return at that time," and excused himself.

These seem to be the general facts of the case but now let us

---

[26] *Examination*, p. 81.

listen to his enemies. Strype[27] said, " He despaired of any
favour at the Revolution and was once got beyond sea in a
fright, but being brought back by the importunities of a
domestic servant he made fresh interest in the Court and
parliament, and bought off the complaints of Mr. Samuel
Johnson and others who suffered by him." Burnet said
" The poor Bishop of Durham, who had absconded for some
time and was waiting for a ship to get beyond sea, fearing
public affronts, and had offered to compound by resigning
his bishopric, was now prevailed to come and, by voting for
the new settlement, to merit at least a pardon for all that he
had done, which, all things considered, was thought very
indecent in him, yet not unbecoming the rest of his life and
character."[28] " Voting for the new settlement," seems to
suggest that he was preparing to escape *before* he voted for the
new regime in the Convention Parliament. This agrees with
Burnet's words, " He ventured out of his retreat to the Convention Parliament, in order to make a merit with the new
Government by voting for it." But Burnet is inaccurate, to
put it mildly, especially about his brother bishops. He also
said, " All our friends had designed that I should be made
Bishop of Durham, Crewe having rendered himself so
obnoxious that he seemed unpardonable." He went on to
say that Crewe sent both to the King and to himself by Lord
Montagu, offering to resign in his favour, trusting to his
generosity to give him £1,000 a year, but the Bishop of
London had asked it of the Prince of Orange a few days after
he came to St. James's, and he could not well deny him anything. Upon this Crewe refused to retire and the matter fell
through, " and soon after the Prince was put on the throne,
and I was made Bishop of Salisbury."[29] Burnet's spite was
undoubtedly increased by disappointment, and the whole story
must be accepted with hesitation. Some corroborative
evidence however is to be found in a newsletter dated March
30th (after he had gone abroad) which stated that the Bishop

[27] Kennet, *Hist. Eng.*, III, p. 597 n.
[28] Burnet, *James II*, p. 457.
[29] Burnet, *Autobiography*. Foxcroft, *Supplement to Burnet*, pp. 496–7.
Burnet was consecrated Bishop of Salisbury March 31st, 1689.

of Durham was about to resign and that Compton was to be translated to Durham.[30]   Birch in his *Life of Tillotson* wrote of Crewe, " He absconded on the abdication of King James, and offered to compound his offences by resignation, particularly to Dr. Burnet." [31]   In a copy of this book in the Routh Collection in the Library of the University of Durham there is a marginal note to this passage, in the hand of Dr. Routh, " As yᵉ Dr says (if true)." Dr. Routh had small belief in Burnet's veracity.

Mr. Speaker Onslow said that Crewe was diverted from resignation by his nephews, Mr. Sidney Wortley Montagu and Mr. Charles Montagu, who were great friends to the new settlement and brought him into it. He was always " a mean man in all respects, but had some court skill."   One of his great-nephews told Onslow that the bishop had given him the following advice : " Nephew, do as I did, when I began the world at Court. Stick firm to some great man there. If he falls, fall with him, and when he rises you are sure to rise with him to more advantage than if you had left him."   The comment follows : " The Duke of York had been his patron, but now the bishop had got his preferment." [32]   The bishop's advice is perhaps not so bad as it might sound to us in the twentieth century. The man who wished to rise in the seventeenth and well on into the eighteenth century needed a powerful patron, and at any rate Crewe recommended loyalty, even if not on very high grounds.

The Bishop of Durham returned to England in July 1689 after a voyage which lasted many days on account of the prevalent calms. He only arrived in London two days before the expiration of the time for taking the oaths. The House of Lords had adjourned three days before the final day. One of his biographers says that the adjournment had been chiefly promoted by Burnet, who hoped that thereby the see of Durham would become vacant and William had promised it to him if the bishop did not take the oaths. There is no

[30] Wood, *Life and Times,* III, pp. 300–1.
[31] Birch, *Life of Tillotson,* 1753, p. 149.
[32] Burnet, *James II,* Oxford 1852, p. 457 n.

doubt that Burnet always had his eye on Durham, but he could hardly have expected such a speedy translation as this would have been, apart from William's promises to Compton. Crewe persuaded " his countryman," Sir Thomas Stamp, to call a guild, and thus he was enabled to take the oaths in the Guildhall on the last day but one. If he had arrived home so recently it is difficult to see how all this was arranged at such short notice. The court was surprised and Burnet was much mortified,[33] and old Lord Falconberg said in the King's bed-chamber that Crewe had acted wisely. Clarendon said that nobody had heard of him for some months, and it was generally said he was gone beyond the sea, but on July 30th he appeared at the Guildhall and took the oaths there.[34] Luttrell, however, noted on July 25th that the Bishop of Durham and Dr. Thompson of Friday Street had taken the oaths.[35]

In August 1689 he paid a visit to Leicestershire, which must mean that he stayed some time at Newbold Verdon, and while he was there it appeared in the public prints and especially in the *Gazette* that while he was abroad he had gone to France; the inference, of course, being that he had gone to St. Germains. Many other injurious things were also published in the same manner. The Whigs were in the ascendant, and any one who had been a friend of James was subject to constant slander, and slanders against Crewe would be popular in high political circles.

When he fled to Holland he committed his library and his manuscripts to the charge of his chaplain Dr. Eyre, who lodged them for secrecy and safety from prying eyes in the house of his tailor, a man named Miller. Unhappily Miller went bankrupt and all that he had was seized by his creditors. Eyre, we are told, died soon afterwards, but the tailor said that Eyre had owed him money and the books had been treated as security for the debt, and Crewe never saw them again.[36]

[33] *Examination*, p. 83.
[34] Clarendon, *Diary*, II, p. 84.
[35] *Luttrell*, I, p. 563.
[36] *Examination*, p. 85. *Memoirs*, p. 26.

The contemporary accounts are not very clear on details, but there seems no doubt that many books were lost together with various papers and sermons, although Dr. Samuel Eyre certainly did not die till 1694. This was not the bishop's only anxiety. Everything he had done in the last reign was being reviewed in a hostile light. About this time Sir William Bowes asked him about some address " intended from Durham, which his lordship was concerned in." This was probably one of the loyal addresses drawn up for the presentation to James. Bowes said he was certain to be asked about it (in the Commons) and enquired what answer he ought to make, to which Crewe replied, " Say all you know." There were spies about too, or at any rate there was fear that there might be. " Narrative Smith " called upon him one day and desired a private interview. Three or four of the bishop's gentlemen were with him at the time. The bishop wished to know what his business was and bade those with him to pay attention to all that passed. He was not going to trust Smith's report of a private conversation, so that gentleman quickly took his leave and went away in confusion much disappointed.[37]

On his return to England Crewe found waiting for him a long letter from Dean Granville, written at Rouen on July 1st. In it he set forth his steadfast loyalty and Crewe must have experienced an uncomfortable moment when he read, " Your lordship, I am sure (which is my comfort) will be none of those who shall load me with reproaches for my dutiful compliances with his Majesty, since your example (which did outrun others) as well as your advice, did powerfully invite me thereto." Granville explained why he had not followed Crewe's example since the previous October, " after your lordship was pleased to present a paper of advice to His Majesty to comply with the designs of the multitude." Granville went on to say that he was astonished at so sudden and unexpected a change, and was one of the last in Durham to give credit to the reports of it. " This change of measures in your lordship . . . did wonderfully weaken me in the discharge of all duties incumbent upon me " and in " several

[37] *Memoirs,* p. 28.

designs which could not be prosecuted, much less accomplished, without the concurrence of the bishop and lord lieutenant." In consequence he was unable to curb or censure those insolent young clergy who in the pulpit attacked both dean and bishop for their obedience to the King. An indiscreet sermon was preached in the cathedral, but all he could do as dean was to refuse to the preacher the customary invitation to his table. " Instead of assistance from those who were sworn to that and much more, I met with reproaches, and was told that I was well-enough served in that my bishop had left me in the lurch." Granville concluded thus : " Grieving that your lordship hath, by doing homage to a superior which I cannot own, absolved me, in a great measure from the canonical obedience, duty and respect, which I did once owe you, and whereby I am capacitated to take greater freedom with your lordship than was lawful for me to do in former letters, as well as debarred of begging your benediction with the same delight I have done formerly."

From Rouen on August 15th Granville wrote also to the vice-dean and prebends bewailing the fact that not a single clergyman within the precincts of Durham had had the courage to support him in the attitude he had taken up. He also wrote the same day to the clergy of his archdeaconry. He reminded them that they had constantly preached the royal prerogative, passive obedience and non-resistance. The accusation of singularity had been thrown against him, on the ground that he was the only dignified clergyman who had followed the King into exile. It was not a new accusation : the non-compliance of the clergy under his authority with the strict order and conformity which he himself had felt bound to observe had rendered him singular for nearly thirty years.[38]

On March 25th, 1689 a licence was issued from Whitehall to Dr. Denis Granville to travel abroad for the benefit of his health,[39] and the King wrote to the sub-dean and chapter informing them that during the dean's absence he should

---

[38] *The Dean of Durham's Reasons for His Withdrawing into France*, Rouen 1689.
[39] *C.S.P.D.*, Warrant Book 34, p. 249.

receive all his emoluments on condition that he found a sufficient substitute.[40] That same year his goods were distrained for debt by the sheriff of Durham, and Sir George Wheler bought his library for £221. Since he refused the oath of allegiance he was deprived of all his preferments on February 1st, 1690. In the December of that year the chapter voted a pension to Mrs. Granville who was left behind in sore distress. In the following February her husband journeyed to England for the last time and obtained a small supply of money. For the rest of his life he lived in poverty in France and he died at last in 1703, loyal to the end.

While he was in Durham Granville evolved in his own mind a scheme of using the cathedral as a training school for the clergy. In the seventeenth century such a thing was unknown. A man went to the university, studied the ancient languages, took his degree and was then thought qualified to study theology for himself. At Oxford or Cambridge he had the society of the learned and the use of the libraries, and the natural student could pursue learning to his heart's content unhampered by syllabuses or examinations. With the select few the system worked tolerably well, it produced the Caroline divines and their learned tomes. But with the man of average or poor intellectual ability it was useless, and there was a large body of clergy who had never been at a university at all. More opportunities for the intellectual advancement of the clergy were needed. (No one, of course, dreamed of anything like devotional training.) Granville was anxious to make the cathedral "the great seminary of young divines for the diocese: and to this end to invite ingenuous young men to be minor canons." Such "according to their seniority, merits and deserts" should have a prior claim to such preferment as the chapter might have at its disposal, and they should further have the right to use the cathedral library. Granville even thought of a scheme for providing lodgings for them in the precincts that they might have the advantages of a collegiate life.

All this we learn from a letter written in 1693 by Sir George

[40] *C.S.P.D.,* King's Letter Book 2, p. 8, March 28th, 1689.

Wheler to the Rev. Hamond Beaumont [41] : " When I last waited on my lord of Durham at Auckland he was pleased to remember him (Granville) at Oxford, when he was an undergraduate, with this advantage that he was then of the same pious and devout temper that he has persevered in ever since." [42]

There were only ten or eleven of the clergy of the diocese who refused to swear allegiance to William and Mary. John Cock, rector of St. Oswald's, Durham and of Gateshead, resigned his preferments.[43] His sermons were published in 1710 with a short memoir by Dr. George Hickes, the nonjuring dean of Worcester. At his desire five hundred copies were distributed among the parishioners of St. Oswald's and St. Nicholas', Durham " as his dying legacy to his parishioners, that when dead he might yet preach to them." He bequeathed a valuable library, to the parish of St. Oswald's, Durham, of several hundred volumes. It was sold in recent years. Thomas Baker [44] was for a long time in great favour with the bishop, but he refused to read the Declaration of Indulgence. In 1690 he retired to his fellowship at St. John's, Cambridge where he was protected by the Earl of Derby. But in 1717 he was dispossessed for refusing the abjuration oath, though he remained in the college until his death in 1740. He was an antiquary and historian of repute. When he resigned his living he wrote to a friend : " I must desire you once more to return my humble thanks to my lord (Crewe) as for all his favours, so particularly that my living has been reserved to me so long : and that my lord may not suffer by it, I have nothing further to desire, only this, that my lord would now dispose of it. I am very sensible of his lordship's favour, and with how much goodness I have been treated in the whole affair, and

[41] Curate of Sedgefield, Official to the Archdeacon of Durham and Rector of Elwick 1672–1701.

[42] Surtees, *Hist. Durham*, I, p. 175.

[43] M.A. Christ's Coll., Camb. Vicar of Doddington, Lincs, 1662–5; Rector of St. Oswald's, Durham, 1665–90. Lecturer of St. Nicholas', Durham, 1675–90. Rector of Gateshead 1687–90.

[44] Durham School. St. John's, Cambridge. M.A. 1681, B.D. 1688. University Preacher 1689. Chaplain to Crewe. Rector of Long Newton 1687–90.

therefore I do now part with it with as much thankfulness as I did receive it. I am not desirous to know my successor : whoever my lord thinks fit to succeed me shall be acceptable to me, and I shall not only be in charity with him but shall have a friendship for him, and if anything further be required of me to make the living more easy to him, I shall be ready to do it upon the least intimation of his lordship's pleasure." [45]

James Hope, Granville's curate at Easington, though he refused the oaths, was left in charge of the parish till the new incumbent was appointed in May 1691. Hope was presented by the constables of Easington on August 10th, 1690 for refusing to pray for William and Mary in the church services. However the constables also reported in his favour that on two different occasions when French privateers attacked the Durham coasts, he had shown great bravery : on one of these occasions two privateers had driven three English ships aground and Hope had been instrumental in saving two of them, and " when all the town except one man forsook him " he continued firing at the French with a fowling piece. The combat of two armed ships against the curate with a fowling-piece deserves an epic poem. When Archdeacon Booth became rector of Easington he employed Hope to collect his tithes and sometimes made use of him as a preacher. But he removed into Yorkshire and there died, and a letter is extant asking the Corporation of the Sons of the Clergy for assistance for his infirm widow aged seventy. [46]

Thomas Davison, vicar of Norton, refused to swear the new oaths of allegiance and in his place Thomas Rudd was appointed. The latter had been curate of Stockton since 1663, and he continued to hold the curacy so as to allow Davison to receive the income of Norton, because he considered him a sufferer for conscience sake. Ralph Grey, curate of All Saints', Newcastle and sometime chaplain to the Bishop of Durham, turned the sermon preached at the coronation of William and Mary into a virulent ballad and had to

[45] Dyer, *Hist. Univ. Camb.*, 1814, II, pp. 250-1. J. H. Overton, *Non-jurors*, 1902, pp. 189-93. Fordyce, *County Palatine of Durham*, I, p. 660.

[46] *Granville*, I, pp. 140-1 n.

answer for it at the King's Bench in October 1690. He refused the oaths, went to France and became a Roman Catholic.[47]   William Richards, lecturer of St. Andrew's, Newcastle, was residing in Newcastle in 1693 as a non-juror.[48] Other non-jurors in the diocese were Jonathan Davison, B.D., lecturer of St. Nicholas', Newcastle, Charles Maddison, vicar of Chester-le-Street, Kendal, curate of Elwick, Luke Mawburn, rector of Crayke, and Johnson of Kellow, but the last-named according to Surtees took the oaths later.

It was expected that John March, vicar of Newcastle would become a non-juror.[49]   He was a high churchman, strongly opposed to nonconformity [50] and was described as " an admirable scholar, a man of strict piety, and a most powerful preacher " who did a great deal to bring Northumberland to some degree of conformity.[51]   In 1689 he found himself engaged in a controversy which was heard of outside the bishopric.   On January 30th, 1689 March preached a sermon before the mayor and corporation in which he advocated passive obedience and non-resistance, called the revolution a rebellion and attacked a pamphlet entitled *An Enquiry into the Measures of Obedience,* written, though March did not know it, by Bishop Burnet.   Burnet's brother, Dr. Thomas Burnet, physician, was a friend of Dr. James Welwood, and after some controversy Welwood published in London, in April of the same year, *A Vindication of the present Great Revolution in England.   In Five Letters between James Welwood, M.D. and Mr. John March, Vicar of Newcastle-upon-Tyne.*   The corporation of Newcastle were paying March £100 a year towards his salary, and on July 15th, 1690 he received notice from the common council that their contribution would be stopped unless he prayed for William

---

[47] *Ambrose Barnes,* p. 433.   *C.S.P.D.,* Greenwich Hospital News Letters 3, No. 76.

[48] Wood, *Ath. Ox.,* II, p. 1072.

[49] Royal Grammar School, Newcastle.   B.A. St. Edmund Hall 1661. M.A. 1664, B.D. 1674.   Vice-Principal St. Edmund Hall 1673.   Vicar of Embleton 1672–9.   Afternoon Lecturer St. Nicholas', Newcastle 1673. Vicar of Newcastle 1679–92.

[50] *Ambrose Barnes,* p. 145.

[51] Mackenzie, *History of Newcastle,* 1827, p. 283.

and Mary by name.[52] In spite of his old loyalty March had taken the oaths by the required date, but it would seem with a bad grace. The day after his death in 1692 the common council ordered that their contribution to the stipend should cease and should not be given to any future vicar.

Very unlike March was Thomas Knaggs, the afternoon lecturer at All Saints', Newcastle, a stout Whig politician. He had a hot controversy with Dr. Henry Atherton, a local physician, a High Churchman with strong views on passive resistance, the author of a work in two parts entitled *The Christian Physician*. By his violent politics Knaggs made for himself many enemies. He must have been a man with but a small sense of humour for he preached a sermon on June 19th, 1689 in which he asked for prayers on behalf of William and Mary and their war against France, and protested against divisions in the Church and against meddling in public affairs. He printed this sermon and thus addressed his parishioners : " A few hot, inconsiderable men among us were very angry after I preached it . . . I lament their malice and pity their ignorance : and seeing wiser men than they were highly satis- fied with the sermon, their peevish reflections shall never trouble me." [53] His opponent, Dr. Atherton, was on Novem- ber 21st, 1693, in the King's Bench, fined £50 and his wife 200 marks for words against the Government.[54]

On July 1st, 1689 the House of Commons had considered the Act of Indemnity. Reference was made to the subject of the Ecclesiastical Commission and it was agreed that Jeffreys, the Earl of Sunderland, the Earl of Huntingdon, Lord Chief Justice Herbert, Sir Robert Wright, Sir Thomas Jenner and the bishops of Durham and Chester should be exempted.[55] Towards the end of the year when William was in Holland, Crewe was introduced to Queen Mary by Dean Tillotson, who had first obtained her leave, and he was graciously received and allowed to kiss her hand. When William returned to England he demurred at this, but Christmas being

[52] *Ambrose Barnes*, p. 438.
[53] *Ibid.*, p. 436.
[54] *Ibid.*, p. 420.
[55] *Luttrell*, I, p. 554.

near and the Queen having interfered, William allowed the bishop to be brought into his presence and to kiss his hand, but when Crewe asked what offence he had committed the King turned away without making any reply.

His name appeared among the thirty-five exceptions in the Bill of Oblivion and amongst the thirty-one exceptions in William's Act of Grace which passed the royal assent on May 23rd, 1690 [56] because their Majesties had so ill an opinion of him.[57] This did him no particular harm but it was a mark of the King's displeasure. Out of this has arisen an incorrect story that he tried to flee the country in consequence. " He did not attempt to go beyond sea till he was excepted out of the Act of Indemnity." [58] " With regard to his attempt to escape, the tradition in Durham some years ago was that he actually hired a Sunderland collier and went over to Holland, but the master of the vessel remonstrated with him and prevailed on him to turn back, instead of going beyond sea." [59] This seems to be a muddled version of Burnet's story about what happened in 1689. Crewe instead of running away spoke in the House of Lords in the debate on the Act of Grace. It was a short speech : " My lords : I am very unfit at any time to speak before your lordships, much more now upon such an occasion as this, when so many thousands have the benefit of this Act of Pardon, and I am to be one of those few that are excepted out of it. I am very far from envying the happiness of those who are thus pardoned : nay, rather I heartily congratulate them upon it, for God forbid that when the King's eye is good mine should be evil. I remember when an Act of this kind was sent down to this House in Treasurer Clifford's time (I then had the honour to sit here); in that Act there was no exception of persons, only crimes were excepted. If the same form had been observed in this, I humbly conceive there would have been more room for justice : I am sure there would have been less reasons for so long a debate as this. My lords, I am very far from going about to justify

[56] Wood, *Life and Times*, III, p. 330.
[57] Birch, *Life of Tillotson*, 1753, p. 149.
[58] *Biographia Britannia*, last edn.
[59] *Ibid.*, 4th edn., 1789.

my own conduct: nay rather I am heartily sorry for it, and beg pardon of Heaven, pardon of all your lordships, and more particularly I ask this reverend prelate's pardon " (here he laid his hand on the Bishop of London's shoulder) " which I have already done in private, and am glad I have an opportunity of doing it again in public before all your lordships. But one great satisfaction to me is that I never had a hand in blood. The truth is, I was hurried on with such a notion of obedience, as I will never be guilty of again, for the greatest king or prince in Christendom. No, my lords, I resolve for the future, to make the laws the standard of my actions, according to the royal example. A golden sentence this indeed, dropped down from the throne above, for I dare be bold to say, 'tis the first time it was ever delivered from that throne. My lords: seeing that this pardon is so necessary for preserving the public peace of this nation, and that you may see how much I am a well-wisher to the good of my own country, rather than I should give any further delay to the passing of it, I will throw myself up for a sacrifice, and am willing the bill should pass."

He then retired and the bill passed and he remained under the exception for some years but nothing else happened. His speech was so applauded that twenty or more of the lords came to him and promised to ask the King to have his name erased. He thanked them for their kindness but said he did not desire them to do so. He used to say privately to his friends that he would have the exception carved on his tombstone. The Earl of Oxford referred in the Court of Requests to the bishop's speech and said that he " spoke like an angel." Lord Macclesfield told Crewe that his speech had saved him. Bishop Bull said that Stillingfleet described the speech as " the most natural piece of oratory he ever heard in his life," and he also said, according to Dr. Sharp, that " it was the best speech he had ever heard in the House." Crewe, however, was quite safe. He had obtained his pardon as we have seen at the end of 1688. The Trotter MS. says that he had a pardon dated a day or two before the time that King William's exceptions took place. So perhaps he had a second. " Judge

Dormer sued it out.[60] Old Wortley produced it in Westminster Hall. Pemberton said, and so did the Attorney-
General, that it was a good pardon." [61]

Danby, now Duke of Leeds, was responsible for placing the
bishop's name on the list of exceptions, and he was accused of
doing it out of revenge. When in 1679 the question was put
in the Lords that Danby should be sent to the Tower, Crewe
with two or three other bishops had refused to vote for him.
Many years afterwards, in 1713 in fact, the bishop and the
Duke of Leeds met on the back stairs of St. James's Palace.
Crewe, who had been with the Queen, was going down and
the duke was going up. " How does your lordship do ? " said
the latter, " I have known you a long time." Quoth the
bishop, " Yes, my lord, you have remembered me since
1679." A full pardon was obtained for Crewe in process of
time by Archbishop Tillotson, partly because of his own
natural kindly disposition and partly at the solicitations of his
friend Dr. William Bates, the Presbyterian minister, who had
been engaged in the bishop's interest.[62]

It is said that as the price of his safety Crewe had to place
no small part of his patronage at the disposal of the Crown,
and in particular the nomination to the prebends of the
cathedral as they became vacant. " He was deprived of the
patronage of the cathedral stalls." [63] " He was forced to
permit the Crown to dispose of, or at least nominate to the
prebends of Durham." [64] Hearne, who was no friend of the
bishop, said : " In King James's reign, he was one of the
Ecclesiastical Commissioners, which was an office that was
very invidious, though perhaps the commissioners went no
farther than the laws of the land and their duty to the King
would justify. Upon the Revolution he was threatened by
King William and his rascally adherents, and to gratify 'em

[60] Robert Dormer 1649–1726. Attorney-General to the Bishop of
Durham 1676. Temporal Chancellor of Durham 1693–1719. Judge of
Common Pleas 1706–26.
[61] *Examination*, p. 75.
[62] Birch, *Life of Tillotson*, p. 150.
[63] Gibbs and Doubleday, *Complete Peerage*, III.
[64] *Biog. Brit.*, last edn. Art. Crewe.

was obliged to dispose of his preferments to such as they recommended." [65]

Such evidence as is available hardly seems to bear out these statements. A State paper of the early part of 1691 referred to the vacancy in the deanery, undoubtedly the best in England, and said, " Here beside the deanery there will be at the King's disposal two good livings, the archdeaconry and a hospital of £800 a year." [66] The deanery was in the King's gift already, and a presentation was made on April 22nd, 1691. The hospital presumably was Sherburn, but Bishop Crewe had conferred this on John Montagu in 1680 and he retained it till his death in 1727. Robert Booth was appointed to the archdeaconry of Durham on May 15th, 1691. Samuel Eyre of Lincoln College, Oxford, was appointed to the third stall on November 10th, 1690. The Lincoln College connection seems to suggest that the Bishop of Durham appointed him. A month previously Crewe wrote to the Rev. James Fynney " My Lord and Lady Burlington (for whom I have a very great service) may be assured that after my Lord Warrington's brother, to whom I am engaged, is served with a prebend of Durham, you shall certainly be the next prebendary there if I live to bestow it." [67] The next appointment to a canonry, however, was that of Theophilus Pickering, who was collated to the fourth stall on June 3rd, 1692, and Fynney had to wait until 1694.

We hear of other interference in the case of two livings in the diocese, but neither of them was in the bishop's gift. On May 27th, 1690 a caveat was entered that no grant should pass concerning the parsonage of Cockfield without notice being given to Christopher Vane Esq. Similarly on August 10th in the following year there was a caveat concerning the rectory of Middleton-in-Teesdale in the county and bishopric of Durham till notice had been given to the Earl of Nottingham. [68] These were probably instances of two great men

---

[65] *Hearne Collections*, Oxf. Hist. Soc., 1884, I, p. 305.
[66] *S. P. Dom.,* King William's Chest, 10, No. 116.
[67] Hunter MSS. Durham Cath. Lib. Letter dated Oct. 13th, 1690.
[68] *C.S.P.D.* Entry Book 73, pp. 9, 12.

using their court influence for the benefit of their friends.
The Crown seems to have claimed the appointment of alms-
men at the cathedral, or as they are called at Durham bedesmen, and a number of petitions for such appointments are
found in the State Papers of William and Anne, but there are
also petitions for similar positions at other cathedrals, as Ely
and Bristol.

Just after the revolution an attempt was made to bring to
an end the palatine and temporal powers of the see of
Durham. It began with an order of the House of Lords
calling for a return of the offices and officers in the various
courts of the Bishopric and for tables of their ancient fees.[69]
There was great opposition from the Bishopric. Two petitions were drawn up to be presented to parliament, though
there is no evidence that they were ever so presented. The
first laid stress on the great antiquity of the palatinate and
urged the convenience of the local courts, where good and
speedy justice could always be obtained without the burden
of a long journey to Westminster. The second set forth that
the suppression of the palatinate courts would be a " manifest
disherison of the people of the county, who were and are born
to the sure use and enjoyment of the laws of the county
(which are always and have been conformable to the laws of
the land) and distributed at their doors, in the courts within
the county, at great ease and little charge." The petitioners
were the tradesmen of Durham who feared the removal of
the courts would be a great blow to their trade.[70]

Crewe caused a statement of " Reasons for continuing the
county palatine of Durham " to be drawn up. The copy
which Hutchinson saw of this was dated February 21st, 1697.
The reasons given were : (1) The county palatine jurisdiction
had existed from William I or at least from Richard I. (2) It
had all the courts of justice and the same royal jurisdiction as
were granted to the Duke of Lancaster by Edward III. (3) It
had enjoyed its privileges, immunities and exemptions, with
only one single intermission, from the seventh year of Edward I

[69] House of Lords MSS. 1689–90, p. 314.
[70] Lapsley, p. 201.

to the reign of Mary when it was restored by Parliament.
The courts of the palatinate had been of great advantage to
the county and city of Durham. (4) All the bishops of
Durham took a solemn oath to maintain the accustomed
rights of the bishopric and county palatine. (5) The present
King when Prince of Orange declared on October 10th, 1688
that he intended, *inter alia,* that the boroughs of England
should return to their ancient prescriptions and charters, and
it was therefore hoped that the county of Durham and the
town corporate should retain their prescribed rights. (6) If in
spite of all this the Government should not think fit to continue the county palatine in the name and person of the
Bishop of Durham : nevertheless it was hoped that the county
would be annexed to the Crown and remain a county palatine
still.[71]

In the end the attempt to do away with the palatine jurisdiction seems to have been dropped. The revolution had been
carried through with surprising ease, but now, many people
were beginning to feel that they had been stampeded into a
change of government, and there was fretful anger on one
side and suspicious hostility on the other. Through 1689 and
1690 efforts were being made in the Bishopric to draw people
from their allegiance to William and Mary, Jacobite papers
were being scattered about, there were stories of gatherings of
disaffected persons, of disturbances here and there, and of
collections made for King James.[72] Lord Lumley wrote to
the Earl of Shaftesbury on June 17th, 1689 complaining that
the commission of the peace and the lieutenancy were not in
the best hands. The country-side was being watched, and
travellers' passes were carefully examined.[73] The new
Government was not very firmly established, and it was no
time for abolishing the ancient magistracies of the palatinate,
a proceeding which could cause bitterly hostile feelings, and
that in a diocese which was on the borders of Scotland. So
the only thing the Government did was to reduce the personal

[71] Hutchinson, I, pp. 695–6. Spearman, p. 38.
[72] *C.S.P.D.* 1689–90, pp. 142, 177, 308.
[73] *C.S.P.D.* 1689–90, *passim.*

powers of the bishop. Richard, Viscount Lumley who had been made Custos Rotulorum of Northumberland in July 1689 [74] was appointed Lord Lieutenant of the county of Durham in the following February.[75] Thus Crewe lost one of his most treasured offices and with it went the Commission of Admiralty.

He had taken the oaths to William and Mary, but with him as with many others it was a bitter thing to do, and his acceptance of the new regime was at the best a grudging one. The Tories were uneasy in their minds and from time to time troubled in their consciences. This was especially the case with the clerical Tories, who at times must have envied the clear consciences of the non-jurors. It was true that James had brought their loyalty to the breaking point, but after all they had preached about obedience their consciences were asking whether there ought to have been a breaking point. But if the Tories were distressed some of the " revolution lords," as they were called, were anything but pleased with the result of their efforts. Ralph Montagu, now Earl of Montagu, Privy Councillor and Master of the Wardrobe, complained to Crewe that King William was " carried about in arms." Aubrey, Earl of Oxford, told the Bishop of Durham that he found the revolution " a rope of sand." These men knew on which side Crewe's real sympathies lay. Even Compton unbent so far as to tell him how he had asked William's permission to entertain Bishop Ken at Fulham, and how the Dutchman had coldly replied at the council table that the Bishop of London had encouraged too many of his enemies. Crewe's reply when Compton told him this was : " That was well worth your pains." [76]

In the days which were never to return Crewe had been in high favour at Court. The Trotter manuscript says of him, " His Court behaviour was such as was the surprise and admiration of all, and soon introduced him with his extraordinary diligence into the favour of the King and his royal

[74] July 8th. *C.S.P.D.*, Warrant Book 34, p. 403.
[75] *C.S.P.D.*, Warrant Book 35, p. 186.
[76] *Examination*, p. 87.

brother. As my lord was in himself agreeable and comely so
his duty and behaviour were so acceptable to His Majesty that
he kept him constantly near his royal person. Their affections
seemed mutual for he was not only admitted to public councils
but in many private consultations and recesses. For some
time none was regarded there but my lord." [77] Now Charles
was dead and James was an exile. Yet Crewe remained
Bishop of Durham, he who has been called " the time serving
favourite of James II." It is by his actions during the short
reign of that king, four years out of the eighty-eight of his
life, that he has been so branded. The accusations against him
may be summed up under three heads—excessive subservience
to James, friendliness towards papists, and final desertion of
the sovereign to whom he had shown such devotion.

Under the first head it may be replied that ever since the
Restoration, and indeed before it, he had been a staunch
royalist, and loyal attachment to the Crown was strong in
multitudes of English hearts. He owed his promotion to the
royal family, the two royal brothers and especially James had
been his personal friends. He belonged to that party in the
Church which most of all disliked puritanism and ultra-
protestantism because they seemed pervaded by heretical and
democratic tendencies. He belonged to a church which had
proclaimed, almost as if it were part of its creed, the supreme
authority of the sovereign. Such a position was maintained
in sermon after sermon and pamphlet after pamphlet.
" Rebellion is as the sin of witchcraft " was a favourite text,
and every January 30th the clergy preached how " hellish
treason " had overcome the martyred King. If the King
showed himself a tyrant they must keep their principles and
suffer at his will, and pray for him to be enlightened, but
active resistance was unthinkable. None were more surprised
than were the seven bishops when James told them their
humble petition was a standard of rebellion. No one was more
surprised than James at the idea that the bishops would even
murmur. The great majority of the Anglican clergy were

[77] *Examination*, p. 107.

surprised and amazed when they saw the nation carried along on a tide of rebellion and most of these were very uncomfortable when that rebellion turned out successful.

As for his friendliness to certain Roman Catholics there was still a Catholic leaven amongst the English people. Though the actual number of openly professing Catholics who went to Mass and confession was small, there were many who had sympathies in that direction, and there were still traces of the old faith to be found amongst the common people. Jacob Bee, the Durham diarist, talked about Corpus Christi and " our Lady day " and there must have been many like him. Since the Reformation the English sovereigns had varied considerably in their religious profession. Henry VIII posed as a Catholic without the Pope, Edward VI was a Protestant, Mary a Roman Catholic, Elizabeth an Anglican of sorts, if she had any religion, James I an Anglican because Presbyterianism seemed to him anti-monarchical, Charles I the only real and convinced Anglican of the lot, Charles II a Deist who died a Catholic. James II would ask himself why he should not hold the faith which was the faith of his fathers for a thousand years, and he was really in earnest about his religion. Crewe and a small number of Anglican divines had less of that hatred of Rome which, increased by the fires of Smithfield and by the Armada, was stirred up annually on the fifth of November, kept at fever heat by hundreds of books and pamphlets, and roused to hysteria and madness by the Popish plot tales. There were Anglican divines in the seventeenth century who in doctrines held a theological position not far removed from that of the Anglo-Catholics to-day. There had always been a small proportion of the English clergy and laity who had vague desires in the way of reunion, who said that the Church of England was not pledged to any uncatholic doctrine, and that the difference between the two churches lay in such matters as the papal power and ecclesiastical discipline. It was said of this period : " The Old Queen Elizabeth Protestants . . . began to grow out of fashion and those of the Laudian stamp were the only men in vogue." [78]   We have no

[78] *Works of the Rev. Samuel Johnson*, London 1710, p. viii.

evidence that Crewe went all the way with these men, but he certainly did not share that morbid horror of Rome that the Puritan party felt: moreover, the Catholics were his royal friend's friends. And to what did his consorting with papists amount? There is the story of his accompanying the papal nuncio to Windsor. He gave a hospitable reception to Bishop Leyburn and seems to have been on friendly terms with him. But he saw the unwisdom of putting Fr. Petre on the council and refused to sit with him. Crewe was a gentleman and, like the King, he believed in religious peace for all. The pity was that few agreed with him.

The third accusation is the most serious because there seemed to be some ground for it. He encouraged the King in his foolish ways and then ratted from the sinking ship. For the first he became an object of abuse to the Whigs and for the second a similar object for the Tories too, even those who made no sacrifices themselves. White Kennet was fairer than most of the Whig writers. He said "The prelates who were most in favour with the King, because he thought them most obsequious to his will, were the Bishops of Durham, Ely and Rochester, and yet hardly one of them would give in to all the following measures of the court." [79] To-day many of us can sympathize with James in his earnest striving to further the cause of his religion. But he was in too much of a hurry. If he had contented himself with his first Declaration of Indulgence all the religious persecution of the eighteenth century might have been avoided: Protestants would have discovered in time that they could live at peace with their Catholic brethren as they did after 1829. But in his hurry he adopted a foolishly aggressive policy. Catholics had served in the army and the position had been winked at. But James called attention to this, flaunted it and brought over Irish regiments in addition, because he wanted an army to put down possible opposition. When he seized Magdalen College for his fellow-Catholics, when he insisted on a savage and uncanonical punishment for Samuel Johnson, who would

[79] *Hist. Eng.*, III, p. 442.

merely have been sent to gaol for sedition to-day, and when he prosecuted the bishops for asking to be excused from reading the declaration which they believed would be a mortal blow to their church, he succeeded in rousing opposition in unexpected quarters.

Now Crewe did all he could to further the King's policy of a general toleration and tried to influence his diocese to support it. He showed himself friendly to individual Catholics. No one to-day would think the worse of him for either of these things. His great mistake was in accepting a seat on the Ecclesiastical Commission. James, though officially head of the Church of England, was a Catholic, and if he had handed over Anglican affairs, such as patronage, to such a body little could have been said. But he made it an ecclesiastical court and attacked Bishop Compton, a dangerous man to attack, as the King would find, and Magdalen College, whereby he alienated the loyal University of Oxford. Crewe sat on it at the King's command and so must bear his responsibility for some of its illegal actions; indeed he afterwards admitted that he had done wrongly. But at last he could go no further. He offered James advice and it was rejected, and he saw that any attempt to influence the King was hopeless. James left England for ever. The Dean of Durham, passionate in his loyalty, followed him; the Bishop of Durham did not. Neither did many others, some of whom like Clarendon had professed their loyalty to the last. A new King came. Crewe disliked the new regime intensely. So did many others, and like many others he submitted to the inevitable, but why he should be singled out for special vituperation it is difficult to see.

CHAPTER VII

IN THE SHADOW

AFTER the revolution Crewe was under a cloud as far as royal favours went, and we only get occasional scraps of information about him. He went down to the Bishopric on July 19th, 1690 and stayed there till September 23rd.[1] It would cause some comment to-day if a bishop stayed in his diocese no more than two months in the year, but Crewe was thought to be very attentive to his episcopal duties. In the same year the office of chancellor and vicar general again became vacant. Mr. William Wilson who had bought it from the Hon. Charles Montagu that year was drowned by the new bridge over the Wear, Prebends' Bridge, on November 27th. Jacob Bee's account is that " Mr. Wilson in the Bailey was drowned Thursday at night as was supposed, and was found the 7th December near Coken Boate, being Sunday, and buried that night in the Nine Altars." [2] Wilson had been a useful man who had acted as steward to Granville, who depended on him to get him out of his financial difficulties and on one occasion wrote to him, " I am not afraid of people's prating that I am governed by *Dean* Wilson." [3] The chancellorship was now the bishop's to dispose of and he appointed another Montagu, but in the very next year James Montagu sold the office for a thousand guineas to Dr. John Brooksbank, who was confirmed in it on September 5th and retained it until his death in 1724.[4]

The appointment to the deanery, vacant by the refusal of Granville to accept the new regime, roused interest in many quarters. It is said to have been offered to Samuel Johnson who refused it as not adequate to his merits.[5] The King con-

---

[1] *Jacob Bee's Diary.* Prebends' Bridge built between 1772 and 1777.
[2] *Ibid.*
[3] March 7th, 1684–5. *Granville,* I, p. 202.
[4] Hutchinson, II, p. 329.
[5] *Zouch's Works,* II, p. 169.

P

sulted some of the leading men at Court, and Lord Falconberg proposed Dr. Thomas Comber, whose claims were supported by the Marquess of Caermarthen and by Tillotson. Comber himself says : " After speaking with the Archbishop and my Lord Nottingham, I did at last accept it." The warrant for the presentation was dated April 22nd, 1691 [6] and he kissed the Queen's hand on May 3rd, was instituted on the 9th of that month and installed in Durham by Dr. Grey on 15th June. He was a Cambridge graduate who had been admitted to deacon's orders at the early age of nineteen. At his living of Stonegrave in Yorkshire, to which he was appointed in 1669, he had shown himself an able and efficient parish priest. East Newton near Helmsley belonged to a Mr. Thornton whom he had converted from Presbyterianism. Comber lived in their house, married their daughter, and his influence on the family is to be seen in Mrs. Alice Thornton's autobiography.[7] He held the living of Thornton in plurality with Stonegrave and a prebend in York Minster, as well as the precentorship. He was a learned man who wrote on liturgical, ecclesiastical, doctrinal and historical subjects, and some of his most important works went through several editions. Thoresby described him as a great antiquary and he is said to have had the knack of getting the esteem of people of very varying views.[8] His influence had been strongly on the side of the opposition to King James, and when in 1687 Bishop Cartwright urged him to persuade the chapter of York to send a loyal address to the King he did exactly the opposite and prevailed on them not to do so. Consequently he was in favour in high quarters and was made chaplain to Princess Anne and to the King and Queen. On becoming dean of Durham he talked about resigning Stonegrave which, however, he retained till the end of his life, and he promised to give up his precentorship also, in spite of the fact that he had financial troubles at the outset, partly because

---

[6] *C.S.P.D.* 1690–1, p. 343.
[7] Surtees Soc.
[8] R. Thoresby, *Diary*, I, p. 165. Overton, *Life in the English Church*, 1885, 1660–1714, p. 90.

DEAN COMBER.

Facing page 214.

considerable arrears were due to him from York and because
at Durham he had to spend large sums on dilapidations, still
an ill-omened word to many clergy. The deanery was in bad
repair and he spent £400 on it, and though £160 had been
allowed him for the purpose the money was never paid. To
add to his annoyances he received very icy letters from his old
friend Granville, who considered Comber as nothing more
than his steward, who would be liable to account for the
revenues of the deanery when the King came back.[9]
Whether Comber found it necessary to be exacting towards
his own debtors we cannot tell, but there was a mysterious
reference to him in a letter dated January 12th, 1695–6 from
D. N. Thynne to John Arnold : " Pray, if it be not too late,
under the article of *Domus mea specus latronum,* put in the
Dean of Durham as well as Worcester." [10]

How thoroughly Crewe was detested by the Whigs is seen
in a newsletter sent to an unknown correspondent in France
on November 17th, 1691, " L'évêque de Durham assiste au
Parlement comme les autres évêques. Il fut même l'autre
jour dans la chambre de la Reyne dans la foule d'une députa-
tion. Sa Majesté fut surprise à voir. Cet évêque qui
s'accommode à tout voudroit bien qu'on luy fît parler du côté
de la Cour à ce que m'a dit l'évêque de Salisbury, mais on le
laisse là pour ce qu'il vaud." [11] A month later he gave the
gossips something else to talk about : he got married, albeit
somewhat late in life. In his young days he was betrothed
to a daughter of Bishop Croft of Hereford, and her marriage
portion, £3,000, had been agreed upon, but she died of
measles just before the time fixed for the wedding. There
was talk at the time that Croft was going to resign the
bishopric out of grief for her loss, " together with a willingness to gratify Bishop Crewe who should have married her." [12]
The statement is in the Verney papers and dated April 14th,
1669, but at that date Crewe was not a bishop and it is diffi-

[9] Comber, *Life of Thomas Comber,* pp. 297, 300, 301. *Autobiography of Mrs. Alice Thornton, passim.*
[10] Downshire MSS., p. 611.
[11] Hist. MSS. Com., Rep. vii. Earl of Denbigh MSS., p. 207.
[12] Hist. MSS. Com., VII. Verney MSS., p. 487.

cult to understand the " willingness to gratify " Crewe, unless there was some idea of his becoming Bishop of Hereford. Croft did not resign and the question therefore did not arise. In 1684 Crewe was paying his addresses to Lady Joanna Thornhill, but without success. In 1691 [13] he was courting Dorothy Forster of Bamburgh, but her parents refused to allow the match because she was too young. She was baptized on September 30th, 1672 so she would be eighteen at the time, usually considered a marriageable age. Crewe himself was fifty-eight. On December 21st, 1691 he married Penelope, the daughter of a well-known loyalist, Sir Philip Frowde of Kent, and the widow of Sir Hugh Tynte.[14] Not much is known about her and her married life seems to have been quite uneventful. She retained the name of her first husband and was known as Lady Tynte until the bishop became Lord Crewe. In 1696 Sir George Wheler published a volume of hymns composed by himself and " adapted to the several hours of prayer and other occasions for the use of a private family." He dedicated the volume to Lady Tynte (or, as he spells it, Tint) " the most virtuous and deserving consort of the Lord Bishop of Durham." He described her as " mistress of most charming conversation," and he referred to her charity in this wise : " At Auckland, the bishop's palace, crowded with poor, sick, lame and diseased neighbours, dispensing cures to each of them, everywhere in Durham her husband's high almoner, dispensing bounty to all that need, displaying her goodness in many a pious domestic and public scene." [15] This volume of hymns was in 1698 bound up with his *Protestant Monastery*, the hymns dedicated to " the Rt. Hon. and Most Excellent the Lady Crewe."

Dean Comber wrote on August 17th, 1692 to the Lord President Caermarthen complaining that in the Bishopric the enemies of the Government were audacious and the friends lukewarm. At the assizes, when a man was tried for wishing confusion to King William, every effort was made to get him

[13] *Examination*, p. 88.
[14] Wood, *Life and Times,* III, p. 379. Luttrell, who calls her " Sir Haswell Tynte's widow." II, p. 326. *Examination*, p. 88.
[15] Zouch, *Works*, II, pp. 170–2.

off. " The judge was solicited by some belonging to the bishop, the jury packed, the King's witnesses baffled by counsel, and neither encouraged by Judge N. (Neville) nor supported by one man on the Bench." King James's health had been openly drunk in the streets " with a reflecting tune " several nights that week, and the bishop had encouraged or at least connived at these proceedings. Comber's grandson said that the bishop never missed any opportunity of doing an ill office to the dean, because he was a supporter of the revolution, but the dean " rose superior to the bishop's malevolence." [16] The cathedral bells being in a very bad condition the dean set on foot a public subscription for a new set, beginning with a handsome donation from himself. In June 1693 an agreement was made with a London bell-founder to cast eight new bells, the total cost to be £300. For some reason or other the bishop refused to give a penny towards it, on which the dean's biographer has the following comment : " From the well-known character of this bishop it is natural to conclude that if those bells had been cast and set up in the reign of James II, and baptized according to the Roman ritual, he would have contributed largely towards the expense of them." [17] It would be difficult to say whether the *odium theologicum* or political hostility most inspired this sentence, but it was Christianity which suffered. Comber's grandson records a similar complaint in 1697, when the fountain belonging to the cathedral chapter needed repair. The dean and canons raised and new cast the cistern, mended the pipes and completely repaired " the house belonging to it," that is the building which enclosed the college water supply. On a similar occasion previously Bishop Cosin had contributed largely, but Crewe refused to give a single farthing.[18] To which it might be replied that Cosin found the whole of the ecclesiastical property in a nearly ruinous condition, but now that most of this dilapidation had been remedied surely the chapter could look after their own property. It would be wearisome to answer all the complaints of the Low Church

[16] Comber, *Life of Thomas Comber*, pp. 308–9, 335.
[17] *Ibid.*, p. 324.
[18] *Ibid.*, p. 354.

Whigs against Crewe; in their eyes he could do nothing right.

It is pleasant to turn from this to note the appointment to canonries of two clergymen who seemed more concerned with their clerical duties and studies than with politics and were a credit to the church of Durham. The first was Theophilus Pickering, who was the seventh son of Sir Gilbert Pickering of Tichmarsh in Northamptonshire, and was a fellow of Sidney Sussex College, Cambridge. He became one of Crewe's chaplains in 1690, and was collated to the fourth stall in 1692, and transferred to the eleventh in February 1705. He was also rector of Gateshead from 1695 to 1705 and of Sedgefield from 1705 to 1711. He had a private income of £1,700 a year which meant that he was a wealthy man for those days, but he expended everything he possessed in hospitality and charity. Amongst his benefactions he gave an organ to Sedgefield church and at the end of his life intended to give a bell to complete a peal of six, but when he died it was found that he had left hardly enough money to bury him and the bell, which had just arrived, had to be returned to the makers at York.

The second was John Smith who was the eldest son of William Smith, rector of Lowther in Westmorland. He received his early education under Christopher Nesse at Bradford in Yorkshire and under Thomas Lawson, a Quaker, and graduated at St. John's College, Cambridge. Ordained in 1680 he became a minor canon of Durham in 1681 and precentor in the following year. In 1686 he accompanied Lord Lansdowne to Madrid as his chaplain and soon after the revolution became chaplain to the Bishop of Durham. He was promoted to the seventh stall in September 1695 and is believed to be the only minor canon of Durham who was ever raised to a major canonry there. He held the rectory of Gateshead for a few months in the year 1695 and in 1704 became rector of Bishopwearmouth. Ralph Thoresby visited the cathedral in 1703 and was received by "the most obliging Dr. Smith," who showed him some of Cosin's MSS.[19]

[19] Thoresby, *Diary*, I, p. 427.

Smith contributed to Gibson's edition of Camden's *Britannia*
much information concerning the diocese of Durham, but his
great work was his edition of Bede, which was published in
1722 in a handsome folio containing all the historical works,
both the Latin text and the Anglo-Saxon translation, with
notes and appendices. But he had not lived to see more than
a portion of the volume in print, for he died at Cambridge
in 1715 and his son George finally saw it through the press.

During the reign of William of Orange the chapter of
Durham found themselves engaged in litigation. There was
an ancient and long continued struggle between the Bishop
of Durham, or his grantees, and the corporation of Newcastle
on the question of the free navigation of the Tyne and the
right of erecting quays and ballast shores on the south side.
It was illegal to throw ballast into the river and so wharves
had to be erected where it might be thrown. (This was the
origin of the Ballast Hills in Newcastle.) The chapter, as
grantees of the bishop, claimed the right to erect a wharf or
ballast quay at Westoe or Jarrow Slake, without the sanction
of the Newcastle corporation. In 1669 the King ordered that
the case should be tried in the Exchequer and after hearing
evidence for six hours the court decided in favour of the
corporation. In 1694 the matter came again before the
Exchequer in the case of " The Mayor and Burgesses of
Newcastle v the Dean and Chapter of Durham and Samuel
Shepherd." Two issues were pleaded; that the defendants
could not erect their intended wharf or quay without the
licence of the mayor and burgesses and that the erection
of such a ballast quay would be detrimental to the river. In
June 1697 a verdict was given on both issues for the plaintiffs
and the court granted a perpetual injunction to stop the
defendants from trying again at either place. On March 17th,
1698 the chapter appealed to the House of Lords, but the
appeal was dismissed on May 7th.[20]

One of the most prominent citizens of Durham during the

---

[20] Bourne, *Newcastle,* 1736, p. 164. Fordyce, *County Palatine of
Durham,* 1857, I, pp. 202–3. Sykes, *Local Records,* I, p. 126. Hutchinson, II, p. 599, where the pleadings are given.

first half of Crewe's episcopate was Sir John Duck, who from a poor butcher's apprentice became a prosperous butcher, a great coal owner and the wealthiest man in the city. In 1680–1 he was mayor of Durham and Crewe made him a justice of the peace that year, much to the annoyance of some of the other justices. In a letter to Gilbert Spearman the bishop asked " Who is that Justice Conyers who refused to sit on the bench with Duck the butcher? " [21] King James made him a baronet in 1687 as a reward for his loyalty to the King's interests. He and his wife were good church people and benefactors of St. Nicholas', Durham; he himself founded Lumley Hospital. Sir John died in 1691 and Lady Duck in 1695. The cathedral authorities were kind to the widow in her last illness and there were sarcastic comments thereon : " Mr. Chancellor Brooksbank wonderfully mortified at my Lady Duck's illness, and Dr. Morton almost killed himself with attending her and preparing her for another world. . . . She died this morning after a month's illness. The landlord (Dr. Morton) had a tedious time as confessor and was called out of bed to see her die. Mr. Chancellor bears it very patiently. It is not known how matters are settled, but the mystery will now be laid open." [22] There are still people incapable of imagining a priest could do his duty to a rich parishioner without ulterior motives.

In 1696 [23] Crewe made a visitation of the chapter. There seems to have been much ill-feeling at the time which the dean " endeavoured to allay, and after divers meetings ordered it " that the trouble was " privately composed," but he complained that " this business cost us £20 in a very dear time and no good was done by it." [24] What the trouble was is not very clear. Certain Articles of Enquiry were issued to " the minor canons, lay clerks, and others the sworn members of the cathedral church," and they were directed to return an answer in writing and signed with their own hands. The questions were :

[21] W. Andrews, *Bygone Durham*, p. 170.
[22] Surtees, *Hist. Durham*, IV, p. 53.
[23] August 25th.
[24] Comber, *Life of T. Comber*, p. 350.

1. Are you careful upon every vacancy in your Quire to recommend such persons as are fit for its services?

2. Is your organist diligent in teaching the choristers and are your service books carefully used and preserved?

3. Is there any person among you who does not duly observe the statutes of this church that are agreeable to the laws of the land, so far as you are respectively concerned therein?

4. Is there anything also concerning the state or government of this cathedral or concerning any member thereof fit to be declared and presented to us at this our visitation?

Thirteen persons signed a brief reply. The first question they answered in the affirmative, and the second also as far as the organist was concerned. The service books, " excepting those belonging to the boys," were carefully used and preserved. To the third and fourth articles they said they had nothing to present.[25]

The Bishop of Durham had voted for the offer of the throne to William and Mary, but he liked them none the better for accepting it. Still Mary was his old master's daughter, and whenever he arrived in London or departed he was accustomed to wait upon her, and when she died he was present at her funeral. He paid similar state visits to William " as much through breeding and common courtesy as the duty of a subject." [26] One can feel sure that he never liked William, and that in his heart of hearts he sympathized with the Jacobites. He was present constantly at Fenwick's trial in 1696 and on the last day of it sat up till three in the morning.[27] In the Lords on December 23rd the third reading of a bill to attaint Sir John Fenwick of high treason was passed by 68 to 61 votes. A protest was signed against the bill on four grounds: (1) that Bills of Attainder were of dangerous consequence to the lives of the subjects; (2) that the evidence was insufficient; (3) that the character of the

[25] Hunter, MSS. Durh. Cath., fol. XI, Nos. 138, 139.
[26] *Examination*, p. 89.
[27] *Memoirs*, p. 33.

witnesses made their evidence suspect and (4) that Fenwick was a man of so little importance that there was no need to proceed to such extremes against him. Forty-one lords signed the protest and amongst them the Bishop of Durham.[28] It was thought in Jacobite circles that he was coming round, and Captain Tempest of Old Durham, a very sturdy partisan of the exiled King, told him that he had orders from James to thank him for his attention to the prisoner and to say that all the past had been forgiven. But Crewe had doubts about Tempest's authority to convey such a message, even if true, and so the captain's efforts proved fruitless.

On November 30th, 1697 died Thomas Lord Crewe, aged seventy-four years, and was buried at Steane. His widow in 1704 married as her third husband Arthur Earl of Torrington, whom she outlived, dying on April 2nd, 1719.[29] By her " practices " the property at Steane had considerably diminished in value; " £3,000 a year was actually lopped off." [30] The writer of the *Memoirs* says that Thomas had cut off the entail about £3,000 a year which belonged to the family.[31] By his brother's death without male issue Nathaniel, as the fourth but eldest surviving brother, succeeded to the title and estates, and he was introduced as a baron into the House of Lords on December 17th and took his seat as such.[32] His is said to have been the first instance in England of the union of a temporal and spiritual peerage, and he was summoned henceforth to Parliament by two writs, one addressed to Nathaniel, Lord Crewe, and the other to Nathaniel, Bishop of Durham.[33] He appeared and voted in either capacity as he pleased and made proxies accordingly.[34] In the journals of the House there is a list of lords who took the oaths on February 10th, 1701. The name of Nathaniel Lord Bishop of Durham is recorded and further down the list Nathaniel

[28] *Protests in the Lords,* 1747, p. 109.
[29] Gibbs and Doubleday, *Complete Peerage,* III, pp. 533-4.
[30] *Examination,* p. 90.
[31] *Memoirs,* p. 33.
[32] *C.S.P.D.,* Will. & Mary, 1697, p. 518.
[33] Cf. MSS. House of Lords 1708-10. Writs of Summons dated April 26th, 1708.
[34] *Examination,* p. 91.

NATHANIEL LORD CREWE.
From the portrait in the Deanery, Durham.

Facing page 222.

Lord Crewe. In the lists of attendance he is sometimes entered as Episcopus Dunelm and D(ominus) Crewe. He seems to have been present in the House with moderate frequency when he was in London and in the earlier years of his membership he had frequently served on committees.

Steane was held from the Crown by a promise of fealty and the rent of a red rose.[35] Henceforth the bishop lived a certain portion of the year at each of his four houses, his " quadruple alliance " as one of his biographers called them, Steane, Newbold Verdon, Auckland and Durham. The bishops of Durham had also a manor house at Darlington close to the river Skerne, and Crewe is said to have been the last of them ever to reside there. Thoresby tells us that it was at a later period turned into a Quaker workhouse.[36]

In the later middle ages there was a constant conflict of jurisdiction between the civil and canon lawyers. Since the Reformation the neglect and ignorance of the canon law had enabled the civil lawyers to increase their grip on the Church. The Bishop of Durham found his officials arrogating to themselves the right of issuing letters dimissory to persons to apply to another bishop for ordination. Here is a letter from Crewe to his chancellor, Dr. Brooksbank :

Arlington West. Jan. 30th, 1698/9.

Mr. Chancellor.

I showed your letter to his Grace of York, who is not at all satisfied with your excuse about Perkins having letters dimissory from your surrogate. I told my Lord Archbishop that I would write for to forbid the granting these letters without my particular approbation : wherein if I cannot be obeyed I will send to such bishops within the province that they would not ordain any persons out of their dioceses without the respective bishops' leave under their own hand. And then the profits, which I doubt are the only reason for granting such letters, will soon fall to the ground. What I write is for

[35] *Life of Edward Montagu,* first Earl of Sandwich, by F. R. Harris, London 1912, p. 10.
[36] Longstaffe, *Hist. Darlington,* 1854, pp. 151, 153.

the good of the church for preservation of our jurisdiction.

I am your very affectionate friend and servant

N. DURESME.[37]

Sir George Wheler was in trouble in the April and May of 1698. At an earlier date he had been accused " by a thankless dependent " of omitting the prayers for the established government. Now " an unworthy personage of his own family " brought a charge of disaffection against " good old Sir George " and made use of " as mean an instrument for so base an end." The unworthy one was Shere, his son-in-law, who accused Wheler of trying to seduce him from his allegiance and to dissuade him from praying for the King in the church service. So the prebendary was arrested, and the Privy Council met several times to discuss what should be done with him.[38] After a time he was released. Crewe and he were great friends; in the following year we have a letter written to him by the bishop from Newbold Verdon.

Sir George Wheler.

I thank you for your kind letter the last post and should have been glad to have seen you before I left Durham. Since my being here I hear that Dr. Comber has taken his leave of you all for a long time. I pray God send him well if he be yet alive. I have forgiven him and I hope he has forgiven you and the rest of his brethren, or else he is unprepared for his great change. We may observe the methods of Providence. God grant we may make a right use of them. The extraordinary pleasantness of the season has kept us here, and will keep us here till the end of next week, and then we shall move for Steane.

My wife and I are your lady's and your

affectionate friends and servants

N. DURESME CREWE.[39]

It will be noticed that the bishop here writes his name with

[37] Hunter MSS., Fol. 8. Letters, Vol. II, No. 85.

[38] Zouch, *Works*, II, pp. 160–1. *C.S.P.D.*, William and Mary, 1698, pp. 58, 234. Surtees, *Hist. Durham*, I, pp. 171–5.

[39] Zouch, II, pp. 175–6.

his double title and spells his secular title with a final *e*. Sir George's wife died in 1703. In 1706 Crewe appointed him to the rectory of Winston and three years later to the important living of Houghton-le-Spring. By his will, dated 1719, Wheler left a chalice to the bishop, " his most honourable patron and benefactor, as an humble and grateful acknowledgement of all his many and great favours conferred upon him above his deserts." If the bishop did not survive him the bequest was to go to Lincoln College, and this was what happened for Sir George Wheler did not die till January 15th, 1724.

The bishop's letter above was dated November 18th, 1699. A week later Dean Comber died at Stonegrave at the age of fifty-five. Things seem not to have been too happy in the cathedral while he was dean. In the following January his successor was appointed in the person of the Hon. John Montagu, fourth son of the Earl of Sandwich and nephew of Bishop Crewe, who had collated him to the mastership of Sherburn Hospital in 1680. In 1683 he became Master of Trinity College, Cambridge, and in the same year prebendary of the fourth stall, which he exchanged for the eleventh in 1692. In 1686 Crewe had made use of him as his commissary for visiting the cathedral chapter and determining an appeal made to him by two of the prebendaries. He held two sittings in the chapter house on July 27th and November 19th of that year and determined the matter in accordance with the bishop's instructions. The deanery, of course, was a Crown appointment, and the warrant for the presentation was issued on December 17th, 1699. On becoming dean Dr. Montagu gave up the headship of Trinity College, Cambridge. " A harmless man," said a scornful young cleric, " if he has meat and clothes and ease he concerns himself little more with the affairs of the world." [40] At any rate he showed no great reforming zeal like that of Granville, nor was he, as far as we know, on bad terms with some of his colleagues as Comber was. He lived in peace and died in 1728 at his house in Bedford Row, London, aged seventy-three years.

[40] *Thomlinson's Diary. North Country Diaries,* I, Surtees Soc., p. 138.

But even with a peaceful dean life cannot always have been very pleasant in the cathedral chapter. In the month in which the new dean was appointed the Rev. Philip Falle was collated to the fourth stall. He was a native of Jersey, of which he wrote a history,[41] and an Oxford man who had held livings in Jersey and in Hertfordshire. At the time of the revolution he was sent by the States of Jersey to bear an address to William and Mary and was by them recommended for a prebend in Durham. It was not given him, however, till 1700 when he was presented to the fourth stall. He had hoped for the eleventh, known as " the golden stall," but Theophilus Pickering had been transferred to that. Falle frequently indulged when in the cathedral pulpit in severe and unjust personal sarcasms against his brother prebendaries, and in consequence was both feared and disliked. After his disappointment in not being promoted to the golden stall [42] he persecuted Crewe with such continual allusions and reflections on his political conduct and his subservience to Court measures that the bishop would never attend cathedral when it was Falle's turn to preach. One instance is particularly recorded in a document in the cathedral library. Falle was ill, or pretended to be so, confined himself to his house, had his knocker tied up, and the pavement before the door littered with straw one morning when it was his turn to preach or find a substitute.

" The bishop who thought himself safe enough from any attack of his adversary for this time, went in full order and dignity to the cathedral, but had scarce taken his place when he saw his old enemy (who had now got him safe in his net) hobbling into his prebendal seat, and at the usual time ascending the pulpit. He chose for his text ' Nathaniel, a man without guile,' and first describing what sort of man was here meant by the expression ' without guile ' he next contrasted the character of the bishop himself under the portraiture of a deceitful man with so many strong strokes that no man could

[41] *An Account of the Isle of Jersey*, London 1694.
[42] He was disappointed again in 1710, when it was given to Fitz-Herbert Adams.

mistake the likeness, but lest they should, concluded his sermon with an apostrophe, ' Was it thou, O Nathaniel, etc.,' which completed his triumph and turned all eyes in the church on the bishop, who sat like a criminal receiving sentence." [43]

The history of the Church of England in the latter part of the seventeenth century is marked by the establishment of societies of various kinds for the increase of religion and morality. The first of such societies is believed to have been established among the clergy of London and Westminster about 1678. Later there began to be formed associations of churchmen united in operation against the prevalent profaneness and debauchery. The first of these Societies for the Reformation of Manners was founded in London in 1692 and led to the formation of similar societies elsewhere. Early in 1699 some of the Northumberland clergy met at Morpeth and agreed to form such a society and, having seen some of the papers of the newly-founded Society for Promoting Christian Knowledge, thought they might profitably correspond with it. [44] In December 1700 a body of twenty keelmen established a Society for the Reformation of Manners in the Sandgate, Newcastle, and agreed in particular to endeavour to put down tippling on Sundays. [45] The object of these societies was to prevent immorality by insisting on a vigorous enforcement of the law. That they did much good in the suppression of vice was admitted by all observers, but on the other hand there was too much encouragement of informers and this roused opposition. Dr. Nathaniel Ellison preached a sermon to the mayor and corporation of Newcastle on " *The Magistrates' Obligation to Punish Vice.*" Clerical societies for mutual edification were also being formed in various places. Archdeacon Booth, who was hoping in 1699 that the Archbishop of Canterbury would command him by letter to form societies of the clergy at his visitation, [46] said in 1700 that the

---

[43] Ex. inform. Mr. Thos. Woodness, Durham; also from Rev. William Baverstock, 1804, Durham Cathedral Library. I am indebted for this reference to Mr. Knight, sub-librarian of the cathedral.

[44] McClure, *A Chapter in English Church History.* Being the Minutes of the S.P.C.K. 1698–1704, London 1888, p. 284.

[45] Sykes, *Local Records,* I, p. 127.

[46] McClure, p. 283.

clergy of the diocese of Durham were anxious to form such and there was nothing wanting but the bishop's countenance which he hoped to obtain.[47] The clergy of the Alnwick deanery were discussing the idea in 1701.[48] The venerable Society for Promoting Christian Knowledge, founded in 1698, has remained to this day and had an early Durham connection, for Archdeacon Morton, Archdeacon Booth and Sir George Wheler were among the early members and Sir William Blackett an early benefactor. Crewe seems to have taken a lukewarm interest in it, for Wheler told Chamberlayne the secretary, that his lordship had taken notice that Dr. Bray's *Apostolic Charity* lacked an imprimatur,[49] and though Booth complained that he had no encouragement to lay before his diocesan the papers of the society and proposed that the Bishop of Chester was the best person to engage him,[50] yet a few months later Wheler told Chamberlayne that he had laid before the bishop the printed accounts and papers, but had not yet thought fit " to press the matter of the society's affairs to him." [51] In August 1701 he reported that Crewe had promised ten guineas towards the expenses of the charter.[52]

The early minutes of the Society for Promoting Christian Knowledge show much correspondence between Chamberlayne, Booth, Wheler, and Ellison of Newcastle. Booth said in 1701, curiously enough in the face of what has already been stated, that they had no Societies for the Reformation of Manners, but if any of the bishops who were members of the S.P.C.K. would write to the Bishop of Durham about them, he does not doubt that he could set up them and the clerical societies in a very few weeks.[53] Wheler thought that all societies should be organized according to ecclesiastical order, they should be parochial, ruri-decanal, archidiaconal, or diocesan. The members should not be too numerous lest

[47] McClure, p. 289.
[48] *Ibid.*, p. 325.
[49] July 2nd, 1700. *Ibid.*, p. 296.
[50] July 22nd, 1700. *Ibid.*, p. 298.
[51] Sept. 14th, 1700. *Ibid.*, p. 302.
[52] *Ibid.*, p. 350.
[53] June 6th, 1701. *Ibid.*, p. 342.

factions arose, and he thought that some of the laity might be gathered in.[54] This appears to refer more particularly to the clerical societies, but a number of people looked askance at these innovations and this may explain why Crewe showed so little enthusiasm for them.

Some account of this movement for social and moral reform at the beginning of the new century can be gathered from the letters sent by various members in the bishopric to the secretary of the Society for Promoting Christian Knowledge. Archdeacon Booth distributed books amongst the Roman Catholics in the hope of converting them and had much reformed Durham by visiting the public houses on Sunday evenings.[55] To the clergy of his archdeaconry he sent copies of certain orders recently issued by the county justices and urged them to be watchful to see that the officers did their duty in suppressing vice. In October 1700 he urged that those who were responsible should set the law vigorously in motion against Catholics and Quakers, and the churchwardens were to act vigorously in cases of wilful absence from church.[56] He was also seeking legal advice about the best way to deal with unqualified persons who taught school, and with people who were not induced to come to church by the statutory fine of one shilling a Sunday : indeed he wanted to know whether he might not proceed against such under the statute which rendered them liable to be mulcted £20 a month.[57]

The bishop took a hand in this reforming process. In the autumn of 1701 Archdeacon Booth told how his diocesan had recently sent for all the constables in the city of Durham and gave them a strict command to preserve good order in the city and to discharge their duty without favour or affection. When he swore in the new mayor he had bidden him to be vigilant in suppressing vice and immorality and to keep a watchful eye over the constables. The Archbishop of Canterbury had heard of this and had promised to write to the Bishop of

[54] March 28th, 1701. *Ibid.,* pp. 327–8.
[55] *Ibid.,* p. 283.
[56] *Ibid.,* pp. 84–5, 289.
[57] *Ibid.,* p. 301.

Durham to thank him for his zeal in promoting a reformation of manners.[58] Booth was vigorously backing up his
bishop. He had obtained a list of public-houses with a view
to suppressing those which were scandalous; he had been
promised the assistance of the mayor and of a wealthy gentleman who had never acted as a justice before, and he had made
a list of honest persons suitable to act as constables.[59] He was
trying to discover a gang of fortune tellers : this, of course,
would come within his duty as a justice. The clergy were to
read royal proclamations and Acts of Parliament[60] against
vice and in particular the Act against adultery was to be read
regularly.[61]

The attempt to force men into the paths of morality might
result, and often did result, as the seventeenth century found
out, in producing an abundance of hypocrites, but in fairness
to the clergy of the diocese of Durham at this time it must be
said that they did not rely by any means entirely on the strong
arm of the law. The letters of Archdeacon Booth and others
to Chamberlayne show us great efforts to instruct people in
better ways. Contributions were raised for a fund to distribute
good books both for the laity and clergy,[62] to establish charity
schools,[63] to provide employment for the poor[64] and to make
arrangements for sermons in neglected churches.[65] The prebends of Durham arranged in the summer of 1700 to visit all
the churches within their jurisdiction, and a group of them
undertook the spiritual oversight of a neglected parish in the
county.[66] Archdeacon Booth tried to arrange for what he
called a clergy feast, the profits of which should go to the
support of the widows and children of the poorer clergy. The
clergy were urged in his visitation to be regular in catechizing
and to ensure that the parents were also present, to have a

[58] McClure, pp. 150, 355, 357.
[59] Ibid., p. 355.
[60] Ibid., p. 289.
[61] Ibid., p. 342.
[62] Ibid., pp. 289, 290, 343.
[63] Ibid., pp. 298, 304, 306, 342.
[64] Ibid., p. 325.
[65] Ibid., p. 315.
[66] Ibid., pp. 289, 315.

particular care for the colliers, whose neglect of religion was grievous, and for persons who lived far from their parish churches.[67]   The archdeacon noted with approval that the Lord's Day was strictly observed in the large towns and that the clergy were not backward in doing their duty.   In one of his letters he said [68] that on the following Sunday he was beginning a monthly celebration of the sacrament in Durham, where they used to have it but twice a year. If the cathedral is referred to it would seem that there had been some slackness since Granville went.[69]   In 1701 Booth said he was trying to get a monthly communion service established throughout his jurisdiction, and he had sent a circular letter to his clergy to cause all young people of the age of sixteen to come every Wednesday and Friday to prepare for their Easter communion and all servants to come on Sundays for the same purpose.[70]

In October 1700 Chamberlayne sent to Booth a copy of a memorial by Dr. Bray representing the state of religion at that time in the American colonies, in the hope that the archdeacon might make use of it to stir up wealthy parishioners. Churchmen were beginning to take thought for their fellow countrymen in our overseas possessions as well as the heathen to be found there.   The Society for the Propagation of the Gospel received its charter on June 16th, 1701 and amongst the earliest members of that corporation were Dr. John Montagu, Archdeacon Booth, Sir George Wheler and Dr. John Smith, now vice-dean.[71]   Crewe however appears to have taken no interest in the new society; his name appears nowhere in its archives.[72]

One more society must be noticed.   In 1709 Mr. Nathaniel Clayton, merchant, and Mr. Deodatus Thirlkeld were the leaders of an effort to establish a local society, the Society of the Sons of the Clergy of the Diocese of Durham.   As first

[67] Ibid., pp. 165–7, 289, 342.
[68] May 3rd, 1700.
[69] Ibid., p. 289.
[70] Ibid., p. 320.
[71] C.S.P.D., 1700–2, p. 358.
[72] Letter to the writer from Mr. J. W. Lyddeker, archivist to the Society.

established it was concerned only with the southern portion of the diocese and its object was to help impecunious clergy and the widows and orphans of the clergy. The first public meeting was held on September 5th that year and a subscription of £5 was raised. A few days later a similar society was formed for Northumberland. The two societies were united in 1725 but the exact relation, if any, between them and the Corporation of the Sons of the Clergy, which received its charter from Charles II in 1678, is not clear. The custom of an annual service in some large church and a special preacher was showing itself in this as in other societies, and so on September 10th, 1711 Prebendary John Smith preached the annual sermon in the parish church of Newcastle.[73]

The last paragraphs show that at this point in its story the church in Durham was showing some increase of life and fervour. As for the Church of England as a whole, ever since the sixteenth century the control of the Church by the state had become more and more deadly, and most of the clergy were content to have it so. The church ceased to have any voice of her own. From 1665 until the end of Charles II's reign the Convocation of York (we are not here concerned with the southern province) met occasionally *pro forma,* did no business and went home again. We read in Bishop Nicolson's diary " May 25th, 1685. York Convocation opened. Bishop of Durham's proxy exhibited his proxy with a protestation: as also did Mr. Beaumont for the archdeaconry. None appeared for Chester or Man, nor any for the chapters of Durham and Carlisle. Adjourned till June 18. On June 18 went to York. Convocation again adjourned." [74] There was a meeting of Convocation in 1687 but no records remain. In 1689 it seems that only four or six members appeared. What was the use? They only came to be prorogued. In 1697-8 the Bishop of Durham nominated three proctors for himself, Dr. John Morton, and the Reverends Charles Neile and John Turner. In 1703-4 the York Convocation returned thanks to Queen Anne for her promise to give her

---

[73] Sykes, *Local Records,* pp. 130–1.
[74] Cumberland and Westmorland Arch. Soc., N.S., I, pp. 30–1.

firstfruits for the augmentation of poor benefices. We do not know whether Crewe was there, but in 1708 a proctor appeared for him at a meeting which was attended by the archbishop, the dean of York and six other members.[75]

Convocation then made no demand on Crewe's services, and he seems now to have taken but a small part in politics, at least we hear little of his attendance in the House of Lords, to say nothing of making speeches there. His name was several times inscribed on protest lists. On March 20th, 1701 the House agreed on an address to the King on the subject of the Partition Treaty, and decided by eighteen votes that the address should not be communicated to the Commons for their concurrence. Twenty-one lords, of whom Crewe was one, signed a protest on the grounds that since the address implied a war for which great supplies would be needed, the Lower House ought to be informed, besides which all other parts of the address were, they held, quite suitable for communication to the Commons. On January 22nd, 1703 the Lords heard counsel on a petition from Robert Squire and John Thompson in relation to an appeal of Thomas, Lord Wharton, and voted that the petition should be dismissed and the two men ordered to answer the appeal. Crewe was one of the eleven members of the House who protested against the decision. On the third reading of an Act for raising recruits for the army and mariners for the navy on March 21st, 1704, the Bishop of Durham joined in a protest, signing his name " Crewe " and not " N. Duresme." [76]

Penelope Crewe died at Steane on March 9th, 1699 in her forty-fourth year and was buried there, and a monumental inscription to her memory was placed in the chapel the following year. The bishop married again on July 23rd, 1700. The bride this time was Dorothy Forster, who was now twenty-seven while the bridegroom was sixty-seven. She was now, as she said herself, " so many years older and by consequence so

[75] *The Records of the Northern Convocation,* Surtees Soc., pp. xcii and 328–9.
[76] *Collection of the Protests of the Lords,* J. E. Thorold Rogers, Vol. I, Oxford 1875.

much wiser and therefore the fitter for his lordship." [77]
She was the daughter of Sir William Forster of Bamburgh
Castle. This Sir William Forster had married Dorothy the
daughter of Sir William Selby of Twizell and of this marriage
there were nine children. William, who died in 1700, was
the eldest, John " of Styford," who died in 1699, the second
and Ferdinando the third of the children. The fifth child was
Frances who married her second cousin, also called Forster,
Thomas Forster of Etherstone, which is about four miles from
Bamburgh, while the ninth was Dorothy who became Lady
Crewe.

Thomas Forster of Etherstone became sheriff of Northumberland and between 1706 and 1710 represented that county
in parliament. Frances and he had fifteen children of whom
two only need be mentioned : Thomas, who became the
General Forster of the rising of 1715, and his sister Dorothy
the heroine of Sir Walter Besant's novel. They were, of
course, nephew and niece of the bishop's wife, but the two
Dorothys have sometimes been confused. There is a portrait
of Dorothy Crewe at Bamburgh and another in the chapter
offices at Durham. She was fair-haired and blue-eyed with
delicate features and a fresh colour and had a pleasant-
tempered expression. She was popularly believed to have
brought a great increase to her husband's already considerable
wealth. Observe the scorn with which Elizabeth Adams wrote
to Sir John Verney on the subject : " I am sorry the Bishop of
Durham's revenues increase upon so sad an account, and
when I see the strange prosperity of some men makes me
wonder, and he is one of them." [78] As a matter of fact it is
doubtful whether Dorothy had much of a portion to bring
to her husband, for her father's estates were very badly
encumbered. Hearne, writing years afterwards, said, " I am
told that Crewe's second wife was sister to Forster the traitor,
that she was the prettiest young woman in England, insomuch
that she was commonly called " pretty Dolly Forster," but that

[77] Nathaniel Lord Crewe by M. C. N. Munro, *Oxford Magazine* 1937,
p. 728.
[78] *Verney Letters of the Eighteenth Century,* ed. Margaret, Lady
Verney, London 1930, I, p. 82.

DOROTHY, LADY CREWE.
From the portrait in the Chapter offices, Durham.

Facing page 234.

she never enjoyed herself after the marriage, but pined away, the bishop being old." [79] One need not dispute her good looks but she was the aunt and not the sister of the Jacobite leader, and if she pined away she took fifteen years about it.

About a fortnight after the marriage, " my Lord Bishop Crewe came from Auckland with his lady, his second wife, and was met with a very great company, both gents, tradesmen and others, besides every street in his way to the castle, the streets and windows clad with people, 'twas almost innumerall, all trades banners were displayed, the mayor and aldermen were there." [80] The banners of the guilds, judging by the arms of the various companies still to be seen in the Guildhall of Durham would add colour to the brilliant procession and civic decorations, while the stately affability of the bishop and the appearance of his bonny bride no doubt contributed to make the day a memorable one in the annals of the city.

Less than a year afterwards a tragedy happened which must have brought great distress to the bishop's wife; her brother was murdered. It was August 22nd, the Newcastle assizes were on and most of the gentry of Northumberland were in the town, among them Ferdinando Forster, then M.P. for Northumberland. The members of the grand jury were gathered that evening in the Black Horse Inn, near the White Cross in Newgate Street,[81] and they were all feeling jovial and convivial when in came Mr. John Fenwick of Rock, singing a song of which the refrain was " Sir John Fenwick's the flower among them," and this seems to have led to an altercation between Fenwick and Forster. The company intervened and the quarrel seemed patched up. But soon after Fenwick had gone, one John Hall of Otterburn arrived and called Forster out of the inn. The latter returned to the company saying that Fenwick had sent him a challenge, whereupon they all trooped out and found the challenger standing in the moonlight by the White Cross. The duel began and in

[79] *Hearne Collections*, Oxf. Hist. Soc., VII, p. 282.
[80] Jacob Bee, *Diary*, August 9th, 1700.
[81] *Monthly Chronicle of North County Lore and Legend*, 1887, I, p. 19.

the course of it Forster slipped and fell on his back whereupon
Fenwick stabbed him to the heart as he lay. There are some
variations of detail, such as that the fight took place next
morning when the two accidentally met,[82] but the main facts
were undisputed and, in spite of the earnest intercession of his
wife, Fenwick was executed at the White Cross, where the
murder had taken place, on September 25th. He was the
owner of Kenton coal mine, and in the fear that the Kenton
and other colliers might attempt a rescue, the gates of the town
were shut during the time of the execution.

King William died on Sunday, March 8th, 1702. One of
Crewe's relatives was deploring the shortness of his reign and
the bishop remarked, " Good truly, I thought it a long one." [83]
On the following Saturday the Princess Anne was proclaimed
in Durham with great rejoicings : the bishop, the chapter, the
mayor and corporation and a great company of people being
present. At a sitting of the Court of Claims Crewe claimed
the right as Bishop of Durham to support the Queen at her
right hand at the coronation, and the claim was allowed.[84]
The supporter on the left hand for this occasion was the
Bishop of Exeter. The bishop's wife as a peeress was
presented to the Queen who declared herself to have a particular regard for her. She even went further and said that
Lady Crewe had an honest face. It was not very gushing ;
she might have given it greater praise without any disregard
for truth. Her husband was to learn that he was not yet to
receive the fullness of Court favour ; when he put in a claim
for the lord-lieutenancy it was refused.

In the times that were past he had been one of the Lent
preachers before the Court for nearly twenty years. In 1704
he was appointed to this office once again : it was told how
the Queen with her own hand had struck the name of the
Bishop of Lichfield out of the list and substituted that of the
Bishop of Durham ; and though the latter begged to be
excused, Anne insisted. Crewe on several occasions showed

[82] Sykes, *Local Records,* I, pp. 127–8.
[83] *Examination,* p. 92.
[84] Luttrell, V, p. 61, April 9th, 1702.

himself diffident about his preaching, but other people praised it. Lord Halifax and others said that his sermon, meaning the one he preached in the Lent of 1704, did him more credit than any one they had ever heard. Lord Bradford and others gave it even more praise, and the Queen personally thanked the preacher. We have unfortunately no means of judging for ourselves. Crewe frequently begged his friends to be watchful after his death lest any works or sermons should be published pretending to be his. So not even the genuine ones were published.[85]

He had a good deal of trouble about preferments. Great men were always asking him to do something for their friends. The Trotter manuscript said he had but few things in his own gift and in these he preferred to be his own master. The editor adds a footnote " Notoriously false. If he compounded, by yielding to the Crown the nomination to his prebends, many of his best gifts were locked up : if the fact was so perhaps Sedgefield, Houghton-le-Spring, Haughton (i.e. Haughton-le-Skerne), Stanhope, Washington and some others were under the same predicament." [86]   But as we have seen there is little or no evidence that either the prebends or the livings were out of his presentation. There is a case in point on the very same page and concerning one of the livings mentioned. The Archbishop of York, the Dean of York, the Earl of Nottingham and the Earl of Guernsey all asked Crewe for the living of Sedgefield for Dr. Finch, and he replied that he hoped they would not be disobliged at his refusal.

In 1703 it came to the bishop's ears that things were in a bad way in the ancient hospital of Sherburn. Dr. Montagu was master, but it was taken for granted that everything could be left to an underling. After the payment of the pensions to the brethren, the wages of the chaplain and some other necessary expenses, the rest of the income fell to the master. Montagu could not be accused of robbing the poor, he was perfectly willing to pay out more that he did, his fault was neglect of duty because he had never realized that it was his

[85] *Examination*, pp. 85–6, 93.
[86] *Examination*, pp. 93–4.

duty. Jacob Bee, the diarist, became poor in his old age and an out pensioner of the hospital, and this is what he has to say about it : " Sherburn House 1702. At Christmas last 1701–2, there was one year's salary due and I got sixteen shillings, and at our Lady-day after there was ten shillings due, and I got five shillings, and that is all I got for £2 10s." [87] In 1703 it appeared that there had been some difficulty in keeping up the numbers of the resident brethren : which shows that life in the hospital must have been the reverse of attractive. The bishop made a visitation and then issued a set of orders and rules for the government of the institution. The brethren were to attend morning and evening prayer and the chaplain was to administer Holy Communion three times a year. Wilful negligence in attendance was to be punished by deductions from allowances, and what was deducted was to be given to the obedient brethren. Serious breaches of rules by the master or his subordinate officials would be dealt with by the bishop. So much for discipline ; the rest of the regulations greatly improved the lot of the in-pensioners, who were to receive more money, more and better food and drink, better provision of bedding, and fuel for individual fires as well as the common fire. All this extra expense was to come out of the master's pocket, and the bishop added " We cannot conclude without doing the present master thus much right and justice, as to let the brethren know, that he is as willing to comply with these statutes and orders as we or you can desire, and that if we had charged more, he would not have thought it too much for such a work of piety and charity." [88] Crewe seems to have settled the affair in a manner which gave satisfaction to all concerned.

Joseph Taylor of the Inner Temple visited Durham in 1705. " The next day after we arrived here," he tells us, " being the 23rd August, which was the thanksgiving day for the success of the Duke of Marlborough in forcing the French lines in Brabant, we had a good opportunity of observing the ecclesiastical grandeur. In the morning the city banners with

[87] *Diary.*
[88] *Collections relating to Sherburn Hospital,* 1771, pp. 199–200.

music before them were carried to the bishop's palace, who came from his country seat on purpose for this solemnity, and attended him to the church door, where the dean and prebends in their habits met him and conducted him to his throne, and the chancellor, Mr. Dormer, being in town that same day, made up the cavalcade. We were entertained at the cathedral with a fine anthem, sung before the Queen at Cambridge, besides other usual performances. . . . There is a temporal chancellor for the law business, who generally comes into town twice a year, attended with a great number of horse, which we saw while we were there, and the bishop seldom travels without a retinue of horse." [89] But church life was not all displays and processions. There was a great deal of serious activity besides, and during these years some very solid work was being done in the direction of what to-day would be called church extension.

The large employers of labour were not unmindful of the spiritual needs of their workpeople, nor indeed were the workpeople unmindful of their own. In 1703 the stewards and workmen belonging to the lead mines adjoining Allenheads built a chapel at that place largely by their own voluntary contributions, Sir William Blackett providing the timber. The following year they built another chapel at Coldcleugh at the head of West Allenwater, near the lead mines. Sir William Blackett built a house at Allenheads, close to the chapel, for the curate in charge, who was maintained chiefly by the workmen's contributions, and an arrangement was made that he should preach on the first Sunday in every month at Coldcleugh and the other Sundays at Allenheads.[90]

When Sir Ambrose Crowley opened his iron works at Winlaton he gathered together a large company of workpeople who came in time to number two thousand souls. In 1705 a chapel of ease was built there, it is believed, on the site of the old St. Anne's chapel which had been destroyed in 1569. The workmen contributed at the rate of half-a-farthing in each shilling of their wages, and the proprietors

[89] Joseph Taylor, *A Journey to Edinburgh*, Edinburgh 1903, pp. 78–9.
[90] Richardson, *Local Historian's Table Book*, 1841, I, p. 335.

gave ten pounds a year, and the money thus raised paid the regular expenses of the chapel and provided an annual income of fifty pounds for the minister. It was a typical eighteenth century church provided with pews, with a gallery at the west end, and a clock turret outside. A pamphlet published in London in 1711 described the building of this church, and by way of a preface contained a letter from Lord Crewe, dated September 23rd, 1710 in which the bishop said that Mr. Jonathan Storey (a prominent local nonconformist) had been very instrumental in this good work.[91] Mr. Storey asked Dr. Nathaniel Ellison of Newcastle, to preach at the opening of the new building, but he refused. Dr. John Smith was also asked but he hesitated and sent to ask the bishop's advice first. There was need for haste for a nonconformist teacher was going to be available the very next Sunday, and if he should be allowed to preach it was feared that covenants might be made between him and the congregation which would effectually cause the loss of some two hundred persons to the Church. There really seemed little fear of this for Storey had applied next to Robert Thomlinson, vicar of Whickham. Ellison had by that time heard that the bishop approved and was quite willing to do anything, but Storey had settled with Thomlinson and would have nobody else.[92]

This Dr. Nathaniel Ellison[93] was vicar of Newcastle, in which town he was a popular preacher: he was also one of the bishop's chaplains. A few of his sermons were printed; one in particular on the subject of Confirmation, preached before the bishop in St. Nicholas', Newcastle, was published in London. When he was made a prebendary of Durham the mayor of Newcastle, Henry Reay, together with the recorder and aldermen, sent a special letter of thanks to the bishop. He seems to have been a man of learning, and made extensive collections of materials for the history of Newcastle

[91] Hutchinson, II, pp. 557–8. Surtees, Durham, II, p. 273.
[92] Thomlinson's Diary, North Country Diaries, I, p. 134.
[93] St. Edmund Hall, Oxford. M.A. 1678, D.D. 1902. Fellow of Corpus Christi College 1682–1721. Archdeacon of Stafford 1686–94. Prebendary of Lichfield. C. of All Saints', Newcastle, 1686–94. Vicar of Newcastle 1694–1721. R. of Whitburn 1704–21. Prebendary of the fifth stall 1712–21.

which Brand saw.[94]   When he died in 1721 he left a number
of his books to Durham cathedral, others to the parish church
of Newcastle and the remainder to his son.

In the south-east corner of the diocese was the little town
of Stockton in which Ralph Thoresby remarked on the
" pretty town house and handsome buildings . . . very prettily
covered with Dutch tiles." [95]   It was growing in importance
and its trade was increasing.   Yet it had only an old chapel
dating from 1234, in a ruinous condition, and too small for
the population.   Thomas Rudd, who had been curate there
since 1663, urged upon his parishioners the necessity of building a new church, and the foundation stone was solemnly laid
on Monday, June 5th, 1710.   A description of the function
has been preserved to us.   After morning prayer Mr. Rudd,
in his surplice, accompanied by four local clergy in their
gowns, followed by the mayor, four aldermen and " a vast
number of people," went to the south-east corner of the site,
and when the stone was well and truly laid recited some
prayers, among which was one used by Laud at the laying of
the first stone of Hammersmith chapel in 1629.   Two years
later (August 21st, 1712) the new church was consecrated by
the Bishop of Durham, the sermon being preached by prebendary John Smith, who referred to that increased zeal for
church-building which was so manifest in Queen Anne's reign.
The church, " a spacious structure of brick," was much
admired at the period when it was built; though few people
admire it to-day.   At a later date galleries were added : the
west gallery and the vestry were built in 1719.   The sum of
£1,625 was raised for the building, of which the bishop gave
£100 : the actual cost was £1,577.[96]   Stockton became a
separate parish in 1713.[97]   Thomas Rudd, after serving the
town nearly fifty years, was inducted to the rectory of Long
Newton in 1712, and George Gibson was made the first vicar
of the new parish.[98]

[94] Bp. Nicholson, *Correspondence*, 1809, I, p. 181. II, p. 463. Ambrose
Barnes, pp. 430, 458.
[95] *Thoresby Diary*, I, p. 142.
[96] See the balance sheet in Fordyce. *County Pal.*, II, p. 160.
[97] Richardson, *Local Historian's Table Book*, I, p. 344.
[98] Surtees, *Hist. Durham*, III, p. 185. Brewster, *Stockton*, p. 120.

Crewe's second marriage had brought upon him a vast amount of financial business. Sir William Forster and his sons had been considerable landowners; the manor and castle of Bamburgh, the townships of Shoreston and Sunderland, the farm known as Bamburgh Friars, the cell of Bamburgh and the tithes, Fleetham in Bamburgh parish, the manor of Blanchland with the monastery, the rectory and monastery of Shotley, the manor of Thornton, houses at Alnwick and elsewhere, Edmund Hills and other lands in the county of Durham, fishing rights on the Tweed and Derwent, and the presentation to four livings and chapelries, all were theirs. In addition the manor of Styford, on the Tyne, near Bywell, was part of the property of William Forster the younger. Altogether the annual value of the family possessions was estimated at £1,314. After the death of Sir William and his sons the property would pass to the co-heirs, Dorothy Lady Crewe and her nephew Thomas Forster, son of her sister Frances. But the property was hopelessly encumbered owing to the careless extravagance of the owners, against whom legal proceedings had begun in 1701, and in 1704 several of the creditors petitioned Chancery to order the sale of the estates for the payment of the accumulated debts, and the court issued a decree accordingly.[99] Lord Crewe gradually bought up all the family property from the Crown for a total sum of £20,697 10s. It took a long time to get everything settled, for the lands were charged with various mortgages and jointures, and when all was paid off there remained only the sum of £1,028 to be divided between his wife and her nephew.[100] The creditors of William Forster exhibited their bills in Chancery in order to have some part of the estate sold for payment of the general debts still remaining, and in July 1708 Lord and Lady Crewe and Thomas Forster sold Styford for £5,500 to John Bacon of Staward. It has been more than once stated that Thomas Forster forfeited all his estates by joining in the " Fifteen." Though in 1705 the court rolls of the manor of Bamburgh spoke of " the Court of

<hr>

[99] *Hist. Northumberland*, VI, p. 329.
[100] *Hist. Northumberland*, I, pp. 165–8.

Nathaniel Lord Crewe and Dorothy his wife and Thomas Forster of Bamburgh, armiger," by 1709 all the property had passed into the hands of his uncle by marriage and he had nothing to forfeit.[101] It was conveyed to Lord Crewe by deed May 15th and 16th, 1709. Bishop Crewe restored Bamburgh castle, which was in a bad state of repair, and by his will the whole Forster property after his death was devoted to charitable purposes.[102]

In 1711 Dorothy Lady Crewe, being the sole survivor of her father's nine children, placed in the chancel of Bamburgh church an inscription to her dear brothers, "William, John and Ferdinand, as the last respect that could be paid them for their true affection to the church, the monarchy, their country and their sister."

In 1705 we hear of Crewe in a new character, new that is to us, that of a match-maker. On May 28th Lady Pye wrote to her cousin Abigail, Harley's sister: "It is said this week will be married our cousin Pye of Farringdon and Mistress Curzon, said to be made by the Bishop of Durham and the young gentleman's own inclinations last year at the Bath, when he was a younger brother."[103] Henry Pye of Farringdon was at this time twenty-two years of age. The bishop had evidently taken a paternal interest in the two young people's love affair.

During the latter part of Queen Anne's reign the Tories being in the royal favour, Crewe came more into prominence. During Dr. Sacheverell's trial in February and March 1710 he was regular in his attendance in the House of Lords and steadfastly opposed the prosecution and all the steps taken to discredit the accused. On March 10th the Earl of Nottingham raised the question, "Whether in impeachment for high crimes and misdemeanours by writing or speaking, the particular words supposed to be criminal are necessary to be expressly specified in such impeachment?" The opinion of the judges was asked and they replied that the grounds of an

[101] *Hist. Northumberland*, I, p. 170.
[102] Gibbs and Doubleday, *Complete Peerage*, III, p. 534.
[103] Welbeck Abbey MSS. IV, p. 186.

impeachment ought to be expressly stated. This was rather a
surprise to them all : it seemed to mean that the impeachment
would have to begin over again, until it was suggested that the
judges' opinion was in accordance with the rules of Westminster Hall rather than the customs of parliament. So next
day they resumed the debate on Nottingham's motion and
decided that in impeachments they were to proceed according
to the laws of the land and the laws and usages of parliaments and appointed a committee to search for precedents.
The committee busied themselves on Monday, March 13th
and next day reported that they had found a parallel case in
Mainwaring's case in the reign of Charles I.[104] A debate
then arose as to whether a question should be put and it was
proposed to adjourn the House, but forty-nine lords including
Crewe voted against the motion which was lost. They next
passed a resolution that it was not necessary that the particular
words should be given and Crewe voted for it.[105]

On the 16th it was proposed " that the Commons have
made good their first article of impeachment against Henry
Sacheverell, D.D." First there was a debate whether the
question should be put. This was carried by 68 to 52. Crewe
was one of the dissentients. It was put and carried and Crewe
was one of those who signed a protest.[106]

There was a discussion about the method of voting. How
could each lord give a plain " Guilty," or " Not guilty," on
the varied articles of the impeachment? Sacheverell might
be thought guilty of some things and not guilty of others.
It was decided that each lord should separately give his verdict
upon the whole impeachment. Again Crewe was one of the
protesters. On March 20th in Westminster Hall sixty-nine
voted the prisoner guilty, while fifty-two, including five
bishops, of whom Crewe was one, voted not guilty. When
the Lord Chancellor cast up the votes and declared the
defendant guilty, forty-seven peers entered a protest, the
Bishop of Durham among them, and thirty-two lords,

[104] Bowyer, *Annals of Queen Anne*, VIII, 1710, pp. 295-7.
[105] *Ibid.*, VIII, p. 299.
[106] Thorold Rogers, *Protests of the Lords*, Vol. I, 1875.

BISHOP CREWE.
From the portrait in University College, Durham.

Facing page 244.

including Crewe, protested against the punishment which was ordered.[107]

There was a widespread feeling in favour of Sacheverell, and the fact that the bishop had voted and protested on his behalf had greatly increased Crewe's popularity in his diocese. When he arrived in the Bishopric a few weeks after the trial the church bells rang in all the towns as he passed and at Elvet Moor just outside Durham he was met by several thousand people. Sir Henry Belasyse, M.P. for Durham, estimated the cavalcade of horsemen alone at five thousand. The gentry and clergy and principal inhabitants of the county of Durham was there, also the guilds with their banners and, as was said, " all who wished well to the bishop and Dr. Sacheverell and all who wished ill to the Government." Mr. Henry Lambton, the Attorney General of the diocese, made a speech expressing the thanks of the county for the bishop's good services to the Church of England and others followed him to the same effect.

Shortly after this there was an episcopal visitation of the cathedral, in the course of which Crewe thus addressed the chapter :

" My brethren of the chapter and clergy, is this another triennial, or rather is it not my primary visitation? So extraordinary has been my reception this year, in this obliging country, justly called the Bishoprick. So that instead of the thirty-sixth year, this may not be improperly styled the first of my translation. Which is enough to set my dial back, and to renew my age, though drawing near that of labour and sorrow, by filling it with joy and exultation. But I pray, my brethren, wherefore is all this? Why? what good have I done more than my duty, if so much? that I should merit this more than double honour, altogether unsought by me, and indeed unthought of, till after I heard of the unanimous and most obliging resolutions of the gentry, clergy and multitudes of others to signalize your approbations of my poor endeavours to serve her sacred Majesty, and the apostolical Church of

---

[107] Bowyer, *Annals of Queen Anne, VIII*, pp. 325-9, 331.

England. A church, which though often struck at in all ages, yet still keeps its ground, holy ground, as being founded on a rock, that is impenetrable and can never be sapped or undermined by its adversaries.

"Neither atheism, deism, nor papism on the one hand, nor the Corahs, Dathans and Abirams, with such like republicans on the other, can ever be able to touch the border of this mount, this rock, without being split and dashed in pieces themselves. While the monarchy with its just prerogatives and the church with its hierarchy and wonted discipline are thus secure from danger, what blessings may we not expect from this most excellent constitution? And more especially under so gracious a Queen, who is the tutelar angel and true Defender of our Faith.

"A Queen who by her exemplary piety, and unparalleled virtue, who by her indefatigable pains and her own particular inspection, labours to convey these blessings safely down to the latest posterity, that they may enjoy the same.

"And now, my brethren, having thus introduced myself here amongst you with this breviate of home occurences, this short narrative of this summer's domestic campaign, I should proceed to that which is more properly the business of the day, expecting your answers to my several articles of enquiry; but your dean being not yet returned, though shortly expected, I shall adjourn this visitation to another day, and because I will not trouble you again with noise and procession, I do appoint it to be at my castle on [108] . . . betwixt the hours of 9 and 12 in the forenoon, and accordingly this visitation is thus adjourned. In the mean time God's blessing light on you all." [109]

In February 1710 Crewe promoted Dr. William Hartwell to the ninth stall in the cathedral, which he exchanged in the following year for the tenth. He was a Lincoln College man and Wood described him as "servant to the Bishop of Durham," [110] which probably means some kind of secretary.

[108] Blank in MS.
[109] *Memoirs*, pp. 31, 32.
[110] Wood, *Life and Times*, III, p. 139.

He was vicar of Stanhope for forty years and died in 1725 in the seventieth year of his age. He seems to have been greatly respected in the diocese. There is a portrait of him in the Town Hall, Durham and in Stanhope rectory, and a long monumental inscription to his memory in Durham cathedral.

CHAPTER VIII

CHURCH LIFE AND PROGRESS DURING CREWE'S
EPISCOPATE

DURING the episcopate of Nathaniel Crewe, especially during
the latter part of it, the church made distinct progress. There
were many difficulties and many adversaries. From 1660 to
1689 church and dissent were at strife. Many churches, if not
standing in ruins, still showed traces of the damage done by
hostile fanaticism in the past, or of long continued neglect,
and large sums had to be spent on repair and redecoration.
Pluralities and absenteeism were the cause of much of the
indifference to religion which was rife in the north county
parishes. Henry Wharton even wrote a *Defence of Pluralities,*
in which he pointed out that some benefices were not worth
more than £5, that many hundreds did not exceed £20, and
some thousands did not exceed £30. All the prebends of
Durham were pluralists. Thus Dr. William Graham, brother
of Richard Viscount Preston, was prebendary of the first stall,
rector of Whickham 1685–1712, Dean of Carlisle 1686–
1704 and Dean of Wells from that date until his death.
Dr. Samuel Eyre of Lincoln College, Oxford, one of Crewe's
chaplains, was made rector of Whitburn in 1686 and prebend
of the third stall in 1690. He held both preferments until
his death on October 23rd, 1694. Dr. James Fynney
succeeded him in his stall, and held it until 1727. From 1690
to 1706 he was rector of Long Newton. From 1706 until
his death in 1724 he was rector of Ryton. In 1695 Henry
Dobson, D.D. of Magdalen College, Oxford was presented
to the sixth stall. He was rector of Boldon from 1692 to
1718, in which year he died in London and was buried in
St. Margaret's, Westminster. Dr. John Bowes, brother of
Sir William Bowes of Streatlam, was collated to the fifth stall
in 1696 and removed to the first in 1712. He was rector
of Elwick 1701–15, and of Bishopwearmouth from 1715 to

1721, in which latter year he died. Robert Offley of Trinity College, Cambridge was for many years chaplain to Crewe. He was presented to the eighth stall in 1704; but he spent most of his life at his rectory of Abinger, in Surrey, where he died and was buried in 1743. Dr. Thomas Eden was another of Crewe's chaplains. He was the son of Sir Robert Eden of West Auckland, and was educated at Trinity Hall, Cambridge. He was a canon of Durham for forty-three years, being in possession of the ninth stall from 1711 to 1715, in which year he exchanged to the seventh. He was rector of Winston from 1709 to 1754, and also of Brancepeth. But pluralism was by no means confined to the prebendaries.

Among the higher placed clergy there were men of considerable intellectual eminence. The prebendaries of Durham were nearly all of them men who had proceeded to the higher theological degrees at the universities : and there were others of the same type who held some of the more important livings. Making a list of all the clergy who held office as incumbents, lecturers or curates during the episcopate of Crewe, and leaving out the prebendaries of the cathedral, who nearly all had livings in the diocese, the present writer has calculated that out of 373 clergy at least 212 were graduates of Oxford, Cambridge or one of the Scottish universities, and at least twenty held higher degrees in divinity or laws, these last being, however, mostly dignitaries. The numbers cannot be asserted to be entirely accurate, the total number given is probably slightly understated, the number of graduates is certainly understated. It is not always easy to find out whether a particular clergyman had a degree or not. But the numbers, imperfect as they are, seem to show that there was a higher standard of education amongst the clergy of the two northern counties than might have been expected. In 1718 Thomlinson noted in his diary about a man named Wood, who was seeking holy orders : " Uncle [1] says the Bishop of Carlisle will scarce ordain him without a degree, especially from this diocese, nor can he recommend a man heartily to preferment

---

[1] John Thomlinson, Rector of Rothbury.

who has not taken a degree." [2] Among the more distinguished of the clergy the following may be noticed here. Of the archdeacons of Northumberland Isaac Basire, who died in 1676, has already been mentioned. His successor was William Turner, D.D., who was a fellow of Trinity College, Oxford and younger brother of Dr. Francis Turner, Bishop of Ely. He was rector of Stanhope,[3] and died in 1685 at the age of about forty-five years. He was followed as archdeacon by John Morton, D.D., one of the canons of Durham. Some held dignities in other dioceses. Cuthbert Chambers, B.D., fellow of Magdalen College, Oxford and rector of Hurworth from 1712 to 1714, was a prebendary of Ripon, where he died and was buried. Samuel Speed, M.A., rector of Whitburn from 1672–5, was a prebendary of Lincoln in 1670 and became a canon of Christ Church, Oxford in 1674. Charles Elstob, M.A., vicar of Merrington from 1676–80, was a prebendary of Canterbury. George Tully, rector of Gateshead 1691–5 and lecturer of St. Nicholas, Newcastle, had been sub-dean of York since 1680. He was described as an eloquent man.

Nicholas Barton, vicar of St. Mary-le-Bow, Durham, 1703–5, became headmaster of Durham Grammar School and died there in 1713. Thomas Rudd, M.A., a pupil of the same school, was headmaster of the Royal Grammar School, Newcastle-on-Tyne for twenty years, 1699–1719. It is told of him that with the backing of Sir Robert Shafto, the recorder, he persuaded the common council of Newcastle to purchase some valuable editions of the classics for the use of the school. In 1719 he returned to Durham as headmaster of the Grammar School and vicar of St. Oswald's. He was also librarian to the dean and chapter and published an edition of *Simeon of Durham*. Richard Parker, Postmaster of Merton College, Oxford, B.A. 1691–2, fellow 1693 and M.A. 1697, was vicar of Ponteland from March to September 1711 and vicar of Embleton 1713–28. He was described as a philologist,[4] and had a reputation as a classical

[2] *North Country Diaries*, I, p. 139.
[3] Wood, *Life and Times*, III, p. 139.
[4] Foster, *Alumni*.

scholar.[5] Francis Woodman or Woodmas, vicar of Bedlington 1696–1719, wrote learned notes on SS. Chrysostom,
Gregory of Nyssa, Basil, Clement of Alexandria and Justin
Martyr. These were never published, but the MSS. are still
in the cathedral library. A mural tablet in Winston church
described Peter Lancaster as "*olim consilarii dein theologi
et demum huius ecclesiæ rector.*" John Balguy, M.A., vicar
of Lamesley 1711–29, was described as "a great preacher and
eminent divine." [6] Thomas Davison, M.A., vicar of Norton
from 1662 to his deprivation in 1690, was some time fellow
of St. John's College, Cambridge. Robert Thornton, M.A.,
the brother-in-law of Dean Comber and rector of Boldon
1691–2, was a fellow of Magdalen College, Oxford.
Dr. Robert Brograve was chaplain to Crewe and succeeded
Dr. William Clagitt at the lectureship of St. Michael's,
Bassingshaw.[7] Samuel Martin, minor canon from 1663–80,
was also vicar of St. Nicholas', Durham and master of the
Grammar School. John Rawlet, B.D., some time lecturer at
St. Nicholas', Newcastle, published some books on theological
subjects and also a volume of *Poetic Miscellanies* in 1687.
Dr. William Cave, rector of Ryton 1676–9, was described
by Ambrose Barnes as a diligent reader in Church history,
and he seems to identify him with the author of *Primitive
Christianity, or the Religion of Ancient Christians in the
First Ages of the Church,* 1672 (dedicated to Bishop Crewe,
then of Oxford), who was vicar of Islington 1662, All-hallows,
Great Thames Street 1679 and Isleworth 1691, and was made
canon of Windsor in 1684,[8] and was a friend and correspondent of Dean Comber. If we referred at length to the clergy
who published sermons, like Richard Werge, M.A., rector of
Gateshead from 1683–7, who published a sermon *The
Trouble and Cure of a Wounded Conscience* in 1685, this
list would be much longer. Perhaps Thomas Dixon, curate
of Whitworth 1662–1703, might be mentioned, since there is

[5] *North Country Diaries*, I, p. 133.
[6] *Chambers Biographical Dictionary.*
[7] Wood, *Life and Times*, III, p. 332. *Fasti*, II, p. 211.
[8] The life in the D.N.B. of this William Cave makes no mention of
Ryton. *Ambrose Barnes*, p. 150 n.

a manuscript volume of his sermons in the cathedral library. John Shaw, B.A., of Queen's College, Oxford was rector of Whalton in 1645 and restored in 1661. In 1662 he was lecturer at St. John's, Newcastle. He published some sermons, one of which, against popery,[9] the corporation of Newcastle published for him. He died and was buried in St. John's, Newcastle, 1689.

There was a great deal of antiquarian and historical learning in the north. Dr. John Smith's edition of *Bede* in the Latin and Anglo-Saxon texts was in preparation during the years with which we are concerned, though his son George Smith did not actually publish it until 1722. Bishop Nicolson of Carlisle noticed in his diary that on December 14th, 1710 Mr. R. Smith of Durham had called upon him and was studying Icelandic. Robert Smith of St. John's College, Cambridge was a relative of Dr. John Smith and it was possible on his account that he was at that time examining what was then called "the Picts Wall."[10] Dr. Hickes the nonjuror published at the Oxford Press between 1703 and 1705 that "stupendous monument of learning and industry," *Linguarum Septentrionalium Thesaurus*. Comber wrote to Hickes, "Yours of November 5th I could not answer till our audit was over. And now I can tell you with satisfaction that upon my proposing your worthy design, the whole body (besides divers other public and private benefactions) cheerfully agreed to encourage your book by making you a present of £20, which I desire you will accept as a testimony how much we value your great and useful pains in restoring the Northern languages and consequently the antiquities writ in these tongues, for which this part of Europe are obliged to you." The Dean adds that he wishes "our MSS. or our company here may invite you down hither." This letter is thus addressed, "For Mrs. Potter at Mr. Boyer's house the

[9] *Origo Protestantium:* Or an Answer to a Popish MS. of N.N.'s London 1677. Dedicated to the Mayor, Recorder, Aldermen and Sheriffs. Another of his publications was: *No Reformation of the Established Religion,* London 1685.
[10] *Transactions Cumberland and Westmorland Arch. Soc.,* N.S., XXXV, pp. 89, 140.

second door on the left hand in Dover Street, London." [11]
Though addressed to Mrs. Potter the letter begins " Dear *Sir* "
and must have been written while Hickes was still in hiding,
that is before 1700, and also before the great work was completed.   It was this interest in antiquities which made the
cathedral library even then begin to be a museum as well.
Sir George Wheler bequeathed to it a cabinet of Greek coins
and medals.   Dean Comber in 1698 persuaded Mr. Morris,
rector of Aldborough to present " many curious medals to
the library."   Christopher Hunter took the degree of
Bachelor of Medicine at St. John's College, Cambridge, in
1698.   After a few years in practice at Stockton he removed
to Durham and began that great work of transcription of the
ancient records of the palatinate to which we owe the great
Hunter collection in the library to-day.   Some of the inscribed
and sculptured Roman stones in the library, particularly those
from Lanchester, came from his collection.

We do not find many curates in the modern sense in the
diocese of Durham at this period.   In the town parishes the
lecturers take their place.   Preaching counted with many
people far more than the sacraments or the prayers, and these
men were primarily preachers; though they might have to
say morning or evening prayer *before* the sermon.   Sometimes
a lectureship was endowed.   Thus at St. Nicholas', Durham,
there was an evening lectureship, the revenue for which came
from a farm at Easington.   Probably the most distinguished
of the evening lecturers at St. Nicholas' Church was John
Cock, vicar of St. Oswald's, who was succeeded in 1690 by
Nicholas Burton, M.A. and he by Henry Porter, M.A.

We hear of John Rawlet, B.D. as a lecturer at St. Nicholas',
Newcastle, and Jonathan Davison, B.D., son of a local alderman, succeeded him in 1686, though he lost his post by
becoming a non-juror.   In 1671 Leonard Shafto was appointed
both forenoon and afternoon lecturer at All Saints', Newcastle.   His duty was to preach on Sunday morning and afternoon and his salary was to be £70.   Nathaniel Ellison was
appointed curate of All Saints' in 1686 at a salary of £130

[11] Letter in possession of the present writer.

per annum, his duty being to preach forenoon and afternoon and to take turns with the Thursday evening lecture.[12] Thomas Knaggs, rector of Merrington 1682–1720, was made afternoon lecturer at All Saints' on December 2nd, 1687,[13] but in 1697 he removed to the rectory of St. Giles-in-the-Fields in London. Then Ralph Emerson succeeded him, at a salary of £80 a year, according to the Town Council Books. In 1698 Leonard Shafto, the son of the morning lecturer of the same name, was appointed morning lecturer at All Saints', Newcastle at a salary of £100 and an additional £10 for a lecture on Thursdays.[14] In 1711 we hear of a sermon at All Saints before the mayor and aldermen by Charles Ward, lecturer there and " an excellent preacher." [15] On July 25th, 1689 Andrew Bates became lecturer of St. John's, Newcastle at a salary of £90 and £10 for his Thursday's turn. He was " a gentleman born of good sound principles " and an excellent parish priest. On the same day the common council appointed William Richards to St. Andrew's at a salary of £20.[16]

Robert Gordon, the Scottish non-juror, who died in 1779, told Bishop Forbes of Ross and Caithness in 1769 that he remembered, when eleven or twelve years of age, he had been in the quire of Durham with a crowd of boys when Lord Crewe was bishop, and he then saw several young people confirmed, but he did not remember that he himself had received that benefit, so he begged Bishop Forbes to supply the defect, which was done next morning in the bishop's bedchamber with only the bishop's wife present beside.[17] This story shows a shocking lack of pastoral care on the part of the clergy responsible for the candidates, and a careless way of administering Confirmation ; a system of things, however, not unusual at the time, as we know from other sources. On the

[12] *Ambrose Barnes*, p. 429.
[13] *Ambrose Barnes*, p. 431.
[14] *Ambrose Barnes*, p. 447.
[15] *Ibid.*, p. 458.
[16] *Ambrose Barnes*, pp. 145, 437.
[17] The Lyon in Mourning, Scottish Hist. Soc., III, 231, quoted in Overton: *The Nonjurors*, 1902, p. 323.

other hand, Dr. Ellison, vicar of Newcastle, preached a sermon before Crewe in St. Nicholas' church in that town, in the course of which he said, " Such is your lordship's pastoral care, that you make not confirmation an appendage to your triennial visitations, but your yearly business in some part or other of your diocese; and this year, particularly, your lordship was pleased to go to many small villages, as well as larger towns. . . . It shows true greatness of mind that your lordship is not exalted by that accession of honour which is devolved upon you, though it be an honour peculiar to yourself, the mitre and coronet scarce having before met together in any other person." [18]

There is no doubt that the ecclesiastical authorities were striving to raise the clergy out of carelessness and slovenliness, which in part certainly were due to the troubled conditions of former years. Granville seems to have had difficulties with most of his curates about keeping rules and rubrics. At Easington and Sedgefield he prescribed that they should say Matins and Evensong daily in the chancel at 6 a.m. and 6 p.m. respectively, except that on all vigils and eves, and on Saturday afternoons Evensong should be said at 3 p.m., and that on Wednesdays and Fridays in Advent and Lent Matins should be said at 9 a.m., and on Rogation days an hour earlier because of the preambulations. They were to preach on all festivals and holy days, and to catechize on Sundays and holy days in the afternoon. The sacrament was to be administered at Christmas, Easter, Ascension and Pentecost, and at least five other times in the year, and no one was to be admitted to communion under the age of sixteen years. In 1679 he issued orders for a monthly communion. The curates were also to instruct people in the rubrics, and to see that all the rubrics were kept and, curiously enough, the King's *Directions to Preachers* were to be read in the congregation at least once a year.[19]   At the archidiaconal visitation of

[18] *Of Confirmation. A Sermon preached before the Rt. Rev. . . . Nathaniel, Lord Crewe.* Published 1701, and dedicated to Crewe.
[19] *Granville*, II, Surtees, pp. 159–61. *Rex Theologus, The Preacher's Guard and Guide*, 1664.

Northumberland at Easter 1684, Isaac Basire, Official of the archdeaconry, issued a number of injunctions. The clergy must be mindful of the duty of catechizing and of presenting schismatics to the authorities. They must say publicly the daily offices, be diligent in the visitation of the sick, at the same time remembering that they also had the care of the whole as well as the sick. They must impress on church-wardens the regular fulfilment of their duties, they must appear regularly at the Easter and Michaelmas visitations, and once a quarter the clergy were to read publicly the Homily against Disobedience and Wilful Rebellion, or else to preach a sermon on the subject.[20] Probably the Rye House plot of 1683 was responsible for the last injunction. On Saturday, April 24th, 1697 the Hon. Robert Booth, Arch-deacon of Durham, and the Rev. Hamond Beaumont, his Official, at Darlington parish church, enjoined a monthly administration of the sacrament and catechizing on every Sunday throughout the year : the catechizing to take the place of the afternoon sermon. They also ordered that the communion table should have rails round it.[21]

Granville was a High Churchman, zealous for the Prayer Book and for obedience to the rubrics. He spoke of " the Blessed Eucharist " [22] and advocated frequent communion. He went to confession himself and heard confessions, though he had some curious ideas about it and set some odd penances, e.g. one of his penitents was told to speak French every day except Sundays and holy days.[23] At Easington on May 3rd, 1682 he urged bowing to the altar.[24] Though he was a high episcopalian, yet when he was abroad he worshipped with the Huguenots, and refused to unchurch them because he held that it was not their fault that they had no bishops.[25]

It has frequently been an accusation against the clergy that

[20] *Granville*, I, pp. 282–3.
[21] Longstaffe, *Darlington*, p. 223.
[22] *Granville*, II, p. 90.
[23] The form used by him in hearing confessions is given *ibid.*, II, pp. 147–52.
[24] *Ibid.*, II, pp. 93–7.
[25] *Ibid.*, pp. 27–36.

they have tended to be over-zealous in asserting their temporal
rights. When these have been perfectly just and legal their
assertion might nevertheless be a cause of offence. Dr. John
Smith while he was rector of Bishopwearmouth from 1704
to 1715 is said to have spent £600 in claiming and recovering
what he believed to be the rights of his parish church. By his
able management the income of the living is said to have been
increased from £300 to £400 per annum.[26] He changed the
old tithe custom of the parish by demanding an additional
agistment tithe or tithe of herbage, sometimes known as the
grazing tithe. He won a decree in favour of his claim and
this affected many other parishes not only in Durham but in
other dioceses. A long account of the case, for example, was
inscribed in the parish registers of Brodsworth in South
Yorkshire. Dr. Grey, his predecessor, had been less aggressive.
At Durham he had always recommended the chapter to keep
to the old rule of Bishop Morton's time in renewing tenants'
leases, namely to be easy with them and to give them every
encouragement. Thus they might avoid the bitterness which
had led to the late unhappy civil wars, of which he himself
had had painful experience, to which also some of the more
rigid clergy had made contribution by the provocation they
gave to the laity.[27]

Very few cases of actual bad conduct seem to have been
recorded against the clergy during this period. An accusation was made against Richard Parker, vicar of Embleton
(1713–28), in the Durham Consistory Court that in October
1714 he had been seen staggering about his parish under the
influence of drink with his parishioners calling after him
" There goes drunken Davy," and he was condemned in costs.
Curiously enough at this very time he was acting on the
commission about the pews in Warkworth church. Probably
the story was not true, for five years later proceedings were
taken against the curate, Alexander Cunningham, who was
accused of insulting and slandering the vicar, in saying that

[26] It is difficult to square this with Ecton's semi-official statement that
the income of the benefice in 1711 was just under £90. *Ecton,* p. 94.
[27] Raine, *North Durham,* p. 333.

he was mad, had been confined for madness, and was a drunkard. Cunningham was also accused of intruding into the parish church and the chapels at Rennington and Rock, dismissing the clerk and putting in another, and taking away the parish register and refusing to return it. Richard Parker is said to have been a friend of Richard Steele and to have written number 474 of the *Spectator*—a paper on the conversation of sporting squires.[28]

It is well known how the Scots prisoners taken at the battle of Dunbar had been herded in the cathedral and to keep themselves warm had made fires of most of the woodwork. Bishop Cosin had spent money lavishly in trying to restore the damage, and his craftsmen had worked hard at the carved work which is the glory of Durham still. Nevertheless in 1705 Joseph Taylor could still see traces of the mischief done fifty years before. Little or nothing seems to have been done after Cosin's time to keep the fabric in good repair, though when on November 20th, 1682 a great wind blew out " one half of the west end of a window in abbey church," [29] which probably means the great west window, we may presume it was restored. In 1693 the eight bells in the great central tower were recast.

Neglect and desolation had caused the prebendal houses also to fall into bad repair and in some cases this state of affairs had not been righted since the Restoration. On December 20th, 1674 there was a very heavy gale and part of the roof of Dr. Brevint's house fell in on the room usually occupied by his daughter, " crushing the very bed flat on the floor." Granville wrote, " We have all, that have been exposed to this west wind, as the houses of this row are, lain in danger of our lives, for the chamber that is fallen seems to us as strong as any standing. . . . I sent out into the College, especially to Bishop Carleton's, whose house is very infirm, to give them notice. And I wish that all that have weak houses would yet leave 'em, the wind, methinks, being not yet allayed." [30]

[28] *Hist. Northumberland*, II, p. 71.
[29] Jacob Bee, *Diary*.
[30] *Denis Granville*, I, pp. 148–50.

Within fifty years after the Restoration, however, all the houses in the college had been repaired and improved, some of them enlarged and some rebuilt.[31] The house of the second stall was rebuilt by Dr. Joseph Naylor and that of the ninth by Sancroft, that of the twelfth by Dr. John Morton, and Dr. John Smith spent £200 in enlarging what Naylor had done. The following story is told of this : " Dr. Morton and Dr. Smith in altering their prebendal houses at Durham (between which stood Dr. Grey's) encroached a little upon his, and the one got a closet and the other a piece of ground from the good old man, who immediately complained to the Body and said he was crucified between two thieves, and expected they would cause these two gentlemen to do him and his successors justice, for he had had so many demands upon him by the needy that he could not expend the money in law which he had appropriated to better uses." [32] Theophilus Pickering altered and improved the house of the eleventh stall, and Philip Falle spent £200 on that of the ninth.

The ancient dormitory was in a ruinous condition, though the roof with its great oak beams still remained. There was built *inside* the dormitory a new house for the fifth stall with its roof underneath and not touching the old roof. The south end of the dormitory was partly removed and " a front door " made, giving access to the college by two flights of steps. Another door opened into the lesser refectory which was made to serve as a dining-room for the new house.[33] Dr. John Bowes, then prebendary of the fifth stall, expended about £1,000 on the work and the chapter allowed him £250 worth of wood for the purpose.

About 1680 Dean Sudbury (1661–84) began to rebuild the old frater or refectory, known in the seventeenth century as the petty canons' hall. He spent some £1,000 or £1,500 on it but died before the work was finished. The building was completed in Dean Granville's time. Sudbury had charged his executors to provide sufficient funds, and this was done by

[31] Cox, *Magna Britannia, sub Durham* where a list is given.
[32] Raine, *North Durham*, p. 333.
[33] Hughes, *Durham Cathedral Library*, 1925, p. xiv.

his heir, Sir John Sudbury. The old dean's purpose had been
to provide housing for a library, and the room has been used
for that purpose ever since.[34] Prebendary Philip Falle presented to this library a collection of sacred music. In 1725
the library was described as " a good handsome room . . . very
well fitted up, but not completely filled with books." Some
ancient stones from Northumberland lay at the entrance to
it. They had been brought from Northumberland by
Dr. Mangey and Dr. Hunter. Lord Harley's chaplain heard
that there were many curious writings amongst their muniments " which my lord could not get a sight of, it being
necessary to have three prebendaries present, and there were
only two at present in the town." [35] Whatever may have been
the regard for the cathedral muniments other documents have
been recklessly destroyed or injured. It is related that during
the first half of the eighteenth century a certain registrar of the
Consistory Court of Durham was in the habit of lighting his
pipe with one of the old wills under his charge, and of glorying
in the deed : " Here goes the testator " was his usual exclama-
tion.[36]

Samuel Pepys possessed a scrap-book in which was his
Calligraphical Collection, consisting of pages or fragments
from MSS. ranging from the eighth to the fifteenth centuries.
Two of these, cut from two MSS. of the Gospels in the
cathedral library, were described as " a present to me from
my most honoured and reverend friends, the dean and
chapter of Durham." There seems evidence that they had
only been lent to him. He certainly never returned them.
The blame really lies with the member of the chapter who
cut them out for him. But old manuscripts were little valued.
The magnificent twelfth century Bible of Bishop Hugo de
Puiset has been shockingly maltreated. The mischief is said
to have been done by the wife or maid of Prebendary Dobson
(1695–1717) " who having his key of the library to go and
play with his child in rainy weather cut out the letters for the
child to play with." [37] Or, as the late Mr. J. Mead Falkner

---

[34] *Hutchinson,* II, p. 344. Sykes, *Local Records,* I, p. 117.
[35] *Hist. MSS. Com.,* Welbeck Abbey MSS., p. 102.
[36] *Notes and Queries,* Series II, February 11th, 1680.
[37] Hutchinson, *Hist. Durham,* II, p. 845 n.

used to tell the story, " cut out the largest illuminated initials from a twelfth century MS. for her children to play with." [38]

Much was done in the way of repairs and enlargements of churches during this period. In the church of St. Mary-le-Bow in Durham there were no services held from 1637 until 1685. On August 29th, 1637 the old arch and steeple had fallen into the street, bringing down with them a great portion of the west end. Other portions had to be pulled down for safety's sake. In 1683 a quite unfounded rumour went round that the church was going to be handed over to the Roman Catholics, so it was determined to restore it and its dilapidated condition was represented to the bishop and chapter. The bishop gave £30, the dean £10, and other sums were raised by subscription and assessment. Altogether the sum of £117 19s. 11d. was expended on repairs and the provision of pews. The church was reopened for service in 1685, but it was not till 1702 that the tower was rebuilt at the expense of the parishioners. [39] The screen was erected by subscription in 1707, and by a legacy of £10 from a Mr. Newhouse, Crewe's arms were carved in the various compartments of the ceiling, where, however, they are no longer to be seen.

The sister church of St. Mary-the-Less, in the South Bailey, remained in a derelict condition. From 1572 to 1742 there was no insitution of a clergyman, " the profits were so small that whoever had the key of the church left him by his predecessor became minister without let or hindrance." In 1681 the sum of £13 was spent on necessary repairs like plastering and glazing, and in 1696 Mr. Smith received £4 10s. for reading prayers in the church for two years and a quarter. [40] The contribution of this parish church to the spiritual life of the city must have been very small indeed.

St. Hilda's, Hartlepool, was a chapelry of the parish of Hart right down to the early nineteenth century. In 1714

[38] J. Mead Falkner in Hughes' *Durham Cathedral Library*, p. xv. A later date for the damage was suggested in a letter by Mr. H. P. Mitchell in *The Times*, Feb. 25th, 1926.

[39] Hunter MSS., *Durham Cathedral Library*, XI, pp. 131-3. Sykes, *Local Records*, I, p. 89.

[40] *Surtees*, IV, p. 45.

S

and 1716 the mayor and burgesses described the church as
ruinous and they obtained a brief in 1719 to collect £1,732 in
order to restore it. The preamble of the brief spoke of the
" general labefactation " of the walls and pillars and described
the chancel as nearly unroofed. Most of the chancel was
ultimately taken down.[41] On September 22nd, 1721 it was
determined that the church should be new flagged, pewed
and whitened. In 1705 a brief was obtained for collecting
throughout the kingdom alms for the repair of Darlington
parish church. The result was disappointing but throws some
light on briefs and their collection. The total sum raised was
£939 10s. 2d., but the expenses amounted to £570 12s. 2d.,
so that the net result to the town was only £368 18s.[42] In
1697 Archdeacon Booth visited Denton chapel and found the
chancel in a state of ruin. Neither the Master and fellows of
Trinity College, Cambridge, who were the impropriators, nor
Sir William Bowes, the farmer of the corn tithes, nor the
vicar of Gainford, who claimed the right to the presentation,
would do anything. Sir Ralph Jenison of Walworth and
Mr. John Hobson of Haughton finally rebuilt it, and in consideration of this charitable deed Jenison was allowed to build
two pews, one for himself and family, and one for his servants,
on the north side of the chancel; and Mr. Hobson one pew
on the south side.[43]

While Dr. John Smith, prebendary of Durham, was rector
of Monkwearmouth between 1704 and 1715 he spent £200
on repairing the chancel. There was a great zeal for galleries
in those days. Sir John Eden erected one in St. Nicholas',
Durham, in 1721. An entry in the registers of St. Hilda's,
South Shields, then a chapelry of the parish of Jarrow, runs :
" Whereas sundry of the masters and mariners of Whitby are
often by their employment obliged to be in Tynemouth
harbour and being then willing (when opportunity invites) to
pay that duty that they owe to God for His great mercies, but
being unwilling to be uneasy to respectable inhabitants in their

[41] *Fordyce*, II, p. 253. *Surtees*, III, p. 116.
[42] Longstaffe, *Hist. Darlington*, 1854, p. 223.
[43] *Surtees*, IV, p. 7.

own seats, they have desired liberty to erect and build a gallery under the furtherest arch save one in the said parochial chapel, at their own proper cost and charges, unto which request, we the minister and chapel wardens and four and twenty do with great willingness consent." This was in 1683. A further gallery was erected at the south end of the " gallery belonging to the masters of Whitby " in 1707, and a third at the east end of the church in 1708. The church since that date has been much altered; in the seventeenth century it was much smaller, and consisted only of a nave and south aisle with an arcade of five bays and no chancel.[44]

In 1694 All Saints' Church, Newcastle, being very ruinous, a cess of £100 was ordered for its repair; but it was not collected that year, and the next year the sum was increased to £150. In April 1704 the vestry discussed building a new gallery between the east and north galleries and no objection was made. In 1712 the gallery at the west end was built, and an organ erected in it. At the north end of this gallery seats were provided for the children of the charity school.[45] In 1710 the common council of Newcastle gave leave to the glassmakers company to erect a gallery at their own charges at the west end of St. Anne's chapel. In the same year the corporation spent over £250 on repairing St. George's porch in St. Nicholas' church.[46] The floor and aisles of St. Andrew's church were flagged in 1707 : hitherto there had been only an earthen floor. The corporation of Newcastle gave £10 towards this.[47] A gallery was built at the west end, at the charge of the parish, in 1711. In 1710 a gallery was erected on the north side of St. John's, and the porch rebuilt.[48] A little before the revolution there had been erected on the Sandhill in front of the Newcastle Exchange, at a cost to the town of nearly £800, a bronze equestrian statue of James II, or as the Common Council Book described it, " a figure of his Majesty in a Roman habit on a capering horse in copper."

[44] Hodgson, *South Shields,* pp. 241–3.
[45] *Ambrose Barnes,* p. 458.
[46] *Ambrose Barnes,* p. 457.
[47] *Ambrose Barnes,* p. 456.
[48] Sykes, *Local Records,* I, pp. 130–2.

During the excitement of the revolution it was thrown into the
Tyne. It was fished out of the water at a later date and the
congregation of All Saints' and St. Andrew's churches asked
for the metal to repair their bells. It was ordered that All
Saints' should have the metal of the horse all except one leg,
which was to be given to St. Andrew's towards casting a new
bell.[49]

Newcastle was a town whose rulers were honourably distinguished by their zeal for the advancement of religion.
Thus the corporation of Trinity House, Newcastle, on January
20th, 1716 ordered that prayers should be read every month
day in their chapel before they proceeded to business, and
that a sermon should be preached every quarter day in the
forenoon. For these duties the chaplain was to be paid £8
a year, with an extra fee of two guineas for a sermon to be
preached on the first Monday of the year.[50] The corporation
of Newcastle was conspicuous for its good works. When
Nathaniel Ellison became vicar of Newcastle in 1694 the
corporation agreed to pay him £80 a year and in addition
£10 a year for a Thursday lecture. In a sermon preached
before the mayor, aldermen and councillors in 1699 Ellison
complimented them on their orders for a stricter observance
of Sunday, and told them that few corporations in the kingdom, if any, contributed so much as they did to churches
and schools. For years past they had given £671 13s. 4d. a
year to churches, and £180 13s. 4d. to schoolmasters and the
chaplain of the gaol.[51] Their charity began at home, but it
went abroad as well. In 1705 they contributed £60 towards
the building of an English church in Rotterdam, and on
July 20th, 1720 they voted £10 towards the building of each
of three churches, at Penrith, Hartlepool and Aberdeen
respectively.[52] There was a proverb in Newcastle that " they
paid nothing for the Way, the Word and the Water," for
the ministers were maintained, the streets paved and the
conduits kept up at the expense of the town.

[49] *Sykes*, I, p. 121.
[50] *Ambrose Barnes*, p. 460.
[51] *The Magistrates Obligation to Punish Vice*. A Sermon to the
Mayor, Aldermen etc. of Newcastle, October 8th, 1699.
[52] *Ambrose Barnes*, pp. 453, 462 n.

The condition of some of the churches in parts of Northumberland was deplorable. Archdeacon Basire in his visitation in 1674 found Hebburn chapel in Bothal parish "most scandalously and dangerously ruinous," the roof split across and propped up with "crutches," the seats upturned and broken; but nothing seems to have been done for many years.[53] Meldon church with broken walls and no roof was not rebuilt till 1736.[54] In 1723 Archdeacon Sharpe found Widdrington chapel in the parish of Woodhorn in a deplorable condition. The one old surplice, the quarto Bible, the Prayer Book, pulpit, font and communion table were described as not fit for use, and there were two old pews.[55] Horton chapel in the same parish was in 1680 presented as "out of repair." At Kirkhaugh in 1682 it was reported that there was no convenient pew in which the minister might read the service and that there was "no pot or flagon for the Communion."[56] A visitation on June 20th, 1707 ordered that the church at Ellingham should be flagged and whitened, and that it should be provided with linen for the communion table, with a decent carpet, and with a flagon and paten, at the expense of the parish. In 1681 the chancel of Newborough chapel in Warden parish was presented as in decay and altogether ruinous. The chapel of Brainshaugh in Shilbottle parish was in 1715 roofless, yet apparently services were held in it occasionally. As late as 1725 the vicar of Norham reported that the church at Branxton was in a sad condition, "not only the decencies but the very necessaries are awanting in it."[57] At Ford the chancel and the churchyard wall were in a ruinous condition, and when George Chalmers became rector in 1689 the church was described as in want of everything necessary for decency and order. In 1725 it was described as "regular and neat, but the chancel wants such decencies as light, whitewashing and flooring."[58] Ilderton

[53] Hodgson, *Hist. Northumberland,* II, ii, p. 130.
[54] *Ibid.,* p. 11.
[55] *Ibid.,* p. 249.
[56] Kirkhaugh Parish Registers.
[57] *Proceedings S.A.N.,* New Series, I, p. 144.
[58] *Ibid.,* p. 145.

parish church was ruinous in 1663 and in 1715 John War-
burton said the only part of it in use was the middle aisle
and that was roofed with turf. Brandon chapel was totally
ruined.[59] The chapel at Cornhill was in bad condition and
without pews or floor. In 1725 Mr. Drake, vicar of Norham,
said of this chapel : " About fifty years ago it had a curate,"
but after his death the vicars of Norham provided a service
every third Sunday in the afternoon.[60] Is it any wonder that
we read such things as " the people turned Dissenters," or
that the whole district was full of them ? In many of these
poor and out of the way parishes the churches had never
recovered from the robbery and devastation of the Reformation.

But we do find an improvement as time goes on. In parish
registers and accounts there are frequent mention of a cess or
assessment levied on the parish for repairs. Thus at Bamburgh on February 2nd, 1676 an assessment was levied of
" two shillings in the pound on land, one shilling on hinds,
sixpence on half-hinds, and tradesmen as they are able," the
proceeds to be used for the repair of the church. There were
other similar assessments in 1680 and 1702 at Bamburgh,[61]
at Felton 1684, and Corbridge 1710 " where the church was
greatly decayed." The chapel at Old Bewick in the parish of
Eglingham was repaired in 1695 at the expense of Ralph
Williamson.[62] George Chalmers in the first few years of his
incumbency at Ford restored the chancel, glazed it, levelled
the floor and rehung the door. An altar was built in 1684
and railed in, and the church bell was sent to Edinburgh to
be refounded.[63] At Bywell St. Peter in 1695 it was agreed
that two cesses of sixpence per plough be laid on the parish
for paving the floor of the church, the one to be gathered on
June 24th, the other on June 29th.[64] There was some correspondence between Archdeacon Basire and Dr. Smith about

[59] *Arch. Ael.* Third Series, XIII, p. 10.
[60] *Proceedings S.A.N.*, New Series, I, p. 143.
[61] *Hist. Northumberland,* I, p. 100.
[62] Sykes, *Local Records,* I, p. 127.
[63] *Hist. Northumberland,* XI, pp. 357-9.
[64] *Hist. Northumberland,* VI, p. 117.

the repair of St. Nicholas' chapel, South Gosforth.[65]   The
lessee of the tithes eventually paid for the repair of the chancel
and the parishioners raised money for the nave.[66]

Not only churches were restored and rebuilt but prebends'
houses and parsonages also. Some of them needed it badly.
When John Thomlinson became vicar of Rothbury in
January 1679 he found the parsonage house uninhabitable,
" for want of a covering to keep it dry," and all the woodwork
was rotten.[67]   Prebendary Robert Grey rebuilt the front of
the rectory house at Bishopwearmouth, which had been much
damaged in the turbulent times.   Dr. John Smith, who succeeded him there, greatly improved the house, and made very
great additions at a cost it is said of £600. Thomas Musgrave
made additions to the rectory of Whitburn.   Thomas Sharp
rebuilt the vicarage of Dalton-le-Dale.   Dr. John Morton
built the parsonage house of Egglescliffe of which he was
rector from 1672 to 1711 ; and while he was rector of Sedgefield (1711–22) he made great improvements there, though
Theophilus Pickering, the previous incumbent, had altered and
improved the house and garden already, as he had also done
at Gateshead while he was rector there from 1697 to
1705.   Dr. William Hartwell was responsible for great
improvements to the rectory house and gardens at Stanhope.
Nathaniel Ellison, vicar of Newcastle-upon-Tyne, in 1694
repaired and enlarged the vicarage in Westgate Street, which
seems to have been in a somewhat dilapidated condition since
the siege of 1644.[68]   James Fynney was rector of Long
Newton from 1690 to 1706 and spent £700 on building a
parsonage there : afterwards, as rector of Ryton (1706–27)
he spent £1,000 on rebuilding the rectory, parts of which
dated back to Elizabeth's time,[69] with suitable outhouses and
high stone walls round the garden and orchard.   Dr. John
Bowes rebuilt the rectory at Elwick.   All the above except
Thomlinson were prebendaries; but there were others who

[65] Bourne, *Newcastle,* 1736, pp. 242–3.
[66] *Arch. Ael.,* Third Series, XIII, p. 12.
[67] Mackenzie, *Northumberland,* 1825, II, p. 61.
[68] Sykes, *Local Records,* I, p. 126.
[69] Fordyce, *County Palatine,* II, p. 669.

were doing the same kind of work. Thomas Nicholson, M.A.,
rebuilt the parsonage house at Stainton where he was incumbent from 1706 to 1749. At Houghton-le-Spring George
Davenport, rector from 1664 to 1677, rebuilt the rectory from
the ground, built the walls round the garden, repaired the outhouses, and added a domestic chapel. In 1702 the dean and
chapter presented Sir George Wheler to the curacy of Whitworth about six miles from Durham. This preferment he held
for five years and during that period he built on it " a convenient house of residence." [70]   Lord Crewe himself was
responsible for repairing, perhaps largely rebuilding, the old
fortress-like vicarage at Redmarshall. Let into the walls of the
modern vicarage, which has superseded it, are two stone slabs,
one bearing the arms of Bishop Crewe, and the other a sundial
with the date 1712, which may possibly be the date of Crewe's
work.

Money was being spent on decorating churches. The
accounts of All Saints', Newcastle, for 1675 show that £8 was
spent on gilding and painting in that year. In February 1685
John Otway, merchant, presented a marble altar to the same
church. By way of a reredos there was a large panel with the
sacred monogram, from which proceeded a cross, above which
was the Hebrew Name of God, surrounded by a golden glory.
Above all there were " representations of three large candles."
On the south side of the sanctuary there was a " prothesis or
credence table." [71]   For some reason or other Protestants
objected strongly to the sacred monogram—the I.H.S. as it is
commonly and wrongly called—to them it was " the Jesuit
symbol." It was considered worth noticing that a plain cross
erected in the village of Esh in 1687 was inscribed with these
letters.[72] Perhaps the fact that there was a Catholic king on
the throne made some of the Anglicans a little more venture-
some. However that may be, the congregation of All Saints'
continued to take pride in the appearance of their church. In
1700 they spent £9 6s. on painting and gilding the font cover
and pulpit. In 1720 the sailors' gallery on the north side was

[70] Zouch, *Works*, II, p. 190.
[71] *Ambrose Barnes*, p. 426.
[72] *Sykes*, I, p. 120.

beautified with four pictures.   At St. John's, Newcastle, in
1710 Robert Percival, pin-maker, beautified the altar at his
own expense, but in 1712 Robert Crow gave a new one.   In
1686 the authorities of St. Nicholas', Newcastle, were presented in the archdeacon's court for not providing a litany
desk and pulpit cloth.   In 1712, however, there was a different
spirit :   the chancel was wainscotted, the altar was " sumptuously adorned," and a carpet, perhaps an altar-cover, was
provided, the carpet alone costing £38.[73]   The churchwardens
of Bywell St. Peter paid " for a table cloth for the communion table, viz. a green carpet 8s., for dyeing the said
carpet and making it, 3s. 6d. for fulling it and wood for the
cushion 2s. 3d."   This was in 1706.   In 1715 they paid a
shilling for mending the King's coat of arms in the church.[74]

In the parish register of St. Nicholas', Durham, there is an
entry that in 1681 John Duck Esq. and Anne, his wife, " out
of their love and kindness to the parish of St. Nicholas have
given a velvet pulpit cloth to be made use of at all times when
sermons are preached."   In 1684 Henry Arrowsmith received
10s. 6d. " for chains for the Ten Commandments," and in
1686 the parish paid £3 6s. 8d. " for the King's arms."   In the
Darlington churchwardens' books occurs the following under
1677 :   " To John Dennis, senior, for writing the Lord's
Prayer and Creed in capital letters, drawing colouring of the
frames and gild :   16s."   At Houghton-le-Spring in 1677
orders were agreed to for an assessment of twenty shillings in
the pound for casting a great bell and making new bell
frames.   The cost was £122 18s. 0½d.[75]   One of the bells at
Sedgefield bears the inscription " Nath. Lord Crewe, Lord
Bishop of Durham.   Anno feriae et mercatus maximae villae
de Sedgefeild restaurationis." [76]

While Prebendary John Smith was rector of Gateshead for
a few months in 1695 he erected choir stalls with his monogram on the end of one and the date of his incumbency on

[73] *Ambrose Barnes,* pp. 457, 458, 462.
[74] Bywell St. Peter Churchwardens' Books.
[75] *Durham Parish Books,* p. 339.
[76] *V.H.D.,* III, p. 341.

another.[77] In 1701–2 the rector and the four and twenty of the parish of Gateshead, finding themselves in arrears with the payments due to Mr. Robert Ellison for the Blue Quarry Spring,[78] ordered that a small and curious ancient bell in their belfry should be presented, by way of settlement of the debt, to Mr. Ellison for the use of Heworth chapel.[79] It is still in use there. A body bearing the name of the four and twenty, or similar title, had considerable influence and authority in several parishes; South Shields, for instance. In 1708 one of the two parish clerks of All Saints', Newcastle, died. At a vestry meeting held on May 23rd, the vicar of Newcastle and the four and twenty being present, it was decided that in future they would only have one parish clerk, and instead they would have a second curate. On January 6th, 1685 the minister and the four and twenty then present, with the churchwardens of Felton, Northumberland, agreed that a cess of 12d. a farm be laid on the parishioners for repairing the church leads, setting up the King's arms and the Ten Commandments and for whitening the church walls.[80]

In St. Nicholas', Durham, in 1684 the congregation paid 4s. 6d. for taking down the organ loft and 2s. 6d. for plastering where the organ loft stood : probably there had been no organ there for many years. Organs were coming into fashion again. The Gateshead churchwardens in 1672 paid £51 to Mr. Roger Preston for making and setting up the organ.[81] About 1676 the corporation of Newcastle contributed £300 towards the erection of the organ in St. Nicholas'. In 1699 they added a trumpet stop, and eleven years later they spent another £200 on the case, and on cleaning and repairing the whole.[82] At Houghton-le-Spring there was an organ, for

[77] Knowles and Boyle, *Vestiges of Old Newcastle,* 1890, p. 147.
[78] Or Greenburn Spring, the upper reaches of the little stream known as Heworth Dene where it nears the Tyne—the Four and Twenty had a lease of it from Robert Ellison for a water supply for the town; R. E. was a Newcastle merchant who had mills and a good deal of land thereabouts.
[79] *Barnes,* p. 452.
[80] Felton Church Registers.
[81] Churchwardens' Books.
[82] Sykes, *Local Records,* I, p. 116.

during 1674 John Hope and his son, the one for tuning and
the other for playing it, received jointly £1 10s. Prebendary
Theophilus Pickering in 1708 gave the organ in a good oak
case, the clock and the gallery and, it is believed, the octagonal
font of black marble [83] to Sedgefield at a cost of £500. We
know the names of the organists of the cathedral; but we even
know the name of one at least of the blowers, for Jacob Bee
in his *Diary,* in his list of deaths has the following note:
"Aug. 1. 1699. George Bullock Bellows Blower in Abbey
Organ, being Lammas." Music in church was not dis-
couraged, though many Puritans disliked it. Ralph Thoresby
visited St. Cuthbert's, Darlington, in 1703 and "was pleased
to find there several young persons met to sing psalms which
they performed very well, with great variety of tunes." [84]

We hear of occasional gifts of communion plate. On
Easter Tuesday, 1676 at the vestry meeting of the parochial
chapel of St Margaret's, Durham, Mr. Samuel Martin, the
minister, presented a silver chalice with the inscription
"*Calix benedictionis Sanctae Margaretae Dunelmensis.
Anno Domini. 1675.*" On the cover were the words "Anno
Domi. 1675." The donor expressed a desire that two new
patens should forthwith be provided by the chapelry.[85] In
1686 Alderman John Hall and his son Jonathan presented
two large silver flagons, and in 1688 Mrs. Mary Fenwick gave
a silver chalice and paten to St. Nicholas', Durham.[86] In
1703 John Spearman of Durham gave a large silver flagon to
Christ Church, Tynemouth,[87] and in 1712 Mrs. Margery
Davison gave a paten to the church at Billingham.[88]
At Norham, however, the churchwardens in 1715 paid
£10 11s. 6d. for a new chalice and paten, and an entry in
the Corbridge Church Book speaks of 2s. 6d. paid for mending
the chalice. In 1670 Sir Gilbert Gerard gave to the chapel
of Greatham hospital a covered cup and paten and a flagon

[83] *Fordyce,* II, p. 333.
[84] Thoresby, *Diary,* I, p. 430.
[85] Vestry Book of St. Margaret's, Durham.
[86] St. Nicholas' Parish Register.
[87] *Hist. Northumberland,* VIII, p. 360.
[88] *Fordyce,* II, p. 309.

of German or Dutch make.[89] At Stockton a chalice and cover were given by William Lee in 1688, and another in 1689 by Thomas Rudd, curate, and Stephen Whitgift, church-warden.[90] A paten was given to the church in 1702 and another in 1711.[91]

In some of the churches the old custom of separating the sexes during service seems to have continued till late in the seventeenth century. It was still the case in Gateshead parish church in 1684 [92] and the gallery there seems to have been occupied by men only. At St. Oswald's, Durham, also the sexes were kept apart, but pews were being granted to individuals and their families and the old system was dis-appearing. At the beginning of 1685 it was decided to erect new seats in the chancel of St. Mary's, Gateshead. The rector, Richard Werge, covenanted not to make any private advan-tage by letting or disposing of these : they were to be " for the public and common use and advantage of the parish-ioners." The accounts for these seats include the items " turning the ball, tin sockets, iron work and the gilding of a candlestick." [93] Private pew-owners seem to have paid for the erection of their pews. Thus Francis Cornforth at the beginning of 1696 paid 8s. " for building his pew." The pews seem to have been liable to forfeiture if the owner ceased to attend church, for in 1706 it was agreed that some of the Gateshead pew-holders might have their seats again if they returned to church, and the substituted persons would then have their money back. By the direction of Sir Richard Lloyd, Official of the Bishop of Durham, the list of pew-holders of St. Hilda's, South Shields, was drawn up in December 1682 by the minister, churchwardens and some of the select vestry. In the church of St. Nicholas, Durham, the mayor and aldermen had seats on each side of the east end of the nave. Adjoining the magistrates' seats were those of the mercers' company, provided by John King in 1678, and

---

[89] *V.H.D.*, III, p. 243.
[90] Or did they only provide it?
[91] V.H.D., III, p. 362.
[92] Accounts Book.
[93] *Ambrose Barnes*, p. 426.

further enlarged and ornamented at the expense of William Grierson in 1698. In the books of the mercers' company of Durham, under date January 5th, 1698, there is a memorandum of an order for a pew to be erected in St. Nicholas' church for the apprentices to sit in, at the discretion of the aldermen, the cost not to exceed fifty shillings.

In 1714 the vicar-general of the diocese appointed Joseph Nicholson, vicar of Whittingham, Richard Parker, vicar of Embleton and Christopher Laidman, as a commission to assign the pews in a gallery recently erected in Warkworth church. Their award was dated November 23rd, 1714. Five years later another commission was appointed consisting of John Thomlinson, Joseph Nicholson and Mark Forster, who drew up an account of all the pews in the body of the church from the choir to the font.[94] In 1721 the minister and churchwardens of Corbridge gave leave to Thomas Reed of Aydon Whitehouse, with his brothers-in-law if they thought fit to join in the expense, to erect a pew on the east side of the north porch.[95]

Denis Granville complained more than once of the way the cathedral was treated. It was a common thoroughfare and people carried burdens through it. Even on Sunday and in the time of service they were walking about the church and making a noise. Boys and young men played rowdily in the cloisters on Sunday afternoons, and on the weekdays in the church itself. On February 11th, 1681 the dean sent some boys to the house of correction for playing on Sunday in the cloisters and playing cards on the communion table. Neither do the clergy appear to have had much sense of reverence. The petty canons could at times be seen sitting on their desks with their backs to the choir. They walked abroad, even to church, in their " studying gowns," and sometimes appeared in dirty and ragged surplices. Mr. Francis Blakeston, vicar of Aycliffe since 1679 and probably still a minor canon, one day felled Richardson, the porter, in the middle of the choir with his staff. Dr. Thomas Smith and Dr. Brevint backed

[94] *Hist. Northumberland*, V, p. 191.
[95] Corbridge Church Books.

Granville in insisting that notice should be taken of this conduct, which rather suggests that some people saw no reason to
do so. The result was that on February 12th, 1681, at the
order of the chapter, Blakeston was made to acknowledge his
fault publicly at the time of divine service. The singing men
seldom wore their gowns under their surplices, and the surplices themselves, in the case of both men and boys, were " so
nasty and dirty as to give offence," while choirmen and boys
alike were guilty of lolling about, sleeping, laughing and
gabbling the service.[96] On June 16th, 1686 Roger Blakeston,
one of the vergers, was made to profess publicly his sorrow for
dishonouring God and the cathedral by drunkenness.[97]

Lord Keeper Guildford, on circuit in the north, visited
York and Durham. He noted in York Minster that " the
gentry affect to walk there to see and to be seen : and the like
custom is used at Durham." [98] Before the sermon people
were accustomed to crowd and push their way up to the
lectern and as soon as the sermon was over they went out.
There was an official dog-whipper, and in the burial register
of St. Mary-le-Bow it is recorded, " Brian Pearson, the Abbey
dog-whipper, buried 6th April, 1722." Complaints were made
that the beadles made no attempt to keep dogs out. Nay, even
beasts were fed on Palace Green, and on occasion wandered
into the church. Outside the building boys persecuted people
for spur money, and by their insolence frightened the timid
from church, and women used the churchyard as a drying
ground for linen.[99]

Among the Granville papers there is a receipt from the
dean to Robert Delaval, who was mayor of Durham from
1686–9, for altar plate lent for the use of the cathedral at the
order of the Bishop of Durham. One basin, two candlesticks,
two flagons, two chalices and two patens were on loan, all of
silver, until such time as the altar plate belonging to the
cathedral of Durham should be changed, and then these were

[96] *Granville*, I, p. 144.
[97] *Granville*, II, p. 135.
[98] North, *Lives of the Norths*, I, p. 174.
[99] *Granville*, II, pp. 161–3.

to be delivered back to Robert Delaval or such person as the bishop should appoint, safe, whole and in good condition as when received. The meaning is obscure but apparently the cathedral authorities intended sooner or later to get a set of altar vessels of better quality than those which had been in use and meanwhile had borrowed these from the corporation; but it was odd that the corporation should have them to lend.

The registers and churchwardens' books of the various parishes show some curious features in church life and customs. The following quaint entry in the registers of Bamburgh tells of a Confirmation held by Crewe in the church there on July 22nd, 1676 when eleven males and three females were confirmed: " Mem : y^t ye most Rev'end father in God did honour Thos. Davison, then presbyter of Bamb· with his attendance and acceptance of a glass of sack, syder and March beer *in honorem parochiae dictae*." The Gateshead books have the following: " 1693–4. Paid Robert Taylor for inviting the clergy to dine with the bishop 1s. Expenses on entertaining the bishop £7 17s." In 1708 " For sweetmeats to entertain the Bishop of Durham 5s." Similarly, the church books of St. Nicholas', Durham, have: " At September 1679 bishop's visitation, in entertainments to the officers of the church, ministers and others 15s." [100] In 1695 at St. Nicholas', Newcastle, the cost of providing " Maccrorones for the bishop's entertainment " was 9d.[101] The refreshments provided for visiting clergy at times would hardly meet with the approbation of modern teetotallers. Take, for example, the following from the churchwardens' books of Darlington : 1675, " For a quart of claret when Mr. Neville preached "; 1677, " For a quart of sack for the minister that came from Westmorland 2s. 6d."; 1690, " A bottle of hock to Parson Tong when he preached." This is almost certainly the Rev. John Tong who was rector of Brancepeth from 1691 till 1727. 1691, " To the parson of Bishopston when he preached one dozen of ale 1s."

We frequently find surplices provided for the parish clerks

[100] *Durham Parish Books,* Surtees Soc., p. 246.
[101] *Ambrose Barnes,* p. 446.

until late on in the seventeenth century: in St. Nicholas', Durham, for example, as late as 1679.[102] Both surplices and hoods seem to have been provided for the clergy, and the parish books enlighten us both as to the material and cost. At Gateshead in 1706 a new hood for the rector, Leonard Shafto, M.A., cost £2 2s. 9d.[103] We have a series of similar entries in the books of St. Nicholas', Durham: 1674–75, " For a new surplice, being ten yards of fine cloth at 2s. 6d. a yard £1 5s. For making, 5s."; 1677–8, " For a new surplice of holland and for making £1 15s. 11d." In 1678–9 repairs were necessary, and we read, " For the minister's and clerk's surplices necks lining, and new cloth for the same 1s. 4d." In 1683–4 we have a more extended account:

" To Robert Johnson for making the hood 3s. 6d.

To Mr. Paxton for calico for a new surplice £1 3s. 9d.

To Mr. Hutchinson for serge for the hood 13s.

To Mr. Morland for the taffety for the lining 10s. 3d.

For the surplice making 7s. 6d,"

while for the year ending April 1697 we have " For silk and making a hood 17s. 6d." [104]

Numerous other quaint entries throw light on parochial life and responsibilities. " For a winding sheet for old widow Longstaffe 1s. 6d." " For two going for the King's touch 1d." [105] " Given the Archbishop Sames (Samos) in Greece, having a commission from the King, 5s." [106] 1674–5, " Paid to Nicholas Stout's wife for twelve burthen of rushes 4s." " For dressing the church against Whitsuntide 1s. 6d." 1684–5, " For carrying rubbish out of the church by the Lord Bishop's order 5s." " To Stephen Taylor for flagging by my Lord Bishop's order £6 7s. 11d." [107] 1694, " Given to a poor Scotch minister at the request of ours for throwing snow off the leads 3s." This was at All Saints', Newcastle, and in the books are a number of items relating to heads of foxes,

[102] *Durham Parish Books*, p. 79.
[103] Churchwardens' Book.
[104] *Durham Parish Books*, pp. 235, 243, 252, 261.
[105] Darlington, 1675.
[106] Darlington, 1678.
[107] St. Nicholas', Durham.

badgers, otters and foumarts (i.e. polecats) placed on the church door.[108] At Bywell St. Peter the churchwardens paid 8d. for one brock and one " fourmert's " head.[109] At Bishopwearmouth John Knaggs was paid four shillings " for whipping the dogs." This was in 1663; but in subsequent years his duties including sweeping the church and keeping the children in order, without, however, any increase of stipend.[110] Incense was in use at St. Nicholas', Durham, till late in the seventeenth century, but not for any ceremonial or devotional purpose. The *Book of Accounts and Reckonings* of that church has the following: 1675–6, " For juniper and frankincense to Robert Henley upon the Lord Bishop's coming into the church 1s." 1677–8, " For dressing of the church at the Lord Bishop's coming to preach 2s." : 1682–3, " For frankincense at the Lord Bishop's coming to the church 2s."

In 1683 and the three following years the same entry appears in the parish books of St. Oswald's, Durham : " Paid for two pairs of gloves to two ministers that assisted Mr. Cock at the communion 4s." One thing that causes some surprise is the amount of wine used at the communion services. A few examples may be given here, though many more might easily be cited. At Gateshead, in the accounts for 1675–6, six quarts of wine and sack are recorded as provided for one communion, the cost being 6s. 9d. At Darlington in 1675 two quarts of claret for the communicants cost 2s. At St. Nicholas', Durham, we find these entries : 1677, " For bread and wine at the communion of Palm Sunday, Skies Thursday, Good Friday, Easter Day and Sunday after 19s. 8d." Here it is interesting to note that there were five communions within fifteen days, and the price of bread and wine is perhaps not so surprising. In 1681, " For bread and wine at the Quarter Communion 9s., ditto Palm Sunday, Good Friday, Easter Day and Low Sunday £1 4s. 8d." In 1683–4, " For bread and wine at the private Communion of the Lord Bishop and the Dean 3s. 1d." In 1691 there was

[108] *Ambrose Barnes,* p. 454.
[109] Churchwardens' Books, Dec. 21st, 1706.
[110] Surtees, *Hist. Durham,* I, p. 230.

T

apparently only one Communion service, for which four
bottles of wine were provided.[111]

Among the collections for charitable purposes the distressed
French Protestants had their share. £4 15s. was collected at
Bishopwearmouth in 1682 and £6 5s. at Houghton-le-Spring,
the last sum collected mostly in pence. A brief for the
reformed episcopal churches in Great Poland and Polish
Prussia resulted in a contribution of 5s. from the congregation
of Bywell St. Peter on November 12th, 1716.[112] *The Church
Book of Bamburgh* has under date November 11th, 1680
"'The names of those that contributed in Belford Chapelry for
the relief of the captive Christians in Argiers." A brief was
issued in 1691 for money for the release of Christians in slavery
in Turkey; and at Darlington parish church the collection
was £1 18s. 2d. A collection was made on February 8th and
12th, 1679 in St. Nicholas', Durham, and throughout the
parish, by special order from the bishop, for the redemption
of some Stockton seamen made prisoners by the Turks.[113] The
books of the same parish make frequent mention of collections for the relief of sufferers by fire. "For the fire in
St. Katherine's near the Tower of London 17s. 9½d.," 1674.
"For a church in Essex rent by lightning and thunder
14s. 10d.," 1675. "For a fire at Walton in the County of
Norfolk 15s. 4½d.," 1675. These were made on receipt of a
brief, but in the case of similar disasters within the diocese the
bishop might issue an order: "For Nicholas Blades, for a
fire at Escomb 15s.," 1676. "For a fire at Hamsterley
18s. 2d.," 1681.[114]

On state occasions the church bells were rung and money
was given to the ringers. On the receipt of the news of the
defeat of Monmouth the bells of St. Nicholas', Durham, were
rung, and the ringers received seven shillings.[115] "For ringing
of a day of thanksgiving for the Queen being conceived with
child" in 1687 the ringers at Billingham were paid 2s. 6d. At
St. Oswald's, Durham, they received 6s. : for ringing for the

[111] *Durham Parish Books*, pp. 241, 248, 258 n.
[112] *Hist. Northumberland*, VI, p. 117.
[113] *Durham Parish Books*, p. 243.
[114] *Durham Parish Books*, *passim*.
[115] *Durham Parish Books*, p. 253.

birth of the unfortunate young Prince of Wales the same sum
was given them, and a further 6s. 6d. for another rejoicing
peal. At Darlington there is a note "To the ringers on
thanksgiving day for the young prince in money ale and coles
7s. 4d." At Houghton-le-Spring the loyal people were lavish;
1688, "Ringing for the young prince 3s. 6d. Drink for
the young prince 7s. 6d. Ringers 8s. To the ringers for
drink 1s. Coals for the bonfire rejoicing for the young prince
10d." In February 1689 they spent 11s. 6d. for the bonfire.
In 1691 "when Limerick was yielded" they spent 2s. and in
1697 the ringers rang for the peace. At Billingham they rang
in 1688 for the King's birthday on October 14th, and so they
did at St. Oswald's, Durham; but a warning note had been
struck when at Billingham they gave 5s. "to the ringers for
powder and drink when the worthy bishops were set at
liberty," [116] and the downfall of the King is marked by the
entry at St. Oswald's, Durham, "For ringing for the Prince of
Orange 6s." [117] A sad story is told in the Staindrop registers.
March 1709, "From this time till 21st November, 1710 no
account at all can be given of the register, by reason of the
carelessness of John Pearson the late clerk. Tho: Lamb,
Curate." [118]

Many churches were accustomed to keep some book like
Fox's *Book of Martyrs* for the edification of good Protestants.
According to an inventory of the possessions of St. Nicholas',
Durham, that church had two large Prayer Books and one
large Bible and three great books chained to two pillars:
Jewel and Harding, Erasmus' *Paraphrase,* and the *Book of
the Proceedings of King Charles I and the Long Parlia-
ment.* [119]

Clandestine marriage was a serious offence. The registers
of the chapelry of Winlaton relate that on September 29th,
1716 William Brockell, clerk, curate of Wycliffe, was admitted
curate of Whorlton on suspension of John Moresby, "a laic

[116] *Surtees,* III, p. 147.
[117] *Durham Parish Books, passim.*
[118] *Fordyce,* II, p. 89.
[119] *Durham Parish Books,* p. 262.

and celebrator of clandestine marriages." [120] We should like to know by what means this laic managed to thrust himself into the curacy, for a John Moresby, if it was the same person, had entered on it in 1677. Ecclesiastical discipline was still in force, and various punishments varying from public penance to excommunication might be inflicted. Thus on March 23rd, 1718 John Thomlinson read publicly a sentence of excommunication against Thomas Hardy and Eleanor Robson. [121]

In the registers of the archdeaconry of Durham will be found a long series of presentments. Taking the years 1673 and 1674 alone, these were amongst the charges dealt with: non-payment of Easter dues, or of assessments for repairs of churches, non-payment of the clerk's wages, not undertaking the office of churchwarden or not fulfilling the duties when appointed, calling the office of churchwarden a roguish office and other abuse, not certifying penances, not rendering accounts as churchwarden, not repairing a churchyard wall, and profanation of a churchyard. Another series of offences will be generally found to have some connection with recusancy such as not attending church, not receiving communion, behaving rudely in church, not having children baptized, women not churched, teaching without licence, conventicling, enclosing a burial-place for sectaries, working or opening shops on holy days, abusive speeches to a minister, not suffering the dead to be buried according to the rubric, scandalous words against the Lord's Prayer and the Creed, unlawful preaching. Some were charged with being Papists, Quakers or Anabaptists. Among moral faults dealt with were fornication, scandalous life, drunkenness, slander, adultery, incest, drinking on the Lord's Day, profanation of Sundays or holy days, drinking or gambling during service time, scolding and swearing. [122]

Special efforts were made to enforce Sunday observance. The Church Book of Bamburgh mentions a number of presentations by the churchwardens for offences under this head

[120] *Surtees*, IV, p. 44.
[121] *North County Diaries*, p. 110.
[122] *Granville*, II, pp. 213–48.

in the years 1681 and 1682, e.g. Thomas Anderson for playing a bagpipe before a bridegroom on Sunday, not frequenting church or receiving the sacrament or sending his children and servants to be catechized; Cuthbert Renwick for absence from church and nutting on several Lord's Days, and Elizabeth Mill for scolding and for drying fish on the Lord's Day. At Bywell St. Peter's in May 1691 John Richley was presented for grinding corn on the Lord's Day.[123]

In order to encourage the woollen trade the law ordered that the bodies of the dead should be wrapped only in woollen. Hence we find entries such as the following: " Mr. Thomas Forster of Ederstone Mid-hall buried in Bamburgh choir June 22, 1678 wrapped in no material but what was made of sheep's wool." [124] " Whereas Mrs. Marie Bowser was buried the 26th of October, 1679 in linen contrary to the Act of Parliament, whereupon Mr. Bowser hath paid the forfeiture of fifty shillings to the churchwardens of St. Mary-the-Less which they have disposed to the poor of this parish and to the poor of St. Margaret's in the Market Place (sic)." [125] There was a similar case of forfeiture for this cause on December 27th, 1684 and many others elsewhere. The Rev. William Eden when he was at Stockton is said to have abolished the practice of burying the bodies of the poor without coffins.[126]

During the latter portion of Crewe's episcopate the diocese witnessed the establishment of charity schools, and a number of people gave gifts or made bequests for educational purposes. The same thing was going on throughout England, the donors being inspired by varying motives. Some regarded schools as a potential defence against popery. Ambrose Barnes, alderman of Newcastle, tells us that " charity schools, founded with a view to opposing and defeating the pernicious effects of the seminaries set up by papists in the reign of King James the Second, first began in this kingdom about 1688." [127] These seminaries had really been few in number and had

[123] *Hist. Northumberland*, VI, p. 117.
[124] The Church Book of Bamburgh.
[125] Burial Register of St. Mary in the South Bailey, Durham.
[126] *Fordyce*, I, p. 160.
[127] *Ambrose Barnes*, p. 454.

collapsed at the revolution, and their number and influence had been greatly exaggerated. Some people, no doubt, desired to counteract by education the danger to the State of an ignorant and vicious populace, but in the main the establishment of the charity schools was the desire of godfearing people that the children of the poor should be taught to read and write, and be instructed in the principles of the Christian religion. "The charity school movement was quite clearly the first great concerted effort for elementary education in England. It resulted in the establishment of a very great number of 'voluntary schools,' many of which were subsequently taken over by the National Society in the early nineteenth century. . . . It is also arguable that they were the first really elementary schools of England." [128] The chapter of Durham cathedral in 1696, in order to encourage the woollen manufacture, bought twelve wheels and sent twelve poor girls to a spinning school which had lately been set up in the city. Comber persuaded the justices in sessions, January 1696, to give the master of the school £50 of arrears in hand, in consideration of £40 a year, which was due from the Bishop of Durham, to keep fourteen poor girls and instruct them in spinning and reading for one year and thereafter a fresh fourteen. Several evil-disposed persons succeeded at length in destroying this excellent charity.[129] By his will, dated 1701, John Spearman, under-sheriff of Durham, left £20 to be used in teaching a poor boy or boys the Church Catechism, the Protestant religion, reading, writing, arithmetic and navigation. Similarly, at Chester-le-Street, by will dated May 10th, 1718 Elizabeth Tewart left certain lands worth £6 a year to a schoolmaster to instruct twelve poor children. At Houghton-le-Spring Dr. Henry Bagshaw, rector from 1677 to 1709, bequeathed certain lands out of the proceeds of which £3 should be paid every year to the principal master of the Kepier Grammar School, and £2 to the usher. Another rector, Sir George Wheler, left £600 for the establishment of a school for twenty poor children, of whom twelve were to be

[128] Prof. E. F. Braley, *Durham University Journal*, XXVIII, p. 187.
[129] Comber, *Life*, p. 548.

clothed; and for repairing the gatehouse, or some other convenient house, in which they might be taught.[130]   A third prebendary of Durham, Dr. Theophilus Pickering, founded the
Anchorage school in Gateshead churchyard.   (The Anchorage
seems to have been used as a school house before this, but what
became known afterwards as the Anchorage school is said to
have used for some years the town toll-booth.)   For this purpose he left £300, the profits of a small colliery which he had
worked in a plot of ground called Bull's Acre.   The master of
the school was to be chosen by the rector of Gateshead for
the time being, and he was to teach the children the Latin and
Greek tongues, writing, casting of accounts, and the art of
navigation.[131]   Edward Kirkby, vicar of Heighington 1684–5,
gave £70 to improve the school there.   Sir Ambrose Crowley
established schools at Winlaton and Swalwell.   At Darlington
in 1715 Dame Mary Calverley assigned to trustees a bond for
£1,000, which she directed to be invested in lands, the rent of
which was to be applied to the maintenance of a charity, later
called the Blue Coat Charity, afterwards established in
that town.[132]   The Durham Blue Coat School for the education of six boys was founded in 1708.   In 1718 it was kept in
two large rooms in the New Place, the house in the corner of
the market-place formerly belonging to the Nevilles.[133]   The
charity school at Stockton was founded by voluntary contributions in 1721.[134]

During the reign of Queen Anne five schools were founded
in Newcastle.   In 1705 Mrs. Eleanor Allan founded in
St. Nicholas' parish a school for forty boys and twenty girls
drawn either from that parish or the neighbouring chapelry of
St. John's.   She also directed that each child on leaving the
school should be presented with a Bible and Prayer Book,
bound together, a copy of the *Whole Duty of Man,* and of
Lewin's *Explanation of the Catechism.*[135]   In the same year

[130] *Surtees,* I, p. 222.
[131] Brand, *Newcastle,* 1789, I, p. 497.   *Surtees,* II, p. 134.
[132] *Sykes,* I, p. 133.
[133] *Surtees,* IV, p. 55.
[134] *Sykes,* I, p. 139.
[135] *Ambrose Barnes,* p. 454.

John Ord founded a charity school for forty boys in the chapelry of St. John's. St. Andrew's charity school for thirty boys, who were to be taught to read English and repeat the Catechism without book,[136] was founded by Sir William Blackett, who died in 1705. The first boy entered in 1708; and the son of the founder, somewhere about 1719, made additional provision for clothing the boys attending the school. In All Saints' parish, or rather chapelry, a charity school was founded in 1709 for forty-one boys and seventeen girls. The boys were to be taught to read and write and cast accounts, the girls to read, knit and sew. Ground for the school house was acquired in the Manors in the year of the foundation. Lastly, in 1712 the Master and brethren of the Trinity House decided to establish a free school.[137]

A free school was founded and endowed by several benefactions at Allendale in 1700, and Richard Coates, who died at Ponteland in 1719, left all his effects to found a charity school for fifteen poor children of that place and to provide the boys with grey coats and caps and the girls with grey capes and petticoats.[138]

Sometimes a sum of money was given and all that was said was that it was to be spent on education. In 1710 John Grainger bequeathed £300 for teaching poor children at Staindrop.[139] The Rev. Christopher Fulthorpe, by his will dated June 30th, 1707, devised property to build a school of which the master was to be a deacon or qualified to become such, and should receive £20 a year for teaching fifteen children from Stainton and Hart gratis. A further £8 a year was to be spent on coats, hats and shoes for four scholars, and 40s. a year for Prayer Books, Bibles and copies of the *Whole Duty of Man* for those who needed them.[140] Vincent Edwards, a graduate of Merton College, Oxford, and incumbent of Embleton from 1680 to 1713, bequeathed to Merton College the school house which he stated that he had built at his own

[136] Richardson's *Local Historian's Table Book*, p. 337.
[137] *Sykes*, I, pp. 129–32.
[138] *Hist. Northumberland*, XII, p. 442.
[139] Fordyce, *County Pal.*, II, p. 91.
[140] Fordyce, *Pal.*, II, p. 285.

expense. He left land and £40 in money for the upkeep of the school at Embleton.[141] In Haydon Bridge, then a chapelry of Warden parish, a school-house and almshouses were founded by the Rev. John Shafto, who was vicar of Warden for fifty-four years until his death in 1697. The purposes of the charity, which was said to have been the fruit of great self-denial, were the education of youth, the maintenance of distressed families and the apprenticing of poor children. The master was to be a Master of Arts and was to have the assistance of an usher. In 1697 the trustees built both the school and the school-house.[142]

A mere list of charitable bequests made in the diocese during Crewe's episcopate would be a wearisome catalogue. Gifts of this kind for the relief of the poor were numerous, there were six at Ryton alone. Bequests of bread were frequent. Alderman John Hutchinson left two houses in Framwellgate to the parish of St. Margaret's, Durham, the rents to provide a shilling a Sunday to be spent on bread. Thomas Cooper left two shillings a Sunday for bread to be given to poor people attending service at St. Nicholas', Durham. Dr. Henry Bagshaw left money for bread to be given at Christmas and Easter to the poor of Houghton-le-Spring. It is still done, and about a hundred and seventy loaves were distributed there at Christmas 1932. John Cock, vicar of St. Oswald's, Durham, 1666–89, and lecturer of St. Nicholas', left £600 to the churchwardens of St. Oswald's to be invested in land, the income to be used in buying Bibles, Prayer Books, *The Whole Duty of Man,* or other books of practical divinity for the poor, for providing clothes and physic for poor persons, for teaching poor boys and girls, and for furnishing apprentices with tools or setting them up in business. He left all his library to the parish and £20 to build a place to contain it. The last was never done, the books remained in the rectory, and in recent years the collection was sold. Francis Callaghan by his will, dated February 7th, 1675 left money to be dis-

[141] *Hist. Northumberland,* II, p. 71.
[142] *Hist. Northumberland,* IV, pp. 415, 421. Hodgson, *Northumberland,* III, ii, p. 387.

tributed to the poor of St. Nicholas' and St. Giles', Durham, twenty shillings to the vicar of St. Nicholas', and £4 yearly for a lecturer or preaching minister there, on condition that a sermon was preached annually on the day of the testator's decease at a public service, before which the bells should be rung, for which duty five shillings should be paid to the ringers. If the lecturer neglected to preach on the stated occasion this part of the benefaction was to cease. John Spearman in 1701 left the rents and profits of certain property to the rector of St. Mary-le-Bow, Durham, on trust that he should perform divine service and administer the sacrament during Lent and on the great festivals to all prisoners in Durham gaol who should be qualified and desirous; and also that the rector should prepare and assist poor criminals under sentence of death in the prison.

The provision of almshouses was one of the favourite methods of showing care for the poor. Several benefactors joined to provide for the establishment of almshouses at Stockton in 1682. They received a licence from Crewe and owed their existence largely to Thomas Rudd, vicar of Norton.[143] These almshouses were erected in the same year and in 1702 James Cook bequeathed £100 to them.[144] In 1688 Sir John Duck founded a hospital for twelve poor persons at Lumley.[145] At present ten tenants live there rent free and receive 1s. a week, but the buildings being " out of keeping with modern requirements "[146] are threatened with destruction. Thomas Cooper, who died in 1703, provided for almshouses for five poor men and five poor women at Sedgefield where he had been a surgeon.[147] Prebendary John Bowes endowed almshouses for twelve poor people at Bishop-wearmouth in 1721. The Jesus College, commonly called at first the Town Hospital, was established in Newcastle by the corporation in 1681. The keelmen of the Tyne in 1700 petitioned the common council of Newcastle for a site for a

[143] *Sykes,* I, p. 118.
[144] Fordyce, *Pal.,* II, p. 167.
[145] *Surtees,* II, p. 167.
[146] *Durham County Advertiser,* Jan. 29th, 1937.
[147] *Sykes,* I, p. 128.

hospital. The lease was taken in the name of the Governor, Wardens and Fraternity of Hostmen and, on the land provided, a building was erected for the use and benefit of the keelmen at a cost of £2,000 and was opened in 1701. The money was raised by the keelmen themselves, each one paying fourpence a tide.[148] That eccentric nonconformist, James Pigg, who was for many years (1666–83) road surveyor for the County of Northumberland, is largely remembered in Newcastle to-day because he erected a pillar at Gosforth covered with texts of scripture and moral maxims, which pillar was known for long as Pigg's Folly. But he should be remembered for his bequest to the sick poor which to this day produces annually a considerable sum for medical charities.[149]

There were numbers of other bequests for the poor, both small and large. Thus George Davenport, rector of Houghton-le-Spring 1664–77, bequeathed £160 for the maintenance of three poor people, £40 to the poor stock of the parish and £10 to be given to the poor at his burial.[150]

Dr. Thomas Wood, Bishop of Lichfield and prebendary of Durham, by his will, November 1690, bequeathed out of his lands and tenements at Egglescliffe a rent charge of £20 per annum, to be employed for the release of such prisoners in Durham gaol as were incarcerated for debts not exceeding £5 each. Under the provisions of the Durham Chancery scheme of 1882 the income of Wood's Charity is now paid to the Discharged Prisoners' Aid Society. In another place there was some regard for prisoners also, for in the Sessions Books for 1687 we find the Rev. John Pye, B.A., rector of Morpeth (1672–91), in receipt of £5 per half year for preaching to the poor prisoners.

---

[148] *Sykes,* I, p. 127.
[149] John Oxberry in *Arch. Ael.,* 4th Series, V, p. 30.
[150] *Surtees,* I, pp. 170–1.

CHAPTER IX

THE LAST YEARS

CREWE lived in the south during the winter, indeed most of the year, but his biographer remarked with some admiration that he was a constant visitor to his diocese for forty years, holding his visitations every three years and his confirmations every year until his health broke down in 1715–16.[1] On the day after Christmas in the year 1710 all the bishops dined together at Lambeth Palace, and it was noted that there were only two absentees, the Bishop of Lichfield, whose wife was ill, and the Bishop of Durham.[2] We do not know the reason : increasing age might well be suggested, but one somehow feels that he would find the atmosphere somewhat glacial among a company of Whig bishops. Early in 1711 there was a bye-election in Leicestershire and Crewe, with Lord Denbigh, Lord Ferrers and others, urged Sir Thomas Cave to stand in the Tory interest with which request Cave complied.[3] We find him at the end of that year being summoned to give his vote in the Lords. The Whigs had captured the Earl of Nottingham and intended to rush the Occasional Conformity Bill through the House of Lords where it had been so often defeated. They " were sacrificing their principles of religious toleration to their factious desire to overthrow the Ministry and the Peace." [4] The Earl of Oxford was trying to whip up his followers. Hence the following letter from the Bishop of Durham, written from Steane on December 4th :

" The honour of your Lordship's commands last post should oblige me to a ready obedience, if old age and the depth of winter would allow me trying the experiment of such a hasty journey. If I know my own heart it is brim full of loyalty and fidelity to the Queen, of unfeigned sincerity for the

[1] *Memoirs*, p. 35.
[2] *Bishop Nicholson Diaries*, p. 143.
[3] *Verney Letters of the Eighteenth Century*, I, p. 323.
[4] Prof. G. M. Trevelyan, *England under Anne*, III, p. 195.

Church, and of a steady adhering to the Constitution; all which, with concern I now perceive by your Lordship, will violently be pushed in matter of the greatest moment. And therefore, though I cannot so suddenly give my personal attendance in Parliament, yet that I may not seem, in such a critical juncture, to decline a service I have hitherto espoused with a more than ordinary zeal, I will presume to appear by proxy at the time desired; in order to which I have here enclosed a temporal one, with a space in it, for your Lordship, if you please, to insert the name of such a Peer as you shall judge most proper. By this your Lordship sees how great a confidence I have in your integrity for the public good." [5] Some of Oxford's friends failed him, certain Scottish proxies did not arrive in time, and the Occasional Conformity Bill passed.

In 1712 the Bishop of Durham was restored to the office of Lord-Lieutenant. It was said that he might have had it twelve months before that, had it not been for Lord Oxford who " kept the bishop back twelve months after the office had been promised him," being unwilling perhaps to displace Lord Scarborough, whose family had a long connection with the county, apart from the fact that he had held the office ever since the revolution.[6] Crewe looked upon it as one of his palatinate rights, though as a matter of fact it had been held only infrequently by his predecessors. He now held it for three years only, for in 1715 he was again succeeded by Lord Scarborough, who retained it until 1721 when he died. When Crewe was sworn in at the Council and kissed the Queen's hand he told her that " as a bishop he prayed for her and as her lieutenant he would fight for her."

The Schism Bill passed the Lords on June 15th, 1714 by 79 votes to 71. Four days previously Crewe was one of seven bishops who supported a proposal to apply the measure to Ireland. He must have returned to Durham soon after that, for Queen Anne died, and on August 1st George I came to the throne and Crewe shortly afterwards proclaimed him at

[5] Welbeck Abbey MSS., Vol. V, p. 121.
[6] *Surtees,* I, p. cxviii.

Durham. Very soon after this, probably on his next return to London, he went to wait upon the King, but was unable to obtain admission to the presence, so he said to one of the people in waiting : " Tell the King that I only came to pay my duty to him, for I have nothing to ask of him." In a day or two George gave orders that whenever Crewe came he should be admitted immediately, and a messenger was sent to him to tell him so. At the coronation on October 20th my lord of Durham was on the King's right hand, though his friends thought he was endangering his own health thereby. Next day, however, he went to see George who remarked that the bishop was less tired than he himself was. Crewe told him that it was the third coronation at which he had been one of the sovereign's supporters, the coronation on the previous day, that of Queen Anne, and that of King James, at which the King said, " Oh, King James ! " The Prince, perhaps with a spice of mischief, asked the bishop where he was at the time of King William's coronation. " Sir," was the reply, " I was then in the Low Countries." In the later years of Anne Crewe had recovered some influence at Court, but now, if he received any royal attention it was only such as might be due to his age and position.

On one occasion, says the Trotter manuscript, " my lord attended the princess and she admired his cane. He told her that with that when he was lord lieutenant he gave the word of command." By the princess must be meant the Princess of Wales, Caroline of Anspach, wife of George afterwards George II. She had arrived in London with her daughters on October 23rd, 1714.[7] She took notice of the bishop's neatness and particularly his cap, and she said that if it were in her power she would remove him to a better cap, presumably an archbishop's mitre. Lord Wharton, who was present, said, " Madam, my lord Crewe is fourscore," to which Crewe replied, " Madam I am more than fourscore, and Lord Wharton remembers me the greater part of the time." Since Wharton died in April 1715 this little incident must have

[7] E. Calamy, *My Own Life*, 1829, II, p. 301.

happened in the winter of 1714–15. Crewe would then be
well over eighty-one and Wharton would be over sixty-six.
There was a general laugh at the bishop's sally and when the
latter asked Wharton why he had told the princess his age his
reply was, "Why you gave me a rub for it." Wharton and
he seem to have chaffed one another on several occasions.
Wharton lost the Lord-Lieutenancy of Ireland in 1709. Some
time after that they met in the House of Lords. "How does
your eminency?" said Wharton, with perhaps a sly hit at the
bishop's alleged popish leanings. "Thank you, my lord,"
said the bishop, "how does your excellency do?" George I,
at his accession, made Wharton a marquess and in 1715 it was
known that he was about to be created a duke. "What must
I call you," enquired Crewe, "your excellency, or your grace,
or what?" "Oh my lord," said Wharton, "no! no! Grace
in the heart, grace in the heart." It was their last jest
together for Wharton died a fortnight later. Crewe's ready
wit appeared on another occasion when the Duke of Argyle in
his presence jestingly asked to be made Bishop of Durham at
the next vacancy. "I hope," said he, "when you are Bishop
of Durham you will bring bishops into Scotland."

There was little humour in the sallies between Crewe and
Burnet; they thoroughly disliked each other. On the occasion
of a divorce between the Earl of Anglesey and his countess,
afterwards Duchess of Buckingham, Crewe supported the
divorce bill in the Lords, upon which Burnet told him rudely:
"You encourage whores." It was during this unsavoury
business in the House that Burnet begged Crewe's pardon,
perhaps for this rudeness, not very willingly probably, but if
he had not done so the Lords showed signs of insisting on it.
Crewe said he had his satisfaction; he meant in seeing his old
enemy thus brought to apologize.[8] Burnet badly wanted to
be Bishop of Durham; he was "gaping for the see for thirty
years." He begged it first from William, and then from
George I, and received promises from both that he should be
appointed to fill the next vacancy. Crewe frequently said

[8] *Memoirs*, p. 34.

that the prayers of the clergy of his diocese on his behalf were redoubled " to keep out such a creature." When Burnet died in 1715 Crewe told George I that he had buried his expected successor. The King, laughing heartily, told him that the air of Durham was good, and that he hoped it would be many years before he named anyone to succeed him. A short time before Burnet's death the two bishops met and Crewe offered his hand, but Burnet said sourly, " I won't give you my right hand," to which Crewe replied, " Then give me your left." Burnet did so, and Crewe said, " Well now, remember we are left-handed friends." [9] But Burnet scored in the long run : he wrote of Crewe : " Bating the dignity of being born of a noble though Puritan family, he had not any one quality to recommend him to so great a post, unless obedience and compliance could supply all other defects. He has neither learning nor good sense, and is no preacher. He was a fawning abject slave to the court ; and thus he was raised, and has been now for above thirty years possessed of the greatest dignity in this church." [10] Thus Burnet got his revenge ; he had the last word, and his malicious fault-finding and slanderous gossip have been accepted as history for two hundred years.

In 1715 the bishopric was disturbed by the rising known as " the Fifteen," a movement which was to bring to Lord Crewe anxiety while it lasted, and bitter grief before the end. There had been Jacobite meetings in London at which plans had been made for the overthrow of the new dynasty, and in August 1715 Captain Robert Talbot travelled northwards to report the resolutions taken. Among the north country gentry who were to be counted upon were the young Earl of Derwentwater and Thomas Forster of Etherstone, Lady Crewe's nephew. Their attitude was known to the Government and messengers were despatched northwards with warrants for their arrest. If they had hesitated before this decided them. At a meeting at the house of Mr. Fenwick of Bywell it was agreed that the only thing possible was to take up arms. On October 6th Forster and about twenty others

[9] *Examination*, p. 97.
[10] Burnet, *Hist. of My Own Times*, ed. O. Airy, Oxford 1900, I, p. 98.

met at Greenrig, at the top of the Waterfalls Hills and were joined by parties led by Derwentwater and Errington, so that now they were sixty strong.

The little troop set out for Rothbury gathering some additions to their ranks at Plainfield on the way. Next day, their numbers still increasing, they went to Warkworth where they were joined by Lord Widdrington and thirty horse. Next Sunday (October 13th) Forster sent Buxton, one of their chaplains, to William Ion, Vicar of Warkworth, ordering him to substitute the names of James III and Mary the Queen Mother for those of George I and his Queen. The vicar refused and went off to Newcastle to report to the authorities there, while Buxton took the services at Warkworth, where James III was formally proclaimed King. Twelve pence a day was publicly offered to recruits, Presbyterians excepted. Proceeding southward on Monday and receiving additions to their numbers on the way, they reached Morpeth three hundred strong, all mounted. Had they been able to accept all those who wished to volunteer as foot soldiers they might have become a formidable force : but they had neither arms nor ammunition, and gallant recklessness is a poor substitute for careful preparation. Still there came a gleam of sunshine in the news that Lancelot Errington, a Newcastle shipmaster, had surprised the fort on Holy Island. It was not a great feat, for the garrison, a contingent changed weekly, sent from the troops at Berwick, only numbered seven, of whom only two seem to have been actually on duty. Moreover, the Governor of Berwick recovered the fort at low tide the next day, and Errington and his men found themselves prisoners in Berwick.[11]

Forster, who received from the Earl of Mar James's commission as a general, now proclaimed James at Morpeth, and then proceeded by way of Hexham, where they were joined by some Scottish horse, to the moor near Dilston. Here there was some idea that they might take Newcastle by a sudden dash, but the magistrates had been warned. All suspected

[11] Raine, *North Durham*, p. 166.

U

persons had been rounded up: the militia and train-bands which had mustered on Killingworth Moor were drawn into the town, the Earl of Scarborough and other gentry collected their neighbours and tenants and hastened thither, seven hundred volunteers were armed as a townguard, the keelmen offered to provide seven hundred more at half an hour's notice, and the gates were walled up.[12] Higher authorities too were busy. A battalion of foot and a regiment of dragoons had been sent hastily from Yorkshire, and Lieutenant-General Carpenter's army was on the way: in fact Cobham's, Molesworth's and Churchill's regiments of dragoons and Hotham's foot were all at Newcastle by the 18th of the month.

While at Hexham Forster's men had seized all the horses and arms they could find in the neighbourhood, especially those which belonged to the supporters of the House of Hanover. As at Warkworth the incumbent refused to pray for James III, so Buxton had to officiate in the abbey. News came that Lords Kenmure, Nithsdale, Carnwath and Wintoun had risen on the other side of the Border and had come south to Rothbury, so on Tuesday, the 19th, the Jacobites proclaimed James at Hexham and set out towards Wooler. Two days later Robert Patten, Curate of Allendale, brought in some volunteers whom he had collected and for his zeal was made chaplain to Forster. Carpenter reached Wooler on the 27th and heard that the enemy had gone to join the Earl of Mar, so for some reason he returned to Newcastle. Forster's army, however, except a number of Highlanders belonging to the Scottish forces on the other side of the Border, suddenly determined to invade England. Marching through Jedburgh they entered Cumberland on November 1st and made their way into Lancashire. Carpenter set out from Durham, marched by way of Clitheroe and attacked them at Preston on the same day as the fight at Sheriffmuir. The result was disaster for the Jacobites.

James, Earl of Derwentwater, was beheaded on Tower Hill on February 24th, and it was believed that he had been

[12] Sykes, *Local Records,* I, pp. 134–5.

buried in the churchyard of St. Giles', Holborn. Either a sham burial took place or the body was disinterred, for it was certainly conveyed secretly to the chapel of Dilston. A priest met the corpse at Sunderland Bridge, two miles from Durham, on March 6th, and at Whitesmocks, in the time of Surtees the historian, there was a farm-house of which the porch was still an object of interest as one of the places where the coffin rested. People flocked all that night from Durham to see it, and for three nights there were continual brilliant displays of the Aurora Borealis, henceforth known in those parts as Lord Derwentwater's lights. Charles Radcliffe, the earl's brother, though condemned to death, escaped out of Newgate. Others also escaped and some were executed. The Reverend Robert Patten, who had preached at Kelso on the text " The right of the firstborn is his," turned King's evidence, wrote a book on the history of the rebellion which went through two editions in 1717, and was ever afterwards held in execration in loyalist circles.[13] Tom Forster escaped out of Newgate, and though £100 was offered for his apprehension, he safely reached the continent. He owed his escape, as every reader of Sir Walter Besant's novel knows, to the persistent courage of his sister Dorothy. He joined James at Avignon in August 1716, took part in some later intrigues in Italy, and was offered a commission in the forces which proposed to rise in 1722 but he died that same year.

There were very many who remembered that the Bishop of Durham had been one of James II's closest friends. When Lord Portland had asked him why he had abandoned James and accepted William as king he had replied that he could not conscientiously do otherwise,[14] but there were those who doubted his conversion, perhaps not without reason. James III, after all, was his master's son, and few people found very strong reason for enthusiasm for the Hanoverian successor. Now his wife's nephew had become one of the principal

---

[13] Patten, *History of the Late Rebellion, with Original Papers and Characters of the Principal Noblemen and Gentlemen concerned in it.* 1717.

[14] *Memoirs,* p. 33.

leaders of a rebellion. The news that a messenger had been sent north with a warrant to seize Thomas, and the fear that he might be arrested, terrified Lady Crewe before the actual rebellion took place. Probably she never knew that it had begun; concern and agitation of mind killed her, for she fell into convulsions and died four days afterwards on October 16th, at the early age of forty-two.

The counties of Durham and Northumberland, the latter especially, had contributed their quota to the band of gallant gentlemen who went out on a hopeless quest, but in neither case was it a large quota. Yet in 1716 after the rebellion had been put down it was reported in Jacobite circles: " Northumberland, Durham and South Scotland almost unanimously well-affected to the King. The main interest is yet entire, especially on the English side, where the whole church Protestant party is yet untouched and is capable to perform their promises." [15] They were mistaken about the Church. Only two clergymen refused the oath of abjuration, which was re-enacted and more severely enforced after the " Fifteen." Abraham Yapp, precentor of Durham cathedral and curate of Witton Gilbert since 1695, became a non-juror, and he was followed by Timothy Mawman, rector of Elton since 1709, in the course of the next year.[16] And these were all.

As time went on the Bishop of Durham and Lord Oxford ceased to be on such friendly terms as hitherto, and when on one occasion the latter sent to the bishop to beg his attendance in the House of Lords, Crewe replied, " Tell him from me that I know the Court as well as he, and longer, and that he does not use me like a gentleman.'' Nevertheless when Oxford was impeached he attended the trial and even sat up all night on his account, at great risk to his own health. The impeachment of the earl had been voted in 1715, but the trial did not take place till 1717. It opened in Westminster Hall on June 24th, and on the second day of the proceedings, which

[15] *Hist. MSS. Com.*, Stuart MSS., IV, p. 55.
[16] Mawman later became a non-juring bishop. Overton, *Nonjurors,* 1902, p. 306.

ST. PETER'S, STEANE.
By permission of Country Life Ltd.

was not until the first of July, because of a quarrel between
the two Houses, the managers of the impeachment did not
appear and the Lords passed sentence of acquittal on all the
charges. It must have meant a great effort on Crewe's behalf
to bear the heat and excitement for so many hours at his
time of life.

His health was breaking. Early in 1716 he was taken ill
in London and retired to Steane. Dorothy was buried there.
After her death he had a settee placed in the chapel and spent
hours in contemplation of the monument he had erected
there to her memory. He expressed to Dr. Grey, his chaplain,
his dislike of a skull the sculptor had placed as a finial, and
Dr. Grey, ever ready to spare his aged patron a moment of
uneasiness, sent to Banbury for the artist and asked if it would
not be possible to substitute a more pleasing subject. After a
little hesitation the sculptor thought he could convert the skull
into a bunch of grapes and this was done.[17]

Crewe paid much attention to his palatine rights and
caused his secretary to make a careful search of the records for
this purpose, but he must have had at times much anxiety and
worry about the property and emoluments of the see, and
sometimes in endeavouring to increase or maintain his rights
suffered through the unwisdom of his legal advisers. Most of
his troubles in this respect seem, according to the information
available, to belong to his last years. Hullam, or Hulam, in
Hesleden parish, was the property of the family of Strode of
Dorset. Towards the end of Crewe's episcopate Serjeant
Strode, the then owner, died. Crewe claimed the estate as
escheated to himself in default of an heir and kept possession
until the heir-at-law, whose name was Evans, brought an
action of ejectment. The bishop had been wrongly advised,
and William Lee, the plaintiff's solicitor, in a very long letter,
told the bishop that one of his predecessors, Anthony Bec,
had in similar circumstances been impeached in parliament.
Threatened with an application to parliament for relief and
with proceedings in the King's Bench, Crewe surrendered

[17] Baker, *Hist. of Northamptonshire*, 1822–41, I, p. 688.

possession and paid a heavy bill for costs and damages. When he paid his money he laid his hand on the head of one of his principal agents and said, "Well, I pay this for *thy* experience." He was so pleased with Lee's ability and plain dealing that some time afterwards he granted to him and his son, by patent for life, the office of registrar in the Durham Court of Chancery.[18]

Another case in which the bishop did not come off well was a dispute about the mines on the manor of Beamish. Mr. Thomas Wray sold the mining rights to Mr. George Pitts. But Crewe claimed the mines, as his predecessors, Morton and Cosin, had done, so he granted a lease of the mines to Mr. Robert Wright and Mr. Musgrave Denison who brought a writ of ejectment against Pitts. The last-named brought an action against them both, uniting with them the Bishop of Durham, in the Court of Chancery, won his case and obtained a perpetual injunction against the bishop, his lessee and successors.[19]

The development of coal-mining in the north in the latter part of the seventeenth century greatly increased the bishop's income, and like other landowners he exercised the right of granting permission to the lessees of the mining rights to carry their coal over his lands; for which convenience a regular rent was charged. The copyholders on the episcopal estates had similar rights, but they could not grant transit rights for more than a year without paying a small fine to the bishop. About 1671 wooden ways called way-leaves were introduced and enabled the coals to be carried more easily and quickly. In consequence of this as time went on fines and rents were greatly increased and men began to make fortunes thereby.

It was asserted that the landlord's claim to mines under wastes and commons, though in some cases this was disputed, was valid; but that to claim mines under copyholds and leaseholds was a new claim, set up within the memory of man. Moreover, some of the landlords were enclosing parts of

[18] *Spearman*, pp. 94–100. *Hutchinson*, I, pp. 697–700.
[19] *Spearman*, p. 89.

commons and claiming the mines underneath.[20] The Bishop
of Durham had been advised to claim mines of coal and
quarries of limestone, and such like, on several enclosed
grounds of his copyhold manors : a claim which had never
been made before. It was perfectly true that they had had
the profits of mines in the waste of some particular manors,
and that by immemorial custom only ; but none of the new
claims, said Spearman, writing in 1729, were more than thirty
years old.

The bishop's advisers had persuaded him to grant leases at
nominal rents to kindred, stewards, servants and favourites.
The new leaseholders proceeded to harry the copyhold tenants
by legal proceedings and interfered with their land. The
lessees got great prices, the bishop " was imposed on " and
reserved no more than 2s. 6d. rent in the leases, and so the
leaseholders were enriched and the tenants were impoverished.
There was, if Spearman is to be believed, a great deal of
corruption among the bishop's entourage. The officials
received large bribes to induce them to persuade the bishop to
make grants or leases of commons. The lessees disturbed the
tenants in their use of the commons and vexed them with suits
and actions. In 1716 a certain William Coatsworth and
another man named Ramsay got from the bishop possession of
the manors of Gateshead and Whickham. In time they
gained control over the way-leaves of the collieries round about
and exercised that control in a grasping and domineering
spirit, charging five shillings for every ton of coal carried over
the lands within their leases. They were believed to have made
£3,000 a year out of one colliery, much more indeed than the
owners themselves received. Bishop Crewe was fully aware of
their oppressive conduct, but he could do nothing as long as
the leases lasted, but in order to safeguard himself he compelled the lessees to give him a bond of £3,000 to indemnify
him for any possible prosecution by injured persons.[21]

Sir Henry Liddell had a lease of coal-mines from Crewe for

[20] *Spearman,* pp. 87, 89.
[21] G. Neasham, *North Country Sketches,* 1893, pp. 269–70. *Spearman,*
p. 112.

which he paid £40 per annum rent. Under a grant of several hundred years standing he made a claim to the wastes and mines on a great part of Gateshead Common, as appurtenant to, and within the ancient boundary of, his manor and lordship of Lamesley and Ravensworth. It was a new claim and Crewe thought his duty to fight it. He had hard usage in the proceedings, and advantage was taken by his opponents of many slips, especially as he was in ill-health. The case was tried in 1715, and the bishop's right to the mines and Sir Henry Liddell's right to the soil and royalties of Blackburn Fell in the parish of Lamesley were established.[22] The case was carried into the House of Lords " and Sir Harry Liddell got it without any opposition almost, not above one speaking in his lordship's favour, and he too but coldly. Sir Harry is zealous for the Government and the bishop a good for naught fellow, and so they scarcely had any difficulty or dispute." This is the view of a conceited junior curate in the diocese who was evidently glad that " the Bishop of Durham had lost a lordship, as he has done two more in the neighbourhood of Whickham." [23] But he was no doubt expressing the Whig idea of law and justice. The Bishop of Durham was " a good for naught fellow," that is, a Tory, so they would soon settle his hash if he came into court. At Oxford they thought differently. When the bishop was at Lincoln College in 1717 an order came from the Court of Chancery for the payment of £1,300 costs in the late suit, but there was no attorney in Oxford who could be prevailed upon to serve the writ.[24] Not that Crewe had any difficulty in paying it ; a considerable lease fell in just at the right time, but no doubt he felt he had had hard measure. He himself was described as one of the best of landlords. His diocese had great reason to acknowledge that truth, as the rents of few of his demesnes or leases were raised during his time.[25]

The visit to Oxford to which reference was made above was

[22] Surtees, *Durham*, II, p. 214. Spearman, p. 89.
[23] *North County Diaries. Diary of John Thomlinson*, p. 105.
[24] *Memoirs*, p. 35.
[25] *Examination*, pp. 104–5.

Crewe's last. He was almost too infirm to travel, but on August 12th, 1717, the anniversary of the day on which in 1668 he had been chosen Rector of Lincoln College, he went there once more. Perhaps because of his great age, and perhaps because of his generosity, his journey thither attracted much attention. A dinner was given him in Lincoln College hall and cost £6 15s. 6d. New table linen was provided for the high table, and the accounts contain also these two entries : " For linen and making cloths and napkins, £2 4s. For wine in hall at entertainment to the Bishop of Durham our benefactor, £3 15s. To the University musick at the same time £1 1s. 6d." On Monday, August 26th Dr. William Stratford, Canon of Christ Church, wrote to Edward, afterwards Lord, Harley that the Bishop of Durham had been for the past fortnight at Lincoln College, and was now in his lifetime vesting in the college the great benefactions he designed for them " to the value, I believe, of £40,000. . . . He drops too, his benefactions of lesser note in other places, amongst them £100 to our library." [26] Hearne noted on the same day this gift of £100 to the new building designed for a library on the south side of Peckwater Quadrangle. Hearne also heard that he had given £100 to Queen's College, and though he was told afterwards that he had been misinformed, the first report was true.[27] Crewe had also given £100 for an altar-piece in the new church of All Hallows and £200 towards the spire, to which sum he added another hundred pounds in the following year. He had augmented the income of the Rector of Lincoln by £20, and that of each fellow by £10 and had further given money to the college for exhibitions. " So that this bishop may be looked upon as a good benefactor to the University of Oxon." [28] On Tuesday, 22nd at 2 p.m., a concert was given in the theatre for the entertainment of their aged visitor, who was present. " This," said Hearne, " was Dr. Charlett's contrivance and is laughed at." Hearne thought that if they provided the concert they should have seen to it that there was

[26] *Welbeck Abbey MSS.*, VII, p. 225.
[27] *Memoirs*, p. 38 n.
[28] *Hearne Collections*, O.H.S., VI, p. 83.

a speech, which ought to have been made by one of the fellows of Lincoln to which college he had been such a benefactor. " I am told the exhibitions he hath given are about twelve and all £20 per annum. He hath likewise augmented the income of four churches, ten pounds each, belonging to that college, viz. All Hallows (now called All Saints), Oxon, St. Michael's, Oxon, Coombe by Woodstock and Twyford in Buckinghamshire." [29] Dr. Stratford wrote again on the 30th : " The Bishop of Durham, good man, never withdraws his benefaction. I, as deputy treasurer, at present am now in possession of the £100." Crewe had also purchased all the houses between Lincoln College and All Hallows to build there accommodation for his new scholars and others. He finally left Oxford on Friday morning August 30th. Stratford wrote, " We mustered up all the horse we could in town to attend him out of the town, and he relishes the respects that have been paid him full well." Stratford seems to have been shocked by the conduct of Thomas Barker of Lincoln College who was in town, and though he owed everything he had to Lincoln College, " he never went to wait on the old gentleman." [30] But Hearne, after mentioning that Dr. Lupton, the bishop's chaplain, was with him in Oxford, says " Old Mr. Giffard tells me that he was formerly well acquainted with the bishop. Mr. Giffard offered to make a visit to his lordship, and the matter was made known to Dr. Lupton, though Mr. Giffard desired that his lordship might know that he was a non-juror. Dr. Lupton when he heard this said that the bishop ' did not care to have a visit from any stranger.' So Mr. Giffard did not go. He was afterwards informed that he did not care to see non-jurors." [31] William Bishop of Gray's Inn, writing to Dr. Arthur Charlett, referred to Crewe's visit : " What the good Bishop of Durham has done lately is wonderfully great and good, and he is commended and praised by all here that wish well to our church and universities." [32]

[29] *Hearne Collections*, O.H.S., VI, p. 84.
[30] *Welbeck Abbey MSS.*, VII, p. 226.
[31] *Memoirs*, p. 39.
[32] August 29th, 1717. *Memoirs*, p. 39.

Dr. William Lupton,[33] who had originally been recommended to the bishop for his chaplain by Dr. John Smith,[34] had been presented by Crewe to the ninth stall in the cathedral in 1715. Nelson described him as a fit model for the preachers of the rising generation.[35] One of his published sermons bears the title "*The Omniscience of God,* a Sermon preached in the Reverend and Right Honourable the Lord Bishop of Durham's Chapel at Steane in Northamptonshire, Oct. 2, 1720 and published at his Lordship's Request." Later he published a volume of sermons preached on several occasions.

Another of the bishop's appointments was that of John Dolben to the sixth stall. This was in April 1718; next year he removed to the eleventh.[36] Edward Harley the younger heard that the former prebend was worth £300 a year.[37] Dolben, who was the grandson of the Archbishop of York of that name, had importuned Crewe for a prebend for a long time, " but was refused, being chaplain to the late Queen, and not of the doctor's degree." These can hardly have been the real reasons : other prebendaries in Crewe's time had been royal chaplains, and certainly some were collated to stalls without doctorates. Moreover, he took his D.D. in 1717, and as he was turned out of the sub-deanery of the Chapel Royal in the following year he begged a prebend again from Crewe, who, according to his devoted unknown friend, exercised his goodness towards his enemy in this way, as he often did, Dr. Dolben and Dr. Morton being instances.[38] Laurence Echard, Archdeacon of Stowe, wrote a *History of England* in three volumes, in which he made some false statements about Crewe and his dealings with Samuel Johnson and several other

---

[33] William Lupton. Fellow Lincoln Coll. M.A. 1700, B.D. 1708, D.D. 1711. Curate of Richmond, Yorkshire, 1705. Lecturer St. Dunstan's-in-the-West 1706. Morning preacher, Lincoln's Inn. Afternoon lecturer, Temple.

[34] *Memoirs,* p. 38.

[35] Nichols, *Literary Anecdotes,* 1812, I, p. 140.

[36] John Dolben, M.A. Christ Church, Oxford, 1707. Rector of Burton Latimer and Vicar of Fyndon, Northants.

[37] *Welbeck Abbey MSS.,* V, p. 559.

[38] *Examination,* p. 105.

matters, and about Dolben's own father, Sir Gilbert Dolben and his actions at the revolution. The third volume of Echard's history came out in 1718, and between that and 1720, when the third edition was published, Dolben, without telling the bishop, wrote to the archdeacon to correct his statements, and the result was a series of alterations and omissions in the text and an appendix consisting of explanations, amendments, apologies and so forth. The new prebendary can hardly have been such an enemy after all.

During the last few years of his life Crewe was unable to undertake any work, he did not appear at all in his diocese and seems to have remained at Steane. Some episcopal duties were performed for him by other bishops. John Thomlinson, for example, was ordained in 1717 by Dr. John Robinson, Bishop of London, on letters dimissory from the Bishop of Durham. An Act of Parliament was obtained dividing Sunderland from Bishopwearmouth and making it a separate parish and a new church was consecrated there by the Bishop of London on September 5th, 1719. The sermon was preached by Thomas Mangey,[39] who was presented to the fifth stall in Durham cathedral, May 11th, 1721. " He gave Dr. Mangey a prebend of Durham, for a flattering dedication prefixed to a sermon which, as Dr. Richard Grey, then his domestic chaplain, assured Mr. George Ashby, he never read. He was fully satisfied with the dedication." [40] The story has been frequently told, and may or may not be true, but one may enquire how Dr. Grey knew that the bishop had never read the sermon. One might also add that there would have been more point in the story if Dr. Mangey had been an unsuitable person for the canonry, which was not the case. The men whom Crewe appointed to the cathedral were almost uniformly representative of a high standard of scholarship and

[39] Thomas Mangey, B.A. St. John's, Cambridge 1707, M.A. 1711, LL.D. 1719, D.D. 1725. R. of St. Nicholas', Guildford 1717, St. Mildred's, Bread Street, and Vicar of Ealing, Chaplain to Bishop of London. He published *Practical Discourses on the Lord's Prayer* and a number of sermons at different times.

[40] Granger, *Biog. Hist.*, 1775, IV, p. 285. *Gent. Mag.*, L, p. 394; LII, p. 551. Nichols, *Literary Anecdotes,* I, pp. 134–6. *Hutchinson,* I, p. 689.

general ability and Mangey in no way came short in these respects.

A little before the consecration of the church at Sunderland, Bishop Robinson, who was at Oxford in the August of that year, paid a visit to Lord Crewe at Steane. When one has seen two eminent prelates in these degenerate days chatting and joking in a third class railway carriage one reads the early eighteenth century story with admiration, using that word, be it understood, in its earlier sense. At five in the morning my lord of London accompanied by the vice-chancellor, Dr. Shippen, Principal of Brasenose, set out for Steane. The Bishop of Durham, having received " Intimation of their Intent," received them with great solemnity in " his princely purple robes." He had provided for them " a very real dinner," having procured for that purpose from his neighbour Mr. Cartwright a fat buck. Good French wine, usually a rarity at Steane, was also brought forth for their delectation. Then in the evening Dr. Robinson and the vice-chancellor returned to Oxford, weary perhaps, but with lively pleasure, we trust, in their recollections of a memorable day.[41]

In the summer of 1719 both the Bishop of Durham and the Rector of Lincoln, Dr. FitzHerbert Adams, were ill. In June the rector managed to make the journey to Steane to see the bishop, who was suffering from an attack of gout in the head, and Dr. William Stratford told Edward Harley that news of his death was expected hourly.[42] A week later, however, it was the rector who was dead. He died of gout in the stomach, and he was buried on June 30th in All Hallows' church. Crewe had always been very good to the fellows of Lincoln College, he promoted them whenever possible to his best ecclesiastical preferments, and he had been a benefactor to the college in many ways. He had given, for instance, in 1699 or 1700 a hundred pounds towards the panelling of the hall, and though he was not the sole subscriber there had been set up over the screen the arms of the see of Durham impaling Crewe, with an inscription " N. Crewe, Lord Bishop of Durham,

[41] *Memoirs*, p. 42.
[42] *Welbeck Abbey MSS.*, VII, p. 255.

sometime Rector." His more recent benefactions must have been fresh in their minds. As a token of gratitude the fellows requested Crewe to name a suitable person as rector. He refused at first, but after the request was renewed two or three times he proposed Dr. Lupton. There were hopes in some quarters that the latter would succeed FitzHerbert Adams,[43] but he is said to have been too strict a disciplinarian to be popular amongst the younger fellows. It has been suggested that Lupton had used his position as Crewe's chaplain to get the bishop to express a wish to see him rector and that the fellows resented this and, even at the risk of offending their benefactor, gave their votes to another candidate.[44] This was Dr. Morley, who was at that time incumbent of a Lincolnshire parish, and had been tutor to many of the younger fellows, who were resolved to have him and won over some of the others. On July 7th the college sent two of the fellows to Steane, bearing a letter to the bishop informing him of their choice and expressing the hope that Dr. Morley would be agreeable to him. Dr. Stratford of Christ Church said they would have done better if they had spared their compliment. Oxford was all agog, and it was expected that the old bishop would be very much displeased, and it was pretty generally believed that Lincoln College would lose much, if not all, of his intended bequests. Everyone knew that the old man was terribly upset at the death of his friend the rector, that he was unable to mention him without tears, and it was reported that he saw no visitors. Fears were widely expressed that his death would be hastened by all these distressing events. " His stomach, which has hitherto been good, fails him and is almost quite gone," which being interpreted signified that his appetite and digestion had failed him and that he was living on a light invalid diet. The octogenarian was sturdier than they thought and was not going to die for another two years. He had seen visitors ; he had received the two fellows who had been sent to tell him the decision of the college. He asked why they had requested him to nominate if they had determined to appoint

[43] *Welbeck Abbey MSS.*, p. 256.
[44] Andrew Clark, *Lincoln*, p. 173.

Dr. Morley. Morley was a stranger to him and he was too
old to make new friends. Dr. Lupton was his friend, but he
had not nominated him for that friend's private advantage :
on the contrary, Lupton would have been financially the loser
by the appointment, but he had suggested him because he
believed that the college would gain thereby.

In spite of this when the election formally took place on
the 8th Morley was unanimously elected. Lupton himself,
Knightley, Adams and William Watts stayed away. One story
is that Watts cast a single vote against Morley, but the register
of Lincoln College says quite clearly that the decision was
unanimous. Further confirmation is to be found in the fact
that Morley, who died in 1731, directed in his will that a
mourning ring should be given to every one of the fellows who
voted for his election, and his executor's accounts show that
nine such rings were provided.[45] Dr. William Watts [46] was
collated to the sixth stall in Durham cathedral at the end of
the following month and was made rector of Hinton in 1720
and of Wolsingham in 1721. It was said that his promotion
was a reward for his vote, but if it was a reward at all, it could
only have been for not voting for Dr. Morley.

The Bishop of Durham was very hurt at the treatment he
had received from the college. Probably he would not have
minded so much if they had not asked him to name the person
he would prefer. When the new rector called on him and
sent up his name, Crewe said he knew nothing of him and
gave him a very cool reception. He was asked whether he
" had any business," to which he replied that he had only
come to pay his respects, and he went away immediately after
dinner. That same day Dr. Watts was made one of the
bishop's chaplains [47] : this perhaps was his reward for his
friendship for Dr. Lupton. Crewe was reported to have
informed the fellows that they must expect no more from
him, that they were very much mistaken if they thought that
what he had already settled upon them was irrevocable, and

[45] *Memoirs*, p. 41 n.
[46] William Watts. Fellow of Lincoln 1706, M.A. 1708, D.D. 1719.
[47] *Memoirs*, p. 41.

that he had designed a benefaction of £30,000, but must now think of placing it elsewhere.[48] In October Stratford reported that Crewe had settled on the university his further benefactions intended for Lincoln College, reserving to himself to appoint by deed or will the uses of it.[49] Quite a number of people seem to have disapproved of the way in which the fellows had behaved to their benefactor, as is to be seen in sundry contemporary letters, among them one from Dr. Lindsay, Archbishop of Armagh, to Dr. Charlett.[50]

In June 1720 Crewe gave a hundred guineas to Worcester College for their chapel, and about a month later he presented portraits of Charles II, Catherine of Braganza, James II, Mary of Modena and himself to the Bodleian.[51] Sunday, July 2nd, 1721 was the fiftieth anniversary of his consecration as Bishop of Oxford. On the next day, at Crewe's invitation, a visit was paid him at Steane by the vice-chancellor, proctors and several heads of houses. They attended " in doctors' robes to solemnize the day with him " and it was arranged that he should receive them in purple velvet [52] but, sneered Hearne, it was " purely to flatter the bishop and try for money," whereby again Hearne betrays his waspishness, being unaware that the visitors came by invitation.[53] Dr. William Lupton preached a congratulatory sermon on the temporal advantages of religion, the text being " Length of days is in her right hand, and in her left hand riches and honour." [54] A magnificent entertainment was provided for the visitors, a band of music playing the whole time. Crewe himself presided at the first table, Dr. Lupton at the second and Dr. Mangey at the third. Comment was made at the time that no English bishop had ever held episcopal office so long, except Archbishop Bourchier of Canterbury, who was a bishop for fifty-two years. Since Crewe there have been others:

[48] *Welbeck Abbey MSS.*, VII, pp. 257–9.
[49] *Ibid.*, p. 262.
[50] *Memoirs*, p. 42.
[51] Hearne, *Collections*, VII, p. 146.
[52] *Welbeck Abbey MSS.*, VII, p. 301.
[53] Hearne, *Collections*, VII, p. 256.
[54] Proverbs iii. 16. Nichols, *Literary Anecdotes*, I, p. 140.

John Hough, first at Oxford, then at Lichfield, then at
Worcester, fifty-two years (1690–1742); Archbishop Harcourt
at Carlisle and York (November 6th, 1791 to November 5th,
1847) was one day short of fifty-six years, and Thomas Wilson
of Sodor and Man (1697–1755), the longest of them all, fifty-
eight years.

Old and feeble and dying as Lord Crewe now was he still
had to be considered. In 1721 a second edition of Anthony
Wood's *Athenæ Oxonienses* was expected from the press. On
his death-bed Wood had entrusted the work to Thomas
Tanner and, as everyone knew of Wood's dislike of the bishop,
there was great eagerness to see what he had said about him
in the added biographies in the new edition. When the work
came out they were disappointed in not finding " so much
scandal as probably they might expect." Tanner told
Dr. Charlett that he believed a good deal of Wood's work
had been burnt before his death. He himself had very considerably expurgated the life of Crewe; he had shown it in
confidence to a certain archdeacon who had talked about it
at Cambridge and hence the expectations of bitter and hostile
treatment. " In short, a northern doctor told me if such a
paper had been in his possession he would have managed it
so as to have got a prebend at Durham," in other words this
northern doctor would have tried to get promotion by a
method of blackmail hardly creditable to the doctor. " My
lord's reputation and character," said Tanner, " is safer in the
hands it is, of one that scorns such mercenary views, and
without such is inclined to let nothing pass which is incon-
sistent with good manners, and that regard that ought to be
paid to his high station in the Church, or, however, to his late
benefactions and charity, which should cover him from many
reflections." [55]

Hearne heard that Tanner had handed Wood's papers to
another person and had had no hand in the edition itself.[56]
Under the date " 28 August 1721, Monday," he wrote, " On
Thursday the vice-chancellor very busy about a new edition

[55] Tanner to Dr. Charlett, April 22nd, 1719. *Memoirs,* p. 44.
[56] *Memoirs,* p. 45.

of *Athenæ Oxonienses* that is come out." He went on to say
that there was a passage in it about the Bishop of Durham
which the vice-chancellor would not for all the world the
bishop should see, since it said that he was first a Puritan,
then a Papist, then an Orangian. Hearne did not think this
could have been written by Wood and thought the new
edition contained many spurious additions. But he went on
to say that the bishop was " an Oliverian and struck in with
the wicked Revolution, and hath always been a Trimmer, and
a very stingy ungenerous man : yet he never was a papist."
Next day Hearne saw the new edition and found that the
words about Crewe were not exactly what he had reported.[57]
In 1737 Dr. Richard Rawlinson informed a correspondent
that he had been assured by Bishop Tanner himself that no
alteration had been made in any one character, except an
omission in that of Bishop Crewe, who was spared as he had
been a great benefactor to the university and to Lincoln
College. He further added that the original manuscript had
been left in the bookseller's hands for many months for the
satisfaction of all those who were curious about it.[58]

Lord Crewe died at Steane on Monday, September 18th,
1721. The end came comparatively suddenly. He had been
feeble and ailing for a long time, but that day he was
suddenly taken worse and died in a few hours, the end coming
at nine o'clock in the evening. He was eighty-eight years of
age and had held the see of Durham for forty-seven years. He
was buried on the 30th in the chapel of the manor house
where lay his two wives Penelope and Dorothy. Hearne, who
a little before had abused him now wrote, " He was an accomplished gentleman as well as a pious and vigilant prelate, of
most excellent parts, which continued entire till his last
moments. His charity was equal to his piety, and as he
abounded in good works through the whole course of his life,
so he hath at his death, bequeathed all the remains, both of
his real and personal estate, to the like purposes." [59] These

[57] Hearne, *Collections*, VII, pp. 272–3.
[58] *Memoirs*, p. 46.
[59] Hearne, *Collections*, VII, p. 281.

contradictory accounts, common enough in all conscience, fail to make the historian's task easier, but it is pleasing to think that for once, the embittered Thomas Hearne had a glimpse of the real character of the dead bishop.

Two others at least bore similar testimony. On July 12th, 1722 Crewe's successor in the see of Durham, Sir William Talbot, translated thither from Salisbury, made his first appearance in his cathedral city, and was welcomed by Dr. Mangey in the name of the dean and chapter :

" My lord, I am, in the name of my brethren, to bid you welcome into this your country, and to wish you the long possession and happy administration of this diocese and county-palatine. It is with satisfaction that we behold you vested with a double character, and can pay respect and duty to you both as our spiritual and civil superior. His Majesty, with a good grace, and great justice, bestows this branch of ancient regalia upon one, whose services to himself have been so many and eminent, and who by descent from noble blood, and an entail of noble qualities, is so well qualified to manage the rights, and support the dignity, of so high a station. But, my lord, your revenues and jurisdiction are not the only subject of our congratulations; but we must likewise add to these, what must be much dearer to you in your spiritual capacity, the good order and regularity of your diocese. We may venture to assure your lordship (and to the steady vigilance of your two immediate predecessors it is owing), that in this see there are as few defects to supply, as few tares of heresy and false doctrine to weed out, as few abuses deserving episcopal correction, as in any other of the kingdom. Your lordship comes now to preside over a laity well affected to our excellent Church and your episcopal character; over a clergy orthodox, and strictly conformable with our canons, articles, and rubricks; and over a chapter, who hath hitherto been so happy, as neither to feel the censure, nor incur the displeasure of their visitor. Since our erection, our body hath never had any contests or disputes of right with their diocesans : there have been no attempts for unbounded power on either side, nor any struggle for unstatutable exemption and independency on ours; but we have all along lived in perfect amity and correspondence with them, as our patrons and spiritual fathers at home, as our guardians and protectors at Court. Such hath been our happiness, my lord, for near two centuries; and we hope for the continuance of it under your lordship's gentle and wise administration. We promise ourselves, that a double portion of that beneficent spirit, with which our ever honoured patron Lord Crewe was blessed, and with which he made all about him happy, rests now upon your lordship. And we have nothing greater to wish you in this world than that you may meet with the same returns of affection and respect from all ranks of men and the like measure of health, long life and prosperity from Divine providence." [60] Sir George Wheler also spoke and referred to " the long widowhood this church hath in a manner sustained by reason of our late excellent bishop's absence, occasioned by his great age and consequential infirmities." [61]

The bishop was buried in the chapel at Steane. Three flat plain black slabs mark where he and his two wives are buried. Towards the south side of the east end are two: that nearest the screen is the bishop's and beside it his second wife's. The inscriptions run :

Here lyeth ye Body
of the Rt. Revd. and Rt. Honble.
Nathanael Ld Crewe
Ld. Bp of Durham
who died Septr. ye 18th
1721
Aged 88.

———

Here lyeth y° Body
of y° Rt. Honble
Dorothy Lady Crewe
Wife of
Nathanael Lord Crewe
and daughter of

[60] Nichols, *Literary Anecdotes*, II, p. 151.
[61] Zouch, *Works*, 1820, II, p. 197.

Sr. William Forster
of Balmbrough in y^e County
of Northumberland K$^{nt.}$
who died Octbr. y^e 16th
1715
Aged 42.

Penelope lies nearer the west end almost opposite to the mural monument to her husband. She has no other memorial than this ledger stone, on which is inscribed:

Here lyeth interred
The Rt. Honble. Penelope
Lady Crewe
Wife of Nathaniel Lord Crewe
Baron of Steane
and Ld. Bishop of Durham
Daughter of Sr. Philip Frowde K^t.
in the County of Kent.
Who dyed in the 44th Year
of her age
The 9th Day of March
in the Year of Our Lord
1699.

Above the inscription are the arms, crest and supporters of Crewe, impaling, *Azure* three lions rampant *or* ducally crowned *gules* within a border *ermine.* Frowde.

The mural monument set up originally to the memory of Dorothy bears an inscription which must have been carved after the bishop's death since it bears his name before hers:

Near this place lyeth ye Body
of the Rt. Revd. and Rt. Honble.
Nathanael Ld. Crewe,
Ld. Bishop of Durham and Baron of Steane,
5th Son of John Lord Crewe,
He was born Jan ye 31, 1633.
was consecrated Bp. of Oxford 1671.
Translated to Durham in 1674.
was clerk of ye Closet and Privy Counsellour

in ye Reigns of K. Charles, ye Second and
K. James ye Second,
and died Sep^er ye 18th, 1721,
Aged 88.

Near this place lyeth ye Body
of ye Rt. Honble. Dorothy Lady Crewe
Wife of Nathanael Lord Crewe,
and daughter of Sir William Forster
of Balmborough in Northumberland K^t.
who died Oct^er ye 16th 1715   Aged 42.

The monument is of variegated marble.   Two circular
Corinthian pillars, with gilt bases and capitals, support an
architrave on which is raised a mitre between two coronets.
Below are the arms of Crewe, *Az.* a lion rampant *arg,*
impaling *arg,* a chevron *vert* between three bugle horns *sable,*
strung *gules,* Forster, with coronet and supporters.   The
inscription is in gold on a rectangular tablet of black marble.

As Crewe died without issue the peerage became extinct.
At the time of his decease his nearest relatives were the
children of his sister, the Countess of Sandwich, one of whom,
Dr. John Montagu, dean of Durham, was a trustee under his
will.   To the youngest of these children, James Montagu, he
bequeathed the manor of Newbold Verdon.   Under the
marriage settlement of Thomas, second Lord Crewe and his
second wife, the estate of Steane devolved on Jemima, wife of
Henry Duke of Kent, his third daughter in all but his first by
the second wife.   The duchess died on July 2nd, 1728, and
during the remainder of his life her widower occasionally
abode there.   He died on June 5th, 1740 and the property
was then sold to Sarah, Duchess of Marlborough, from whom
it passed to Earl Spencer.

The greater part of the manor house, about two-thirds of it,
was pulled down before 1750, the remainder was for a long
time a farm-house, but about 1890 when the house was sold
by the Spencers to Captain Alcock, this portion was restored
and considerable additions made.   The chapel, too, was not
destroyed, and in 1752 after repair and restoration at the

expense of Elizabeth, Countess of Arran, and William Cartwright of Aynhoe, was reopened for services. The preacher
at the reopening was Dr. Richard Grey, Crewe's old chaplain,
now Rector of Hinton with Steane, and his text was the text
which Mr. Speaker Crewe had caused to be inscribed over
the chapel door : " Holiness becometh Thine house, O Lord,
for ever." [62]

[62] *A Sermon Preached at the Opening of Steane Chapel* . . . on the
Renewing Divine Service and on Sunday, May 3rd, 1752. London 1754.

CHAPTER X

HIS NAME LIVETH

It is difficult to estimate Crewe's character fairly because so much of our information about him has come from his enemies. The Whigs hated him because he had so openly showed his loyalty to James. After 1688 the Tories hated him because he had accepted the new order of things. So had most of the Tories but it made no difference. Bishop White Kennet, the historian, disliked him for the former reason. That prejudiced gossip Burnet detested him for his Toryism. Anthony Wood, the Tory, has expressed the view of him which has generally been accepted since then, so much depends on how you state a thing : " When he saw that the Prince of Orange was likely to prevail he began to flinch and desert his master." [1] Wood had personal reasons for his dislike; Crewe had ousted his friend John Curteyne, with good reason, from his fellowship; moreover, he seems to have had jealous feelings about the bishop's successful career. Burnet also had a personal reason : he wanted the bishopric of Durham and didn't get it. This is his character of Crewe : " Though the Lord Crewe, both father and son, his father and brother, were two very worthy persons, yet he is in all respects a reproach to his birth and family; he is a very weak man, has no learning and less virtue, and is a fawning abject flatterer. He was raised by the king's favour in the former reign; but he found quickly that he was an insignificant man; he desired me in the time of his favour to go much to the Bishop of Durham to make somewhat of him. I went once or twice, but I found him so excessively weak that I told the duke that nothing could be made of him, so I gave over all further commerce with him. He waits only for a fair opportunity to declare himself a papist; for he has no religion at all. Yet when the business of the exclusion was on foot the

[1] Wood, *Ath.*, II, 1177.

Earl of Essex assured me that they knew if it had come near an equal division that he would have voted for it." [2] Burnet's prophecy in this passage never came true. As for what Lord Essex may or may not have said it may be replied that it is not wise to take too seriously a bitter remark of a disappointed party man after a defeat in the House.

Some hostile writers have even found fault with his generosity. Hutchinson admitted his beneficence but added that " his charity was sometimes observed to be exerted with too much ostentation." [3] This probably refers to the prevailing custom of inscribing his name or his arms on some of his gifts, a custom by no means peculiar to Crewe. A hostile writer referring to the above quoted sentence from Hutchinson said : " This encomium would have been more just if the bishop's generosity had not been displayed so late in life : and indeed, if it had not been for the most part posthumous. His benefactions during the space of forty-seven years were not to be compared with those which in eleven years had flowed from his predecessor in the see of Durham." [4] The sneer about his posthumous charities might be answered by remarking that even then he was not obliged to leave his money for such purposes, he had plenty of relatives who would no doubt gladly have received it.

Hearne accused Crewe of being rude and ungrateful. Dr. Cave in the second volume of his *Historia Literaria* spoke in high terms of Bishop Richard de Bury and added *utinam opulenta ista sedes semper haberet talem episcopum,* " which no doubt," said Hearne, " is a just reflection upon the present Bishop of Durham to whom the said Dr. Cave had dedicated some of his works, which that bishop had not acknowledged, as he was obliged in honour to have done." [5] Hearne also adds that when Crewe was under a cloud, Dr. Hudson, that he might do the bishop some honour, as well as gratefully commemorate Bishop Skirlaw the founder of the fellowship

---

[2] *Burnet's Original Memoirs,* H. C. Foxcroft's Supplement to Burnet, Oxford 1902, p. 212.
[3] Hutchinson, *Hist. Durham,* pp. 562–4.
[4] Kippis in *Biog. Brit.*
[5] *Hearne Collections,* O.H.S., I, p. 111.

he held, dedicated the first volume of his *Greek Geographers* to him, " for which he was no more considered by that bishop than by the others he has dedicated to." There is much virtue in this last clause. Books, dedicated with a fulsome preface to a patron, in the hope that he would contribute largely to the cost of publication, might, *pace* the shades of Dr. Samuel Johnson, become a nuisance to a wealthy man, and if he were of a sensitive disposition might appear to him a mild form of blackmail. Hearne was a cross-grained fellow like Anthony Wood, a High Churchman, and an unbending Tory and he disliked Crewe. " I can say no more of this bishop than that in compliance with the fashion of the age he is a digamist," [6] said he, though he did say more elsewhere.

The view of Lord Crewe's life and character thus set forth by hostile witnesses in his lifetime has lasted until our day. It was expressed by Mandell Creighton in the *Dictionary of National Biography.* The late Professor Gwatkin said that the two worst of Charles II's promotions to the episcopate were Wood of Lichfield and Crewe of Durham.[7] Even the National Portrait Gallery describes him quite unnecessarily as " time serving," although it is not the custom of that institution as a rule to supply epithets to the names of the persons whose portraits hang upon its walls. Now a writer who pleads for a reversal of a traditional condemnatory judgment always lies open to the accusation of whitewashing. Be it so : a great many traditional conceptions have been altered in modern times, and to wipe off mud is not the same thing as white-washing.

It is difficult to realize the mental confusion of many people generally loyal to the Stuart house during the events of the end of 1688 and the beginning of 1689. Only the Whig leaders knew what they really wanted. Most people believed that William had not come seeking the crown. The King had been very difficult, they thought, but the King's son-in-law was coming over; something would be done and matters would be

[6] *Hearne Collections*, O.H.S., I, p. 305.
[7] H. M. Gwatkin, *Church and State in England to the Death of Anne,* 1917, p. 380.

straightened out. William came, but with an army, the King
fled, the party in power put William and Mary on the throne,
and when it was all over people sat up and gasped at the
breathless rush of events and the final result. There was fear
that the triumphant Whigs would take revenge for those whom
they considered the martyrs of the Rye House plot, and Crewe
retired abroad. However, a proscription was avoided and he
could go back to Durham. His master's daughter was on the
throne and he would as far as possible ignore the Dutchman,
so he contented himself with things as they were. He did not,
as many did, give lip service to William and letter service to
James. He had hitherto taken comparatively little interest in
politics; henceforth he took still less. He was faithful to his
master's daughters while they lived. The Hanoverians came
in and there was nothing to do but accept them. At heart his
sympathies were with the Jacobites, though he took no part
in plots or rebellions. The story is told that almost in his last
moments he cried out to Richard Grey, his chaplain, " Dick,
Dick, don't go over to them," but the story may be apocry-
phal. He could think of his old masters with affection,
even though he had been disillusioned; certainly he had
none of the romantic loyalty of Granville, or of those who in
after years shed their blood for a lost cause. He had an
Englishman's common sense and common sense is never
romantic.

Nathaniel Crewe had his weaknesses. There was something
of the great prelate about him. The Anglican bishops few in
number, members of the Upper House, and courtiers all, had
retained this worst side of episcopacy through and since the
Reformation. This was one of the great objections of the
nonconformists against episcopacy—they called it prelacy.
There were exceptions, of course, like Ken of Bath and Wells
and Thomas Wilson of Sodor and Man. Those were the days
when the lords of the council and all the nobility were treated
with respect and even adulation not given to common men.
Crewe had in addition his rank as a baron and the considerable remains of his palatine powers. One sees this lordly
attitude peeping out at times, but it came natural to him and

perhaps he is hardly to be blamed. At times one feels a certain coldness in his nature, partly perhaps due to his high position, which led to a certain fastidious withdrawal from the common touch, and perhaps even there was a tinge of shyness in it.

He was certainly kind to his friends. The first time Tillotson preached before Charles II it was through Crewe's influence, and afterwards he persuaded the King to order the sermon to be printed, to make Tillotson a royal chaplain, and to send him personally to Tillotson with the news. He used his influence to get Dr. South promoted to Westminster and to Christ Church, Oxford. In his earlier days he seems to have been friendly with Stillingfleet; in 1668 we find them exchanging Court duties.[8] Spearman complained that his appointments to prebends in Durham were exercised in such a way that he had a majority of his friends in the chapter and so a useful check on the bishop's actions was removed. It is true that he promoted many men from Lincoln College to stalls in his cathedral and that some of them were his devoted friends : it is also true that he gave stalls to men like Morton and Falle who certainly were not. In any case it is not easy to see in what way the chapter could have been a check on the bishop's doings. Spearman, in spite of his occasional criticisms, thought well of him, and expressed an intention, never carried out, of writing the lives of " those three good bishops, Morton, Cosin and Crewe." Crewe was always a good-natured man, but there were times when he had to refuse the too frequent applications made to him by great men for promotion for their friends, and so he sometimes gave offence.

In the seventeenth century high position and great hospitality went, as a rule, hand in hand, and Crewe's hospitality at Durham and Auckland was on a lavish scale. When Francis North, Lord Guildford went as judge of assize on the northern circuit " the bishop carried his lordship to his ancient seat called Auckland, and the entertainment was in all points while his lordship stayed in the palatinate . . . truly great and

[8] *C.S.P.D.* Car. II, 238/183, April 23rd, 1668.

generous." Crewe was the first Bishop of Durham to entertain His Majesty's judges at his own expense, and his successors continued the custom until the founding of the
University of Durham in the nineteenth century, and the
judges still have official lodgings in the ancient castle, now
University College.

Crewe's career at Lincoln College implies that he was
prominent among his fellows for his learning. Spearman tells
a story, however, intended to show how little he was
acquainted with the practice of the law, though he does him
the justice of prefacing it with " it is said." Crewe was in one
of his own courts and " hearing John Doe called desired that
he might not be condemned in the matter before the court
until he could be heard : but being told that John Doe was
only a man of straw he blushed at his mistake and seldom or
never appeared on the bench after." [9] Knowing as we do
what the exercise was which was required of Crewe for his
degree of Doctor of Laws we need not be surprised that he
was ignorant of the fictions of legal practice. The story at
least shows a fairness of mind and a kindly heart.

He has been described as a good judge of men and a patron
of learning [10] and he had a ready wit. He was an acceptable
preacher : and people who should have been capable of
judging spoke well of his sermons. Archbishop Sharp said
that he had a talent for writing, so that it is all the more to be
regretted that not one of his discourses has come down to us,
but he gave instructions to his friends to be careful that after
his death nothing should be published under his name. He
probably feared that spurious editions or garbled versions of
his writings might come forth from the press.

His servants said he was the best of masters and his tenants
that he was a good landlord, and his diocese had good reason
to acknowledge the truth of the last statement, for on few of
his lands were the rents ever raised during his time. He felt
it a duty to his successors to maintain his palatine rights. For
this purpose he caused careful search to be made in the

[9] *Spearman*, p. 103.
[10] Zouch, *Works*, II, p. 157.

ancient records of the see and from the extracts thus collected
Spearman composed the first part of his *Enquiry*.[11] He
was not, however, merely a great lord. According to his
lights, and they were the lights of the seventeenth century, a
time when bishops were expected to spend a great part of
their time in London, he was a pastoral bishop who visited his
diocese regularly, entertained his clergy freely, visited distant
parishes for Confirmation instead of confining himself to
certain centres, and spent money with an open hand. When
he died his personal property was only £400, but he
bequeathed all the revenues of his extensive landed property
to be used in ways which have benefited the church and the
poor ever since.

It has been said that many men have been canonized for
works of beneficence greatly inferior to those of Nathaniel
Crewe. Whatever the truth of this, it it true to say that during
his lifetime his generous deeds were many and that since his
death innumerable people have had cause to bless his name.
To give a complete list of his benefactions would be impossible.
In Durham cathedral he repaired the episcopal throne, and
his arms are carved on the door at the bottom of the steps to
it. The organ, organ case and carved screen given by Cosin
and Crewe were taken down in 1846. Some of the woodwork found its way to University College, Durham, and a part
of the organ went to the chapel of that college. Recently the
chapter has been able to reassemble from different quarters
the middle portion of the screen on which the organ case
stood. At present it stands in the south aisle of the nave, and
it is so high that there is no room for the great shield of arms
of Crewe, the mitres on either side of it being five feet in
height.

In Durham castle he spent large sums on repairs and in
beautifying the place. He extended Tunstal's chapel by two
bays and placed a fine bell in the Tunstal turret.[12] He adapted
some of the older rooms, the present state rooms, if he did not

[11] *Hutchinson*, I, p. 695.
[12] *Durham and Northd. Arch. Soc.*, V, p. clxxix.

DURHAM CASTLE IN THE TIME OF CREWE.
From a painting in University College, Durham.

Facing page 323.

build them,[13] and he did some repairs to the keep and the north-west turret. A picture in the small state room shows the castle as it was before Wyatt's restoration, and the Norman windows on the south side before Bishop Trevor altered their shape and covered over the worn masonry with eighteenth century ashlar. In the courtyard is seen the bishop's coach with its six black horses : while a trumpeter waits to give the signal to depart. In the castle chapel is a prayer book bound in royal red, with two interlacing C's showing they came from the Chapel Royal of Charles II. These were given by Crewe. At Auckland castle in the year of the revolution he erected the organ and organ loft in the palace chapel.[14] The church of St. Andrew, Bishop Auckland, possesses and still uses a beautiful set of silver altar vessels given to it by Crewe on the occasion of its episcopal jubilee. To the corporation of Durham he presented a silver tankard, six silver candlesticks, a silver loving cup and cover, and a silver whistling pot and cover. To Lincoln College in 1717 he continued his past kindness by giving the sum of £474 6s. 8d. per annum to increase the incomes of the rector, fellows, chaplain, scholars and Bible clerk.[15] He did not leave so much to Lincoln as he originally intended, being hurt by their refusal to elect his candidate rector, and so some of the proposed gift went to the university. There is in the college a Bible given by him, also bearing on the cover the royal crown and Charles II's monogram of two interlacing C's,[16] and evidently from the Chapel Royal. He also contributed to the new buildings of Queen's College, Oxford. The spire of the church of All Saints', Oxford, fell in the year 1700, demolishing the roof, and Crewe subscribed £200 for the spire and £100 for the altar piece : this church had close associations with Lincoln College. The year before he died he gave to the church at Steane a handsome set of silver vessels for the altar, consisting of a paten and chalice, flagon and alms-dish engraved with

---

[13] H. Gee in R. S. Rait's *Episcopal Palaces of York*, 1911, pp. 184–6.
[14] M. E. Simpkins in Rait, *Ep. Pal.*, pp. 84–6.
[15] S. A. Warner, *Lincoln College*, London 1908, p. 16.
[16] *Ibid.*, p. 65.

his mitre and coronet; a marble altar, with crimson velvet to cover it, and similar velvet for the reading desk and pulpit. The chalice is of silver and measures 7 inches in height, $3\frac{1}{2}$ inches across the bowl and 4 inches across the foot, and bears the inscription "Gift of Rt. Hon. Nathaniel, Lord Crewe, for use of Parish Church of Steane. Anno 1720." Here also he presented a Bible and Prayer Book which had been " diligently handled " by King Charles II. The Bible is dated 1660 and has a fine engraved title page. That in the library of the University of Durham has some slight differences in the engraving and is dated 1659. He gave £100 to the Westminster dormitory, and in 1719 made handsome augmentations to the hospitals of Brackley, Hinton, Durham and Auckland. At Newbold Verdon he founded a free school and some time after 1715 another free school at Bamburgh.

By his will signed on June 24th, 1720 he left his property in trust to Dr. John Montagu, Dr. Morley, rector of Lincoln College, Dr. William Lupton, Dr. Thomas Eden, and Dr. John Dolben. To each of his trustees he gave a dozen silver trencher plates, to the poor of the city of Durham £200, to the poor of Bishop Auckland £300, to every one of his domestic servants a year's wages above what was due to them. To various friends and servants he left legacies, among which was one of £30 to his coachman John Coventry and £10 to Coventry's wife. In addition he left to John Coventry an annuity of £10 a year to survive to his wife and Thomas their son. The trustees were to pay £20 a year up to eight years to each of the twelve exhibitioners of Lincoln College, Oxford, that he had already named and appointed, and to such as should be elected after his decease; to the eight poor scholars of Trap and Marshall in Lincoln College and to the Bible clerk there so much as would increase their endowment to £10 a year each; and to the rector of the college £20, and to the fellows £10 each yearly. He bequeathed to the minister of the parish of Bamburgh and his successors £40 yearly; to the minister of St. Andrew's, Bishop Auckland, £30 yearly; £10 a year each in augmentation of twelve poor livings in the diocese of Durham; £10 each annually to the four parishes of

All Saints' and St. Michael's, Oxford, Combe, Oxfordshire and Twyford, Bucks, for catechizing the youth in those parishes; to the alms people at Durham and Bishop Auckland and others named, an augmentation of forty shillings a year each. To the schoolmaster of North Verdon he left £20 a year; and he bequeathed £30 to build a school house at Newbold Verdon; £10 a year for the relief of the widows and children of poor clergymen deceased within the hundred of Sparkenhoe; £6 a year for the maintenance of a charity school at Daventry; £100 a year to the mayor and aldermen of Durham for charitable uses; £20 a year to a schoolmaster to teach thirty boys at Bishop Auckland and £30 a year to clothe the boys. All his bequests were to be free of tax. Any surplus funds out of his property were not to be used by the trustees to augment any of his benefactions to Lincoln College, the University of Oxford or the city of Durham but to such other charitable uses as his trustees should appoint.

By a codicil to the will, dated September 17th, 1721 he gave *inter alia,* to Edward Wortley, late ambassador to Constantinople, his silver cistern; to James Montagu his gilt tankard; to Ralph Trotter the picture of Dorothy, Lady Crewe; to Dr. William Lupton Kneller's portrait of himself in his baron's robes; to the mayor and aldermen of Oxford a dozen silver plates; a silver dish for the altar of Newbold Verdon and £30 towards the altar piece there; and to his secretary, Mr. Richard Grey, his palatine and episcopal silver seals and seal manual. All his books Crewe left for such uses as he should appoint and for want of appointment as the trustees should think fit. No one knows what became of his books and papers after his death. Probably, like his plate and carriages, they were disposed of by his trustees; but no trace of them has been left except that in the Bodleian Library is a volume [17] of John Parkhurst's *Epigrammata Juvenilia* bearing his autograph, " Nath. Crew." There is a note in it written by Anthony Wood: " This book following did belong to Mr. Nathaniel Crewe of Linc. Coll. afterwards Bishop of

[17] Wood, 334, No. 2.

Y

Durham : who exchanged it, amongst others, for other books of Joseph Godwin, a book seller at the upper end of Cat Street. I afterwards bought it of him." [18]

Crewe left to the University of Oxford the sum of £200 per annum to be used as the chancellor, masters and scholars should think fit. There was a great deal of squabbling and controversy over it. On July 12th, 1722 the late bishop's will was read in convocation. " Mr. Whiteside of the Museum " told Hearne that Mr. Grey of Lincoln College, who was " a sort of secretary to the bishop," give it under his hand, and offered to give an oath to the vice-chancellor, that the bishop designed that the sum of £30 a year should be set aside for a professor of experimental philosophy and that his twelve exhibitioners should be allowed the benefit of two of his courses of lectures.[19] From Whiteside he heard a little later that month what decision had been made about the apportionment of the gift, but in September there was a meeting of heads of houses, where in spite of much disagreement, they settled on a different arrangement.[20] Nothing seems to have come of this either, for on Wednesday, June 6th in the following year the vice-chancellor proposed that a certain annual sum should be paid to the public orator, the reader in poetry, the reader in philosophy, and the registrar of the vice-chancellor's court. There was great opposition, and he solemnly declared to the house that what he suggested was in accordance with the late bishop's own intention. Nevertheless his proposals were thrown out one after the other, and seeing they would refuse everything he went no further. Stratford said that only a few Christ Church men were present and that they readily voted for what was reasonable, though they would have opposed some other things which it had been intended to bring forward. The vice-chancellor had become thoroughly unpopular because of certain of his dealings with University College, and anything he proposed would be

[18] Wood, *Life and Times,* I, note, p. 450.
[19] Hearne, *Collections,* VII, pp. 286, 382.
[20] *Ibid.,* pp. 386, 399, 400.

thrown out right or wrong. " Nothing," said Dr. Stratford, " will go down during this man's mayoralty." [21]

The university authorities seem to have been undecided about the application of the bishop's bequest nearly ten years later, for among the papers in the Tanner MSS. there is a sworn deposition by Richard Grey, formerly Crewe's domestic chaplain, that the bishop had several times expressed his intentions in the matter and had once commanded him to write them down. His firm belief was that amongst other things which he could not recollect so long afterwards, the testator had desired his bequest to be expended in the following way : £30 per annum as stipend of a reader in experimental philosophy, an addition of £30 per annum to the stipend of the professor of music, an addition of £60 per annum to that of the public librarian, £10 a year in books for the Bodleian Library and £10 a year to the vice-chancellor. Also he desired that £20 a year each should be given to the university orator and the poetry lecturer, " who in consideration thereof should be obliged alternately to make a speech in commemoration of the benefactors to the university in the public theatre once in the year, upon the day in which this speech should be spoken. He likewise intended an entertainment should be made for the heads of houses, doctors, professors, proctors and those who were to be sharers of his benefaction and should be present at the said speech. For which entertainment was to be allowed yearly the sum of ten pounds." [22]

This last desire of Lord Crewe is still annually fulfilled. At the Encaenia in June the vice-chancellor invites the doctors, proctors, heads of houses and those about to receive honorary degrees " to partake of Lord Crewe's benefaction " in his own college before the ceremony. The " entertainment " by custom consists of champagne and strawberries, after which they go in procession to the Sheldonian Theatre. The Creweian oration is delivered in alternate years by the professor of

[21] Hearne, *Collections,* VIII, pp. 84–5. *Welbeck Abbey MSS.,* VII, pp. 360–1.
[22] Tanner MS. 314, f. 203.

poetry and the public orator, and though mainly a commemoration of benefactions, yet by long tradition it deals also
with the chief events in the university during the past year.
Here is the first paragraph of the oration delivered by the
professor of poetry in 1935 :

Depromite, quæso, Academici, chartulas istas quas cæri-
moniarum ordine inscriptas in sinu fertis : evolvite : quæ
contineant paullulum, si voltis, considerate. Hic nobilis
Episcopi Dunelmensis Nathaniel Baronis Crewe nomen præ-
clarum duobus locis invenietis memoratum : primo, quo pro
larga sua munificentia cum Baccho tum Pomonæ sacrum
instituisse dicitur, cui nonnulli τῶν καθ' ἡμᾶς παχέων non
sine summa voluptate nuper adfuerunt ; altero, quo hunc
sollemnem Benefactores nostros honorandi ritum posteris
instaurandum curavisse. Inter quos ipsius fundatoris nomen
in primis commemorare gaudeo ; hoc solum mihi contionanti
scrupulum iniecit quod cum paucis vestrum hunc diem adhuc
Baccho hilarare contigerit, contionem iam omnes pariter
exaudietis.

The bishop's will provided that when any one or two at the
most of his trustees should die, then the survivors should
within three months elect one or more clergymen to serve as
trustees, provided that they should never be more than five in
number, of whom the Rector of Lincoln College was always
to be one. One of the earliest acts of the first three executors
was to fulfil the clause in the will endowing twelve parishes in
the diocese of Durham with an additional £10 a year. The
parishes chosen were Lanchester, Pittington, St. Helen's,
Auckland, Barnard Castle, Witton-le-Wear, Shotley, St. Mary-
le-Bow, Durham, Grindon, Castle Eden, Hartlepool, Hamsterley and Darlington.[23] The church of the abbey of Blanchland was in 1752 repaired and made into a chapel-of-ease by
the trustees. During the eighteenth and nineteenth centuries
Crewe's castle of Bamburgh became the headquarters of a
most noble charitable work. Dr. John Sharp, Archdeacon of
Northumberland, who became a trustee in 1758 conceived

---

[23] Allan MSS., Durham Cathedral Library, VI, p. 4.

the idea of applying a portion of the surplus income to the assistance of the poor, the establishment and maintenance of schools and the relief of necessitous seamen. Bamburgh castle, which for over a century had been falling more and more into decay, was during Sharp's lifetime repaired and rendered habitable, the archdeacon himself bearing the expense. The plan was to adapt the keep to be used as the headquarters of the Crewe charities and to complete the buildings for schools and other benevolent institutions. Dr. Sharp himself resided in the keep for a great part of the year in order to give personal superintendence, and to prevent the cost of the great building becoming a burden upon the trustees he conveyed to them in 1778 some lands and tenements near Bamburgh, the income of which would be available for the maintenance of the fabric; on his death also bequeathing additional funds for the purpose. A library was established in the castle in 1778 by the trustees who purchased the books of the Rev. Thomas Sharp, incumbent of Bamburgh, who died in 1772. When Archdeacon Sharp died in 1792 he left to this library his own books and a great part of the collection which had previously belonged to his grandfather, John Sharp, sometime Archbishop of York. Considerable additions have been made to the library since then.[24] The library, however, was only a small part of the activities at the castle. Corn was ground for the poor at the windmill, there was a granary well stored for their use in hard times and a grocer's shop where goods were sold to them at cost price. At the infirmary a thousand patients a year received medical assistance. There were rooms and beds for shipwrecked sailors. The coast was patrolled in stormy weather and watch was kept from one of the towers for ships in distress. For the benefit of the fishermen a bell was kept ringing on stormy nights from a turret of the keep; during fogs a signal gun was fired from a turret every fifteen minutes for the benefit of ships in danger near the rocky coast. In the castle there were separate schools for boys and girls numbering together about

[24] Catalogue of the Library of Bamburgh Castle, printed by the Order of the Trustees of Lord Crewe, London 1856.

two hundred. Some thirty poor girls were maintained alto-gether in the institution until sixteen years of age and trained for domestic service.[25]

By judicious management the income of the trust increased considerably so that by 1850 it was about £9,000 per annum. Time has, of course, brought changes. A scheme for Lord Crewe's general charity was approved by orders of the Court of Chancery on June 29th, 1875 and June 17th, 1876. Another scheme was established by order of the Charity Commissioners on March 31st, 1896, and a further scheme on August 12th, 1898. In 1894 and succeeding years the £100 set aside for apprentices was paid by the Crewe trustees to the trustees of the Apprentice Charity, and a further scheme for the latter charity was approved on May 7th, 1901. The castle was purchased by Lord Armstrong in the latter part of the nineteenth century and a good deal of restoration and alteration was carried out by him about 1894.

Under the scheme at present in force for Lord Crewe's charity the trustees are the Rector of Lincoln College, two representative trustees appointed by the Bishop of Durham, one representative trustee appointed by the Bishop of New-castle, and three co-optative trustees, one of whom shall be a clergyman resident in the diocese of Durham and one a clergyman resident in the diocese of Newcastle. The pay-ments under Lord Crewe's will are still made. The trustees are authorized to continue any payments to public elementary schools, or to the repair or construction of churches on any land belonging to the charity. They may apply a sum not exceeding £200 in providing medical and nursing for the sick poor resident in the parish of North Sunderland as long as there is land in the parish belonging to the charity. Every year they had to pay £100 to the owner for the time being of Bamburgh Castle in aid of crews and ships in distress and shipwrecked sailors in maintaining a fog gun or signal at Bamburgh Castle, but this duty has been within the last few years taken over by the Trinity House. Dr. Sharp's library is

[25] W. S. Gibson, *A Visit to Bamburgh Castle*, 1850.

CREWE'S SEAL.
Photograph by C. H. Hunter Blair Esq., F.S.A.

Facing page 331.

to be kept up and facilities provided for its use by the clergy and others in the diocese of Durham and Newcastle. The income of the funds representing Dr. Sharp's gift is to be applied primarily to this purpose. The residue of the charity is divided into nineteen parts, of which eleven are applicable to the diocese of Durham and eight to the diocese of Newcastle, the money to be used for the benefit of the clergy in each diocese by the augmentation of their stipends, or by assistance in the education of their children, or in times of sickness.

How Crewe would have rejoiced had he lived to see all this. A friend wrote of him, " As his stronger years were active for the public, so his later time was well spent in pious and charitable benefactions. His riches, honours, park houses and all worldly advantages, as they were derived from his friends, so did he no less esteem their names, and constantly and gratefully remembered them, with an affectionate veneration. Many were the families he raised and greatly God preserved him." [26]

* *Examination*, p. 107.

APPENDIX I

In the name of God Amen.

Nathaniell, Lord Crewe, baron of Steane in the county of Northampton and lord bishop of Durham being of sound and disposeing mind and memory. Praised be God for the same. Doe make publish and declare this my Last Will and Testament in manner following that is to say In the first place I returne my Spirit to God that gave it most humbly begging pardon for all my Sins in and through the alone merits of my blessed Saviour Jesus Christ declaring myself to be a true Protestant of the Reformed Church of England as now by Law Established. And my Body I comitt to the earth from whench it was taken in the hope of a joyful Resurrection at the Last Day when all shall be called to an account before the great Tribunall. *And as* to my Funerall I desire that it may be a decent and private manner and the expense thereof not to exceed 500£ and my Body to be Interred in the Buryall place at Steane next to my dearest and truly Vertuous and Religious Wife Dorothy, Lady Crewe. *As* to my Mannor of Newbold Verdon and all other my lands and heredita-ments in the county of Leicester from and after my decease I have given the same to James Montague Eldest Son of my Nephew the Honorable Charles Montague Esq and his Heirs Male as by deed will appear. *Item* I do hereby give devise and bequeath unto my neice the Honourable Mrs Anne Joliffe,

Widow, Eldest daughter of the Right Honorable Thomas, Lord Crew deceased and to her
heires and Assigns for ever. *All* that my
messuage or Tenement or farme with the
appurtenances comonly called or known by
the name of Stevens or Cassanson Farme.
And all those meadows and lands and hereditaments whatsoever to the same Messuage
or Farme belonging or appurtaineing or there-
with now or late used, occupyed or Enjoyed
situate Standying Lyeing and being in the
Comone Fields Liberties Precincts Territoryes
and parish of Lawford in the County of
Essex being Lett at the yearly rent of Sixty
Five pounds or thereabouts and now or late
in the possession of John Boreham his Assignes
or Under tenants. *And whereas* my Mannor
of Dalehall in the said County of Essex and
all Lands and Hereditaments therto belonging
comonly called Dalehall being together of the
yearly value of £130 or thereabouts are now
mortgaged for the principle Sume of £1,500.
And whereas I owe my nephew the Honorable Edward Carterett Esqre upon Bond the
principle sume of £500. *Now* my Will is and
I doe hereby direct and appoint that both the
said Sume of £1,500 and £500 and all
Interest now due and to be due for both the
same Sumes shall be paid and discharged out
of my said Manor of Dalehall and out of the
Lands and Hereditaments thereunto belonging and not out of my personall Estate. And
I doe hereby Charge my said Manor of Dalehall and all my lands and hereditaments
thereunto belonging with the payment of the
said Sumes of £1,500 and £500 and with the
Interest now due and to be due for both the
same Sumes of £1,500 and £500. *Item* I

Dalehall.
Charged with £1,500
& £500 to Edward
Carterett Esqre

doe hereby give devise and bequeath unto my
said Nephew the Honorable Edw. Carterett
and to his Heires and Assignes for ever my
said Manor of Dalehall and all my said Lands
and Hereditaments thereto belonging comonly
called Dalehall charged neverthelesse as aforesaid with the payment of the said Sumes of
fifteen hundred and 500 with all Interest due
or to be due for the same, But if my said
Nephew Edwd. Carterett shall after my decease to take and accept of my said Manor of
Dalehall and the Lands and Hereditaments
thereunto belonging by me devised to him as
aforesaid by reason of the charges thereupon
THEN and in such case I do hereby give and
devise my said Manor of Dalehall and all the
Lands and Hereditaments thereunto belonging charged nevertheless as aforesaid unto the
Honorable John Montague doctor in Divinity
and deane of Durham the Reverend John
Dolben doctor in Divinity and Prebendary of
the cathedrall church of Durham the Reverend
John Morley doctor in Divinity and Rector of
Lincolne Colledge in the University of Oxford
the Reverend William Lupton doctor in
Divinity and Prebendary of the said Cathedrall church of Durham and the Reverend
Thomas Eden doctor of Lawes and Prebendary of the said Cathedrall church of
Durham their Heirs and Assignes. But if it
shall happen my said Mannor of Dalehall and
the Lands thereunto belonging shall not be
sufficient to answer and pay all the Charges
payments and money charged thereon Then
my will is and I doe in such case direct and
order that all such sume and sumes of money
as shall be wanting to make good the De-
ficiency of any money payments and charges

Dalehall devised over to the Trustees if Ed. Carterett refuses to take it with the charges thereon.

charged on my said Mannor of Dalehall and
the Lands thereunto belonging shall be made
up and supplyed to the said John Mountague
John Dolben John Morley William Lupton
and Tho. Eden and their Heires out of any
of my personall Estate and as to my Mannor

of Plegdon Hall in the parish of Henham in
the said County of Essex from and after my
decease I have granted to my Nephew
Thomas Cartwright of Aynoe in the said
County of North'ton Esq and his Heires and
Assignes for ever as by deed will appear.
Item I doe hereby give devise and bequeath
unto the said John Mountague John Dolben
John Morley William Lupton and Tho : Eden

their Heirs and Assignes (whom I doe hereby
make appoint and nominate my Trustees for
the performeing of all and every the Trusts
and Confidences in this my Last Will contained) All those my Mannors of Balmbrough
and Blanshland with their rights members and
appurtenances in the County of Northumberland and in the County of Durham or in
either of them and alsoe my Advowsons
Donations and Right of Patronage and Pren-
sentation of and the Churches of Balmbrough
and Shotley and to either of them in the said
Countyes of Northumberland and Durham or
in one of them and all and every other my
Mannors Advowsons Messuages Cottages
Mills Mines Quarryes Meadowes Pastures
Closes Woods Underwoods Fishings Fisheryes
Tythes Rectoryes Rents Services Lands Tenements and Hereditaments whatsoever with
their and every of their rights members royal-
tyes priviledges and appurtenances scituate
Lyeing and being renewing or to be had
received or taken in or within the several

Townes Feilds Libertyes parishes precincts or Territoryes of Balmbrough Blanshland Shorut on Sunderland Shorston Heatham Beadnell Berwick Burton Newham Bradford Fryars Lucker Warinford Monsin Warinton uggle Budle Acton Cowbyar Broomshill haugh Briskside alias Birkside Shildon Hadderyburne Shotley Westhaugh-head Westhaugh Hoof Easthaugh head Easthaugh Hoof Thornton Edmondshill Hunsdornoorth Holy Island Norham in any or every of them in the said Countyes Northumberland Durham or in either of them or elsewhere in the said Countyes of Northumberland and Durham or in either of them of which any person or persons whatsoever now is or are seized in Trust for me my Heirs and Assignes or for the use of me my Heirs and Assignes in the said countyes of Northumberland and Durham or in either of them and which I lately purchased and are of the yearly value of Thirteene Hundred and Twelve pounds Thirteene Shillings or thereabouts To have and to hold my same Mannors Hereditaments and premisses with their rights members and appurtences unto the said John Mountague John Dolben John Morley William Lupton and Tho. Eden their Heires and Assignes upon and under such Trusts and to and for such uses Ends intents and purposes as I shall hereafter by this my last will

A dozen of Silver Trencher Plates to each of the Trustees.

direct and appoint. *Item* I give to each and every of my Trustees before named a dozen of Silver Trencher Plates. *Item* I give for the poore people of the Citty of Durham and

200^{ll} to the poore of Durham. 300^{ll} for the poor of Aukland.

Suburbs the rest of the Sume of 200^{ll} to the poore of Bishop Aukland in the said County of Durham 300 to be distributed amongst them in such proportions as my Trustees before named or the major parte of them shall think fitt. *Item* I give to M^r. Richard Stonehewer M^r. Ralph Trotter and M^r. Francis Pewterer and for every one of my domestick servants as shall receive wages from me and be Liveing with me at my death one whole yeares wages over and above the wages due to them respectively and to Jane the Wife of John Coventry my coachman besides her yeares Wages as aforesaid and alsoe over and above the Wages due to her the sume of 10. *Item* I give to M^r. John Wallis and M^r. Richard Grey Clerks eighty pounds apeece. *Item* I give to my Nephew the said Deane of Durham 100 to buy him Mourning all which Legacyes I direct shall be paid within 12 monethes next after my decease. *Item* I give to my servant Mr. Tho. Baty besides his yeares Wages as above and alsoe over and above the Wages due to him the sume of 100 to be paid him within 12 monethes after my deceas. *Item* I give to my Nephew the Honorable James Mountague the elder Esq who was with me beyond sea at the Revolution the sum of 100 to be paid him within six monethes after my decease. *Item* I give the sume of 30 to build a Schoolehouse at Newbold Verdon aforesaid to teach the Children of the same parish in gratis to write and read unlesse I shall build such schoolehouse in my life. *Item* I do hereby nominate and appoint Mr John Gilbert of Newbold Verdon aforesaid to be First Schoolemaster at Newbold Verdon aforesaid. *Item* I doe hereby order will and direct whatsoever person or persons who shall be at all times for ever hereafter Owner or Owners of my Capitall Messuage

Marginal notes:

yeares wages to servants

Jane Coventry 10

Mr. Wallis & Mr. Grey 80 apeece.

Dean of Durham 100

Mr. Baty 100

The Honble. James Monntague Sen. Esq 100

30 for a schoole at Newbold Verdon

Mr. Gilbert Schoolemaster

Owner of Mannor House at Newbold Verdon to choose Schoolemasters or Mannor House in Newbold Verdon aforesaid for the time being shall from time to time and at all times forever after my decease as often as occasion shall require Nominate Elect and Choose a Schoolemaster and Schoolemasters who shall teach gratis the children of the parish of Newbold Verdon aforesaid to write and read which said Schoolemaster or Schoolemasters shall be subject and liable to such orders Removals and Regulations as to the said Owner or Owners of my said Capitall Messuage or Mannor House in Newbold Verdon aforesaid for the time being shall from time to time seeme meete and convenient. *Item* I doe hereby give unto my coachman John Coventry besides his wages due to him and besides his yeares wages as aforesaid during his life the yearly sume of 10 and from and after his decease I do hereby give unto Jane Coventry his wife the yearly sume of 10 during her life and from and after their deceases and the decease of the survivor of them I do hereby give unto Tho : Coventry son of the said John Coventry dureing his life the yearly sume of Ten Pounds the same sums of 10" to be paid to them respectively in manner as aforesaid out of the Rents of my said Mannors Lands and Hereditaments in the said Countyes of Northumberland and Durham without any deduction or abatement for Taxes or any other matter or thing whatsoever by halfe yearly equall payments. *Item* I doe hereby declare that I have given and devised my said Mannors Advowsons Lands and Hereditaments in the said countyes of Northumberland and Durham as aforesaid Upon Trust and Confidence that they the said John

10 Anno to John Coventry his wife and son Thomas for life successively

Mountague John Dolben John Morley William Lupton and Tho. Eden and the

survivors and survivor of them and the Heires and Assignes of the survivor of them doe and shall from time to time and at all times for ever hereafter as occasion shall require nominate present such person and persons to the said Churches of Balmbrough and Shotley and to either of them as the said John Monntague John Dolben John Morley William Lupton and Tho: Eden their Heires and Assignes shall think fit and convenient and upon this further Trust that the said John Monntague John Dolben John Morley William Lupton and Tho. Eden and the survivors and survivor of them and the Heires and Assignes of the survivor of them doe and shall out of the Rents issues and profits of my said Mannors Hereditaments and premisses in the said Countyes of Northumberland and Durham for ever hereafter pay or cause to be paid the yearly sume of 20 to each and every of 12 Exhibitioners of Lincolne Colledge in

the University Oxford which I have already named and appointed or which I shall hereafter name and appoint and to each and every of 12 Exhibitioners to be Elected and chosen after my decease as herein after mentioned who shall be Undergraduate Comõners in Lincolne Colledge aforesaid and who are or shall be Natives of the Diocesse of Durham and for want of such Natives of Northallertonshire or Howdenshire in the County of York or of Leicestershire and particulerly of the parish of Newbold Verdon or the Diocese of Oxford whereof I was formerly Bishop or of the County of North'ton in which County I was Borne and my Will is and I doe hereby

direct that such Exhibitioner and Exhibitioners
on any Vacancy or Vancancyes of any Exhibitioner or Exhibitioners by me already
named and appointed or to be by me hereafter named and appointed upon any other
Vacancy or Vacancyes whatsoever shall be
from time to time and at all times for ever
after my decease Elected and chosen by the
Rector and Fellowes of Lincolne Colledge
aforesaid for the time being or by the major
parte of them and to Enjoy the said Exhibitions or Annuall payments for Eight yeares if
they shall respectively soe long continue
Resident in the Colledge aforesaid and noe
longer unless they have Leave from the Rector
of the Colledge aforesaid for the time being
to be absent which I desire he will not grant
but upon reasonable cause and I doe hereby
direct that as often as any Vacancy or

When Exhibitioners
on Vacancyes to be
chosen

Vacancyes shall happen of such Exhibitioner
or Exhibitioners others shall be Elected in
their Roome within three monethes in manner
as aforesaid and upon this further Trust that
the said John Mountague John Dolben John
Morley William Lupton and Tho : Eden
their Heires and Assignes doe and shall out
of the Rents Issues and profits of the said
Mannors Lands and Hereditaments in the
said Countyes of Northumberland and Durham devised to them as aforesaid for ever
hereafter pay the Annuall Sumes hereafter
mentioned that is to say Unto the Minister of

To the Minister of
Balmbrough 40 p.
Anno

the said parish Church of Balmbrough in the
said County of Northumberland and his successors the yearly sume of 40 And to the
Minister of Saint Andrews Church in Aukland in the said County of Durham and his

successors the yearly sume of 30 and the yearly sume of 10 apeece for the Augmentation of 12 poore Rectoryes Viccaridges small Liveings or Curacyes in the Diocese of Durham such as shall be by any writeing or writeings codicill or codicills under my hand and seale to be attested by Three or more Credible Witnesses from time to time direct and appoint and in default thereof to and for the Augmentation of 12 such poore Rectoryes Viccaridges small Liveings or Curacyes within the Diocese of Durham aforesaid as the said John Mountague John Dolben John Morley William Lupton and Tho: Eden and the survivors and survivor of them and the Heires and Assignes of the survivor of them shall direct and appoint *and* unto the Ministers Lecturers or Curates of the parishes of All Saints and Saint Michaells in Oxford of Twyford in the County of Bucks and of Comb in the County of Oxford which belong to Lincolne Colledge aforesaid and to their severall successors for the time being the severall yearly sumes of 10 apeece for Catechizing youth within the same respective parishes *and* unto the poore schollars of Trap and Marshall in Lincolne Colledge aforesaid being Eight in number such Annuall sums as will make up and increase their respective Schollarships may be all alike in their respective yearly values and to the Bible Clerke of Lincolne Colledge aforesaid such Annual sume as will make up and increase his sallary to the yearly sum of 10 Includeing what he already receives on Account of his said Clerkship *and alsoe* the yearly sume of 20 to the Rector of the said Colledge and the yearly

z

20 to the Rector and 10 apeece to the Fellowes of Lincolne Colledge

sum of 10 apeece to each of the said Fellowes of the said Colledge which benefactions I give to the said Rector and Fellowes of Lincolne Colledge and to the Colledge aforesaid being the place where I had my education and of which Colledge I was first Fellow and

40ˢ apeece to the Almspeople of Durham Aukland Brackley and Hinton.

afterwards Rector *And* each of the Almesmen and Almeswomen in each of the Hospitalls in Durham and Bishop Aukland aforesaid of the foundation of Bishop Cosins and to each of the six almeswomen in the Hospitall in Brackley in the said County of North'ton of the Foundation of my Honoured grandfather Sʳ Tho : Crew and to each of the two Almeswomen in the Hospitall in Hinton in the said County of North'ton of the Foundation of Elisha Hele Esq the severall yearly sumes of Fourty shillings apeece *and* to such

20 to the Schoolemaster of Newbold Verdon.

Schoolemaster of Newbold Verdon aforesaid for the time being the yearly sume of 20 *and* to the Trustees for the time being of the Hundred of Sparkenhoe in the said County of Leicester for the Releife of the Widowes Orphans and Children of poore Clergymen

Sparkenhoe 10 for releife of Widowes and children of Clergymen.

deceased and to their successors the yearly sume of 10 to be by the said Trustees and their successors distributed for the Releife of Widowes Orphans and Children of poore Clergmen deceased within the said Hundred in such proportions as the said Trustees and their Successors shall think fit *and* unto the Minister and Church Wardens of the parish

Daventree 6 for a Charity School

of Daventree in the said County of North'ton and to their successors the yearly sume of six pounds to be by them paid and applyed for and towards the support and maintenance of a Charity Schoole to teach poore Children of the said parish of Daventree to read English

and write all which said Annual payments I
will and direct shall be for ever hereafter in
manner following that is to say unto the said

When all the pay-
ments to commence.
Almesmen and Almeswomen by quarterly
equall payments that is to say on the Feasts of
Saint Michaell the Arch-Angell Saint Thomas
the Apostle the Annunciation of the Blessed
Virgin Mary and Saint John the Baptist The
first payment thereof to begin and to be made
at such of the said Feasts which shall first and

All moneyes given to
Lincoln Colledge to
be paid to the
Burser.
next happen after my decease and all other
the Annual payments by half yearly equall
payments that is to say at the Feasts of Saint
Michaell the Arch-Angel and the Annunciation of the Blessed Virgin Mary the First payment thereof to begin and be made at such of
the same two last mentioned Feasts which shall
first and next happen after my decease *and* I
doe hereby will order and direct that all the
said Annuall payments by me directed to be
paid to the said Rector Fellowes Exhibitioners
poore schollars of Lincolne Colledge aforesaid and to the said Ministers Lecturers or
Curates of All Saints Saint Michaell Twyford
and Comb aforesaid and to the Bible Clerke
shall be from time to time received by the
Burser of the said Colledge for the time being
as other Rents of the said Colledge are by him
received to be by him paid for the uses aforesaid and for noe other uses whatsoever whom
I doe hereby direct shall give security to pay
the money comeing to his hands by virtue of
this will to the uses aforesaid to the satisfaction of the Rector and Fellowes of the
Colledge aforesaid *and* my will is and I doe
hereby direct that all the said Annuall pay-

All Annuall payments
without deduction for
taxes etc.
ments for ever hereafter shall be made without any deduction or abatement whatsoever

for Taxes Charges or Assessments for or by reason of any Act or Acts of Parliament already made or hereafter to be made or by reason or meanes of any other payments matter or thing whatsoever and to begin to be made in manner as I have herein before directed *and whereas* the Right Honble Lady Stawell hath a Rent charge of 350 p Anno for her Life issueing out of my said Mannors Lands and Hereditaments in the said Countyes of Northumberland and Durham *now* my will is and I doe hereby order and direct the surplus rest and residue of the Rents and issues and profits of my said Mannors lands and Hereditaments in the said Countyes of Northumberland and Durham if any after the

Surplus of the Rents during the Lady Stawell's Life to such uses as my Lord shall direct and for want thereof to such uses as the Trustees think fitt.

said Annuall payments shall be paid but not before shall during the Life of the said Lady Stawell be paid disposed and applyed by the said John Mountague John Dolben John Morley William Lupton and Tho : Eden and the survivors and survivor of them And I doe hereby give and devise the same to and for such Charitable use and uses as I shall hereafter by any writeing or writeings Codicill or Codicills under my hand and seale to be attested by Three or more Credible Witnesses from time to time direct and appoint And for want of such direction and appointment to and for such Charitable use and uses as the said John Mountague John Dolben John Morley William Lupton and Tho : Eden and the survivors and survivor of them and the Heires and Assignes of the Survivor of them shall from time to time direct and appoint subject neverthlesse to the provisoe herein after contained concerning the same *and* from and after the decease of the said Lady

Stawell but not before I doe hereby order and

How the surplus of
the rents disposed
after the Lady Sta-
well's death.
direct that all the surplus rest and residue of
the Rents issues and profits of my said Mannors Lands and Hereditaments in the said
Countyes of Northumberland and Durham
and after the said Annuall payments shall be
made but not before shall be from time to
time and at all times for ever thereafter paid
applyed and disposed by the said John
Mountague John Dolben John Morley
William Lupton and Tho : Eden and the

200 p Anno after
the Lady Stawell's
death to be paid for
such publick use of
the University of
Oxford as my Lord
directs and for want
thereof as the Chan-
cellor Masters and
Schollars think fitt.
survivors and survivor of them and the Heires
and Assignes of the Survivor of them and I
doe hereby give and devise the same to and
for the uses and purposes and under the
Trusts and confidences hereafter mentioned
that is to say *Upon Trust* and confidence that
they the said John Mountague John Dolben
John Morley William Lupton and Tho. Eden
and the survivors and survivor of them and
the Heires and Assignes of the survivor of
them doe and shall from time to time and at
all times for ever after the decease of the said
Lady Stawell pay the yearly sume of 200 part
of the said Surplus rest and residue of the said
Rents Issues and profits of my said Mannors
Lands and Hereditaments in the said County
of Northumberland and Durham after the
said Annuall payments shall be made but not
before unto the Chancellor Masters and
Schollars of the said University of Oxford for
the time being and their successors to be by
them paid applyed and disposed to and for
such publick use and uses of the said University of Oxford as I shall hereafter by any
writeing or writeings Codicill or Codicills
under my Hand and Seale to be attested by
Three or more credible witnesses from time to

time direct and appoint And for want of such
direction and appointment To and for such
publick use and uses of the said University of
Oxford as the Chancellor Masters and Schollars of the University aforesaid for the time
being and their successors shall from time to
time direct and appoint *and alsoe* that they,
the said John Mountague John Dolben John
Morley William Lupton and Tho : Eden and
the survivors and survivor of them and the
Heires and Assignes of the survivor of them
doe and shall from time to time and at all
times for ever after the decease of the said
Lady Stawell pay the further yearly sume of
100 other part of the said surplus rest and
residue of the said Rents Issues and profits of
my said Mannors Lands and Hereditaments
in the said Countyes of Northumberland and
Durham after the said Annuall payments
shall be made but not before unto the Mayor
and Aldermen of the said Citty of Durham
for the time being and to their successors to
and for such Charitable use and uses of the
said Citty of Durham and suburbs thereof as
I shall hereafter by any Writeing or Writeings
Codicill or Codicills under my hand and Seale
to be attested by three or more Credible Witnesses from time to time direct and appoint
And for want of such direction and appointment To and for the putting and placeing out
such and soe many poore Children of the said
Citty of Durham and Suburbs thereof Apprentices to such Trade or Trades as the said
Mayor and Aldermen of the said Citty of
Durham for the time being and their Successors or the major part of them shall from time
to time direct and appoint *And Alsoe* that the
said John Mountague John Dolben John

100 p Anno after
the Lady Stawell's
death to be paid to
such uses of the
Citty of Durham as
my Lord directs and
for want thereof for
the putting out poore
children Apprentices
within that Citty.

Morley William Lupton and Tho : Eden and
the survivors and the survivor of them and the
Heires and Assignes of the Survivor of them
doe and shall from time to time and at all
times for ever after the decease of the said
Lady Stawell pay the further yearly sume of
20 other parte of the Surplus rest and residue
of the said Rents Issues and profits of my said
Mannors Lands and Hereditaments in the
said Countyes of Northumberland and Durham after the said Annuall payments shall be
made but not before to a Schoolemaster to
teach gratis Thirty such poore Boyes of the
parish of Bishop Aukland aforesaid to read
and write and who shall be taught for soe
Long time and noe Longer as the Minister
Churchwardens and Vestry of the said parish
and their Successors for the time being shall
from time to time Elect nominate direct and
appoint *and* that they the said John Mountague John Dolben John Morley William
Lupton and Tho : Eden and the Survivors and
Survivor of them and the Heires and Assignes
of the Survivor of them after the said
Annualle payments shall be made but not
before doe and shall from time to time and at
all times for ever after the decease of the said
Lady Stawell alsoe pay the further yearly
Sume of Thirty pounds other parte of the
surplus rest and residue of the Rents and
profits of my said Mannors Lands and Hereditaments in the said Countyes of Northumberland and Durham to and for the cloathing
of Thirty such poore Boys soe to be taught to
read and write as aforesaid in such manner
and with such distinction of Habit as the said
Minister Churchwardens and Vestry of the
said parish of Bishop Aukland and their Suc-

Marginal notes:

20 p. Anno after
the Lady Stawell's
death to a Schoole-
master at Bishop
Aukland.

30 p Anno after the
Lady Stawell's death
to cloath 30 poore
Boyes at Bishop
Aukland.

cessors for the time being or the major parte of them shall from time to time direct and appoint *and* my Will is and I doe hereby order and direct that the said John Mountague John Dolben John Morley William Lupton and Tho : Eden and the Survivors and Survivor of them and the Heires and Assignes of the Survivor of them shall from time to time and at all times for ever after my decease and the decease of the said Lady Stawell as often as occasion shall require Nominate Elect and choose a Schoolemaster and Schoolemasters who shall for ever hereafter teach gratis the 30 poore Boyes of the parish of Bishop Aukland aforesaid to write and read as aforesaid which same Schoolemaster or Schoolemasters shall be Subject and Liable to such orders Removalls and Regulations as to the said John Mountague John Dolben John Morley William Lupton and Tho : Eden and the survivors and survivor of them and the Heires and Assignes of the Survivor of them shall from time to time seeme meete and convenient. *Item* after the decease of the said Lady Stawell all the rest residue and remainder of the said surplus of the said Rents Issues and profits of my said Mannors Lands and Hereditaments in the said Countyes of Northumberland and Durham if any after all the said Annuall payments shall be made but not before I doe hereby Will order and direct shall at all times for ever after the decease of the said Lady Stawell be paid applyed and disposed by the said John Mountague John Dolben John Morley William Lupton and Tho : Eden and the survivors and survivor of them and the Heires and Assignes of the survivor of them And I doe hereby give and

devise the same to and for such Charitable use
and uses as I shall hereafter by any writeing
or writeings Codicill or Codicills under my
hand and Seale to be attested by Three or more
Credible Witnesses from time to time direct
and appoint And for want of such direction
and appointment To and for such Charitable
use and uses as the said John Mountague John
Dolben John Morley William Lupton and
Tho : Eden and the survivors and survivor of
them and the Heires and Assignes of the
survivor of them shall from time to time direct
and appoint *and* my Will is and I doe hereby
direct that all the said Last mentioned Annuall

payments of 200 to the said University of
Oxford of the said 100 to the said Mayor and
Aldermen of the said Citty of Durham of the
said 20 to the said Last mentioned Schoolemaster and of 30 for the cloathing of the said
Thirty poore Boyes as aforesaid shall for ever
after the decease of the said Lady Stawell be
made without any deduction or abatement
whatsoever for Taxes Charges or Assessments
for or by reason of any Act or Acts of Parliament already made or hereafter to be made
or by reason or meanes of any other payments
matter or thing whatsoever by half yearly
equall payments that is to say the Feasts of
Saint Michaell the Arch Angel and the
Annunciation of the Blessed Virgin Mary The
First payment thereof to begin and be made
at such of the same two last mentioned Feasts
which shall first and next happen after the
decease of the said Lady Stawell *Provided*
alwayes and my Will is and I doe hereby

order and direct that the Surplus rest and
residue of the Rents Issues and profits of my
said Mannors Lands and Hereditaments in

the said Countyes of Northumberland and
Durham by me before devised to be applyed
and disposed of by the said John Mountague
John Dolben John Morley William Lupton
and Tho: Eden and the Survivors and
Survivor of them and the Heires and Assignes
of the Survivor of them as aforesaid for such
Charitable uses as they shall direct shall not
at any time for ever hereafter either during
the life of the said Lady Stawell or after her
decease be paid given disposed of or by any
wayes or meanes whatsoever applyed by the
said John Mountague John Dolben John
Morley William Lupton and Tho: Eden and
the survivors and survivor of them and the
Heires and Assignes of the survivor of them or
by any of them either for the Increase or
Augmentation of any of the Guifts Charityes
or Benefactions by me before given to the said
University of Oxford to Lincolne Colledge
aforesaid and the said Citty of Durham aforesaid or the suburbs thereof or for any other
use or uses Charity or Charityes whatsoever
or to or for the said University of Oxford
Lincolne Colledge aforesaid and the said Citty
of Durham or suburbs thereof or of any or
either of them. *Item* I give to the said John
Mountague John Dolben John Morley
William Lupton and Tho: Eden the several
Mourning to Trustees sumes of 12 apeece to buy the Mourning over
and above the legacyes I have herein before
given them. *Item* I give to the said John
Wallis Richard Grey Ralph Trotter Richard
Stonehewer Francis Pewterer and Tho. Baty
Mourning to servants the several sumes of 10 apeece to buy them
Mourning over and above the Legacyes I have
herein before given them. *Item* I give to my
servants Mr. James Peters Mr. Edward Grey

and Mr. Benjamin Hilton the severall sumes of 10 apeece to buy them Mourning if they shall be respectively Liveing with me at my decease. *Item* I give to my servants Tho. Elston George Carleton John Bradford Tobias Jackson and Richard Clapham if they shall be respectively Liveing with me at my decease the severall sumes of Eight pounds apeece to buy them Mourning over and above the Wages I have given them as aforesaid. *Item* I give to the said Jane Coventry if she shall be Liveing with me at my decease the sum of 8 to buy her Mourning over and above the Legacyes I have herein before given. *Item* I give to each of my Livery Men-servants that shall be Liveing with me at Steane aforesaid at my decease and to each of Maidservants that shall be Liveing with me at Steane aforesaid at my decease the severall sums of 7 apeece to buy them Mourning over and above the Wages I have given them as aforesaid. *Item* I give to my servants John Buttery William Jackson William Braggens and Mary his Wife if they shall be respec-tively Liveing with me at my decease the several sumes of Foure pounds apeece to buy them Mourning over and above the wages I have given them as aforesaid. All which last mentioned Legacyes for Mourning I will and direct shall be paid within one moneth after my decease. *Item* I doe hereby give unto the said Chancellor Masters and Schollars of the University of Oxford aforesaid the Pictures of King Charles the Second and of Queene Katherine his consort and of King James the second and of Queene Mary his consort all drawn by Mr. Ryley and now being in the drawing Roome at Steane aforesaid to be

The pictures of King Charles the 2d & his Queene & of King James the 2d & his Queene to the University Oxford.

placed in such place in the said University as
the said Chancellor Masters and Schollars

shall think fit. *Item* my Will is and I doe
hereby direct that the communion plate and
all the Furniture belonging to the Chappells
of Durham and Bishop Aukland which were
left by my predecessor Bishop Cosin shall be
carefully transmitted by my Executors to my
Successor to the Bishoprick of Durham for the
use of the same Chappells immediately after
my decease and the Election of my successor
to the Bishoprick aforesaid *and* untill such
time as there shall be a successor Elected to
the Bishoprick aforesaid I doe hereby direct
that the Deane and Chapter of Durham
aforesaid for the time being shall have the
Care and Custody of the same Communion
plate and Furniture *and* my further Will is
that the Organ now being in the Chappell in

Bishop Aukland aforesaid which I erected at
my owne charges and costs shall be and
remaine and I doe hereby give the same
organ for the use of the same Chappell *and* to
the intent my said Mannors Lands and Hereditaments in the said Countyes of Northumberland and Durham may for ever hereafter
be conveyed and assured to and for the uses
and upon and under the Trusts aforesaid my
Will is and I doe hereby order and direct that
when any one or two at the most of my said

Trustees or of any other person or persons to
be hereafter Elected Trustee or Trustees for
the purposes in this my Last Will contained
shall happen to dye That then the Survivors
of them or the major part of the survivors of
them shall within Three moneths after such

death or deaths Elect one or more Clergyman
or Clergymen and noe other person or persons

whatsoever to be Trustee or Trustees in the Roome of him or them soe dyeing as they in their discretion shall think fit soe as such Trustees doe never Exceed Five in number and which said person or persons soe to be Elected Trustee or Trustees shall have the same powers and authorityes to all Intents and purposes whatsoever as the Trustees appointed by this my last Will and shall alsoe within Three monethes after such Election grant and convey All my said Mannors Lands and Hereditaments in the said Countyes of Northumberland and Durham by me before devised for the purposes aforesaid To the use of the Surviveing Trustees and of such person or persons soe to be Elected and chosen Trustee and Trustees and of their Heires and Assignes to and for the uses and purposes and under and subject to the Trusts and Confidences by me herein before directed and appointed as aforesaid the Charges of which Conveyances I direct shall be paid out of the Rents of my said Heriditaments devised to my Trustees as aforesaid. *Item* my Further Will is that the Rector of Lincolne Colledge aforesaid for the time being shall be at all times for ever hereafter one of my Trustees And therefore I doe hereby order and direct when the said John Morley shall happen to dye that then my present and future Trustees their Heires and Assignes doe and shall within Three monethes after the respective death and deaths of the said John Morley and of all future Rector and Rectors of Lincolne Colledge aforesaid Elect and choose such person and persons as shall be at all times for ever hereafter Rector and Rectors of Lincolne Colledge aforesaid for the time being to be Trustee and Trustees in the

Rector of Lincolne Colledge always to be a Trustee.

Roome of such Rector or Rectors soe dyeing and which said Rector and Rectors of Lincolne Colledge aforesaid soe to be Elected Trustee or Trustees as aforesaid shall have the same powers and Authorityes to all Intents and purposes whatsoever as one of the Trustees appointed by this my Last Will And I doe further direct that the surviveing Trustees doe and shall within Three monethes after such election grant and convey all my said Mannors Lands and Hereditaments in the said Countyes of Northumberland and Durham by me before devised for the purposes aforesaid To the use of the surviveing Trustees and of such Rector of Lincolne Colledge aforesaid for the time being soe to be elected and chosen Trustee and of their Heires and Assignes Neverthelesse to and for the uses ends Intents and purposes and under and subject to the Trusts and confidences by me herein before directed and appointed or to be by me hereafter appointed as aforesaid. *Item* I doe hereby give unto the Most Noble Henry Duke of Kent and to my Neece his Dutches All my Household goods and Furniture and

Pictures in my House in Steane aforesaid and in the outhouses thereunto belonging all my Bookes and Plate Excepted and except the Foure Pictures as I have herein before devised to the Chancellor Masters and Schollars of the University of Oxford aforesaid and except all my Scrutores Truncks Desks and Boxes whatsoever my will being that my said Bookes Plate the said Foure excepted Pictures and the said Scrutores Truncks Desks and Boxes shall not passe to the said Duke and to his Dutches by this my Last Will. *Item* I doe hereby give

all my Bookes unto and for such use and uses

as I shall hereafter by any Writeing or Write-ings Codicill or Codicills under my hand and Seale to be attested by Three or more Credible Witnesses from time to time direct and appoint and for want of such direction or appoint-ment To and for such use and uses as the said John Mountague John Dolben John Morley William Lupton and Tho: Eden and the Survivors and Survivor of them and the Heires and Assignes of the Survivor of them shall direct and appoint. *Item* I doe hereby give to the said James Mountague son of my said Nephew Charles Mountague All my Household Goods Furniture and Pictures in my House in Newbold Verdon aforesaid and in the outhouses thereunto belonging. *Item* all the Furniture and Bookes and Communion plate now used in the Chappell or in the parish Church at Steane aforesaid I doe hereby give for the use of the said Chappell or parish Church *And* my further will is and I doe hereby direct and appoint that the said John Mountague John Dolben John Morley William Lupton and Tho: Eden and the Survivors and Survivor of them and the Heires and Assignes of the Survivor of them and all succeeding Trustee and Trustees their Heires and Assignes shall be satisfyed and paid for their Charges and Expenses which they any or every of them shall be put unto Lay out or Expend in or about the Execution of all every or any of the Trust or Trusts aforesaid or by reason of any matter or thing whatsoever any wayes relating to or concerning this my Last Will or the Trusts herein contained *And* that neither the said John Mountague John Dolben John Morley William Lupton Tho: Eden or the Survivors or Survivor of them or the

Marginal notes:

direct and for want thereof as the Trus-tees shall direct

Household goods at Newbold to Mr. Mountague.

Furniture to the Chappell of Steane.

Trustees charges to be paid.

Heires or Assignes of such Survivor or any succeeding Trustee or Trustees shall be any wayes charged or chargeable for any more money than what every one shall severally and actually receive Nor shall be any wayes Answerable or chargeable the one for the other nor for the act or acts deed or deeds Receipts defaults or miscarriages of the other. *Item* all the rest residue and remainder of my personnal Estate whatsoever and wheresoever if any I doe hereby give and bequeath unto the said John Mountague John Dolben John Morley William Lupton & Tho. Eden and to the Survivors and survivor of them to be by them or the major parte of them applyed and disposed of to and for such charitable use and uses as the said John Mountague John Dolben John Morley William Lupton and Tho : Eden or the Survivors or Survivor of them or the major parte of them shall from time to time think fitt. *Item* I doe hereby make and constitute the said John Mountague John Dolben John Morley William Lupton and Tho : Eden Executors of this My Last Will and Testament *In Trust* neverthlesse for the uses and purposes aforesaid hereby Revoakeing all former Wills by me heretofore made *In Witnesse* whereof I the said Lord Crewe Lord Bishop of Durham have to this my Last Will and Testament set my hand and Seale this Foure and Twentyeth day of June in the yeare of our Lord one Thousand Seaven Hundred and Twenty.

Codicil.

I Nathanael L. Crewe Lord Bishop of Durham having made my last Will and Testament bearing date June 24 1720 Do hereby make this Codicil as part thereof as fully to be observed as if therein contained

that is to say Imprimis I give to my niece the
Honble Mrs. Cartwright my finest set of
Damask Linen. Item I give to Mr. Edw.
Wortley late Ambassador to Constantinople
my silver cistern. Item I give to Mr. James
Montagu my Gilt Tankard. Item I give to
Mr. R. Trotter the Picture of Dorothy Lady
Crewe. Item I give to my servant Mr Thomas
Baty all my cloaths and Wearing Apparel.
Item I give to Dr. Wm. Lupton my Picture
drawn by Sir G. Kneller in my Barons Robes
now hanging in my great Parlour. Item I
give to Mrs. Eliz. Cartwright my set of course
knives and forks and spoons. Item I give to
the Mayor and Aldermen of the City of Oxford for the time being one Dozen of my
Silver plates for the use of the Corporation.
Item I give one of my silver plates such a one
as I have given to Steane chapel for the use
of the Altar at Newbold. Item I give ten
pounds to Mr. Andrew Crewe for mourning.
Item I will that my Trustees provide all
necessary wearing apparel for Charles Franks
during his apprenticeship and when he is out
of his time I give him five pounds. Item I
give to my secretary Mr. R^d. Grey my Silver
Seals that is to say my Palatine and Episcopal
Seals and Seal Manual. I declare this to be a
part of my last will anything in my said will or
in any former will to the contrary notwithstanding. In Witness whereof I have hereunto set my hand and Seal this 17 day of Sept.
1721. And WHEREAS in my will I have left
my books to be disposed of as my Trustees
shall direct I do hereby declare my meaning
to be that they shall not be sold but given and
distributed as they or the major part of them
shall think fit. In Witness whereof I have

hereunto set my hand and seal this said 17
day of September in the year of our Ld 1721.
                                    N.D.C.
Signed Seald and Delivered and declared to
be part of his will by the Ld. Bishop of
Durham in the presence of
    Wm. Halifax
    Caleb Byard
    John Jones [1]

---

[1] Bodleian MSS., Add. C. 303, f. 209.

APPENDIX II

NUMEROUS portraits of Crewe still exist. Probably the following list is not complete.

1. *In the Gallery of the Bodleian Library.* Robed as a peer. Painted by Kneller in 1698. This portrait was afterwards engraved by Faber.

2. *Lincoln College Hall, Oxford.* One in the *Rector's Lodgings,* probably the original of the one at Blanchland. Two in the Hall: one in baron's robes, one in bishop's surplice, of date 1674.

3. *Bamburgh Castle.* (1) Crewe as a young man in cassock and bands. (2) As a bishop, with a coronet beside him, and a book bound in blue in his hand.

4. *Cuddesdon. The Bishop's Palace.* In the dining hall. Crewe in ordinary walking dress.

5. *Durham. Chapter Library.* Crewe as a bishop. Cf. 3 above.

6. *Durham. University College. Senior Common Room.* Crewe as a bishop, probably soon after he came into the Crewe title.

7. *Durham. University College Hall.* Crewe as a baron.

8. *Durham. Mayor's Chamber, Town Hall.* Crewe as a bishop.

9. *Durham. Deanery.* Crewe as a baron.

10. *Durham. Chapter Offices.* As in the Court Room at Bamburgh with lawn sleeves, black scarf, coronet beside him, a book bound in blue in his hand.

11. *National Portrait Gallery*. As a bishop.

12. *Bishop Auckland Castle*. As a bishop.

13. *Blanchland*. In episcopal robes, with right arm extended and placed near him a mitre and coronet, and behind him a sword (said to be by Lely).

14. *Aynho* (the home of the Cartwrights—his collateral descendants). In baron's robes, a fine portrait and bears the clear signature of G. Kneller. It is possibly the picture from which Loggan made his engraving.

15. *Odell Castle*. Portrait of Crewe as a young man, believed by Lord Armstrong to be a copy of that at Bamburgh.

A mezzotint of Crewe was engraved by Francis Place and is rare. There is a copy in the offices of the Bishop's Secretary, Durham.

There are portraits of Dorothy Crewe at Bamburgh and in the Chapter Offices, Durham. They represent her in a light blue dress with a dark blue mantle or overdress.

ENGRAVINGS OF CREWE

1. By Faber, from Kneller, fol. 1727.

2. By Loggan, from Kneller.

3. By Place, fol.

4. By White, fol.

5. In *Oxford Almanack* 1733.

6. In Hutchinson's *Durham*. The portrait in the *Examination* is from Hutchinson's *Durham*.

APPENDIX III

A FEW notes on the religious opposition which faced the
Anglican Church may throw further light on the condition of
ecclesiastical affairs in the northern diocese during the period
under review.

The struggle with recusancy broke out spasmodically from
time to time but not, as a rule, so violently as in other parts
of the country. The number of openly practising Catholics
seems to have been small, but the influence of the Roman
Church lingered in unexpected quarters and there were many
sympathizers. In 1674 a hundred and forty-two Roman
Catholics were proceeded against in the court of the Archdeacon of Durham.[1] Semple and Veitch, the Covenanters,
both described Northumberland as full of Papists. One
schedule of names gave 106 for Northumberland and eighty-
two for Newcastle, but there must have been many more than
these. In 1685 Fr. Pearson, S.J., was priest-in-charge of a
mission which had existed in Durham at least since 1590, and
he built a chapel and opened a seminary in the Old Elvet, but
the revolution destroyed his work, and though he returned at
a later date very little could be done. Celia Fiennes said of
Durham, "There are many Papists in the town, popishly
affected and daily increase." Defoe said that he found the
town of Durham " full of Roman Catholics who lived peace-
ably and disturbed no one," and he saw them going as openly
to Mass as Nonconformists to their meeting-house.[2] The
parish registers of St. Oswald's, Durham, speak of " Mr.
Ferdinando Ashmole, a popish priest living with the Lady
Margaret Ratcliffe in Old Elvet, buried April 4th, 1712," and
" Mr. Ralph Jennison, a popish priest, aged about 80, buried

---

[1] *Granville*, II, pp. xxi–xxiii.
[2] Defoe, *Tour*, II, p. 658.

in Harbour House Chapel, March 10th, 1718." In Anne's reign there were said to be thirteen Jesuits at work in the counties of Durham, Northumberland and Cumberland.

About 1681 Fr. Philip Leigh, a Jesuit, and Mr. William Riddell, a secular priest, were busy on Tyneside, and "a sufficiently spacious chapel and well-frequented school" were erected in Newcastle at the back of the "White Hart" in the Flesh Market, now called the Corn Market, but they were closed at the revolution. Thomas Riddell of Fenham was one of the leading Catholic laity and in 1683 was in jail with some seventy other Newcastle and Northumbrian recusants. In 1684 John March, Vicar of Newcastle, preaching before the mayor and corporation, spoke of the increase of Roman Catholics in the town.

In 1687 Bishop Leyburn confirmed 360 persons in Newcastle alone. Writing in 1701 to Mr. Chamberlayne, the secretary of the Society for Promoting Christian Knowledge, Archdeacon Booth said that the Papists were "the most formidable of all the dissenters both for Quality and Great Estates." In East Chapelry there are twenty-seven families, in Brancepeth parish twenty, in Coniscliffe thirteen and in Durham a very great number.[3] The grand jury of Durham on January 15th, 1702 presented two persons for being Roman Catholics, and about forty for being reconciled to the Church of Rome. They stated that Mass was said in St. Oswald's and St. Giles' parishes in Durham, and at Tanfield, Croxton and Norton, and they presented the constables of those places for dereliction of duty.[4] In a return to the House of Lords in 1705 there were said to be twelve Catholics in St. Andrew's Ward in Newcastle, fifteen in St. Nicholas' and twenty in St. John's. When the chapel in the Flesh Market was closed at the revolution, the chapel in the town house of the Radcliffe family in Newgate Street was probably used. The disastrous "Fifteen" led to the confiscation of the Radcliffe property, and what was known as the "House in the Nuns," that is, a house on the site of the old convent of St. Bartholomew in Newgate

[3] *Minutes and Correspondence*, S.P.C.K., p. 342.
[4] *Ibid.*, pp. 167-8.

Street, became the chapel. There is a tradition in Catholic
circles that the Benedictines had a chapel on the quayside for
some years down to 1688. There was also a Benedictine
mission at Chester-le-Street and Birtley.[5] There were some
Roman Catholics in Bishopwearmouth, for the parish books
record, under 1678: " for going to Durham with popish
recusants 1/6." Except when professional informers appeared
upon the scene, or there was some local or national panic, the
tendency increased to let Catholics alone. The returns of
numbers of Catholics, or other details, given from time to time
were often farcical. Thus, in 1696 there was an order from
the Privy Council to search for arms and stores belonging to
Papists and recusants; this is the return from Chester Ward:

> *Item,* one rusty musket and a rapier of John Smith of
> Ashe.
> *Item,* at Ashe, in Sir Edward Smith's pound, one old
> black horse, wall-eyed, but is not his, but Mr. Salvin's
> of Croxdale." [6]

Nonconformity does not seem to have been particularly
strong in the two counties during this period, though it was
undoubtedly increasing. In 1674, in the court of the Archdeacon of Durham, proceedings were taken against twenty-
one Baptists, twenty-six Quakers and thirty-three persons
whose special denomination is not given. The ecclesiastical
authorities seem to have been more vigorous that year than in
the immediately preceding and succeeding years. Generally,
however, a careful watch was kept for disaffected people. On
July 11th, 1678 the Government received information from a
certain Captain Brabant that Lord Balmerino was lodging in
Durham in the house of one Rackett, who was a notorious
fanatic, and kept company with none but fanatics and dis-
contented people.[7] Rackett is heard of several times. After
the Rye House Plot dissenters were treated with increased
severity. On August 7th, 1683 the grand jury of Northum-

[5] W. Vincent Smith, *Catholic Tyneside,* 1930.
[6] Surtees, *Hist. Durham,* I, p. cxx.
[7] *C.S.P.D.,* 405, No. 68.

berland urged the execution of all laws against recusants.
Dean Granville reported to the Archbishop of Canterbury that
there was greatly improved conformity in the bishopric; if
the Nonconformists met at all, it was in small parties at night,
" according to the example of the primitive Christians"; to
which the archbishop replied, " No, it was not like the primitive Christians, but like thieves and robbers to do mischief."

On Sunday, September 28th, 1684 died John Richardson,
a malt man and tanner in Framwellgate, Durham. A grave
was opened for him in the choir of St. Margaret's church, but
as he was an excommunicated Nonconformist, the bishop
refused leave for him to be buried there, so the grave was
closed up and he was buried in his own garden at Cater-
house.[8] John Shaw of Newcastle preached a sermon in 1685
published under the title of *No Reformation of the Established Church*. In it he said that Nonconformists complied
with the law so far as to come to church for the sermon. Many
of them, he affirmed, " dispute, scruple, deny and undervalue
the authority of the church, rebel against its governors,
associate, pack juries in a design to ruin the church, and as
opportunity serves, take to a conventicle." In 1699 Archdeacon Booth preached a sermon before the mayor and aldermen of Durham in which he urged them to put the laws
against dissenters into execution.[9] In 1701 he said there were
only three settled Presbyterian meetings within his jurisdiction,
and they were not frequented by any persons of note. The
Independents, who were inconsiderable in number, joined
with them.[10] A few years previously Celia Fiennes, visiting
Durham, had found a congregation of Nonconformists in a
meeting-house near the river with at least three hundred
persons present. It was said that in 1715 there were twenty-
seven Nonconformist congregations in Northumberland and
nine in the county of Durham, but as the writer wrongly states
that there were no Baptist congregations and further ignored
the Quakers, the estimate is not very helpful.[11]

[8] Jacob Bee, *Diary*.
[9] *Minutes*, S.P.C.K., p. 283.
[10] *Minutes*, S.P.C.K., p. 342.
[11] Bogue and Bennett, *Hist. Dissenters*, II, p. 98.

Quakers were to be found in most parts of the diocese, as we learn from the lists of prosecutions. During the years 1674 to 1690 the total of fines and distraints on them in the two counties amounted to over £1,800.[12] In 1686 three hundred and twenty-three were convicted as recusants in the county of Durham alone. In the city of Durham they had a meeting-house in the parish of St. Nicholas as early as 1700, and there are some references to them in the registers, e.g. " William Heighington and Margaret Crosseck were married at the Quakers' meeting house, 3 April 1700 " : "Elizabeth Marchell buried at the Quakers' meeting house, 15 January 1705." Archdeacon Booth complained that the Quakers were very numerous in the trading towns, but he was able to record in 1701 that several individuals had been recently won over to the church.[13] The Quakers in Gateshead had their original meeting-place in Pipewellgate, but in 1660 they moved to a place near the Tolbooth which was in the centre of High Street. In 1689–90 this meeting was licensed at the quarter sessions.[14] In 1698 they purchased premises in Pilgrim Street, Newcastle, and moved thither in the following year. In 1684 the parish books of Gateshead have the entry " For carrying twenty-six Quakers to Durham £2 17. 0." Even after the days of toleration had begun there were strong prejudices against them, and in 1719 the Curriers' Company of Newcastle ordered that no member should take a Quaker as an apprentice on pain of forfeiting £100.

Nonconformity in South Shields claims to date back to 1662, and it may be so. The first chapel of which there is any record was the Scotch church in the Long Bank, facing down Mile End Road, built in 1718.[15] There was a general Baptist congregation there [16] from the time of the Commonwealth.[17] Lewis Frost, a Newcastle Baptist, was part-owner of the Lay Farm. The meeting-house of the Baptists seems to have been

[12] Besse, *Sufferings of the Quakers*.
[13] *Minutes*, S.P.C.K., p. 342.
[14] *Ambrose Barnes*, p. 44.
[15] Hodgson, *South Shields*, p. 265.
[16] Whitley, *Minutes of the General Baptist Churches*, 1908, I, p. lvii.
[17] Hodgson, *South Shields*, p. 277.

the ancient chapel or burying-place east of Laygate, on the site now occupied by Holy Trinity schools. The little group seems to have lasted at least till 1734.[18] Robert Linton, a proprietor of several salt pans, was one of the most prominent Quakers in South Shields.

Nonconformity seems to have been comparatively strong in Sunderland. Not coming to church, not paying Easter dues, not receiving communion, keeping shops open on holy days, attending conventicles, "being schismatics and offenders against all order," the usual charges in fact, are heard of from time to time.[19] In the latter part of the seventeenth century the Baptists are believed to have held their meetings in a house in the Low Street near the Black Bull Quay. Scottish Presbyterians settled in Sunderland early in the eighteenth century, and for their use the Corn Market Chapel was built in a narrow court on the north side of the High Street. It was capable of seating five hundred and fifty people, and was the first Nonconformist place of worship to be built in Sunderland. The Rev. George Wilson was the first minister.[20] In 1701 it was said that there were thirty Quaker families in the town. There was a Quaker meeting in Bishopwearmouth, but their house was burnt down in 1688; it was rebuilt and licensed in 1698.[21]

There was a Presbyterian congregation in Stockton at least as early as 1688. The Rev. Thomas Thompson was ordained to minister to a Unitarian congregation there in 1688, and they built a meeting-house at the north end of the High Street in 1699.[22] The Unitarian congregation in Wellington Street claims a continuous connection with them. In 1701 there were said to be thirty families of Quakers in the town.[23] Not far from Stockton is Norton, where in 1676 Mary Whiting, sister of the Quaker preacher, John Whiting, visited the Friends who lived in that parish, died and was buried there.[24]

[18] Hodgson, *South Shields*, p. 101.
[19] Fordyce, *County Pal. Durham*, II, pp. 403, 444.
[20] Fordyce, II, pp. 445, 448.
[21] Mackenzie and Ross, I, p. 293.
[22] Fordyce, II, p. 165.
[23] *Minutes*, S.P.C.K., p. 342.
[24] John Whiting, *Persecution Exposed*, 1715.

John Rogers, ejected from Barnard Castle, preached in Teesdale and Weardale, set up a conventicle in Darlington in 1672 and died in 1688.[25] There were Quakers in Darlington in the early days of George Fox's movement and Darlington was long known as the Quaker town. There were twenty Quaker families counted there in 1701. Ralph Thoresby expressed his regret at seeing the bishop's manor house in Darlington turned into a Quaker warehouse.[26]

Jonathan Storey helped to establish the first Nonconformist place of worship at Winlaton and preached the first sermon in it.[27] There were twelve families of Quakers at Staindrop at the opening of the eighteenth century. The Baptists claim 1652 as the date of the still existing churches at Hamsterley, Rowley and Blackhill.[28] The meeting-house at Hamsterley was erected in 1715 on ground given for a nominal consideration by Mr. Thomas Dawson of Brakenhill. The Baptists do not seem to have had a large following in county Durham. Archdeacon Booth in 1701 calculated their adherents within his archdeaconry as a hundred and fifty.[29]

Several of the more distinguished Nonconformist ministers were found in Newcastle. Such were John Pringle, ejected from Eglingham at the Restoration; John Thompson, ejected from Bothal; Thomas Wilson, ejected from Lamesley; Robert Leaver, ejected from Bolam, and others. Richard Gilpin, who had been ejected from Greystoke in Cumberland, lived in Newcastle as a physician. There he wrote his *Demonologia: a Treatise of Satan's Temptations,* London 1677. His meeting-house was outside the Close Gate, between it and Skinnerburn. In 1694 William Pell, M.A., Magdalen College, Cambridge, ejected from Stainton in 1662, became his assistant, but he died in 1698, and was succeeded by Timothy Manlove, who had already ministered to dissenters at Durham, Pontefract and Leeds. It was he who had

[25] Fordyce, II, p. 25.
[26] Thoresby, *Diary,* I, p. 430.
[27] Hutchinson, II, p. 558.
[28] *Baptist Handbook.*
[29] *Minutes,* S.P.C.K., p. 342.

objected to Thoresby's increasing habit of going to Church of England services.[30] He died on August 3rd, 1699, and Thomas Bradbury became Gilpin's assistant,[31] but Gilpin himself died a few months later, on February 13th, 1700, and Benjamin Bennett took charge of what was considered the chief Nonconformist congregation in Newcastle,[32] and in 1715 he, with his assistant, Nathaniel Fancourt, had seven hundred hearers. In 1717 John Gee left £6 a year to the minister of the Nonconformist meeting-house without the Close Gate. Later this congregation moved to Hanover Square, and from thence to New Bridge Street. Though Gilbert and his followers were Congregationalist, the Unitarian congregation in Newcastle claims to have been founded by Richard Gilpin, and they still have the communion cups inscribed " Church Plate, Dr. Richard Gilpin, pastor, 1693."

William Durant was another ejected minister. He had a congregation at his house in Pilgrim Street. He married a sister of Sir James Clavering and was a well-to-do man. He died in 1681 and was buried in his own garden. Richard Pitts was minister of a Baptist congregation in Newcastle from 1689–98.[33] The Baptist churches in Osborne Road, Jesmond and Westgate Road, both claim a history reaching back to 1650.[34] There was a meeting-house on the Tuthill Stairs before the revolution; it was not originally Baptist, but was purchased for the Baptists in 1720.[35]

In 1706 a Presbyterian meeting-house was erected on some leasehold ground in the Castle Garth. The register of baptisms begins in 1708 when a Mr. Dawson was their minister. This congregation was connected with the Presbyterian Church of Scotland.[36] John Lowe had one of the Presbyterian congregations in the Castle Garth in 1715, with eight hundred adherents. William Holbrook had another Presbyterian con-

[30] Ambrose Barnes, pp. 445, 448–9.
[31] Bogue and Bennett, III, p. 491.
[32] Ambrose Barnes, pp. 450–2, 456.
[33] Ambrose Barnes, p. 437.
[34] *Baptist Handbook.*
[35] Ambrose Barnes, p. 461.
[36] Ambrose Barnes, p. 455.

gregation in Newcastle, with two hundred members; and about the same time (1715) the Groat Market meeting-house was built for the Presbyterians to whom William Arthur ministered. This congregation also numbered about two hundred.[37]

In 1698 Thomas Barnes, probably the younger son of the well known Nonconformist alderman, Ambrose Barnes, was ordained an Independent minister in Newcastle. In 1715 there is said to have been only one Independent congregation in the town with a membership of about a hundred.[38]

There was a great influx of foreign Protestants on the banks of the Tyne in the seventeenth century especially round Byker, where they established glass factories and other works. Some of these foreign families, like the Tyzackes and the Tittorys, became Quakers. Nonconformity was perhaps stronger in north than in south Northumberland, and some of the gentry gave their support. Sir William Middleton of Belsay, who made his house a place of refuge for them, and Sir Thomas Liddell were dissenters, and could always be looked to for help and protection by their co-religionists.

The Covenanting movement in Scotland also had some influence in Northumberland, for Covenanters on occasion sought refuge over the Border. William Veitch escaped after Rullion Green to England and after a time settled down at Stanton, near Morpeth. He had a secret hiding-place in his house, and though his meeting was broken up by William Ogle and Sir Thomas Horsley in August 1677, they could not find him. In 1679, however, he was arrested and sent back to Scotland.[39] Gabriel Semple exercised a great influence round Ford, where the past neglect of the Church had given the Presbyterians a hold, and their numbers greatly exceeded those of the church-people. Semple returned to Scotland in 1690, but his influence lived after him.

From Ovingham in 1662 Thomas Trewren or Trurant was ejected, and in 1672 was licensed as a Congregational teacher

[37] Ambrose Barnes, pp. 455, 459. Bogue and Bennett, II, p. 98.
[38] Ambrose Barnes, pp. 447, 459.
[39] Hodgson, *Hist. Northumberland*, II, ii, p. 110.

in his own house in that parish, but the Nonconformist centre was finally established near by at Horsley-on-Tyne by Robert Blunt, a Cambridge man, who ministered there from 1682 to 1715 and built the meeting-house. Blunt had been ejected from Ponteland. Ambrose Barnes obtained for him a yearly allowance out of the legacy of Philip, Lord Wharton. It is uncertain whether the meeting-house was built before or after the revolution,[40] but the present Congregationalists of Horsley claim direct connection.[41]

At Alnwick there was a Nonconformist congregation founded by Gilbert Rule and the present Presbyterian congregation claims to date back to 1662.

John Lomax, ejected from Wooler, opened a house in North Shields as a Presbyterian meeting-place in 1672, and a church was established on Magnesia Bank, now called Thornhill Lane, in 1688. The Scottish church in Howard Street, North Shields, claims descent from it.[42] There was a Quaker meeting-house at Cullercoats.[43]

There was a Baptist congregation at Hexham and the Baptist congregation at Stocksfield began in 1652.[44]

At Ponteland the Ogles and the Horsleys were Presbyterian. The house of John Ogle at Kirkley was licensed in 1672. Meetings were also held at the house of George Horsley of Milbourne Grange.

At Morpeth a conventicle had been kept by John Lomax in 1681,[45] and Jonathan Harle or Harley, M.D., preached there for a long time. Later he settled at Alnwick. He was a learned scholar, and John Horsley wrote his life.[46] In 1709 John Horsley settled as a Presbyterian minister and schoolmaster at Morpeth, and there he wrote his *Britannia Roma*, " till lately the best and most scholarly account of any Roman province that had been written anywhere in Europe." [47]

[40] *Arch. Ael.*, 2nd series, XIII, p. 33.
[41] *Congregational Year Book.*
[42] *Arch. Ael.*, 3rd series, II, p. 33.
[43] Sykes, I, p. 112.
[44] *Baptist Handbook.*
[45] *Arch. Ael.*, 3rd series, II, p. 33.
[46] Ambrose Barnes, pp. 442–3.
[47] Sir George Macdonald in *Arch. Ael.*, 4th series, X, p. 1.

Meeting at first in a private house the Presbyterians of Morpeth built themselves a meeting-house in 1721.[48] At a visitation held at Morpeth on June 14th, 1682 seventeen Quakers
were presented, and James Hedley was described as their chief
speaker.[49]

Nonconformity was fairly strong in the north of the county.
Luke Ogle, a Presbyterian minister ejected from Berwick,
settled for some years on a small property at Bowsden, near
Lowick, but in the reign of James II he returned to Berwick
and gathered a congregation, to which he ministered until his
death in 1696. A meeting-house at Barmoor, not far away,
was built during the ministry of his successor, William Bird.

In Eglingham parish in 1672 the house of Patrick Bromfield at Harehope was licensed for the Presbyterians. Bromfield
had been ejected from Ellingham in 1662. Several other
houses were licensed in and after 1689, but about 1693 a
chapel was opened at Branton and became the centre of
Presbyterian worship for the district. Timothy Punshon, a
graduate of Edinburgh, was minister there until 1716.

The Stamfordham congregation had been founded by John
Owens, one of the ejected, who in 1684 was imprisoned for
conventicling. A house in Dalton, nearby, was licensed for a
Presbyterian congregation, but from 1688 to 1691 they had a
regular minister, John Dyart, a graduate of Glasgow, who was
accustomed to take a pair of pistols into the pulpit and lay
them beside him. Robert Youll, an Edinburgh graduate and
author of *The Nature and Extent of the Covenant of Grace*,
was minister of this congregation from 1699 to 1715.[50]

A Presbyterian congregation was founded in 1697 at
Branxton by Aaron Wood : a place of worship was built in
1703, and Wood ministered in it until 1731. At Wooler there
was a Presbyterian congregation founded in 1702 by John
Barnes. At Chatton the house of Thomas Tindale was
licensed for Presbyterian services in 1701.

Special burying-places began to appear. The Society of

[48] Hodgson, *Hist. Northumberland*, II, ii, p. 441.
[49] *Ibid.*, II, Vol. I, p. 93.
[50] *Hist. Northumberland*, XII, pp. 197–8.

Friends had burial places in Newcastle (in the Sidegate), in Durham, Gateshead, South Shields, Bishopwearmouth, at North Shields (in Coach Lane), West Boldon, Whickham and Cullercoats.[51] Scottish Presbyterians, like the Quakers, refused to bury in Anglican burial grounds, " their religious opinions and a saving of expense kept them from making interments in the established churchyards." Baptists and independents felt the same, hence the setting apart of land on the Ballast Hills, Newcastle, as a Nonconformist burying place.[52] Dissenters were punished for burying their dead in a garden, and for refusing to bring them for Anglican burial. Thus, a number of parishioners at Bolam got into trouble for having a burial place in the garth of the church other than that provided by law.[53]

[51] Arch. Ael., 2nd series, XVI, p. 189.   Hodgson, South Shields, p. 98.
[52] Newcastle Records, Series IX, p. 170.
[53] Arch. Ael., 2nd series, XIII, p. 33.

INDEX

B 2

Crewe, Nathaniel—*contd.*
Against Danby, 105; Raises troops for the Border, 106; Entertains Monmouth, 107; Duke and Duchess of York, 108; The justices, 111; Preacher before the King, 113 –14; Offered Archbishopric of York, 125; Grants new Charter to Durham, 130; At Coronation of James, 143; Dean of Chapel Royal, 144; Privy Councillor, 145; Ecclesiastical Commissioner, 147; Samuel Johnson, 154; Accused of being Roman Catholic, 165; The papal nuncio, 165; Spied on, 166; Advocates toleration, 172–4; The Bishops' petition, 177; Sermon on birth of Prince of Wales, 179; Receives pardon, 181; Makes peace with the bishops, 183; His memorial to James, 184; Voted for abdication, 189; Refused to sign the Association, 189; Goes to Holland, 190; Pardon, 190; Question of resignation, 192–3; Takes oaths to William and Mary, 193; His books, 195; Exempted from Act of Indemnity, 201; Speech in House of Lords, 202; His patronage, 204; "Time-serving," 208–10; Crewe as a bishop, 213; Becomes a Baron, 222; In House of Lords, 233; Sermons, 236, 237; Buys Forster property, 242; Visitation of the Cathedral, 245; Votes for Sacheverell, 245; Subscribes to St. Mary-le-Bow Church, 261; Confirmation, 275; Last years, 288; Lord Lieutenant again, 289; Crewe and Wharton, 290; Crewe and Burnet, 291, 292; Impeachment of Oxford, 296; Palatine Rights, 297; At Lincoln College, 300, 305; Weak health, 306; Death, 310; Character, 311, 312, 316; Epitaph, 312, 313; Arms, 314; Benefactions, 322, 328–31; His books, 325; His Will, 332–58; Portraits, 359; Engravings, 360; Trustees, 328–31

Crewe, Penelope, 216, 233, 313;
Crewe, Randolph, 1, 2, 315;
  Samuel, 6, 37; Temperance, 3, 110; Thomas, Sir, 2, 3, 6, 25; Thomas, 2nd Lord, 6, 110, 222; Walgrave, 6
Croft, Bishop of Hereford, 23, 24, 215
Crookham Affray, 97
Crosby, John, 19
Crosseck, Margaret, 365
Crow, Robert, 269
Crowley, Ambrose, 51, 239, 283
Croxdale, 363
Croxton, 362
Cullercoats, 370, 372
Cunningham, Alexander, 257, 258; Peter, 43
Curteyne, John, 316
Curzon, Lady, 7; Mistress, 243

d'Ada, Ferdinand, Count, 164, 165
Dalton, an informer, 112, 113
Dalton-le-Dale, 267, 371
Danby, Earl of, Marquess of Caermarthen, Duke of Leeds, 40, 91, 94, 104, 108, 118, 185, 204, 214, 216
Danby Wiske, 151
Dangerfield, Thomas, 104
Darlington, 48, 58, 100, 107, 122, 256, 262, 269, 271, 275, 277, 279, 283, 328, 367
Dartmouth, Lord, 136
Davenport, George, 268, 287
Daventry, 325
Davis, Dr., 170
Davison, Alexander, 136; Jonathan, 200, 253; Margery, 271; Thomas, 199, 251, 275
Dawson, Thomas, 367
Declaration, of Indulgence (1st), 162, (2nd), 175, 177; of Lords Spiritual and Temporal, 186
Decoration of Churches, 268
Defoe, Daniel, 61, 361
Delaval, Mr., 131; Sir Ralph, 52; Robert, 274
Denbigh, Lord, 288
Denison, Musgrave, 298
Dennis, John, 269
Denton, 262
De Puiset, Hugo, Bishop of Durham, 52, 260
Derby, Earl of, 186, 198
Derwentwater, Lord, 293, 294

PRINTED IN GREAT BRITAIN BY THE FAITH PRESS, LTD., LEIGHTON BUZZARD